DATE DUE

NOV 2 0 1995	
MAR 1 2 1997	
FEB - 3 1998	
MAR 4 1999	
MAY - 5 1999	
MAY 2 5 2001	
APR - 8 2003	

Past and Present Publications

Epidemics and ideas

From plague to AIDS, epidemics have been the most spectacular diseases to afflict human societies. This volume examines the ways in which these great crises have influenced ideas, how they have helped to shape theological, political and social thought, and how they have been interpreted and understood in the intellectual context of their time.

The first chapters look at classical Athens, early medieval Europe and the Islamic world, in order to establish the intellectual traditions which influenced later developments. Then there are contributions on responses to different epidemics in early modern and modern Europe, where western notions of 'public health' were defined; and chapters on the ways in which disease was perceived outside Europe, in India, Africa and the Pacific, where different intellectual traditions and different disease patterns came together. The final chapter brings us back home, looking at the ways in which policies towards AIDS have been formulated in the 1980s and drawing striking parallels as well as contrasts with the social construction of disease in the more remote past.

Past and Present Publications

General Editor: PAUL SLACK, *Exeter College, Oxford*

Past and Present Publications comprise books similar in character to the articles in the journal *Past and Present*. Whether the volumes in the series are collections of essays – some previously published, others new studies – or monographs, they encompass a wide variety of scholarly and original works primarily concerned with social, economic and cultural changes, and their causes and consequences. They will appeal to both specialists and non-specialists and will endeavour to communicate the results of historical and allied research in readable and lively form.

For a list of titles in Past and Present Publications, see end of book.

Epidemics and ideas

Essays on the historical perception of pestilence

Edited by
TERENCE RANGER
and
PAUL SLACK

CAMBRIDGE
UNIVERSITY PRESS

Published by the Press Syndicate of the University of Cambridge
The Pitt Building, Trumpington Street, Cambridge CB2 1RP
40 West 20th Street, New York, NY 10011-4211, USA
10 Stamford Road, Oakleigh, Victoria 3166, Australia

First published 1992

Printed in Great Britain at the University Press, Cambridge

A catalogue record for this book is available from the British Library

Library of Congress cataloguing in publication data

Epidemics and ideas: essays on the historical perception of
pestilence / edited by Terence Ranger and Paul Slack.
     p.   cm. – (Past and present publications)
Includes bibliographical references and index.
ISBN 0 521 40276 X
1. Epidemiology – History.   I. Ranger, T. O. (Terence O.)
II. Slack, Paul.
RA649.E65   1992
614.4′9 – dc20   91-19775 CIP

ISBN 0521 40276 X hardback

UP

Contents

Contributors   *page* vii
Preface   ix

1   Introduction   1
    PAUL SLACK

2   Epidemic, ideas and classical Athenian society   21
    JAMES LONGRIGG

3   Disease, dragons and saints: the management of
    epidemics in the Dark Ages   45
    PEREGRINE HORDEN

4   Epidemic disease in formal and popular thought
    in early Islamic Society   77
    LAWRENCE I. CONRAD

5   Plague and perceptions of the poor in early modern Italy 101
    BRIAN PULLAN

6   Dearth, dirt and fever epidemics: rewriting the history of
    British 'public health', 1780–1850   125
    JOHN V. PICKSTONE

7   Epidemics and revolutions: cholera in nineteenth-century
    Europe   149
    RICHARD J. EVANS

8   Hawaiian depopulation as a model for the Amerindian
    experience   175
    A. W. CROSBY

9   Plague panic and epidemic politics in India, 1896–1914   203
    RAJNARAYAN CHANDAVARKAR

10   Plagues of beasts and men; prophetic responses to
     epidemic in eastern and southern Africa   241
     TERENCE RANGER

11   Syphilis in colonial East and Central Africa: the social
     construction of an epidemic   269
     MEGAN VAUGHAN

12   The early years of AIDS in the United Kingdom 1981–6:
     historical perspectives   303
     VIRGINIA BERRIDGE

     Index   329

Contributors

VIRGINIA BERRIDGE is Senior Lecturer at the London School of Hygiene and Tropical Medicine and Deputy Director of the AIDS Social History Programme. Her publications include *Opium and the People. Opiate Use in Nineteenth-Century England* (1981).

RAJNARAYAN CHANDAVARKAR is Assistant Director of Research in History at the University of Cambridge, and a Fellow of Trinity College. He is the author of *The Origins of Industrial Capitalism in India. Business Strategies and the Working Classes in Bombay, 1900–1940* (1992).

LAWRENCE I. CONRAD is Lecturer in the History of Medicine at the Wellcome Institute, London. He has written several articles on epidemic disease in the Islamic and pre-Islamic Near East, and edited (with Averil Cameron) *The Byzantine and Early Islamic Near East*, I: *Problems in the Literary Source Material* (1991).

ALFRED W. CROSBY is Professor of American Studies at the University of Texas in Austin. His books include *The Columbian Exchange. Biological and Cultural Consequences of 1492* (1972) and *Ecological Imperialism. The Biological Expansion of Europe 900–1900* (1986).

RICHARD J. EVANS is Professor of History at Birkbeck College, University of London, and the author of several works on German history, including *Death in Hamburg. Society and Politics in the Cholera Years, 1830–1910* (1987).

PEREGRINE HORDEN is a Fellow of All Souls College, University of Oxford, and author (with Nicholas Purcell) of *The Mediterranean*

World. Man and Environment in Antiquity and the Middle Ages (forthcoming).

JAMES LONGRIGG is Senior Lecturer in Classics at the University of Newcastle upon Tyne. He has written articles on Greek medicine and anatomy, and is currently completing a book on *Greek Rational Medicine*.

JOHN V. PICKSTONE is Director of the Wellcome Unit and Centre for the History of Science, Technology and Medicine at Manchester University, and author of *Medicine and Industrial Society. A History of Hospital Development in Manchester and its Region, 1752–1946* (1985).

BRIAN PULLAN is Professor of Modern History at the University of Manchester. His books include *Rich and Poor in Renaissance Venice* (1971) and *The Jews of Europe and the Inquisition of Venice, 1550 to 1670* (1983).

TERENCE RANGER is Rhodes Professor of Race Relations at the University of Oxford, and a Fellow of St Antony's College. He is the author of *The Historical Study of African Religion* (1972) and *Dance and Society in Eastern Africa* (1975), and editor (with Eric Hobsbawm) of *The Invention of Tradition* (1983).

PAUL SLACK is Reader in Modern History at the University of Oxford, and a Fellow of Exeter College. His publications include *The Impact of Plague in Tudor and Stuart England* (1985) and *Poverty and Policy in Tudor and Stuart England* (1988).

MEGAN VAUGHAN is Rhodes Lecturer in Commonwealth Studies at the University of Oxford, and a Fellow of Nuffield College. She is the author of *The Story of an African Famine* (1987) and *Curing their Ills. Colonial Power and African Illness* (1991).

Preface

The chapters in this volume are, with one exception, revised versions of papers delivered to the Past and Present conference on 'Epidemics and Ideas' held in Exeter College, Oxford, on 21 and 22 September 1989. The exception, chapter 7 by Richard Evans, was originally published in *Past and Present*, no. 120 (August 1988). The Past and Present Society is grateful to the Wellcome Trust for a grant towards the expenses of the conference. The Editors also wish to thank those who gave papers on that occasion, and especially Virginia Berridge, Lawrence Conrad and Peregrine Horden who stepped in to fill gaps in the programme at a late stage. We owe a considerable debt finally to all those who commented and contributed to discussion at the various sessions, and who have generously allowed us to draw on their remarks in our own contributions to this volume.

T.O.R.
P.A.S.

1. Introduction

PAUL SLACK

In an article on 'Cholera and Society in the Nineteenth Century', published in *Past and Present* in 1961, Asa Briggs issued a 'call for further research' into the social history of epidemics. It is a call which has not gone unanswered in the thirty years since the appearance of Briggs's article, and of the book by Louis Chevalier on which he drew.[1] There have been historical monographs, not only on cholera in different towns and countries,[2] but also notably on plague,[3] many of them very much in the Briggs–Chevalier tradition, showing how societies coped with, reacted to and interpreted short-term but intense epidemic crises. One aim of the Past and Present Conference of 1989, whose papers are printed in this volume, was hence to return to the subject and survey the development of the field.

There have, of course, been many other advances in the history of medicine and disease since 1961 which have helped to enrich the

[1] *Past and Present*, no. 19 (1961), pp. 76–96; L. Chevalier (ed.), *Le Choléra: la première épidémie du XIXe siècle* (La Roche-sur-Yon, 1958).

[2] For example, C. E. Rosenberg, *The Cholera Years. The United States in 1832, 1849 and 1866* (Chicago, 1962); R. E. McGrew, *Russia and the Cholera, 1823–1832* (Madison, 1965); R. J. Morris, *Cholera 1832. The Social Response to an Epidemic* (London, 1976); M. Durey, *The Return of the Plague. British Society and the Cholera, 1831–32* (Dublin, 1979); F. Delaporte, *Disease and Civilization. The Cholera in Paris, 1832* (Cambridge, Mass., 1986); R. J. Evans, *Death in Hamburg. Society and Politics in the Cholera Years, 1830–1910* (Oxford, 1987).

[3] For example, E. Carpentier, *Une ville devant la peste: Orvieto et la peste noire de 1348* (Paris, 1962); B. Bennassar, *Recherches sur les grandes épidémies dans le Nord de l'Espagne à la fin du XVI siècle: problèmes de documentation et de méthode* (Paris, 1969); C. M. Cipolla, *Cristofano and the Plague. A Study in the History of Public Health in the Age of Galileo* (London, 1973); M. W. Dols, *The Black Death in the Middle East* (Princeton, 1977); J. T. Alexander, *Bubonic Plague in Early Modern Russia. Public Health and Urban Disaster* (Baltimore, 1980); P. Slack, *The Impact of Plague in Tudor and Stuart England* (London, 1985); A. G. Carmichael, *Plague and the Poor in Renaissance Florence* (Cambridge, 1986).

study of major pestilences in the past. They have sprung partly from that broadening of the historian's agenda which has characterised research over the past thirty years, and from a recognition that several flourishing areas of historical inquiry – from the history of population to the history of material and mental culture – share a common interest in the subjects of health and disease. The social history of diseases which are not, or not always, the cause of short-term epidemic crises – diseases which can be endemic or chronic, such as syphilis and tuberculosis[4] – has been illuminated. There has been novel and fascinating work on disease 'exchanges' between different continents and on their implications for the history of whole populations and for ecological balances between men and their environment.[5] There has been a growth of new sub-disciplines – medical anthropology[6] and the social history of medicine[7] – which have contributed massively to our understanding of disease and health-care in different societies. In European and American historiography there has been much interest in instruments of medical and social control, from hospitals to medical ideologies, and in definitions of 'illness';[8] and in English historiography there has been a welcome focus on the standpoint of the sufferer, the patient.[9]

The chapters in this volume have naturally been influenced by these various new approaches to medical history. They illustrate in particular the value of case-studies drawn from outside as well as from within Europe, and they are sensitive to the importance of

[4] For example, A. M. Brandt, *No Magic Bullet. A Social History of Venereal Disease in the United States since 1880* (Oxford, 1987); L. Bryder, *Below the Magic Mountain. A Social History of Tuberculosis in Twentieth-Century Britain* (Oxford, 1988); F. B. Smith, *The Retreat of Tuberculosis 1850–1950* (London, 1988).

[5] W. H. McNeill, *Plagues and Peoples* (Oxford, 1977); A. W. Crosby, *The Columbian Exchange. Biological and Cultural Consequences of 1492* (Westport, Conn., 1972); A. W. Crosby, *Ecological Imperialism. The Biological Expansion of Europe 900–1900* (Cambridge, 1986).

[6] See, for example, G. M. Foster and B. G. Anderson, *Medical Anthropology* (New York, 1978).

[7] The new journal *Social History of Medicine* (Oxford, 1988–) contains and reflects the exciting work now being done in this area.

[8] Inspired by the work of Michel Foucault, beginning with *Folie et déraison: histoire de la folie à l'âge classique* (Paris, 1961) and *Naissance de la clinique* (Paris, 1963), and by Susan Sontag, *Illness as Metaphor* (London, 1977).

[9] See, for example, R. Porter (ed.), *Patients and Practitioners. Lay Perceptions of Medicine in Pre-Industrial Society* (Cambridge, 1985).

'perceptions' – the ways in which disease has been interpreted or 'constructed' in the past. All of the contributions focus, however, on major epidemic episodes. For epidemics are especially susceptible to comparative study because they are common to all continents and cultures; and they raise particularly broad issues in the history of ideas because they support, test, undermine or reshape religious, social and political as well as medical assumptions and attitudes. AIDS has been a recent reminder – in countries complacent about their success in banishing the major infections – of how wide the intellectual repercussions of epidemics can be.[10] The chapters in this volume show that they had a similar 'shock effect' in the past: conflicting with Islamic notions of a benevolent all-ordaining God in Conrad's Near East, challenging bourgeois optimism in Evans's nineteenth-century Europe, highlighting what was 'coercive or implausible' in the varied intellectual orthodoxies of Ranger's Africa.[11] Past epidemics continue to throw a peculiarly sharp light on the ideologies and mentalities of the societies they afflicted.

I

Even the most cursory perusal of the chapters which follow will show that the shocks of epidemics elicited very similar responses in very different historical and geographical contexts. So much so that Richard Evans wondered, half seriously, in the course of the conference whether there was not a common 'dramaturgy' to all epidemics. Were we simply learning that there was a fundamental and often repeated human response to such biological events, a familiar set of perhaps involuntary social reflexes? Was there anything more interesting to be discovered than that apparent truism?

Almost all epidemics were seen by contemporaries, for example, as being transmitted from person to person and as arising from particular, usually filthy, local conditions: notions of 'contagion' and 'miasma', of a more or less undefined kind, were combined. Again and again 'stench' lay at the root of disease.[12] Common social responses – and intellectual justifications for them – followed

---

[10] See below, p. 322–3, and the special number of *Social Research*, 'In Time of Plague', 40 (Autumn 1988).

[11] Below, pp. 86, 154, 173, 268.

[12] Below, pp. 34, 36, 112–13, 154, 171, 191–3. Cf. V. Nutton, 'The Seeds of Disease: An Explanation of Contagion and Infection from the Greeks to the Renaissance', *Medical History*, 27 (1983), p. 19.

from these assumptions. Flight from an infected place was usual, and had to be defended (or attacked) since it took people away from charitable, neighbourly or political duties.[13] Carriers of disease were identified and scapegoats stigmatised: foreigners most often, as in Renaissance Italy and modern Hawaii, since epidemic disease came from outside, but also inferiors, carriers of pollution of several kinds, among whom disease had its local roots – untouchables in India and ex-slaves in Africa, for example, or Jews at the time of the Black Death (though less commonly in Europe in later outbreaks of plague).[14] For their part, the inferiors themselves thought epidemics the consequence of plots by external enemies, or governors and elites, to 'poison' the poor.[15]

If social prejudices became polarised under the stress of an epidemic, so too did attitudes toward religion. From the plague of Athens onwards, people either sought solace in religious practices or fled from Gods which had failed them to what Pullan calls 'a kind of antinomianism'.[16] The forms of religious satisfaction also repeated themselves. At one extreme was the view that God sent plague as a punishment or a martyrdom which could not be resisted, an attitude which went hand in hand with a popular fatalism in the face of disaster. At the other pole were collective ritual practices – from Merovingian and Renaissance processions to participation in ecstatic or prophetic cults in Athens and Africa – which held out the promise of effective action, even if (in gathering people together) such rites conflicted with other assumptions about the kinds of defence responses which epidemics called for.[17]

In other words, epidemics like other afflictions and disasters present and presented common dilemmas, arising from the need to explain and combat them; and the answers repeat themselves in

[13] Slack, *Impact of Plague*, pp. 41–4. See also below, p. 94.
[14] Below, pp. 113, 189, 235, 259; comments by Richard Palmer and Brian Pullan at the conference.
[15] Below, pp. 22, 116–17, 163, 224.
[16] Below, pp. 44, 121, 252.
[17] Below, pp. 77–99 *passim*, 109, 37, 241–68 *passim*; I. N. Wood, 'Early Merovingian Devotion in Town and Country', in D. Baker (ed.), *The Church in Town and Countryside*, Studies in Church History XVI (Oxford, 1979), p. 66. For processions as sources of controversy, see below p. 105; R. Palmer, 'The Church, Leprosy and Plague in Medieval and Early Modern Europe', in W. J. Sheils (ed.), *The Church and Healing*, Studies in Church History, XIX (Oxford, 1982), pp. 98–9; C. M. Cipolla, *Faith, Reason and the Plague in Seventeenth-Century Tuscany* (Ithaca, 1979), pp. 55–6; C. M. Cipolla, *Public Health and the Medical Profession in the Renaissance* (Cambridge, 1976), pp. 36–7.

history. Nevertheless, as the various forms of religious ritual indicate, intellectual and social responses assumed a different shape in different social, cultural and political contexts. Conrad shows that early medieval Islamic discussions of plague were to a large degree separate from the historical reality of the disease, which had indeed (if only temporarily) disappeared by the time many of them were written. They were 'part of a greater overarching discourse in which epidemic disease itself was not necessarily the issue of primary concern'. The same might be said about Christian discussions of identical problems of divine justice and social obligation, though they took a subtly different form.[18] Chandavarkar and Vaughan find British responses to epidemics reflecting deep-seated colonial anxieties about India and Africa, just as Crosby and Vaughan again demonstrate the importance of missionary perceptions of indigenous cultures and moralities. As Berridge says, epidemics are interpreted according to 'pre-existing agendas' of questions which arouse anxiety and debate.[19]

II

Reactions to epidemics also took different forms according to the nature of the disease involved, a topic which deserves more detailed consideration than there is space for in this volume. One significant variable is the novelty, or alternatively the familiarity, of the disease. The intellectual challenges posed by epidemics were greatest when they plainly came fresh and new from outside, like plague in fourteenth-century Europe, many of Ranger's epidemics in Africa, or AIDS in the modern West.[20] Endemic infections or persistent chronic diseases like Horden's malaria or some of Pickstone's fevers presented different problems. Some epidemic diseases, of course, change from one to the other, like syphilis and smallpox in many societies, and AIDS arguably in our own, so that the definition of an 'epidemic' may often be problematic.[21]

[18] Below, p. 81. Cf. Slack, *Impact of Plague*, pp. 36–41.
[19] Below, pp. 211, 273, 299, 182, 315. For colonial attitudes, see also D. Arnold, 'Cholera and Colonialism in British India', *Past and Present*, no. 113 (1986), pp. 118–51, and the interesting studies in D. Arnold (ed.), *Imperial Medicine and Indigenous Societies* (Manchester, 1988).
[20] Below, pp. 250, 323. Cf. p. 150–1.
[21] Cf. C. E. Rosenberg, 'What Is an Epidemic? AIDS in Historical Perspective', *Daedalus*, 118, no. 2 (1989), pp. 1–17.

A second variable is the violence of the epidemic, which can be measured in a number of ways. Total mortality and morbidity are obviously relevant. There is a distinction between epidemics of plague in European cities which often killed more than 20 per cent of populations, and those of cholera which rarely killed half that proportion.[22] We usually know less than we would like about morbidity, however, and the violence of reactions does not always follow the violence of death or sickness in any neat relationship: extreme crises may inhibit all but fatalistic responses. The intensity of an epidemic depends also on its time-scale, whether it lasts days, months or years, plague again being exceptional in late medieval and early modern Europe in the total number of casualties recorded in two or three months.

Thirdly, we need to know something about the geographical and social incidence of the epidemic in question. Agreed communal responses may be easier to find if diseases are universal, or at least random, than if they are socially selective or concentrated, as they commonly are, in towns, suburbs or slums. Socially selective afflictions, on the other hand, allow authorities to distance themselves from the phenomenon – with the result that they either pay little heed to them, as in Chandavarkar's Bombay once plague was demonstrably a disease of the poor by 1902,[23] or define them as 'problems' and identify 'targets' for attack. Most productive of all for government responses seem to be epidemics with a definable local incidence but which nevertheless – being infectious – pose a perceived threat of breaking out of their bounds and striking the elite. This was the case with plague in European cities in the early modern period, and with cholera in the nineteenth century.[24]

Finally, in order to have a rounded picture of the dimensions of an epidemic, we need to set it in its 'disease-environment', to relate it to the 'background levels' of mortality and morbidity. It is important to recognise also that patterns of mortality and morbidity may vary in different ways and not necessarily move in the same direction over time. In early modern Europe, before the stabilisation of mortality in the eighteenth century, violent epidemics and acute infections may

---

[22] Below, pp. 111, 170–2. Cf. Slack, *Impact of Plague*, pp. 5, 174, 308.

[23] Below, p. 209. See Slack, *Impact of Plague*, p. 240, for hints of a similar reaction to plague in Tudor London.

[24] Slack, *Impact of Plague*, pp. 192–5; A. G. Carmichael, 'Plague Legislation in the Italian Renaissance', *Bulletin of the History of Medicine*, 57 (1983), pp. 519–25; below, pp. 110–11, 157.

have gone hand in hand with – and to some extent have been responsible for – low levels of morbidity for the survivors.[25] Where background morbidity is high, on the other hand, as in colonial Africa, concentration on epidemics by contemporaries or historians may have diverted attention from chronic diseases and more important problems of background health.[26]

A stimulating article by Mary Dobson has recently shown how complex the variations in disease-patterns in different parts of the world can be, and how they can be changed by movements of infection between them. In colonial New England low background mortality combined with infrequent but intense epidemics may have contributed to a peculiar fear of death. On the other hand, the disease 'jungles' created elsewhere by Professor Crosby's 'Columbian exchange' may have led to a greater tolerance of sickness and death, as well as to the initial cultural shocks for which Crosby argues in the case of Hawaii in this volume.[27] We need to pay attention also to the ways in which different kinds of crisis as well as different diseases reinforce one another. From the plague of Athens to the epidemics of nineteenth-century Europe and Africa, war and famine have aggravated and helped spread disease, and contributed to social and ecological crises.[28]

In general the studies in this volume and other work suggest that the most radical responses may be expected to follow epidemics which are novel, violent and intense, random (at least as initially perceived), and associated with other social disturbances. A developed reaction, such as a public health 'campaign', however, depends on familiarity, though not too much familiarity. If a violent epidemic occurs only once, it produces a single shock which may quickly be forgotten: the devastating influenza epidemics of 1557–9 in England and 1918 in the USA and elsewhere are nicely comparable examples.[29] On the other hand, familiarity may breed contempt. In some relatively closed societies illnesses such as yaws or

---

[25] J. C. Riley, *Sickness, Recovery and Death. A History and Forecast of Ill Health* (London, 1989), p. 156 and *passim*.

[26] A point made by Paul Weindling at the conference.

[27] M. J. Dobson, 'Mortality Gradients and Disease Exchanges: Comparisons from Old England and Colonial America', *Social History of Medicine*, 2 (1989), pp. 291–2; below, pp. 175–201, *passim*.

[28] Below, pp. 26, 161, 245, 254.

[29] Slack, *Impact of Plague*, pp. 308–9; A. W. Crosby, *America's Forgotten Pandemic. The Influenza of 1918* (Cambridge, 1989), ch. 15.

malaria may be so common as scarcely to be classed as illnesses at all. Some comparison with healthier regimes or periods is needed for the identification of disease. In early modern Japan, for example, there was a much more 'cataclysmic' view of measles, which invaded in major epidemic waves, than of smallpox, which was so common that it held few terrors.[30] Developing responses over time seem to require, besides familiarity, the maintenance of tension, such as is achieved by intense, repeated, but infrequent epidemics, with a definable but not immutable selective incidence.

III

It is possible, therefore, to build up profiles of different epidemic episodes, by recognising what Charles Rosenberg has called 'the individuality of disease entities',[31] and relating them to the environments in which they flourish; and one may go on from there to look at likely intellectual responses. So superficial a feature as the symptoms of an infection may have profound social and intellectual effects: the physical horrors of plague, syphilis and cholera account in large part for the revulsion which has given them a leading place in the history of epidemics (in contrast to influenza, for example). Different diseases exist, and different microorganisms affect their human hosts and human society in different ways. Yet epidemics are also themselves intellectual 'constructs' which, once formulated, have a history, vitality and resilience of their own. One of the chief lessons of the studies which follow is the extent to which man-made images of pestilence have shaped responses to it, whether or not they have been what we would regard as 'accurate' or 'rational' depictions of the phenomenon. The persistence of these representations is not the least consequence of that familiarity with particular epidemics which has just been referred to.

The ways in which Dark-Age dragons 'embody' rather than symbolise disease, in Horden's striking phrase, is one example, and

---

[30] E. H. Ackerknecht, *Medicine and Ethnology* (Baltimore, 1971), p. 141; A. B. Jannetta, *Epidemics and Mortality in Early Modern Japan* (Princeton, 1987), pp. 105, 125, 134.

[31] C. E. Rosenberg, 'Cholera in Nineteenth-Century Europe', *Comparative Studies in Society and History*, 8 (1966), p. 453, quoted in Arnold, 'Cholera and Colonialism', p. 119.

the same might be said about demons and devils in other contexts.[32] But 'plague' itself is a particularly telling case. Chandavarkar notes that bubonic plague was far from being the worst infectious disease in Bombay, though it produced the greatest scare, and the same phenomenon has been noticed in western Europe and elsewhere. Bubonic plague certainly had its own peculiar terrors; but much of the fear of it may be attributed to the wider associations of the term 'plague', as well as to collective memories of the history of the particular disease – so that the French in the 1890s were afraid of riots in Marseilles where the great crisis of the 1720s could still be recalled.[33]

Past histories may indeed shape present perceptions, as Berridge suggests in the case of AIDS. It is notable how Thucydides's description of the plague of Athens, with which this book opens, produced echoes again and again in literary depictions of later epidemics, some of whose authors may have had access to the Greek historian or to writers who borrowed from him, from Lucretius onwards.[34] Hence, one can never be entirely sure about the extent to which chroniclers of epidemics concentrated on social dislocation, the failure of doctors, flights to and from religion, rumours of poisoned wells, and similar phenomena simply because Thucydides and later writers down to Defoe taught them to look for them. It is a possibility which historians need at least to be aware of. Longrigg shows below how Thucydides's own account of plague was a carefully crafted narrative, consistent with his wider view of history and his vision of the disintegration of Greek society; and Giulia Calvi has similarly argued that official chronicles of the Florentine

---

[32] Below, p. 71. Cf. Jannetta, *Epidemics in Early Modern Japan*, p. 134; R. Crawfurd, *Plague and Pestilence in Literature and Art* (Oxford, 1914), p. 3.

[33] Below, pp. 202, 207 (France); Palmer, 'The Church, Leprosy and Plague', p. 79; N. G. Owen (ed.), *Death and Disease in South-East Asia. Explorations in Social, Medical and Demographic History* (Oxford, 1987), pp. 211, 235 (comparing plague and influenza in Java). For controversy over quarantine in Marseilles in 1851 because of memories of 1720, see Delaporte, *Disease and Civilization*, p. 191.

[34] Below, pp. 327, 22–7; Crawfurd, *Plague in Literature and Art*, p. 71; G. Deaux, *The Black Death 1347* (London, 1969), pp. 20, 46, 87; Dols, *Black Death in the Middle East*, pp. 14, 53, 297; Carmichael, *Plague and the Poor*, p. 154 n. 16; and for English references, W. Boghurst, *Loimographia ... 1665*, ed. J. F. Payne (London, 1894), p. 5; W. G. Bell, *The Great Plague in London in 1665* (London, 1951), p. 299. The first English translation of Thucydides was Bishop Sprat's, *The Plague of Athens* (1667). Cf. D. Defoe, *A Journal of the Plague Year*, ed. L. Landa (Oxford, 1969), p. xxxix.

plague of 1630 are discourses shaped by analogies between the city's history and 'the inevitable trajectory of the illness'.[35]

The 'pox' has similar reverberations down the centuries, and presents similar intellectual boundaries and barriers to understanding, even when redefined as a 'venereal' or 'sexually transmitted disease'. Vaughan shows that British observers of syphilis in Uganda were encumbered by the baggage of inherited assumptions about moral disintegration and dangerous female sexuality to the extent that they at first ignored the evidence that the disease was present in an endemic, non-venereally transmitted form. As she says, AIDS has been 'socially constructed' in much the same way.[36]

In short, one of the purposes of this symposium is to show that the interaction between epidemics and ideas does not proceed only in one direction – from biological challenge to intellectual response. It is much more complicated, and interesting, than that. David Arnold writes of cholera that

> Like any other disease, [it] has in itself no meaning: it is only a micro-organism. It acquires meaning and significance from its human context, from the ways in which it infiltrates the lives of the people, from the reactions it provokes, and from the manner in which it gives expression to cultural and political values.[37]

IV

A second purpose of this collection is to illustrate how Arnold's cultural and political values, the interpretations and images attributed to epidemics, have varied from context to context and how they have changed over time. Early historical accounts of 'The Conquest of Epidemic Disease' generally saw change over time as a Whiggish progress in which popular superstitions and folklore were replaced, first, by government regulation in the interests of public health, more or less informed by the theories of doctors, and then by

---

[35] G. Calvi, 'A Metaphor for Social Exchange: The Florentine Plague of 1630', *Representations*, 13 (Winter 1986), pp. 139–40. For an extension of this approach, see the same author's *Histories of a Plague Year. The Social and the Imaginary in Baroque Florence* (Berkeley, 1989); and also J. S. Amelang (ed.), *A Journal of the Plague Year. The Diary of the Barcelona Tanner, Miquel Parets, 1651* (New York, 1991).

[36] Below, pp. 278, 281, 299. Cf. C. Quétel, *History of Syphilis* (Oxford, 1990); S. L. Gilman, *Disease and Representation* (Ithaca, 1988), ch. 14.

[37] Arnold, 'Cholera and Colonialism', p. 151.

a triumphant biological and medical science, influencing both public and private arenas.[38] Even when the notion of progress over time was questioned, the three elements could be seen in association, and often in contention, in particular situations, usually colonial ones. It remains useful for purposes of discussion to distinguish 'popular', 'government' and 'medical' elements in the equation which produces ideas of epidemics; but the chapters below show that each needs to be looked at carefully and reassessed.

First, much anthropological work has shown that traditional popular systems of healing have their own validity and rationale.[39] They may appear to combine elements which, according to western medical ideologies, should be kept separate: an insistence on hygiene justified on religious rather than bacteriological grounds, for example.[40] But they are 'rational' in their own terms. They are often sensitive to the wider environment in which disease occurs, aware – as for example in the cases of Merovingian bishops and native African elites – of the ecological importance of drainage. They may be eminently practical and empirically sensible, as with the road blocks used in the Dark Ages against the spread of plague or the vaccination and isolation practised in Africa against smallpox.[41] Indeed, outside authority sometimes imposes non-rational ideas of epidemics on sensible traditional reactions, as in the case of the Islamic insistence on the futility of flight from plague or the missionary and colonial introduction of morality into African attitudes towards venereal disease.[42] It is commonly only when ordinary protections and precautions fail that people turn to more

[38] C. E. A. Winslow, *The Conquest of Epidemic Disease* (Princeton, 1943), and L. F. Hirst, *The Conquest of Plague. A Study of the Evolution of Epidemiology* (Oxford, 1953), Part I, exemplify this approach (in their contents as well as in their titles).

[39] See, for example, V. W. Turner, *Lunda Medicine and the Treatment of Disease* (Rhodes-Livingstone Museum Occ. Paper 15, Lusaka, 1963); R. and E. Blum, *Health and Healing in Rural Greece* (Stanford, 1965); U. MacLean, *Magical Medicine. A Nigerian Case-Study* (London, 1971); J. Buxton, *Religion and Healing in Mandari* (Oxford, 1973). G. Prins, 'But What Was the Disease? The Present State of Health and Healing in African Studies', *Past and Present*, no. 124 (1989), pp. 159–79, is an interesting discussion of some of the intellectual issues involved in such approaches.

[40] See F. L. K. Hsu, *Religion, Science and Human Crises* (London, 1952), pp. 14, 41, 45–6, 75, for examples from an outbreak of cholera in China in 1942; and S. B. Hanley, 'Urban Sanitation in Pre-Industrial Japan', *Journal of Interdisciplinary History*, 18 (1987–8), pp. 1–26, for the way in which private and public notions of cleanliness effectively interacted in Japan.

[41] Below, pp. 73, 247–8.

[42] Below, pp. 94, 294.

extraordinary religious or social outlets for anxiety, and even then the ritual propitiation of deities and the reassertion of communal values or prejudices may be vitally important as social therapy.[43]

As Berridge says, therefore, 'panic' is rarely a helpful concept in the analysis of reactions to epidemics.[44] It begs too many questions by implying spontaneous, unthinking social behaviour. Chandavarkar demonstrates in the case of Bombay that panic is intelligible only in the light of specific pressures and suspicions in particular epidemic circumstances. Moreover, the phenomenon is much rarer than some historians have assumed. Both Chandavarkar and Evans show that there were riots during epidemics, but epidemics did not cause major social and political upheavals. Disturbances in time of plague and cholera were reactions to the strict controls and police regulations imposed by apparently insensitive and uncaring authorities. They can be correlated with the severity of government regulations and with the failure of governments to persuade people of the reasonableness of their actions. They arise from what Chandavarkar calls the 'political conjuncture' of epidemics.[45]

Government reactions, the second element in our equation, are not therefore neutral in their impact; and the studies below show that they were extremely mixed and clouded in their motivation. First formulated in the fight against plague in late medieval and early modern western Europe, they rested from the beginning on the assumption that the preservation of society from disease was a fundamental duty of government. But, as Pullan shows, the ways in which that preservation was accomplished were shaped by social prejudices, by fear as much as pity with regard to the poor. Mass evacuation from plague-infected houses, incarceration of the sick at home or in *lazzaretti*, the imposition of *cordons sanitaires* and quarantine were all means of shutting away various kinds of danger to 'public health'. Even when these mechanisms were abandoned or qualified, in the early nineteenth century, that was arguably as much the result of pressure from mercantile and trading interests as a

---

[43] Below, p. 255–6; comment by D. Arnold at the conference.
[44] Below, p. 323. The phenomenon is arguably overstated, for example, in J. Delumeau, *La Peur en occident (XIVe–XVIIIe siècles). Une cité assiégée* (Paris, 1978), ch. 3.
[45] Below, pp. 162–3, 165, 206, 220–1. See also Slack, *Impact of Plague*, pp. 295–303; Calvi, *Histories of a Plague Year*, ch. 4; and for an example of a cholera riot in Italy as late as 1910, F. M. Snowden, 'Cholera in Barletta, 1910', *Past and Present*, no. 132 (1991).

consequence of an awareness that they were less effective against diseases like cholera than they had been against bubonic plague.[46]

Pullan and Evans are doubtful whether these aggressive but irregular assaults on epidemic disease had any lasting effect on administrative structures or attitudes to health, and there is much to be said for their view in the short term.[47] Taken together, however, their chapters show that over the centuries these devices combined to reinforce existing fears of poverty and dirt, and by their very repetition encouraged other 'campaigns' by European governments to protect public health. There were programmes to improve sanitation and even apparently successful regulations against cattle plague.[48] By the nineteenth century these attitudes were being exported to European colonies overseas, and there reflecting imperialist concerns – about manpower and national degeneration at home, and about 'native' dangers abroad. 'Sanitary and medical science', as Chandavarkar puts it, was part of colonial 'statecraft'.[49]

As this suggests, by then our third element – medical science – had come into the equation, and this too was less neutral and value-free, less clearly 'scientific', than its exponents believed and believe. Pickstone shows that by the early nineteenth century in Britain there were rival clusters of medical attitudes and theories, alternative 'structures of knowledge', determining public approaches to epidemics. The old, uneasy marriage of miasma and contagion had broken up under intellectual investigation. Yet, paradoxically, the new Chadwickian ideas, which were partly associated with anti-contagionism, produced a programme for government action as decisive as the quarantine programme of the past; and 'sanitary science' was certainly as influenced by social prejudices as the disciplines of 'medical police' on which it built.[50]

---

[46] Below, pp. 106–7, 115, 119–20, 166–7. Cf. D. Panzac, *Quarantaines et Lazarets. L'Europe et la peste d'Orient (XVIIe–XXe siècles)* (Aix-en-Provence, 1986), pp. 102–6.

[47] Below, pp. 121, 153, 171.

[48] J. C. Riley, *The Eighteenth-Century Campaign to Avoid Disease* (London, 1987); J. Broad, 'Cattle Plague in Eighteenth-Century England', *Agricultural History Review*, 31 (1983), pp. 104–15.

[49] Below, pp. 284–5, 214. Cf. pp. 314, 327–8; Delaporte, *Disease and Civilization*, pp. 194–5.

[50] Below, pp. 125–48 *passim*. See Delaporte, *Disease and Civilization*, ch. 7, for similar controversies in France, and, on medical police, G. Rosen, 'Cameralism and the Concept of Medical Police', *Bulletin of the History of Medicine*, 27 (1953), pp. 21–42.

At the end of the nineteenth century, with the rise of bacteriology, there were new opportunities for confident public action, based partly on that respect for specialist expert knowledge which came with the 'medicalisation' of western societies.[51] Modern 'bio-medicine' could be as blinkered and as politically inspired as its intellectual predecessors, however. Chandavarkar notes the initial hostility to Simond's rat-flea hypothesis with regard to plague, for example, and David Arnold stressed in discussion the way in which international conferences in the late nineteenth century encouraged major campaigns for the eradication of epidemic diseases. Paul Weindling commented that by then the 'military model' of public health was triumphant: 'invasive organisms' were attacked by 'campaigns', by single solutions like 'magic bullets', by 'corps' of medical experts, and often with the priorities of military health in the minds of colonial and would-be colonial powers.[52]

The alternative model, Weindling argued, was an 'interactionist' one, partially exemplified in Berridge's picture of reactions to AIDS, where a 'policy community' developed, resting in part on public discussion, popular education and self-help. This had its roots in the past, of course: in the process of 'medicalisation' itself; in the politics of western democracies where, as in Hamburg in 1896, health became a political issue; and in religious and medical debates over how far states could justifiably control and coerce their citizens, as for example in Britain in the 1900s and in Uganda in the 1940s.[53] Berridge's story also shows how complex these interactions can be, how much they depend on power relationships between various interest groups and on the prestige given to particular elements by public position and access to resources. The control of epidemic threats in democracies requires an acceptance of the pluralism of different approaches to health, and a recognition of the complexities of those popular, administrative and medical ideologies and frames of mind, which are illustrated in the chapters which follow.

[51] Below, p. 172. For the concept of 'medicalisation', see J.-P. Goubert (ed.), *La Médicalisation de la société française 1770–1830* (Waterloo, Ontario, 1982), and cf. C. Jones, 'Montpellier Medical Students and the Medicalisation of 18th-Century France', in R. Porter and A. Wear (eds.), *Problems and Methods in the History of Medicine* (London, 1987), pp. 57–80.

[52] Below, pp. 215–16; comments by D. Arnold and P. Weindling at the conference.

[53] Below, pp. 303–28 *passim*, 171, 291. The issue of public knowledge and debate as against the private discussion of 'experts' is well explored in W. Muraskin, 'The Silent Epidemic: The Social, Ethical and Medical Problems Surrounding the Fight against Hepatitis B', *Journal of Social History*, 22 (1988), pp. 277–98.

V

A final theme which may be drawn from this volume is, nevertheless, the enormous historical importance of the 'government' element and the 'military' model, of those campaigns to eradicate epidemic disease which began in western Europe and which became the medical and political orthodoxy which was carried from there to the rest of the world. Their historical influence on attitudes can scarcely be exaggerated, and though their impact on epidemic disease is often open to argument, they can claim some spectacular successes, against bubonic plague possibly, at least in the West,[54] and, more certainly and world-wide, against smallpox. The historian of epidemics and ideas must ask how so powerful an intellectual model originated.

As already suggested, we must look for an answer to western European reactions to plague in the years after the Black Death. The first health commissions, the first boards of health, were set up in the face of epidemic disease, in Venice and Florence in 1348; and they developed into permanent magistracies monitoring and regulating civic health: in Milan in the early decades of the fifteenth century, in Venice in 1486, in Florence in 1527. The first isolation of shipping occurred in the Italian Adriatic colony of Ragusa in 1377, and the quarantine of suspect maritime commerce developed from there. In 1374 there were bans and controls on commerce overland also, in Milan and Mantua, the beginnings of more rigid regulation in the following century. In 1374, in Milan again, the *contacts* of those infected, as well as the sick themselves, were isolated, and between 1450 and 1470 many of the city states of northern Italy set up isolation hospitals, *lazzaretti*, in further attempts to prevent contagion. In the end, a whole armoury was in place which could be adapted for use against other epidemic threats as well as plague.[55]

Two features of these developments are noteworthy. First, though spreading over most of western Europe, to England in the sixteenth century and Russia by the seventeenth, for example, they all began

[54] Slack, *Impact of Plague*, pp. 313–26; J. N. Biraben, *Les Hommes et la peste en France et dans les pays européens et méditerranéens*, 2 vols. (Paris, 1975–6), II, pp. 86–90, 173–5; Panzac, *Quarantaines et Lazarets*, pp. 89–92, 101; D. Panzac, *La Peste dans l'empire Ottoman 1700–1850* (Louvain, 1985), pp. 510–12.
[55] Cipolla, *Public Health and the Medical Profession*, pp. 11–18; Carmichael, *Plague and the Poor*, pp. 105–6; R. Palmer, 'The Control of Plague in Venice and Northern Italy, 1348–1600' (Univ. of Kent, PhD thesis, 1978), p. 31 and ch. 3; Carmichael, 'Plague Legislation', pp. 511–13; Biraben, *Les Hommes*, II, *passim*.

in the city states of northern Italy. Secondly, they were not an immediate response to the major, initial blow of the Black Death of 1348–50: they arose gradually out of experience of the later waves of epidemics which followed. The defences adopted in 1348–9 by Italian cities were old familiar sanitary regulations, concerned with civic hygiene: regulations designed to prevent contagion and the transport of infection came later.[56] We still need a thorough investigation of the origins of western concepts about the regulation of public health, but these facts of timing and location perhaps provide some clues which can be interpreted in the light of the earlier discussion.

First, we might look at the nature of the epidemic threat. The massive initial mortalities of 1348–50 certainly had an impact, but it was (to adopt Crosby's term) a cultural shock rather than a stimulus to administrative innovation. The Black Death provoked extreme religious reactins, including a revival of eschatological prophecies (as in Ranger's Africa); it led to a redirection of benevolence, towards chantries, for example; and to that obsession with death, guilt and the need for penance in the face of divine wrath, which can be seen in much of the art and literature of the later Middle Ages. It is possible to overstate the novelty of these changes. Recent work suggests that they had begun before 1348; the Black Death was not a clean break with the past. But it did powerfully reinforce cultural developments which were beginning in reaction to the other economic and social dislocations of the early fourteenth century, developments which – without plague – might have petered out.[57]

It took more than one initial shock to produce new methods of controlling epidemics, however. That kind of innovation rested on experience of repeated outbreaks of the same disease; it required the observation that the threat came always from outside (and, as Boccaccio had noted in 1348, from the East), so that states could be warned of its approach and take precautions; and it depended upon

---

[56] Carmichael, 'Plague Legislation', p. 510; J. Henderson, 'Epidemics in Renaissance Florence: Medical Theory and Government Response', in N. Bulst and R. Delort (eds.), *Maladie et société (XIIe–XVIIIe siècle)* (Paris, 1989), p. 167.

[57] See, for example, R. E. Lerner, 'The Black Death and Western European Eschatological Mentalities', *American Historical Review*, 86 (1981), pp. 533–52; K. L. Reyerson, 'Changes in Testamentary Practices at Montpellier on the Eve of the Black Death', *Church History*, 47 (1978), pp. 253–69; A. Smart, *The Dawn of Italian Painting 1250–1400* (Oxford, 1978), pp. 106–10 (modifying the influential thesis of M. Meiss, *Painting in Florence and Siena after the Black Death* (Princeton, 1951)).

a cool perception of the selective incidence of plague in the less serious epidemics which followed 1348. Ann Carmichael has stressed that the administrative attack on contagion came in the later fifteenth century, not the later fourteenth, that it owed much (as Pullan shows) to the association which could then be observed between plague and poverty and that it may have owed something to observation of epidemics other than plague which were more obviously contagious.[58] It certainly came late, as the result of a learning process.

Learning processes bring us back, of course, to ideas. For why did not the same developments occur outside western Europe wherever epidemics had similar features? A comparison between Moslem and Christian reactions to plague perhaps takes us part of the way towards an answer. Conrad argues below that contagion remained a divisive issue for Islam, and that its role was not unanimously rejected; but he also shows the dominance of the Islamic belief that plague was a martyrdom or a mercy, which Moslems should not resist. Michael Dols has contrasted this with the Christian insistence that plague was a punishment for sins which could be identified and remedied. The Christian notions of original sin and divine chastisement therefore predisposed men to action: to search out the targets of epidemics, often to find scapegoats, but also to identify the physical as well as moral sources of disease – unruly public assemblies, vagrants and beggars, disorderly slums.[59] Whatever the effect of Christianity, by the seventeenth century Christians themselves proudly contrasted their own sensible precautions with 'Turkish fatalism'; and Daniel Panzac has shown how, in practice, the Ottoman Empire suffered severely from plague because of its failure to adopt quarantine and *cordons sanitaires* until the 1830s and 1840s – when, paradoxically, they were being weakened or abandoned in the West.[60]

If Christianity arguably made a difference, why should change have come particularly in the towns of northern Italy? Much must

[58] Carmichael, 'Plague Legislation', *passim*. Cf. F. Hildersheimer, *La Terreur et la pitié. L'ancien régime à l'épreuve de la peste* (Paris, 1900), pp. 52–3, and for the kind of traffic which was observed to bring plague into Florence in 1630, Calvi, *Histories of a Plague Year*, pp. 21–58.

[59] Below, p. 98; Dols, *Black Death in the Middle East*, pp. 285–98; Slack, *Impact of Plague*, p. 49; Panzac, *La Peste dans l'empire Ottoman*, pp. 310–11.

[60] Slack, *Impact of Plague*, pp. 250, 336; Panzac, *La Peste dans l'empire Ottoman*, ch. 16.

be attributed to the nature of urban society in this most urbanised part of western Europe. Its international trading links were important: in the cases of Ragusa and Venice most obviously, commerce brought plague along familiar routes from the East. By contrast, closed societies may neither suffer invasions of plague nor therefore need defences against them: Tokugawa Japan with its ban on most foreign trade and lack of quarantine precautions is a classic example.[61] The towns of northern Italy were also well supplied with medical personnel and hospitals – some for the isolation of lepers (another western debt to theology perhaps).[62] Yet it is important to stress that doctors and physicians played little or no part in the developments we have been discussing. Physicians were not prominent on boards of health until the sixteenth century, and even then they were the servants of the state, giving advice at its bidding. Their presence was not a vital factor: physicians had, after all, served some classical and Byzantine towns without inspiring regulations against epidemics.[63] It was the secular civic administration which took the lead, and our theme therefore leads us to the nature of the unique corporate activism of the early modern European city state.

This is obviously a much bigger subject than can properly be dealt with in a few words here. A great deal seems to have depended, however, on power and competition: on a concentration of political authority in a very few hands, on the one side, and on competition and emulation amongst such powers, on the other. Carmichael concludes that, in the fourteenth century, 'only city states dominated by a powerful ruler seemed to explore alternatives in plague control'; Florence, by contrast, never attacked plague in that century 'with the kind of aggressive legislation used by the Visconti of Milan or

[61] Jannetta, *Epidemics in Early Modern Japan*, pp. 168, 191–7. Japanese cities did, however, have effective procedures for regulating civic hygiene: Hanley, 'Urban Sanitation'.

[62] See, for the Florentine example, K. Park, *Doctors and Medicine in Early Renaissance Florence* (Princeton, 1985); J. Henderson, 'The Hospitals of Late-Medieval and Renaissance Florence: A Preliminary Survey', in L. Granshaw and R. Porter (eds.), *The Hospital in History* (London, 1989). On leprosy, see Palmer, 'The Church, Leprosy and Plague', *passim*, and S. N. Brody, *The Disease of the Soul. Leprosy in Medieval Literature* (Ithaca, 1974).

[63] Park, *Doctors and Medicine*, p. 97; Carmichael, 'Plague Legislation', p. 513; Henderson, 'Epidemics in Renaissance Florence', pp. 169–70; R. Palmer, 'Physicians and the State in Post-Medieval Italy', in A. W. Russell (ed.), *The Town and State Physician in Europe* (Wolfenbüttel, 1981), pp. 56–7; V. Nutton, 'Continuity or Rediscovery? The City Physician in Classical Antiquity and Medieval Italy', in *ibid.*, pp. 9–46.

the Gonzaga lords of Mantua'. By the second half of the fifteenth century, however, the Medicean regime in Florence was borrowing projects like *lazzaretti*, John Henderson argues, as 'an oratorical flourish to boost the reputation of the city'.[64] Here were small states rivalling one another to excel their neighbours in their care for the welfare of their citizens and in their success in keeping out the neighbours' infections. It was a story repeated on a larger stage by later Renaissance princes, from Henry VIII (or rather Cardinal Wolsey) in England and Philip II in Spain to Catherine the Great of Russia, all of whom sought advice from physicians on the latest government measures against plague; and it was echoed on a smaller stage by the German states which developed rival ideas of 'medical police' in the eighteenth century.[65]

It is a story which also calls to mind E. L. Jones's discussion of the 'European miracle', and his broader argument that the services uniquely provided by the governments of the West – including attempts at 'disaster-management' – rested on competition between the rulers of relatively small European states, first cities and then nations.[66] One might be tempted to take the story back in time also, and perhaps to connect it to R. I. Moore's argument for the importance of 'persecution' – of lepers amongst others – in forming the identity of the princely states of western Europe in the two centuries before 1348; related processes of communal definition and the erection of comparable social boundaries seem to have been involved in some of the early developments in public health after 1348.[67] Much of this may seem speculative, but it is intended to show the wider ramifications of our subject, and its importance for political as well as intellectual history. What is certain is that we can tie what was arguably the most historically influential interaction of

[64] Carmichael, 'Plague Legislation', p. 512; Henderson, 'Epidemics in Renaissance Florence', p. 173.
[65] Slack, *Impact of Plague*, pp. 201, 218–19; D. C. Goodman, *Power and Penury. Government, Technology and Science in Philip II's Spain* (Cambridge, 1988), pp. 214–15; V. Nutton (ed.), *Medicine at the Courts of Europe* (London, 1990), pp. 202–3; Rosen, 'Cameralism and the Concept of Medical Police', *passim*. On the origins of the latter, see G. Oestrich, *Neostoicism and the Early Modern State* (Cambridge, 1982), pp. 156–9, and H. J. Cook, 'Policing the Health of London: The College of Physicians and the Early Stuart Monarchy', *Social History of Medicine*, 2 (1989), pp. 1–2.
[66] E. L. Jones, *The European Miracle* (Cambridge, 1981). Much of Jones's argument is relevant here: see especially, pp. 32, 140–3, 233, 237–8.
[67] R. I. Moore, *The Formation of a Persecuting Society* (Oxford, 1987).

epidemics and ideas to the Italian city states of the late fourteenth and fifteenth centuries, and hence to what George Holmes has called 'one of the most momentous moments of birth in the history of the West'.[68]

[68] G. Holmes, *The First Age of the Western City 1300–1500* (Inaugural Lecture, Oxford, 1990), p. 21.

2. *Epidemic, ideas and classical Athenian society*

JAMES LONGRIGG

My focus of attention is the great plague of Athens. However, before analysing the impact of the plague upon contemporary Athenian society, I should like, if I may so describe it, to examine Athenian impact upon the plague. More specifically, I wish to examine Thucydides's treatment of the plague. Thucydides provides our only contemporary account.

The Peloponnesian War broke out in 431 BC. In the early summer of the second year of the war the Peloponnesians again invaded Attica and laid waste to the countryside, whose inhabitants had taken refuge within the Long Walls. The city consequently became seriously overcrowded. Thucydides himself mentions this over-crowding (*The Peloponnesian War*, Book II, Chapter 52) and Aristophanes, with comic hyperbole, speaks in the *Knights* (792ff) of the refugees squatting in casks and birds' nests. A few days after the incursion of the Lacedaimonian army into Attica plague broke out in Athens – a pestilence, we are told, of unprecedented mortality.[1] The plague raged ferociously during that year and the next. It subsided and then broke out again in 427 BC, wiping out, it appears, one third of the population of the city (a higher proportion, incidentally, than that of medieval London carried off by the Black Death).

The spread of the plague to Athens and its impact upon that

Research for this paper was begun while I was a Member of the Society of Fellows at Durham in the Summer term of 1988 and completed in the following year during tenure of a Wellcome Research Fellowship in the History of Medicine. I am grateful to the Small Grants Research Committee of the University of Newcastle upon Tyne for a subvention which enabled me to consult works in the Wellcome Library at London.
[1] For attempts to identify this disease see my article 'The Great Plague of Athens', *History of Science*, 18 (1980), pp. 209–25.

overcrowded city is described by Thucydides in the second book of his *History of the Peloponnesian War* (Chapters 47–54):

[47] In the first days of summer in the second year of the war the Lacedaimonians and their allies, with two-thirds of their forces as before, invaded Attica. (Their commander was Archidamos, king of the Lacedaimonians, son of Zeuxidamos.) They settled down in their positions and laid waste to the country. They had not been many days in Attica when the plague first began to appear among the Athenians. It was said to have struck even before this in many places, both in the vicinity of Lemnos and elsewhere. However, nowhere was a pestilence remembered as being so virulent or so destructive of life as it was in Athens. For neither were the doctors, who were the first to offer treatment in ignorance of the disease, able to ward it off (their own mortality indeed was especially heavy inasmuch as they approached the afflicted most frequently). Nor was any other human skill of avail. Equally useless were prayers in the temples, consultations of oracles and so forth. Finally, overcome by their sufferings, the sick ceased to resort to such practices.

[48] The plague first originated, so it is said, in Ethiopia above Egypt and then descended into Egypt and Libya and much of the Persian Empire. It fell suddenly upon Athens and attacked in the first instance the population of the Piraeus; giving rise to the allegation that the Peloponnesians had put poison into the reservoirs (there were not yet any wells there). Later it also arrived in the upper city and by this time the number of deaths was greatly increasing. The question of the probable origin of the plague and the nature of the causes capable of creating so great an upheaval, I leave to other writers, with or without medical experience. I, for my part, shall merely describe its nature and set down its symptoms by which it might be recognised if it should ever break out again. I caught the disease myself and observed others suffering from it.

[49] It is generally agreed that the year in question was particularly free from other kinds of disease. If anyone had an illness prior to the onset of the plague all its symptoms were resolved into it. Others, from no prior observable cause, but in good health, were suddenly attacked in the first instance by violent heats in the head; their eyes became red and inflamed; the inner parts, such as the throat and the tongue, immediately

became blood-red and the breath unnatural and malodorous. These symptoms were followed by sneezing and hoarseness and in a short time the pain descended into the chest, producing a severe cough. Whenever it settled in the region of the heart, it upset it and there ensued evacuations of every kind of bile named by the doctors accompanied by great distress. Most patients then suffered an attack of empty retching, producing violent spasms; in some cases soon after the abatement of the previous symptoms, in others much later. Externally the body was neither excessively hot to the touch, nor pale in appearance, but flushed and livid with an efflorescence of small blisters and sores. Internally the heat of the body was such that the victims could not endure even the lightest coverings or linens; they preferred to go naked and would have liked best to throw themselves into cold water. Many of the sick who were not cared for actually did so, plunging into the water-tanks driven by their unquenchable thirst. It made no difference whether they drank little or much. They continually suffered distress through sleeplessness and their inability to rest. At the height of the disease the body did not waste away, but surprisingly withstood its ravages. Consequently the majority succumbed to the internal heat on the seventh or the ninth day before their strength was totally exhausted. Or, if they survived this critical period, the disease would descend to the bowels, where a severe ulceration occurred coupled with an attack of uncompounded diarrhoea, which in many cases ended in death from exhaustion. For the disease, seated at first in the head, began from above and passed throughout the whole body; if the patient survived its worst effects, it left its mark upon his extremities; it attacked the genitals, fingers and toes; many escaped with the loss of these, some also lost their eyes. Some rose from their beds seized momentarily by a total loss of memory and failed to recognise themselves and their friends.

[50] The nature of the disease was beyond description: in general its individual attacks were more grievous than human nature could endure, and in the following particular respect, especially, it revealed that it was something out of the ordinary. Though there were many unburied corpses lying around, the birds and beasts that prey upon human bodies either did not go near them, or died after tasting them. As evidence for this: there was a conspicuous disappearance of such birds; they were not seen

about the bodies, or indeed at all. But it was the dogs rather, being domestic animals, that provided an opportunity to observe this effect.

[51] If we pass over many other peculiarities as it manifested itself differently in individual cases, such was the general nature of the disease. Throughout the duration of the plague none of the ordinary diseases attacked the population as well: or, if any did, it ended in this. Some died in neglect, others in spite of being given every care. No single 'cure', as it were, established itself as the one which had to be applied to benefit the sick (for what helped one, harmed another). No bodily constitution, whether strong or weak, was conspicuously capable of resistance; but the disease carried off all alike, even those treated with every medical care. The most terrible aspect of the malady was the despondency of the afflicted when they realised that they were falling sick (for their minds immediately turned to despair and in the majority of cases they gave themselves up for lost instead of resisting). Most terrible, too, was the fact that having caught the infection through caring for one another they died like sheep. This was the cause of the greatest mortality. For, if they were afraid to visit one another, they expired with no one to look after them. (Many houses were emptied through lack of anyone to do the nursing.) Alternatively, if they did visit the sick, they also perished – especially those who made any claim to goodness. For their shame did not allow them to spare themselves from entering the houses of their friends at a time when even their relatives, overcome by the size of the disaster, were wearied of the funeral dirges for their dead. But still, it was those who had survived the disease who showed the more pity to the dying and the suffering because they themselves had previous experience of it and were themselves by this time confident of their immunity. For the disease did not attack the same person twice, at least not fatally. Such people both received the congratulations of the others and they themselves in the elation of the moment also entertained to some extent a vain hope that for the rest of their lives they would never die of any other disease.

[52] In addition to their existing distress, the crowding into the city of people from the country also caused the Athenians further hardship, and this especially affected the newcomers. Since there were no houses available for them and they had to live in stifling

cabins in the hot season of the year, they perished in utter disorder: corpses and the dying lay one upon the other and half-dead people reeled about in the streets and around all the fountains in their desire for water. The sacred places, too, where they had camped, were full of corpses of those who had died there. As the disaster pressed so overpoweringly upon them, men, not knowing what was to become of them, became contemptuous of everything, both sacred and profane. Burial customs, which had previously been observed, were all thrown into confusion and they buried their dead each as they could. Many, through lack of the necessary materials due to the fact that many members of their household had already died previously, resorted to shameful modes of burial; some would hurl their own dead upon another's pyre and set fire to it, forestalling those who had raised it; others would throw the corpse they were carrying on top of another that was already burning and depart.

[53] In other respects, too, the plague was responsible for first introducing a greater degree of lawlessness at Athens. Men ventured more readily upon acts of self-indulgence which had formerly been concealed. They saw rapid changes of fortune when the prosperous suddenly died and those who previously had nothing in a moment inherited their wealth. Regarding life and wealth alike as transitory they thought it right to live for pleasure and to enjoy themselves quickly. No one was eager to persevere in what was esteemed as honour, considering it uncertain whether he would live to attain it. But it was generally agreed that the pleasure of the moment and all that contributed to it was honourable and expedient. No fear of the gods or law of men restrained them. For, on the one hand, seeing that all perished alike, they judged that piety and impiety came to the same thing; and, on the other, no one expected that he would live to be brought to trial and punished. They believed the penalty that had already been passed upon them and was hanging over their heads to be far greater and that it was reasonable, before it fell, to get some enjoyment out of life.

[54] Such was the calamity that befell the Athenians and caused them great distress, with their people dying within the walls and their land ravaged without. In their distress they naturally recalled, among other things, this verse which the elders said had been uttered long ago:

'A Dorian war shall come and with it death'.

There was controversy, however, whether the word used by the ancients had been 'dearth' and not 'death'. At the present time the view that the word was 'death' naturally prevailed. For people made their recollection fit their experience. But, I imagine, if ever another Dorian war should come upon us after the present one and a dearth should ensue, people will, in all probability, recite the verse accordingly. Those who knew of it, recalled, too, the oracle given to the Lacedaimonians in answer to their enquiry whether they should go to war; the god answered if they made war with all their might victory would be theirs and said that he himself would assist them. So they surmised that what was happening tallied with the oracle: the plague began immediately after the Peloponnesians had invaded; it did not enter the Peloponnese to any extent worth mentioning; it ravaged Athens most of all, then the other most populous places. Such was the history of the plague.

In Chapter 58 of this book Thucydides describes how this deadly disease was carried from the stricken city to infect the Athenian forces investing Potidaea:

[58] In the course of the same summer, Hagnon, son of Nicias, and Cleopompus, son of Cleinias, colleagues of Pericles, taking the forces which the latter had employed against the Peloponnese, immediately set out on an expedition against the Chalcidians in Thrace and against Potidaea. On their arrival they brought siege-engines to bear against Potidaea and tried every way to take it. But, in their attempts to take the city and in other respects, their success was incommensurate with the scale of their preparations. For the plague broke out there and sorely distressed the Athenians. It so ravaged the army that even the soldiers of the earlier expedition, who had previously been in good health, caught the disease from Hagnon's troops ... Hagnon, therefore, withdrew with his fleet to Athens, having lost by plague in about forty days 1,050 hoplites from a total of 4,000. The soldiers of the previous expedition remained in position and continued the siege of Potidaea.

And in the following book (III.87) he records the return of the plague and estimates the military losses caused by it:

[87] During the following winter the Athenians suffered a second attack of the plague. It had never completely abated, but there had been some remission in its virulence. The second

outbreak lasted no less than a year, the first lasted two. Nothing did more harm to Athenian power than this. For no less than 4,400 heavy infantry in the ranks and 300 cavalry died of it, as well as an indeterminable number of common folk.

Several later writers, poets as well as historians, have paid this powerful and moving account of the sufferings of the Athenians in their beleaguered city the most sincere form of flattery and adopted it as a literary model for descriptions of plague in their own works. Lucretius, for example, bases his own account of the Athenian plague at the end of the sixth book of the *De rerum natura* (vv. 1138–286) very closely upon that of Thucydides, and Virgil follows suit in his portrayal of a cattle plague in Italy in the third book of the *Georgics* (478ff). Amongst historians, Diodorus Siculus and Procopius might be singled out especially. The former follows Thucydides not only in his own account of the Athenian plague (*World History* XII, 45 and 58), but also employs him as his model when describing the epidemic which befell the Carthaginians investing Syracuse in 387 BC (*ibid.* XIV, 70.4–72 see below). Procopius, the historian of the reign of Justinian, adopts as much material from Thucydides as circumstances permit in describing an outbreak of bubonic plague at Constantinople in AD 542 3 (*Persian Wars* II.22 3).

As was seen above Thucydides first tells us that the plague was held to have originated in Ethiopia, spread thence to Egypt and Libya and into most of the Persian Empire. It was next reported in the neighbourhood of Lemnos and thence brought to Attica. It attacked first the population of the port of Piraeus, giving rise to the rumour that the Peloponnesians had poisoned the water reservoirs. When it reached the upper city, he grimly records, the number of deaths was greatly increased. Since Thucydides himself fell victim to the disease (see II.48 above) it is commonly assumed that he was in Athens in 430 BC and was thus an eye-witness to the harrowing scenes he describes. We should not, however, overlook the possibility – and I stress that it is *only* a possibility – that he might have contracted the disease in the north when it was brought to Thrace by Hagnon's troops sent to reinforce those besieging Potidaea. It may be recalled that Thucydides had an estate and gold-mining concessions in Thrace and much of his military service seems to have been located there. If Thucydides had based his description of the social effects of the plague upon the stricken city, not on autopsy, but upon hearsay evidence, then some rather puzzling anomalies in his account would be more comprehensible. For example, he tells us that men became totally disillusioned with conventional religion (II.53); yet, as Mikalson has pointed out,[2] the state continued to make dedications to the gods after military victories. Thucydides also declares that all burial rites were entirely discarded and men buried the bodies as best they could (Chap. 52); but Plutarch tells us (*Pericles* 36) that Pericles attended several funerals in the early years of the plague and tombs were erected by the state for Melisandros in 430/29 (Paus. I, 29, 7; Thuc. II. 69), for Pericles, who died in 429 (II.65), and for Phormio in 428 (Paus. I, 29, 3). And at II.34.7 Thucydides observes that public funerals for the dead were 'held throughout all the war'. It may be doubted, then, that conditions at Athens were quite as desperate, even throughout the initial (and presumably most severe?) period of the plague, as Thucydides's description might lead one to assume.

It is noteworthy too – and not a little puzzling – that Thucydides provides our only contemporary account of the plague. No other unequivocal contemporary reference to the plague occurs elsewhere either in inscription or in literature.[3] Thucydides apart, the first explicit reference to the plague occurs in Plato's *Symposium* 201D, written many years later. It is curious, for example, that Aristophanes should have made no mention of the plague in the catalogue of ills caused by the war recited in the *Acharnians*, produced in 425 BC. To explain this puzzle it has been suggested that the plague was too painful an episode for contemporary reference. (Thucydides's account would, presumably, not have been completed, or, at any rate, not have been released, until several years after the disease had run its course.)

Diodorus Siculus, who has clearly used Thucydides's description of the Athenian plague as a model for his own account, describes an epidemic which afflicted the Carthaginians investing Syracuse in 397 BC. It is illuminating to compare the two. Diodorus writes:

After the Carthaginians had captured the suburb and plundered

---

[2] J. D. Mikalson, 'Religion and the Plague in Athens, 431–423 BC', in A. L. Boegehold *et al.* (eds.), *Studies Presented to Sterling Dow on his Eightieth Birthday*, Greek, Roman and Byzantine Studies, Monograph 10 (Durham, North Carolina, 1984), p. 219.

[3] It has been conjectured that there are references to the Athenian plague at Sophocles, *Oedipus Tyrannos*, 26 and 180, and at Euripides, *Helen*, 1327.

the temple of Demeter and Core, a disease fell upon their army. This god-sent calamity was increased by the crowding of tens of thousands into the same place; by the time of year, which was very conducive to disease, and, in addition, by the extraordinary heats prevailing that summer. It seems probable that the place, too, had something to do with the intensity of the trouble; for when the Athenians had earlier occupied the same camp, many of them had perished from disease, the place being marshy and low-lying. At first, before sunrise, owing to the coldness of the air from the marshes, shiverings were produced in the body, while the heat of mid-day naturally had a stifling effect upon such a crowd gathered together in such a confined space.

This malady, then, first attacked the Libyans, many of whom died; the dead were buried at first, but afterwards, when their numbers increased and those attending the sick were seized by the disease, none dared to approach the sufferers. Thus, aid being withdrawn, there was no more help against the trouble. Owing to the stench of unburied corpses and the putridity arising from the marshes, the disease began with catarrhs; later swellings super-vened about the throat, succeeded shortly afterwards by fevers, muscular pains in the back, and heaviness of the legs. Thereafter followed dysenteries and small blisters over the whole surface of the body.

Such was the experience in the majority of cases. Others were afflicted by madness and a complete loss of memory; they would walk about the camp out of their minds striking anyone they met. In general, as it turned out medical assistance was of no avail, both because of the intensity of the disease and the suddenness with which death arrived; for the victims died on the fifth day, or on the sixth, at the latest, enduring terrible tortures so that those who had fallen in the war were universally regarded as blessed. For in fact those who attended upon the suffering fell victims to the disease; consequently the plight of the sick was terrible, since none would help them in their trouble. For not only did strangers desert one another, but brothers were compelled to abandon brothers and friends friends through fear for themselves. (*World History*, XIV, 70.4–71)

The extent to which Diodorus models his account upon that of Thucydides is plain for all to see; but in sharp contrast to Diodorus's description, the rationality of Thucydides's account is immediately apparent. Unlike Diodorus, who regards the Syracusan epidemic as a 'god-sent calamity' in retribution for the plundering of the temple of Demeter and Core, Thucydides makes no attempt to account for the onset of the plague in terms of the anger of affronted deities.

Thucydides's rational, careful, detailed description of the symptoms of a disease is, for its time, rare – indeed, unparalleled, outside the writings of the Hippocratic *Corpus*. Accordingly, it is no surprise to find that many scholars believe that the historian has been influenced here by contemporary medicine. C. N. Cochrane, for example, maintains that Thucydides has adapted the principles and methods of Hippocratic medicine to the interpretation of history and believes that in his account of the plague Thucydides follows precisely Hippocratic procedure.[4] Some years later K. Weidauer, pointing to the parallel usage of certain key terms in both Thucydides and certain of these medical treatises, arrives at a similar conclusion.[5] And, more recently, D. L. Page in a well-known article has sought to determine 'how far the Greek is expressed in the technical terms of contemporary medical science'.[6] Page concluded that the great majority of the nouns, adjectives and verbs in Chapter 49 do in fact recur as standard terms in the medical writings of the fifth and fourth centuries BC. One can hardly take exception to this conclusion. However, it would be most unwise to take the further step, as do some scholars,[7] and infer that Page's survey shows that Thucydides has founded his description of the plague upon a strict use of contemporary technical medical terminology. For, as Adam Parry has pointed out, the great majority of the words discussed by Page appear in common and even poetical usage as well as in the medical writers.[8] Parry's conclusion that 'the vocabulary of the description of the Plague is not entirely, is not even largely, technical' may be accepted, for then, as now, terms in popular use were employed in medical treatises and medical terms, in their turn,

---

[4] *Thucydides and the Science of History* (London, 1929), pp. 16, 27.
[5] K. Weidauer, *Thukydides und die hippokratischen Schriften* (Heidelberg, 1954).
[6] 'Thucydides' Description of the Great Plague at Athens', *Classical Quarterly*, n.s., 3 (1953), p. 97.
[7] See, for example, A. W. Gomme, *Historical Commentary on Thucydides*, II (Oxford, 1956), p. 150; C. Lichtenthaeler, *Thucydide et Hippocrate vus par un historien-médecin* (Geneva, 1965), p. 33; and J. Scarborough, 'Thucydides, Greek Medicine, and the Plague at Athens', *Episteme*, 4 (1970), p. 80.
[8] Adam Parry, 'The Language of Thucydides' Description of the Plague', *Bulletin of the Institute of Classical Studies*, 16 (1969), pp. 106–18.

were adopted in popular speech. It was not, in fact, until Hellenistic times that systematic attempts were made to establish a technical terminology when the Alexandrian anatomists were constrained to invent new terms to describe the discoveries they had made in the course of their pioneering dissections of the human body.

However, if it is impossible to prove the influence of contemporary medicine upon Thucydides upon a linguistic basis, evidence of this influence is not lacking elsewhere. Thucydides himself reveals some familiarity with medicine when he records that during the course of the plague there occurred 'evacuations of bile of every kind for which the doctors have a name' (II.49). Despite his evident disinclination to enter into technicalities here, there can be no doubt of his awareness of current medical belief in this regard. A similarity between Thucydides and the Hippocratic doctors may also be seen in that it was characteristic of the latter to exalt prognosis over diagnosis, as Cochrane pointed out. For them the object of accurate observation and recording was prognosis, the understanding in advance of the course which the symptoms would follow, the foreknowledge of the development of the disease from beginning to end.

It may be remarked that in precisely the same spirit, Thucydides declares that his object is not to inquire into causes, but to describe the nature of the plague and set down its symptoms so that one who had foreknowledge of the disease would not fail to recognise it should it ever strike again (II.48.3). This same emphasis upon prognosis can be clearly discerned in Thucydides's conception of history in general. In Book I Chapter 22, for example, he announces the prognostic purpose of his History when he declares that it will be sufficient for him if his work is judged useful by those who will want to know clearly what has happened and what will someday probably happen again in the same or a similar way. Again, that he feels it incumbent upon himself to describe in such detail the symptoms of the disease would itself naturally seem to suggest medical influence.

In view of these affinities, there seems to be no good reason to doubt that Thucydides is familiar with contemporary medical literature and has been influenced by the spirit of Hippocratic medicine. But, notwithstanding this influence, it would be unwise to conclude that his rationality of approach was itself derived exclusively from contemporary medicine. Thucydides is himself manifestly a child of the Enlightenment and the writing of History had itself, in any case, felt, at an earlier date, the influence of Ionian natural philosophy, when Herodotus, the Father of History, enrolled himself within this tradition and adopted Ionian rational attitudes to describe an earlier war.

Thucydides's account of the plague, however, is no mere medical digression. It is not just a simple attempt to record in the manner of the *Epidemics* (albeit on a larger scale) the course of a disease which happened to occur at the beginning of the Peloponnesian War. It constitutes rather an important and integral part of his *History of the Peloponnesian War*. Thucydides has realised the important role played by the impact of the plague in Athens's ultimate defeat. Not only did the plague have a serious adverse affect upon Athenian military man-power; but it also, Thucydides believes, adversely affected, both directly and indirectly, Athenian leadership and policy during the war. Pericles, it seems, died of the plague and, it appears, Alcibiades was later impeached under legislation initially introduced during and as a result of the plague. Thucydides has recognised, as many modern historians have not, the importance of medical factors in the history of warfare. Thucydides's treatment of the plague as an integral part of the history of the Peloponnesian War can also explain why, although he gives a detailed, albeit explicitly conjectural, account of the origin and spread of the disease, he is less interested in its subsequent progress after its deadly assault upon Athens. Since its impact upon the Peloponnese was negligible, it thus had no major adverse effect upon the Peloponnesian war-effort. The disease became, therefore, no longer significant to his central theme and is summarily dismissed.

It should be noticed, too, that Thucydides's account of the plague is subordinated to his general historiographical principles. His harrowing description of the plague is dramatically exploited for historiographical purposes. The stark and immediate contrast between the optimism and confidence of the Funeral Oration and the grim ravages of the plague is heightened by their being deliberately set in tight juxtaposition. Again, this careful location of the description of the plague cheek by jowl with the Funeral Oration enables Thucydides to illustrate forcefully the deep-seated conviction, which permeates his History, that there is an unpredictable principle, an incalculable element, inherent in human affairs. The plague is the unforeseen factor which undermines Periclean policy. It may be accepted that this arrangement was hardly accidental.

Furthermore, Thucydides's theme is the disintegration of Greek society. He is describing the processes by which social and political violence can undermine reason. The plague serves as a catalyst which expedites these processes. His description of its effects is, therefore, subordinated to his overriding theme and ought not to be simply regarded as the product of an entirely clinical outlook totally detached from humane and ethical considerations.

It would, however, be going far too far to maintain, as a colleague once provocatively argued, that the plague-description itself is a purely literary invention for this express historiographical purpose. Thucydides would hardly have declared that his intention was to leave to posterity a description of the symptoms, whereby the disease could be recognised, should it ever recur, if it was, in fact, a figment of his own imagination. Furthermore, as has been seen, Thucydides's whole methodology in history is itself markedly influenced by the procedures of contemporary medical science. He saw human history as a 'great case-book of social pathology' and sought in his account of the Peloponnesian War to depict as accurately and objectively as possible the true course, the symptoms and the causes of that long malaise. His careful description of the symptoms of the plague epitomises both his general historiographical methodology and his historical purpose. Had he applied the same analytical procedures to a purely imagined event of that war, a fiction devised for a purely historiographical purpose (the plague), he would surely have run a grave risk of seriously weakening his proud claim to have written a History which was to be a 'possession for ever'. And in this connection, too, we must not overlook the fact that Thucydides is describing a *contemporary* war, where particular invention would inevitably lead to general disbelief.[9]

In addition to winning praise for his rational and clinical description of the plague, Thucydides has also recently been given credit by Poole and Holladay for making two important observations, which have not yet been properly recognised.[10] These two scholars believe that 'Thucydides was the first of extant writers to enunciate clearly

[9] In addition to the above arguments it may be noted that Plutarch, Pausanias and Diodorus Siculus all record information about the plague not found in Thucydides. While some of this information may well be described as 'inventive elaboration', it is clear that not all of it falls within this category.

[10] J. C. F. Poole and A. J. Holladay, 'Thucydides and the Plague of Athens', *Classical Quarterly*, 29 (1979), pp. 282–300.

the doctrine of contagion'[11] and to describe the phenomenon of acquired immunity. They assert that 'one searches the Hippocratic corpus in vain for any suggestion that the authors understood contagion' and confidently maintain that Thucydides 'certainly owed nothing to contemporary medical thinking'.

To be sure, Thucydides observes that the doctors and those who nursed the sick often contracted the disease themselves (II.47 and 51). He also records that, at the siege of Potidaea, soldiers already investing the town and previously unaffected by the plague, caught the disease from the reinforcements brought by Hagnon (II.58.2). The phenomenon of acquired immunity and its specificity is described at II.51.6 where it is stated that recovery from an attack of the plague prevented (or, at any rate, reduced the severity of) further attacks, but did not, as some foolish people believed, protect against other diseases. Thucydides manifestly deserves praise for his accurate observation and detailed description of these particular effects of the plague. But Poole and Holladay, nevertheless, in my opinion, overpress the evidence here. Although Thucydides certainly observes and records the *fact* of contagion, this is not to say that he clearly enunciated the *doctrine* of contagion or possessed an '*understanding* of contagion and immunity' or had any conception at all of its true cause.[12] And, in any case, by his own evidence Thucydides reveals that he was not unique in recognising the phenomenon of contagion. For at II.51.5 he states quite explicitly that a number of his contemporaries were afraid to visit one another and that those whose sense of moral obligation transcended their fear and drove them to nurse their friends were especially vulnerable to the disease.[13] Thucydides may well have been the first to describe in writing specific immunity and the phenomenon of contagion; but his own evidence reveals that the idea that one could contract the

[11] This quotation actually comes from R. Crawfurd, *Plague and Pestilence in Literature and Art* (Oxford, 1914), p. 37, but it is cited with approval by Poole and Holladay ('Thucydides and the Plague of Athens', p. 295 n. 52), who similarly speak of Thucydides's 'understanding of contagion and immunity' (p. 299).

[12] The same state of affairs is apparent half a century later. Isocrates records (*Aegineticus* 390, 29) that when Thrasylochus fell ill with phthisis, his friends warned a relative, who was determined to look after him, that many who had tended those similarly afflicted perished themselves of the disease. But there is no suggestion that this warning was given on the basis of any *understanding* of contagion.

[13] With J. Solomon, 'Thucydides and the Recognition of Contagion', *Maia*, 37 (1985), pp. 121–2.

disease from someone already affected by it was a matter of general knowledge within the Athenian populace.

The assertion that Thucydides 'certainly owed nothing [in this respect] to contemporary medicine' may also represent misplaced confidence on the part of Poole and Holladay. They claimed, as was seen above, that 'one searches the Hippocratic corpus in vain for any suggestion that the authors understood contagion'. Their use of the term 'understood', however, prejudges the issue. No Hippocratic author has anticipated this achievement of nineteenth-century biological science. But, as we saw, *observation* of the *phenomenon* of contagion is very different from *comprehension* of it and it is upon this more restricted level that Poole and Holladay should have made their assessment.

In the first book of the *Epidemics* an outbreak of epidemic disease on the island of Thasos is described as follows:

In Thasos, during Autumn, about the time of the equinox, towards the setting of the Pleiades, there was abundant rain, soft and continuous, with southerly winds. The winter southerly, light north winds, droughts; on the whole the winter was springlike. Spring was southerly, cool with light showers. Summer for the most part cloudy, no rain. Etesian winds were few, light and irregular.

All atmospheric conditions had been southerly with drought, but early in the spring conditions changed to their opposite and became northerly and a few people were stricken with remittent fevers which were very mild. A few had haemorrhages which were not fatal. Many had swellings around the ears, some on the one side, some on both; in most cases without fever and the patient was not confined to bed. Some also experienced a slight fever. In all cases the swellings subsided harmlessly. In no case was there suppuration such as is common with swellings from other causes. The character of the swellings was spongy, large and spread widely, without inflammation or pain. In all cases they disappeared without a sign. Boys, young men and men in their prime were afflicted – mainly those who frequented the wrestling-school and the gymnasia. (Few women were attacked.) Many had dry coughs without expectoration; their voices were hoarse. Soon after the onset of the disease, but in some cases after an interval, painful inflammations developed sometimes in one, sometimes in both testicles, sometimes with fever, sometimes not, causing much suffering to the majority of patients. But, in other respects, people were free from the sort of ailments that require medical assistance. (*Epidemics* I, 1 (II.600–602L))

The symptoms just described, which include swellings in the regions of the ears and which, in the case of some males, were coupled with the added complication of a painful orchitis, strongly suggest that the disease was mumps.[14] Our author tells us that few women were affected; its main victims were youths, young men and men in their prime – for the most part those who frequented the wrestling-school and the gymnasia. Despite the scepticism of Poole and Holladay, it is very hard to believe that there is not, at least, an implicit recognition here of the fact of contagion.[15] The traditional Hippocratic view was that epidemics were 'miasmatic' in origin, i.e. were caused by air polluted by some unhealthy exhalation[16] – a widespread belief which still survives in the term 'malaria'. But, to explain this disease upon such a miasmatic basis, it would be necessary to assume either that the gymnasia and wrestling-school were all located in an insalubrious area or badly ventilated, and set apart from private dwellings. In the present instance the medical writer has evidently realised that some males, who came into contact while taking exercise, picked up the infection from one another; whereas the women, who stayed at home, were less prone to catch the disease. It may be of some significance that the epidemic is described as having occurred at Thasos, the island where Thucydides was himself stationed in 424 BC. But, in view of the controversy regarding the dating of Hippocratic works – not to mention the difficulty in determining when the different parts of Thucydides's History were written – it would not be wise to go further and draw any firm conclusions regarding influence between medicine and history here.

---

[14] See E. Ebstein, 'Klassische Krankengeschichten: II. Der Mumps bei Hippokrates', *Kinderärztliche Praxis*, 2 (1931), pp. 140–1, and M. D. Grmek, *Diseases in the Ancient Greek World* (Baltimore and London, 1989), p. 336.

[15] Cf. Poole and Holladay, 'Thucydides and the Plague of Athens', p. 298. But see H. E. Sigerist, *A History of Medicine*, II (New York, 1961), pp. 330–1; and H. Diller, 'Stand und Aufgaben der Hippokratesforschung', *Jahrbuch der Akademie der Wissenschaften und der Literatur* (Mainz, 1959), p. 286 (repr. in *Antike Medizin*, ed. H. Flashar (Darmstadt, 1971), p. 49).

[16] See, for example, *Nature of Man* 9.44ff: 'But whenever an epidemic of a single disease is prevalent, it is clear that the cause is not regimen but what we breathe and that this gives off some unhealthy exhalation'; *Breaths* 6.19ff: 'so then whenever

It is time now to describe the impact of the plague upon Athenian society. Thucydides's account, we might note in passing, affords several interesting parallels with the later impact of the Black Death – one of the many diseases with which the plague has been identified. Just as the plague is reported to have made its first appearance in Attica at a port, so in the Middle Ages the Black Death, allegedly, was brought by twelve galleys to the harbour-city of Messina. Thucydides in the same chapter (48) records the belief that the plague was caused by the Peloponnesians poisoning the water reservoirs. In like manner, during the ravages of the Black Death, the Jews were accused of causing this epidemic by poisoning the wells. (Presumably this charge was largely due to the latter's more hygienic habit of drawing their drinking water from running streams.) The teachings of the established church also fell into disrepute and such hysterical excesses as the flagellant movement and dancing mania (St Vitus's Dance) spread over medieval Europe. Similarly, in fifth-century Athens, under the impact of the plague, there is some evidence to suggest that men turned increasingly away from conventional forms of religion, and orgiastic and ecstatic cults, such as Bacchanalianism, the worship of the Phrygian 'Mountain Mother', Cybele, and that of her Thracian counterpart, Bendis, and the mysteries of the Thraco-Phrygian deity, Sabazius, were all enthusiastically embraced.[17] There can be little doubt that the plague played an influential role in creating conditions ripe for these developments.

One of the reasons which contributed to the decline in the belief in the Christian faith during the Black Death was the craven behaviour of members of the priesthood. Putting survival before duty, they fled

the air has been infected with such pollutions (miasmasin) as are hostile to the human race, then men fall sick'.

[17] It is difficult to determine precisely when a particular cult practice became established within a society or when, once established, its popularity increased. However, in common with a majority of scholars I am persuaded that in the last third of the fifth century BC Athens witnessed a widespread interest in foreign and ecstatic cults and that the plague played an important contributory role in creating the conditions which fostered this development. The Cult of Bendis was accorded state recognition at the Piraeus in 430/29 BC. The Adonia is first mentioned by Cratinus (Frg. 17 P. C. G.) and Aristophanes speaks of him in 421 as already dead (*Peace* 700). Cybele is referred to at *Birds* 877 (414 BC) as is Sabazius, who is earlier mentioned at *Wasps* 9 (422 BC). Aristophanes, apparently, wrote a whole play, the *Horae*, about these foreign gods in which, according to Cicero (*De legibus* II, 37), 'Sabazius and certain other foreign gods were put on trial and sentenced to be banished from Athens.'

the onset of bubonic plague. The French physician, Guy de Chauliac, records that the doctors, too, 'out of fear of infection, hesitated
to visit the sick', and adds 'even if they did, they achieved nothing'.[18]
If the interpretation placed by the scholiast[19] upon the
rather knotty piece of Greek at the beginning of II.47, which
describes the situation of the Greek doctors at the outbreak of the
plague, is correct, we should then have a fifth-century medical
counterpart to this cowardly behaviour in the Middle Ages. According to this view, which has found some favour in modern scholarship,[20] the doctors only treated the sick during the initial stages of
the epidemic. But, once the lethal nature of the disease had been
recognised, they ceased treating the afflicted in order to save their
own skins. This somewhat cynical interpretation seems preferable to
the one traditionally adopted, viz. 'the doctors at first were helpless',
since the latter implies that, although ineffective at first, the doctors'
treatment ultimately became more successful. But there is no
suggestion elsewhere that the doctors subsequently achieved greater
success in combating the disease. A third possibility, however, seems
to me best and has been adopted in my translation: viz. the sick
sought medical help in the first resort but, when they realised that
neither medicine, nor any other human art or science, could help,
they then turned to the gods for aid.[21]

However, as Thucydides records, religion proved to be no more
efficacious. Prayers made in the temples, consultations of oracles
and so forth proved to be equally useless. Ultimately, he tells us,
men became totally disillusioned with conventional religion, since it
was thought to make no difference whether one worshipped the gods
or not, since believer and non-believer perished alike. The impact of
the plague, then, upon a traditional theology at Athens, already
weakened under the influence of Ionian natural philosophy in the
course of the preceding century, was considerable. Although the
Ionian natural philosophers had not directly attacked traditional
Homeric theology, their substitution of natural explanations for

---

[18] See *La Grande Chirurgie*, ed. F. Nicaise (Paris, 1890), p. 171.
[19] The scholiast remarks εἰ γὰρ ᾔδεισαν ὅτι λοιμὸς ἦν, οὐκ ἄν ἐπεχείρουν ῶ – 'if they
    had known that it was plague, they would not have attempted to treat it'.
[20] See, for example, C. Lichtenthaeler, 'οὔτε γὰρ ἰατροὶ ἤρκουν τὸ πρῶτον θερα-
    πεύοντες ἀγνοίᾳ', *Hermes*, 107, 3 (1979), pp. 270–86.
[21] See Diodorus Frg. XXX, 43 (Dindorf) who observes that when the doctors'
    therapy fails, their patients resort to incantations and prayer. See, too, Pliny,
    Naturales Historiae XXX, 98.

phenomena previously held to be the result of the supernatural activity of anthropomorphic deities had clearly weakened the authority of the Olympian gods. This implicit rejection of the Epic pantheon, however, was followed by an explicit attack. Xenophanes of Colophon, employing for this purpose natural modes of explanation in the manner of his Ionian predecessors, assailed the Homeric pantheon on two basic counts: its anthropomorphism and its immorality.[22] This attack upon traditional theology was followed by a no less vigorous onslaught upon traditional religious and cult practices by Heraclitus of Ephesus, who criticises them as foolish or illogical. Following Xenophanes, he ridicules the anthropomorphism and idolatry of contemporary religion and points out the absurdity of praying to statues. Such a procedure, he adds trenchantly, is like carrying on a conversation with a house.[23] But the most striking instance of his attack upon cult practices appears in his terse statement that 'corpses are more fit to be cast out than dung'.[24] Here, in three words, we have a calculated dismissal of all the immense concern manifested within Greek culture for the proper observance of burial rites.

In Chapter 52 Thucydides records that under the onslaught of the plague 'men became indifferent to every rule of religion and law'. The weakening of the normal restraints of religion and piety may be clearly seen in his description of the occupation of the temples by squatters unable to find accommodation in the crowded city. When these unfortunates were stricken by the plague, they died there. Under more normal circumstances holy places were not only kept clear of death, but even those who had had recent contact with the dead were banned from the precincts. Now, we are told, men had

---

[22] See Frg. 14: 'But mortals think that the gods are begotten as they are, and have clothes and a voice and a body like theirs' (*D.K.*21B14); Frg. 15: 'But if oxen and horses and lions had hands and could paint and produce works of art as men do, horses would paint the forms of the gods like horses, oxen like oxen, and make their bodies in the image of their several kinds' (*D.K.*21B15); Frg. 16: 'The Ethiopians make their gods black with snub-noses; the Thracians give theirs blue eyes and red hair' (*D.K.*21B16); Frg. 11: 'Homer and Hesiod have attributed to the gods all things that are a shame and a disgrace among mortals, thefts and adulteries and deceptions of one another' (*D.K.*21B11).

[23] See Frg. 5: 'When defiled with blood, they seek to purify themselves with new blood, as though one who has stepped into mud were to wash with mud. One would seem to be mad, if one were observed doing this. They also pray to these statues, as if one were to carry on a conversation with houses, not recognising the true nature of gods or demi-gods' (*D.K.*22B5).

[24] νέκυες γὰρ κοπρίων ἐκβλητότεροι (*D.K.*22B96).

become so indifferent that refugees were not only allowed to squat in the temple, but were even permitted to die there, and, having died, their corpses were left where they lay. Heraclitus's terse dismissal of the due observance of traditional burial rites doubtless caused a considerable frisson amongst his contemporaries and, only a decade before the outbreak of the plague, Sophocles had written a tragedy which turned upon this very point: viz. whether Antigone should follow the unwritten laws of the gods and perform a token burial of her brother, or yield to the tyrant's edict forbidding burial. Now, so Thucydides records (II.52), with disposal the paramount problem, men simply tossed their own dead onto another man's pyre and went off.

Thucydides also attributes to the influence of the plague 'the beginnings of a state of unprecedented lawlessness' (II.52). In Ancient Greece the laws had previously been regarded as having been divinely established, or, as in the case of Athens herself, instituted by a divinely inspired law-giver. Not only did the influence of Ionian natural philosophy weaken men's faith generally in the Olympian gods, but the very evolutionary nature of the cosmogonies propounded by the philosophers to explain the origin and operation of the world had itself diminished the authority of the laws and moral standards. In consequence, these were no longer regarded as god-given, but rather held to be the result of primitive forms of social contract. According to these theories of human progress, which developed as a corollary to natural explanations of the origin of life (including human life), social and political groups were formed initially to serve as a common defence in a hostile environment. Then, language and laws were developed by mutual agreement. Laws, customs and standards of behaviour, therefore, which had previously been regarded as absolute, universal and of divine institution, came to be regarded as merely local and relative, as having been adopted purely to meet the needs of particular people at particular times.[25] The abiding interest of the Greeks in other cultures with their different customs and morality also contributed to this growing belief in moral relativism. Now, under the stress of the plague, Thucydides records, 'no fear of the gods or law of man had a restraining influence' (II.53). In so dire a situation what counted most was the pleasure of the moment.

[25] It may be observed that even the laws of burial came to be regarded as another cultural product, a consequence of progress. See Moschion Frg. 6, 30–3 Nauck.

However, not all men, evidently, lost their belief in conventional religion. Some, having survived the horrors of the plague, were clearly driven to seek more powerful aid and turned to the healing-cult of Asclepius, the son of Apollo. In 420 BC, during the Peace of Nicias, the first possible opportunity, Asclepius, in the guise of his sacred snake, was solemnly inducted into Athens and lodged at the house of Sophocles until a temple could be built for the god.[26] During the last third of the fifth century BC Asclepius was transformed from a hitherto fairly minor cult-hero into a major god. There can be little doubt that the impact of the plague played a major role in promoting the spread of his influence over the Ancient World.

Perhaps the clearest testimony to the strength of the survival of more traditional beliefs and of conservative hostility to the spread of the Enlightenment may be seen in the hysterical fuss, some years after the plague, which attended the mutilation of the Hermae and the subsequent discovery that Alcibiades had been involved in a parody of the Eleusinian Mysteries (VI.28). Further evidence of reaction against the Enlightenment may be seen in the series of successful prosecutions at Athens for impiety during the last third of the fifth century BC. To the piously inclined, to offend the gods by denying, or even questioning, their existence, by replacing them by theories of natural causation, by criticising them for immorality, by mutilating their statues, parodying their forms of worship, openly provoking them at impious dinner-parties, or even by calling the sun a red-hot stone, was risky enough in peace-time, but in war it practically amounted to treason and helping the enemy since such behaviour would alienate the gods from one's cause. Had not Hesiod pointed out long ago that often a whole city suffers for the

---

[26] I.G.II² 4960. It is noteworthy that shortly after the outbreak of the plague, the Athenians mounted an abortive expedition against several places in the Peloponnese including Epidauros, the site of Asclepius's main sanctuary (II.56.4). Doubtless, as Gomme points out (*Historical Commentary on Thucydides*, II, p. 163), there were good strategic reasons for doing so, but it would be unwise in the light of subsequent events to discount religious motivation altogether here and underestimate Athenian desire to have access to this god of healing. It is interesting to observe that over 130 years later, when Rome was similarly racked by plague and all human efforts had proved unavailing, the senate, too, sent a delegation to Delphi to supplicate the aid of Apollo. On this occasion the god advised them to seek the aid of his son, Asclepius, who accompanied them back to Rome in the guise of his sacred snake (Livy, xxix, 1).

sins of a bad man?[27] According to Plutarch a decree was passed which made 'those who do not acknowledge divine things or who give instruction about celestial phenomena' liable to indictment for impiety, and during the next thirty years many leading intellectuals at Athens were impeached in a series of heresy trials.[28] This decree of Diopeithes seems to have been originally levelled at Anaxagoras with the specific aim of discrediting Pericles through his friendship with the philosopher. Even if the underlying motivation were political, however, the charge clearly reflects the state of popular opinion at the time. Clearly Anaxagoras would not have been impeached on grounds for which popular support would not have been forthcoming. Our sources seem to indicate c. 432 as the date of the decree. Adcock,[29] however, followed by Gomme[30], has argued for the later date of 430 and has persuasively sought to connect it with 'the emotions evoked by the Plague'. This later dating makes better sense both on psychological and on historical grounds: the theologically more conservative regarded the plague as a punishment sent by the gods (see Diodorus Siculus, XII, 58, 6 above) and Thucydides himself observes that Pericles became very unpopular for a time largely because of the plague (II.64).

Some further evidence of the strength of these traditional beliefs may be seen in the Athenians' purification of Delos, Apollo's sacred island, in 426 BC (see I.8 and III.104) by removing the dead and forbidding future births and deaths on the island. Although Thucydides himself rather dismissively describes the Athenian action as

---

[27] *Works and Days* 238–45.
[28] Plutarch, *Pericles* 32. As presented here by Plutarch the decree has evidently undergone a certain amount of rewriting. Its genuineness has been attacked on the grounds that Plutarch is our only source and there is no reference to it in other writers who might have been expected to mention it had it been known to them. But neither singly nor together are these objections sufficient to justify rejection of Plutarch's testimony. (Both of them, it might be observed, could equally be levelled at the plague itself, which is also recorded in a single source and is similarly not mentioned in contexts where one might expect to find reference to it.) K. J. Dover ('The Freedom of the Intellectual in Greek Society', *Talanta*, 7 (1975), pp. 24–5) is hostile to Plutarch's evidence here and regards it at best as not more than a proposal made by Diopeithes 'on some occasion (e.g. the plague) ... and ... transmitted to posterity ... by a reference in a speech'. While even this minimal acceptance is sufficient to support the point I am seeking to make here, Dover, in my opinion, is too sceptical both on this particular issue and in his treatment of the evidence regarding the heresy trials generally.
[29] *Cambridge Ancient History*, V (Cambridge, 1973), p. 478.
[30] Gomme, *Historical Commentary on Thucydides*, II, p. 187.

'doubtless due to some oracle',[31] Diodorus is more expansive and specifically links this act of piety with the plague which, he tells us, the Athenians attributed to supernatural causation.[32] Thucydides also records here that the Athenians revived the ancient festival of the Delian Games, which had been held in honour of Apollo and Artemis. Furthermore, Pausanias tells us that Apollo was given the epithet 'Alexikakos' ('Averter of Evil') for having 'stayed the pestilence which afflicted the Athenians at the time of the Peloponnesian War'.[33]

In summary, we may conclude that the effects of the plague upon classical Athens were considerable, widely ranging and even diametrically opposed. Both politically and militarily its impact was severe. In addition to the serious drain upon man-power,[34] Pericles probably died as a direct result of the plague in 429 BC and, Thucydides tells us, his policies fell into the hands of ambitious demagogues who lost control over the actual conduct of affairs. Indirectly, the plague was responsible, too, for the loss of Alcibiades, who was impeached for impiety in accordance with legislation which, it has been maintained, was initially introduced under stress of the plague. Socially and morally, the plague was responsible for

[31] III.104: κατὰ χρησμὸν δή τινα.

[32] XII.58.6. οἱ δ' 'Αθηναῖοι διὰ τὴν ὑπερβολὴν τῆς συμφορᾶς ἐπὶ τὸ θεῖον ἀνέπεμπον

[33] I,3,4. Pausanias is here referring to the statue of Apollo Alexikakos in the Agora at Athens, which he says was made by Calamis. This evidence has been rejected by modern scholars on the grounds that Calamis's artistic activity seems to belong to the first half of the fifth century BC. (On Calamis see, for example, P. Orlandini, *Enciclopedia dell' Arte Antica, Classica e Orientale*, IV (Rome, 1961), pp. 291–4, and B. Ridgway, *The Severe Style in Greek Sculpture* (Princeton, 1970), p. 87.) But it should be noted that Pausanias does not state that the statue was 'set up on the occasion of this pestilence' (*pace* e.g. Gomme, *Historical Commentary on Thucydides*, p. 160), only that it was believed that Apollo was accorded this epithet for having stayed the pestilence. It is perfectly possible that this epithet could have subsequently been associated with a statue of Apollo which actually pre-existed the outbreak of the plague.

[34] As was seen above (III.87), Thucydides tells us that during the second outbreak of the plague 4,400 hoplites (i.e. out of a total of about 13,000) and 300 cavalry (out of about 1,000) died of the disease. Since it is usually the case in an epidemic that there is a higher mortality among the very old, the very young, the poor and the sick than among the richer and the able-bodied, one might be tempted to assume that the proportion of the dead throughout the whole population was even higher than this – but caution would be wise since we learn at II.51.3 that strong and weak constitutions proved equally incapable of resisting the disease. (On the above statistics see Gomme, *Historical Commentary on Thucydides*, II, p. 388.)

the subversion of many of the norms of civilised behaviour. As in the case of the Black Death, where fear of the disease led to the stricken being abandoned to their fate, so, too, in Athens, Thucydides records, the sick died unattended. He further informs us that normal burial rites were not observed and the dead were denied a proper funeral. Under stress of the plague, men became disillusioned with conventional religion and rejected with it traditional restraints of law and morality. In effect, the plague served as a catalyst and accelerated the dissemination of those ideas most characteristic of that period of intellectual ferment, the fifth-century Enlightenment. However, it should not be overlooked that at the same time – contrary to the impression we are given in Thucydides's main account – the plague also helped to engender a reactionary backlash amongst the more conservative-minded, who were manifestly most anxious to avoid giving further offence to the gods and who sought, especially, to propitiate Apollo. There can be little doubt that the catastrophe of the plague, in addition to destroying the traditional religious beliefs of some, served also to heighten the more conventional religious sensitivities of others.

3. Disease, dragons and saints: the management of epidemics in the Dark Ages

PEREGRINE HORDEN

Dragons exist. Let us begin with the effort of imagination necessary to make that assertion plausible. Let us entertain the idea that never having seen a dragon may reflect only narrowness of experience. Others have, if not encountered the beast, at least come close to doing so. Here is the opening of a paper by the anthropologist Dan Sperber, appropriately entitled 'Apparently Irrational Beliefs'. It takes the form of a quotation from his field diary:

> [*Dorze, Southern Ethiopia*]
> *Sunday 24 viii* 69
>
> Saturday morning old Filate came to see me in a state of great excitement: 'Three times I came to see you, and you weren't there! ... Do you want to do something? ... If you do it, God will be pleased, the Government will be pleased. So?'
> 'Well, if it is a good thing and I can do it, I shall do it.'
> 'I have talked to no one about it: will you kill it?'
> '*Kill*? Kill what?'
> 'Its heart is made of gold, it has one horn on the nape of its neck. It is golden all over. It does not live far, two days' walk at most. If you kill it, you will become a great man!'
> And so on ... It turns out Filate wants me to kill a dragon. He is to come back this afternoon with someone who has seen it, and they will tell me more ...[1]

Filate did not return – to the anthropologist's embarrassed relief.

I am grateful to Edward Hussey, Emily Kearns, Gwyn Prins, Nicholas Purcell, Richard Smith and Ian Wood for advice and references on various matters. I am particularly indebted to Peter Brown for commenting on my draft.
[1] D. Sperber, *On Anthropological Knowledge* (Cambridge and Paris, 1985), p. 35.

A report of another dragon narrowly missed can be found in Carlo Levi's classic *Christ Stopped at Eboli*, a description of his exile by the fascist government to a remote Lucanian village. In a nearby hillside church with a miraculous Madonna 'were preserved the horns of a dragon which in ancient times had infested the region'.

Everyone ... had been to see these horns, but unfortunately I could not fulfil my wish to do so. The dragon, they told me, once lived in a cave near the river; it devoured the peasants, carried off their daughters, filled the land with its pestiferous breath, and destroyed the crops, until life ... became impossible.

Only the effort of a mighty prince emboldened by an apparition of the Madonna enabled the villagers to return to their homes. In the mid-1930s peasants still made pilgrimages to gaze at the vanquished monster's horns. 'Nor would it be strange if dragons were to appear again today before the startled eyes of the country people.'[2] For them as for old Filate – and doubtless for numerous others still – dragons exist. They are a part of nature: a cause of environmental disaster. In addition, as part of some divinely created order, they may bear a weighty symbolic charge. They may have to be interpreted as well as slain. For Sperber's and Levi's informants, however, the brute fact of dragons' natural existence seems to be primary. The heroes who slay them may please God or the government. But their achievement is above all to have made normal life possible once again – by removing an ecological hazard.

I

I begin in the recent past, with identifiable individuals and their ostensibly uncluttered beliefs, as an attempted corrective to the habitual procedure of those who study dragons academically. It is all too easy to dismiss Filate or the Lucanian villagers as simply the passive beneficiaries of a vast and diverse heritage of legend accumulated over millennia – as if nothing in their immediate experience could have contributed to the formation of their beliefs.[3] Such easy

---

[2] *Christ Stopped at Eboli* (Harmondsworth, 1982), pp. 110–11. Cf. F. Huxley, *The Dragon: Nature of Spirit, Spirit of Nature* (London, 1979), p. 5.

[3] Huxley, *The Dragon*, is an attractive compendium. Useful collections of references, and full bibliographies, can be had from *Reallexikon für Antike und Christentum*, IV (Stuttgart, 1959), *s.v.* 'Drache', and the briefer entries in *Lexikon des Mittelalters*, III (Munich and Zurich, 1986), *s.v.* 'Drache', and *Encyclopedia of Religion*, IV (New York and London, 1987), *s.v.* 'Dragons'.

dismissal permits historians to ignore particular circumstances in favour of a large, undifferentiated 'background' of world mythology, and to indulge in a superficial comparativism. It also encourages them to treat notions about dragons far more as part of the history of symbolism than as an aspect of the history of science, of everyday ideas about nature. Such beliefs, like other manifestations of apparent irrationality, can then be summed up in one or more of the ways that philosophers and anthropologists have variously proposed: as pre-logical, as expressive or metaphorical, as semi-propositional, culturally relative, and so on – not to be taken entirely seriously.[4] The most absurd and otherwise inexplicable ideas can be allocated to folklore – as if, for the remoter past, that term possessed any sociological precision or explanatory power.[5]

In what follows, comparative mythology cannot wholly be avoided. But I hope to rescue at least one associated group of recorded dragons from this undisciplined realm and restore them to a possible local context – which I shall, at this preliminary stage, crudely describe as the malarial (or at least miasmatic) swamp. I want to envisage these dragons less as symbols with meanings than as animals with effects. I want to take seriously the epithet 'pestiferous' that, in Lucania and elsewhere, has so often been applied to them, and to ask what consequences so doing may have for our appreciation of the role of heroic dragon-slayers. And, so far as is possible when considering the early Middle Ages, I want to evoke the immediate ideological and material surroundings in which belief in pestiferous dragons might be sustained. These ambitions do not entail a positivist confidence that the genesis of myths or legends can be adequately accounted for by reference to specific historical events. Instead, they involve an attempt at what has (rather suitably for present purposes) been dubbed an 'epidemiology of representations' – an attempt to see why certain images or ideas prove more

---

[4] M. Hollis and S. Lukes (eds.), *Rationality and Relativism* (Oxford, 1982). See also D. Sperber, *Rethinking Symbolism* (Cambridge, 1975); and D. Sperber, 'Is Symbolic Thought Prerational?', in M. Foster and S. Brandes (eds.), *Symbol as Sense* (New York, 1980), pp. 25–44. Contrast C. R. Hallpike, *The Foundations of Primitive Thought* (Oxford, 1979), ch. 4; P. Veyne, *Did the Greeks Believe their Myths?* (Chicago and London, 1988).

[5] For the variety of folklorists' approaches to hagiography, from which much of the evidence for what follows here is drawn, see W. W. Heist, 'Hagiography, Chiefly Celtic, and Recent Developments in Folklore', in *Hagiographie, cultures et sociétés IVe–XIIe siècles* (Paris, 1981), pp. 121–41.

'contagious' than others and become part of a community's common stock.[6]

I do this as a way of advancing three general propositions, albeit to unequal extents. The first – admittedly hard to defend using medieval evidence – is that malaria has yet to be given due prominence by historians of morbidity and crisis mortality. After a long period in historiography during which the disease was invoked to explain far too much – the decline of states, the vicissitudes of the economy and the like – we have only quite recently settled down to an appreciation of its complex ecology, its more subtle demographic effects and the conditions under which its incidence may grow to epidemic proportions.[7] The second and third propositions are interrelated, and provide the justification for my subtitle, 'the management of epidemics'. The second proposition is that while much attention has been given to the iconography of medicine, too little has been devoted to representations of disease. Historical notions of contagion have been discussed, but not ideas of the diseases being transmitted. There is a history here that has yet to be examined in more than desultory fashion. It would begin in antiquity with such arresting items as the Greek personification of diarrhoea possibly referred to by (?pseudo-)Empedocles, the Roman *Dea Febris* and Robigo, and the beggar who embodies disease in the *Life* of Apollonius of Tyana. And it would continue right through to

---

[6] D. Sperber, 'Anthropology and Psychology: Towards an Epidemiology of Representations', *Man*, n.s., 20 (1985), pp. 73–89. On the perils of adducing historical evidence for dragon combats, see F. W. Hasluck, 'Dieudonné de Gozon and the Dragon of Rhodes', *Annual of the British School of Athens*, 20 (1913–14), pp. 73–6; L. Dumont, *La Tarasque* (Paris, 1951), pp. 13–14, on the 'rationalising' of processional dragons. See more generally F. Graus, *Volk, Herrscher und Heiliger im Reich der Merowinger* (Prague, 1965), pp. 11ff, 28ff.

[7] Examples of those who invoke malaria to explain too much: W. H. S. Jones, *Malaria and Greek History* (Manchester, 1909); A. Celli, *The History of Malaria in the Roman Campagna from Ancient Times* (London, 1933); C. Laderman, 'Malaria and Progress: Some Ecological and Historical Considerations', *Social Science and Medicine*, 9 (1975), pp. 587–94; L. Bruce–Chwatt and J. de Zulueta, *The Rise and Fall of Malaria in Europe* (Oxford, 1980). Correctives: L. W. Hackett, *Malaria in Europe* (London and Oxford, 1937); P. A. Brunt, *Italian Manpower* (Oxford, 1971), appendix 18; P. Toubert, *Les Structures du Latium Médiéval*, 2 vols. (Rome, 1973), II, pp. 363–4; M. D. Grmek, *Diseases in the Ancient Greek World* (Baltimore and London, 1989), pp. 275–83. Historical demographers have unfortunately done little work on the disease. There are few European equivalents to the publications of M. J. Dobson. Cf. ' "Marsh Fever": The Geography of Malaria in England', *Journal of Historical Geography*, 6 (1980), pp. 357–89; 'Mortality Gradients and Disease Exchanges: Comparisons from Old England and Colonial America', *Social History of Medicine*, 2 (1989), pp. 259–97.

relatively modern times.[8] This history might be thought to constitute evidence of the management of epidemics in a *conceptual* sense. A potent image, pre-eminently such as that of the dragon, provides a means of reducing to a single 'contagious' representation an involved aetiology that is perhaps barely accessible to modern experimental science.[9] The third proposition, to which I can return only briefly at the end, concerns the management of epidemics at a *practical* level. It is that the means of controlling a potentially epidemic disease (such as malaria) may in the past have been less formal, less medical or technological in character than has usually been supposed – at least by medievalists and ancient historians.

II

I have introduced dragons and the management of epidemic disease. I must now present my saints. As with the dragons in question, I shall focus on one particular saint and adduce others more briefly for clarification. The principal is in some respects not the one who best exemplifies my argument. But I shall begin and end with him (turning to other saints in between) both because he has already

---

[8] Three types of disease (dry, putrefactive, wet) haunt 'the meadow of disaster': H. Diels and W. Krantz, *Die Fragmente der Vorsokratiker*, 6th edn, 3 vols. (Berlin, 1951), I, p. 360, B121; three types of fever (presumably quotidian, tertian and quartan) appear as three women in the autobiography of Guibert of Nogent, *Self and Society in Medieval France*, ed. J. F. Benton (New York and Evanston, 1970), p. 141; cholera, smallpox and plague as three demons in modern Athenian folklore: J. C. Lawson, *Modern Greek Folklore and Ancient Greek Religion* (Cambridge, 1910), pp. 21ff. The spirit of an epidemic apparently takes the form first of a beggar then of a huge rabid hound in Philostratus's *Life* of Apollonius of Tyana, IV, 10 (Loeb edn, I, pp. 362-6). Other ancient disease personifications: Roman *Dea Febris* and Robigo, see G. Wissowa *et al.* (eds.), *Paulys Real-encyclopädie der classischen Altertumswissenschaft*, *s.vv.* 'Febris', 'Robigalia'; Greek equivalent: K. Deichgräber, 'Parabasenverse aus Thesmophoriazusen II des Aristophanes bei Galen', *Sitzungsberichte der Deutschen Akademie der Wissenschaften zu Berlin: Klasse für Sprachen, Literatur und Kunst* (1956), no. 2, pp. 34–8. Pestilence as tornado-like column of vapour: 'Life of St. Teilo', *The Text of the Book of Llan Dav*, ed. J. G. Evans and J. Rhys (Oxford, 1893), p. 107. S. Thompson, *Motif-Index of Folk Literature*, 2nd edn, 6 vols. (Copenhagen, 1955–8), III, pp. 131–2, F493. An Indian comparison: E. C. Dimock Jnr, 'A Theology of the Repulsive: The Myth of the Goddess Sītalā', in J. S. Hawley and D. M. Wulff (eds.), *The Divine Consort: Rādhā and the Goddesses of India* (Boston, Mass., 1982), pp. 184–203.

[9] Cf. M. Last, 'The Importance of Knowing about Not Knowing', *Social Science and Medicine*, 15 B (1981), pp. 387–92, on the preferred absence of systematic knowledge in a traditional medical culture. Sperber, 'Anthropology and Psychology', pp. 85–6.

been the subject of an influential study and because his sphere of operation can be mapped with relative clarity. He takes his place in a long line of dragon-slayers and tamers of whom the Babylonian god Marduk is perhaps the oldest, St George is the best known and the anthropologist Dan Sperber is (in a sense) the most recent. His name was Marcellus and he probably became bishop of Paris during the first part of the fifth century, dying in about 436. (The ecclesiastical historian must tread cautiously here because there is a little room for doubt about the saint's historicity. Dragons exist, but bishops may be mythical creatures.[10]) In the present context, however, it is the later representation of Marcellus rather than the original reality that is mainly important. For information about this we must turn to his sole biographer.

Venantius Fortunatus, himself a bishop as well as a major poet and hagiographer, was commissioned to write a *Life* of Marcellus by one of the saint's successors as bishop of Paris, Germanus.[11] Since Fortunatus dedicated his work to Germanus, he must have completed it by the time of Germanus's death in 576. He was thus writing well over a century later than the events that he describes, and in somewhat different cultural surroundings. (During the sixth century much of Gaul passed under the political control of the Merovingian Franks.) Also, he was clearly short of material. The *Life* of Marcellus fills no more than six pages in the standard edition.[12]

There was an additional source of embarrassment. Marcellus was

---

[10] M. Vieillard-Troiekouroff *et al.*, 'Les Anciennes Eglises suburbaines de Paris (IVe–Xe siècles)', *Paris et Ile-de-France*, 11 (1960), p. 122; E. Griffe, *La Gaule chrétienne à l'époque romaine*, rev. edn, 3 vols. (Paris, 1964–6), I, p. 305.

[11] On Fortunatus, see W. Wattenbach and W. Levison, *Deutschlands Geschichtsquellen im Mittelalter: Vorzeit und Karolinger*, 2 vols. (Weimar, 1952), I, pp. 96–9; P. Godman, *Poets and Emperors: Frankish Politics and Carolingian Poetry* (Oxford, 1983), ch. 1; J. M. Wallace-Hadrill, *The Frankish Church* (Oxford, 1983), pp. 82–8. See also R. Collins, 'Observations on the Form, Language and Public of the Prose Biographies of Venantius Fortunatus in the Hagiography of Merovingian Gaul', in H. B. Clarke and M. Brennan (eds.), *Columbanus and Merovingian Monasticism*, British Archaeological Reports international ser. CXIII (Oxford, 1981), pp. 105–31. On Germanus the essential references are collected in R. Van Dam (trans.), *Gregory of Tours: Glory of the Confessors* (Liverpool, 1988), p. 93 n. 99. On possible reasons for the promotion of Marcellus's cult, A. Lombard-Jourdan, 'Du nouveau sur les origines chrétiennes de Paris: une relecture de Fortunat', *Paris et Ile-de-France*, 32 (1981), pp. 125–60.

[12] *Vita Marcelli, Monumenta Germaniae Historica* (hereafter *MGH*), *Auctores Antiquissimi* (hereafter *AA*), IV, 2, ed. B. Krusch (1885), pp. 49–54. General context: Wallace-Hadrill, *Frankish Church*; R. Van Dam, *Leadership and Community in*

of humble origin (born to 'mediocris parentibus'). And by the sixth century it had become widely abhorrent that a future prince of the church should not (in Lady Bracknell's phrase) 'rise from the ranks of the aristocracy'. Indeed, for such a common fellow as Marcellus to have clawed his way up the ecclesiastical hierarchy could only be accounted a miracle.[13] But that, of course, exactly fitted the hagiographer's requirement. Marcellus was to be portrayed as a saint. The performance of miracles before or after death was, and remained, the one essential sign of sanctity. The personal details of the man's life were less important than his conformity to type.[14]

I shall briefly survey Marcellus's few recorded miracles. The last of these is the one that is of particular interest here. But the character of the others provides a useful hint of things to come. The miracle that heralds Marcellus's entry into the priesthood occurs when the saint is challenged by a smith to determine the weight of a piece of red-hot iron. Marcellus takes it in his hand and volunteers a very precise measurement – which is later proved accurate. Such scientific know-how and immunity to extreme physical discomfort are what we have learned to expect of the early medieval holy man.[15] The second miracle resembles that wrought by Christ at the marriage of Cana. Marcellus is drawing water from the Seine. He offers some to his bishop so that he can wash his hands. The water promptly turns to wine. Although the bishop uses it to give communion to all present, the quantity of wine remains undiminished. Many of those who have tasted it, moreover, are subsequently cured of their ailments. Some time later the same bishop is struck dumb when he orders the flogging of a disobedient priest. Marcellus's intercession enables him to regain the power of speech. Who better, then, to

Late Antique Gaul (Berkeley, Los Angeles and London, 1985); P. J. Geary, *Before France and Germany* (New York and Oxford, 1988).

[13] *Vita Marcelli*, 4 (p. 50). On the attempted aristocratic monopoly of bishoprics and sanctity in Merovingian Francia see Graus, *Volk*, pp. 362ff; M. Heinzelmann, *Bischofsherrschaft in Gallien*, Beihefte der Francia V (Zurich and Munich, 1976); Collins, 'Venantius Fortunatus', p. 114; Geary, *Before France and Germany*, pp. 123ff.

[14] Gregory of Tours, *Liber Vitae Patrum*, preface, *MGH, Scriptores Rerum Merovingicarum* (hereafter *SRM*), I, ed. Krusch *et al.* (1885), p. 662 (for the various writings of Gregory, all subsequent page references are to this edition). Wallace-Hadrill, *Frankish Church*, p. 79.

[15] *Vita Marcelli*, 5 (p. 51). Background: P. Brown, *Society and the Holy in Late Antiquity* (London, 1982), pp. 103–52. For Roman Gaul and Francia, see C. Stancliffe, *St Martin and his Hagiographer* (Oxford, 1983); Van Dam, *Leadership and Community*.

succeed the man as bishop on his death? While bishop, Marcellus performs those miraculous deeds of patronage and protection that the age expected from its heroes. For example, a prisoner is miraculously released from his chains and then, absolved by Marcellus, he is freed from the greater bondage of sin.[16]

What is striking about these miracles is that they mostly involve mastery of nature. Marcellus can turn the water of the Seine into health-giving wine, an easier feat in his time than it would be now but admirable nonetheless. Such an achievement benefits the whole community, not just select individuals. From Marcellus this community learns to expect a quasi-scientific expertise, a swift and practical solution to problems, an enhancement of corporate well-being. That much is confirmed by Marcellus's last miracle, 'illud triumphale mysterium'.

This is the story as Fortunatus tells it.[17] A noble woman of sullied reputation dies blind and is placed in her tomb. A dragon or monstrous snake (*draco, serpens inmanissimus, belua*) sets about devouring her body. Members of her family, still nearby, hear the noise and rush to the tomb. They see a huge monster leave the tomb, uncoiling itself and whipping the air with its tail. Terrified, they abandon the place – even to the point of migrating from their homes ('de suis sedibus migraverunt'). When Marcellus is informed, he gathers the people of Paris together. He orders them to stand within sight of the tomb and marches forward to do battle. The dragon comes out of the wood (to which it has presumably retreated) and returns to the tomb; Marcellus prays; and the dragon approaches him with bowed head and trailing tail to ask pardon. Marcellus subdues it by striking its head three times with his pastoral staff and putting his stole around its neck. 'Thus,' Fortunatus writes, 'in a spiritual theatre [or perhaps arena], with the populace looking on, he alone fought with the dragon.' Amazed by his performance, the audience of this theatre runs up to have a closer look at the captured enemy. Then, with the bishop leading, almost three thousand people form a procession with the dragon at its head and they celebrate the monster's exequies. Marcellus then reprimands the somehow still

---

[16] *Vita Marcelli*, 6 (p. 51), 8–9 (pp. 52–3). On the liberation of prisoners, see F. Graus, 'Die Gewalt bei den Anfängen des Feudalismus und die "Gefangenenbefreiungen" der merowingischen Hagiographie', *Jahrbuch für Wirtschaftsgeschichte*, 1 (1961), pp. 61–156; E. James, ' "Beati Pacifici": Bishops and the Law in Sixth-Century Gaul', in J. Bossy (ed.), *Disputes and Settlements* (Cambridge, 1983), pp. 33–6.

[17] *Vita Marcelli*, 10 (pp. 53–4).

living beast, and tells it to stay either in the desert or in the sea. The dragon disappears.

This edifying tale has been analysed before. Most influentially, Jacques Le Goff made it the subject of a substantial paper that he originally published in 1970.[18] As in a number of his other works, Le Goff was here concerned to elaborate a distinction between clerical culture and popular culture. The clerical culture of the early Middle Ages portrays the combat with the dragon in relatively simple terms, as involving an embodiment of the Devil or of paganism. In doing so, this culture is attempting to transform, as Le Goff puts it, 'a monster that had formerly carried one of the most complex symbolisms in the history of culture'. Popular culture, for Le Goff, embraces this complexity. The people in Marcellus's spiritual theatre had 'invested the same symbol with an ambiguous value as a result of a long series of contaminations and metamorphoses'. The potential sources of these are vast. Le Goff ranges from China to Ireland, across what he distinguishes as Germano-Asiatic, Graeco-Roman and autochthonous dragon lore. He then writes confidently: 'underlying all these traditions, do we not find the quasi-universal serpent-dragon common to all primitive beliefs and myths? Was not the Merovingian dragon above all a monster of folklore which had resurfaced during an interregnum between two beliefs, when pagan culture was fading before the Christian cultural system had really taken root?' And he concludes that the story of Marcellus's taming of the dragon is essentially a foundation myth. The bishop's victory represents the subjugation of the hostile forces of nature. Marcellus's miracle makes possible both cultivation and settlement.[19]

My purpose is far more to supplement this analysis than to quarrel with it. There is much to command immediate assent. First, Le Goff notes that two different stories involving dragons appear to have been run together in the narrative of the saint's last miracle.

[18] 'Ecclesiastical Culture and Folklore in the Middle Ages: Saint Marcellus of Paris and the Dragon', first published in L. de Rosa (ed.), *Ricerche Storiche ed Economiche in Memoria di Corrado Barbagallo*, 3 vols. (Naples, 1970), II, pp. 51–90. I have for convenience used the translation: *Time, Work, and Culture in the Middle Ages* (Chicago and London, 1980), pp. 159–88. In what follows it will be clear that I am overwhelmingly indebted to Le Goff's piece as an abundant source of references and ideas, and also that I am not concerned with the second half of his paper (pp. 174ff), on the later medieval cult of Marcellus.

[19] Le Goff, 'Marcellus', pp. 162, 172.

The opening story – of the adulteress whose entombed corpse the monster devours – has a history of its own that need not be pursued here.[20] We should certainly register the implied correspondence between the various elements in Fortunatus's paragraph: between the woman's loss of moral and sexual integrity, the violation of her tomb (which should have been a place of order and repose), and the disruption of the whole pattern of settlement.[21] Yet it is the dragon as communal enemy rather than individual nemesis that dominates the narrative and demands attention. Secondly, Le Goff rightly points out that in the later of the two stories Fortunatus hardly represents his hero's dragon as diabolical in character. There is not, perhaps, 'a total absence of symbolic interpretation'.[22] Fortunatus after all emphasises the 'spiritual' aspect both of the weapons that the saint deploys – prayer, crook and stole, frail fingers – and of the context in which he performs – a theatre or arena. In the saint's injunction to the monster to confine itself to the desert or the sea, moreover, there is a strong hint of a formula of exorcism.[23] Yet, overall, the dragon-slaying saint does appear 'in his worldly role as chief of an urban community'. Thirdly, when seen in the widest context, the dragon is certainly a 'polyvalent' creature. Late antique and early medieval Christianity could not avoid bearing the imprint of a number of traditions in which Marcellus's combat is foreshadowed. And these traditions do imply the freeing for human occupation of an initially unpromising site and the taming of natural forces.[24]

There are, however, two aspects of Le Goff's analysis that seem to me to hinder understanding of the significance of the saint's dragon-taming for sixth-century Parisians. The first of them is the sheer number of dragon legends that we are offered by way of background. There are no established criteria of relevance to Fortunatus's

---

[20] *Ibid.*, p. 162 nn. 12, 28. Cf. 'Apocalypse of Paul', *New Testament Apocrypha*, ed. E. Hennecke and W. Schneemelcher, 2 vols. (London, 1963–5), II, p. 783 n. 4.

[21] I owe the point to Peter Brown.

[22] Le Goff, 'Marcellus', p. 164.

[23] Cf. the prayer of exorcism (misattributed to St Basil) quoted by C. Mango, *Byzantium* (London, 1980), p. 160, from J. Goar, *Euchologion sive Rituale Graecorum* (Paris, 1647), pp. 730–1; A. Franz, *Die kirchlichen Benediktionen im Mittelalter*, 2 vols. (Freiburg im Breisgau, 1909), II, pp. 547ff.

[24] Cf. P. Boglioni, 'Il Santo e gli Animali nell'alto medioevo', *Settimane di Studio . . . Spoleto*, 31, 2 (1985), pp. 970ff. Contrast H. Delehaye, 'Euchaïta et la Légende de S. Théodore', in W. H. Buckler and W. M. Calder (eds.), *Anatolian Studies Presented to Sir William Ramsay* (Manchester, 1923), p. 131.

text. It is not therefore clear that, say, the Egyptian Seth or Cadmus of Thebes exerted any great pressure on the minds of sixth-century Franks. Nor can we be confident that Asiatic dragons were beginning to make a discernible impact on the Franks' repertoire of monstrous imagery during the Merovingian period.[25]

The second difficulty arises from the sharp distinction that Le Goff draws between his two cultures, and his tendency to represent each of them as homogeneous. Perhaps there was a determinate clerical culture in the early Middle Ages – a culture that derived its ideas about dragons from the Bible, the Fathers and the earliest hagiography. But if so, it was far from speaking with one voice on the subject. As Le Goff himself reveals, there was for example a tradition of scientific thinking about monsters in which the indebtedness to antiquity is as striking as the absence of diabolical symbolism.[26] A satisfactory definition of popular culture proves even more elusive. For Le Goff it seems to be, on one hand, the residue of ancient mythology, a collection of 'quasi-universals' that survive more or less unchanged across millennia until they can be recorded by folklorists. On the other hand, it is apparently so amorphous that it must be defined in negative terms. It is non-clerical – which means that it is what cannot be found in the standard encyclopaedias of Christian thought. It is not literate   so that it breaks surface in the historical record of the early Middle Ages only when the repressive culture of the dominant class (clerical culture) is in disarray, and drops its literary guard.

Everything that we have learned in recent years from historians of cult practice, of language, of 'lay literacy', of the interaction between the written and the oral, of clerical and monastic taste in supposedly folkloric material, suggests that this Marxian typology is inadequate.[27] I would prefer to conceive Fortunatus's account of Marcellus

---

[25] Cf. Gregory of Tours, *Liber in Gloria Martyrum*, preface (p. 487); *Liber de Passione et Virtutibus Sancti Juliani Martyris*, 5 (pp. 566–7). E. Salin, *La Civilisation mérovingienne*, 4 vols. (Paris, 1949–59), IV, pp. 207ff, 241ff.

[26] Le Goff, 'Marcellus', pp. 166–7; *Reallexikon für Antike und Christentum, s.v.* 'Drache', cols. 226–7; Collins, 'Venantius Fortunatus', p. 97.

[27] P. Brown, *The Cult of the Saints* (London, 1981), ch. 1; R. McKitterick, *The Carolingians and the Written Word* (Cambridge, 1989); B. Stock, *The Implications of Literacy. Written Language and Models of Interpretation in the Eleventh and Twelfth Centuries* (Princeton, 1983); P. Wormald, 'Bede, "Beowulf" and the Conversion of the Anglo-Saxon Aristocracy', in R. T. Farrell (ed.), *Bede and Anglo-Saxon England*, British Archaeological Reports XLVI (Oxford, 1978), pp. 32–95.

less as a focus of tension between two widely differing cultures than as a point on the single spectrum of possible beliefs about monsters that formed part of the essentially unitary culture of Merovingian Francia. On this spectrum there is certainly room for the use of the dragon as pure symbol (metaphor rather than metonymy, to recall Jakobson's antithesis[28]). But at the heart of most propositions involving dragons is an acceptance of their material existence. In preparing his *Life* of the saint, Fortunatus needed oral testimony, for he had little or nothing in writing on which to base his narrative.[29] But there is no evidence that his informants were mainly the old Filates of sixth-century Paris. Nor are there any clear signs that he found his information ideologically repugnant – even though he was among the most educated men of his day. Recounting Marcellus's final miracle, he moves back and forth between the metaphorical and the metonymic within the space of two lines of text. His *Life* of the saint was, like all his hagiography, designed for both clerical and lay consumption. It would have been read annually to Parisian congregations, perhaps as part of the liturgy, on the day commemorating Marcellus's death. Its audience formed what has usefully been called a textual community. That community should, I believe, provide our frame of reference.[30]

III

I now wish to propose a reading of Fortunatus's text that takes its cue less from supposed universals of myth and folklore or models of cultural conflict than from a shared sense of locality between saint and populace, hagiographer and audience. The case that I hope to make cannot be properly supported in even the limited fashion with which medievalists must generally be content. As far as Marcellus is concerned, I have to go beyond, though I trust not against, the evidence. I cannot hope for 'glory' according to Humpty Dumpty's wilful definition – that is, 'a nice knock-down argument'. I certainly do not propose a complete revaluation of all early medieval dragons

---

[28] R. Jakobson, 'Two Aspects of Language and Two Types of Aphasic Disturbance', in R. Jakobson and M. Halle (eds.), *Fundamentals of Language* (The Hague, 1956), pp. 55–82.

[29] *Vita Marcelli*, 2 (p. 50). Does the mention of the date of the saint's death at the very end of the text suggest access to an episcopal list?

[30] Collins, 'Venantius Fortunatus', pp. 107–8; Stock, *Implications of Literacy*.

or even of the few on which I shall concentrate, but, rather, a hint of one particular pressure exerted upon those who spoke or wrote about them: the pressure of an epidemic upon an idea.

Recall first, from his earlier miracles, Marcellus's ability to assess the capacity of nature and turn possible harm to certain benefit. Recall in addition the report that the dragon whips the air with its tail, and that its ferocity compels Parisians to abandon their homes. Fortunatus identifies these Parisians as the dead woman's *familia*, but that may have been a device to harmonise the two stories that he or his informants had conjoined. Certainly by the end of his account the monster has become the 'public enemy'. The dragon seems to appear on the outskirts of the city. When it has left the woman's tomb it retreats to the woods. After subduing it, however, Marcellus banishes it to either desert or sea ('aut deserta ... aut in mare'), in effect to water or wasteland. Thereafter, not even traces (*indicia*) of it are to be found.

To begin to clarify the possible implications of these ecological touches, we must look for analogues. An immediate comparison is suggested by Fortunatus himself, who concludes that 'Gaul should admire Marcellus as Rome does Silvester'.[31] The legend of Pope Silvester has usually been studied in connection with that renowned forgery, the Donation of Constantine. There is one version of the legend in which the pope manages to subjugate a dragon that lives in a rocky cave under the Capitol. When the heathens see that the monster really has at last been overcome, they convert to Christianity. The pope's battle with the dragon appears in this context to be equivalent to his victory over paganism. But there is another version of the legend, apparently favoured within Rome, according to which Silvester's dragon was a giant serpent washed ashore when the Tiber flooded. The pope's task becomes one of leadership in the response to natural disaster, the consequence of flooding.[32] Something of the perceived extent of the challenge is revealed by events in Rome in the time of Pope Gregory the Great.

Gregory of Tours, writing only a few years after the occasion that he purports to describe, recounts what his deacon told him on returning from Rome in 590. In November of the previous year the Tiber had flooded the city, destroying the papal granaries and a number of churches. 'A great school of water snakes swam down the

---

[31] *Vita Marcelli*, 10 (p. 54).   [32] Le Goff, 'Marcellus', p. 168 with nn. 45–7.

river to the sea, and in their midst was a tremendous dragon as big as
a tree-trunk, but these monsters were drowned in the turbulent salt
waves of the sea and their bodies were washed up on the shore.' An
epidemic ensued – of plague. The first to succumb was Pelagius, the
reigning pontiff. His successor, Gregory the Great, led the people in
penitential processions. There was no dragon to combat: it had
already died. But the association of dragons with the linked disasters
of flooding and pestilence is noteworthy. (According to Gregory,
torrential rains were among the signs preceding the arrival of plague
in Gaul.)[33]

To determine Fortunatus's sources for the *Life* of Marcellus is not
my aim. But it is a useful connection to make, a check on relevance,
that he might have known Gregory's account. He might also have
known the story, much later preserved by Isidore of Seville, about
Donatus, a bishop of Epirus who would have been a near-contemporary of Marcellus. This bishop was said to have slain an enormous
dragon whose breath and body turned the air putrid.[34]

Fortunatus's own work provides a further illuminating analogue
of his story of Marcellus. It comes from his *Life* of St Hilary. The
saint is passing the island of Gallinara, which lies opposite Albenga
on the Ligurian coast. Coastal dwellers tell him of the innumerable
serpents that infest the island, making settlement impossible.
Although it is within sight of the mainland, its inaccessibility makes
it seem further away than Africa. The serpents flee, however, at the
sight of the saint. Hilary uses his episcopal staff as a marker to divide
the island into two parts. The serpents are restricted to one sector,
and cannot again trouble the other, even though a portion of the
island – including, presumably, some of the sector now available for
settlement – 'is not so much land as water' – lake or swamp. In
contrasting Hilary with Adam, the hagiographer does here gloss
these serpents as diabolical. But he emphatically ends this chapter in
his narrative with the assertion that Hilary has opened up the island
for human occupation.[35] And we might add, in a gloss of our own,
that he has done it through some kind of technological insight. He

[33] *Libri Historiarum*, X, 1 (pp. 406–7); X, 23 (p. 435); quotation adapted from the
translation by L. Thorpe, *Gregory of Tours: History of the Franks* (Harmondsworth, 1974), p. 543. Cf. Gregory the Great, *Dialogi*, III, 19, ed. A. de Vogüé,
Sources Chrétiennes, 3 vols. (Paris, 1978–80), II, pp. 346–8.
[34] *Chronicon*, 107, ed. J.-P. Migne, *Patrologia Latina*, LXXXIII, col. 1051; Le Goff,
'Marcellus', p. 167.
[35] *Vita Hilarii*, 10, ed. Krusch, *MGH, AA*, IV, 2, p. 5.

manages the threat posed by the snakes; he knows where to draw the line between the safe and unsafe parts of the island.

After such analogues, it will be asked, what of St George? A late version of his career, preserved in the *Golden Legend,* has the saint living in a great swamp near the town of Silene in Libya. The inhabitants are daily being killed by the dragon's breath, and the survivors offer up their children to appease it until none is left but the king's daughter. The rest of the story is now familiar. But it would not have been so in the sixth century. The cult of George had indeed spread to Gaul – despite papal prohibition. But his fight with the dragon was apparently not then part of his legend.[36]

If we must exclude St George, there are nonetheless other Frankish hagiographical dragons that can helpfully be set alongside the one challenged by Marcellus. In the story of the conversion of the martyr Afra, a Carolingian text, a dragon is to be found living near a spring in the Julian Alps. It allows no one to drink there; indeed its breath kills all who approach. It is not simply a manifestation of the Devil, for only a ruse of Narcissus, the bishop involved, transfers into its body the demon that has been possessing Afra.[37] The pestilential quality of the monster is not always so explicit. But the dragons or serpents (it would be a mistake to distinguish between them too carefully) that are quite often reported as infesting wells or other sources of water are clearly capable of a variety of harms: they can do more than coil and bite.[38]

Gregory of Tours, for example, includes in his anthology of local saints, the *Book of the Life of the Fathers,* the curious tale of the hermit Caluppa. He is one day confronted in his cave by two enormous dragons. Gregory pronounces one of them stronger than the other and thus 'the very chief of every temptation', the Devil. While the saint is conquering this animal with the power of the cross, the second monster entwines itself around his legs. It too is expelled from the cave (by prayer). But as a parting shot it lets out 'a formidable noise from its rear end', filling the little cell with a great stink. For Gregory, such eructation must, again, be a sign of the Devil's work: he appears far more reluctant than Fortunatus to

---

[36] *Reallexikon für Antike und Christentum,* cols. 245–6; Gregory of Tours, *Liber in Gloria Martyrum,* 100 (pp. 554–5).

[37] *Conversio Afrae,* 7, ed. Krusch, *MGH, SRM,* III (1896), p. 60. Contrast the allegorical interpretation in *Reallexikon für Antike und Christentum,* col. 248.

[38] Cf. *Vita Iohannis Abbatis Reomanensis,* 2, ed. Krusch, *MGH, SRM,* III (1896), p. 507: serpent infests a well.

accept the metonymic character of his sources, even though the hermit was his near-contemporary and, at the end of the story, the reader is left wondering why two diabolical dragons, unequal in strength, should have been included.[39] The dragon's lingering stench may have been differently construed by those who transmitted the story. Gregory himself, moreover, is happy elsewhere to adopt a naturalistic account of a giant serpent that inhabits a field. It has been devastating an entire region, causing widespread panic and depopulation. The saint who deals with it is no less than the Apostle Andrew. As the serpent dies, it coils itself around an oak tree, and vomits a river of blood – and poison. The apostle goes on to bring back from the dead one of those whom the serpent has smitten.[40]

In another piece of hagiography, ostensibly Merovingian but perhaps a Carolingian forgery, the young St Amand frees a whole island from imminent danger by miraculously compelling a huge snake to retreat to its cave.[41] In this account the nature of the threat is not specified at all. But some idea of its possible consequences may perhaps be gained from a different part of the *Life*, where the 'ingens plaga' ('great disaster' – or perhaps 'great plague') visited upon those who ignore the saint's preaching is described with a certain vividness: 'houses collapsed, fields were made into solitudes, even small towns and forts were destroyed, and hardly anyone remained in these regions of those who had despised the preaching of the man of God'.[42] The two episodes in the *Life* are not directly connected – unless, that is, one ignores the naturalistic tone of the author and interprets both as signs of the Devil's work. But the second one (just quoted) does show us that the hagiographer envisaged the saving power of the saint in terms of corporate material well-being. And his evocation may suggest, to the incautious, nothing so much as the aftermath of some epidemic.

---

[39] *Liber Vitae Patrum*, XI, 1 (pp. 709–10), trans. E. James, *Gregory of Tours: Life of the Fathers* (Liverpool, 1985), pp. 88–9. *Libri Historiarum*, V, 9 (p. 199). Cf. Wallace-Hadrill, *Frankish Church*, pp. 81–2.

[40] *Liber de Miraculis Beati Andreae Apostoli*, 19 (p. 837). On the matter of authorship, and the original that was adapted, see K. Zelzer, 'Zur Frage des Autors der Miracula B. Andreae Apostoli und zur Sprache des Gregor von Tours', *Grazer Beiträge*, 6 (1977), pp. 217–41.

[41] *Vita Amandi*, 2, ed. Krusch, *MGH*, *SRM*, V (1910), p. 440, trans. J. N. Hillgarth, *Christianity and Paganism, 350–750* (Philadelphia, 1986), p. 140. On the question of authenticity, see I. N. Wood, 'Forgery in Merovingian Hagiography', *Fälschungen im Mittelalter*, MGH Schriften XXXIII (Hanover, 1988), V, pp. 371–2.

[42] *Vita Amandi*, 19 (p. 443), trans. Hillgarth, *Christianity*, p. 146.

I must clearly not urge too strongly a purely nosological explanation of this cluster of sources. But a loosely connected group of recurrent images can be said to have emerged. The dragon makes its home in fields or standing water of some kind. It prevents access to the pure spring. Its insides or its exhalations are lethal. It is in the strict sense of the word epidemic, affecting not just individuals.[43] It can cause widespread depopulation. Sometimes it is an embodiment of the Devil – though that need hardly make it any the less pestiferous, for the Devil is quite capable of causing epidemics, whatever form he assumes.[44] The texts invoked present something rather different from foundation myths, partly because in some there is already habitation in the area where the dragon wreaks its destruction, partly because the making available of an area of land that occurs in others does not apparently signify the origin of a determinate settlement. The dragon-slayer is the figure who renders safe a whole route or area, who demarcates the waste and the habitable, contains the environmental hazard and, it can be added, given the dragon's noxious breath, makes the area salubrious.

This attempt to capture the implications of the hagiography may be strengthened by looking at evidence that does not specifically relate to dragon-slaying. One form of dragon is a monstrous snake. It is we, not early medieval commentators, who make a distinction of terminology (and ontology) between the two. Snakes, of whatever size, can obviously be harmful, both individually, as the remedies for snake bite in the medical texts of the early Middle Ages remind us,[45] and collectively. The image of snakes infecting the whole world with their poison goes back at least to the Emperor Diocletian's Edict against the Manichaeans.[46] And we can perhaps relate to it one of the more curious anecdotes in the *Book of Histories* by Gregory of

[43] Cf. *Lacnunga*, 80, ed. J. H. G. Grattan and C. Singer, *Anglo-Saxon Magic and Medicine* (London, 1952), pp. 152–5: origin of diseases in pieces of serpent smitten by Woden.

[44] Gregory of Tours, *Liber Vitae Patrum*, XVII, 3–4 (pp. 730–1).

[45] See Marcellus Burdigalensis, *De Medicamentis Liber*, XXXV, 8, ed. M. Niedermann and E. Liechtenhan, Corpus Medicorum Latinorum V, 2 vols. (Berlin, 1968), II, pp. 588–90; W. Bonser, *The Medical Background of Anglo-Saxon England* (London, 1963), ch. 20. Cf. Sulpicius Severus, *Dialogi*, I, 25, ed. C. Halm, Corpus Scriptorum Ecclesiasticorum Latinorum, I (1866), p. 177.

[46] P. Brown, *Religion and Society in the Age of Saint Augustine* (London, 1972), p. 95. Cf. Eusebius, *Historia Ecclesiastica*, VII, 31. The image's subsequent history is examined in P. Courcelle, 'Le Serpent à face humaine dans la numismatique impériale du Ve siècle', in R. Chevallier (ed.), *Mélanges d'archéologie et d'histoire offerts à André Piganiol*, 3 vols. (Paris, 1966), I, pp. 343–53.

Tours. The discovery in the mud blocking a drain of a snake and rat, fashioned in bronze and presumably pagan cultic objects, heralds the infestation of the city by large numbers of both animals, and a 'plague' of fires.[47]

A further passage in Gregory's writings deserves consideration in this context.

In the territory of Javols there was a mountain ... that contained a large lake. At a fixed time a crowd of rustics went there and, as if offering libations to the lake, threw [into it] linen cloths and garments that served men as clothing. Some [threw] pelts of wool, many [threw] models of cheese and wax and bread as well as various other objects ... They came with their wagons; they brought food and drink, sacrificed animals, and feasted for three days.[48]

The models may have been votive offerings of the kind that had long been an established feature of cultic practice in Gaul. And the whole episode is frequently cited as an example of how cunningly bishops in Francia dealt with enduring instances of rural paganism.[49] For the bishop simply diverted the revellers into a church that he had built nearby. But his mildly ungrammatical exhortation, 'nulla est religio in stagnum' – literally and most effectively translated as 'there is no religion in a lake' – can perhaps be taken as an indication of a more general problem that the Frankish church had to confront: an awareness of the potentially dangerous forces – dragons certainly among them – that could issue from standing water and that would require propitiation. Without reverting to Le Goff's interpretation of dragon combats as no more than symbols of the church's victory over paganism, we could nonetheless see Marcellus's great victory as another way of proclaiming: 'nulla est religio in stagnum'. The destructive power of waste or water could be far more effectively dealt with by a bishop than by a model made of cheese. The celebrations could signal not just temporary appeasement of that power (as in Gregory's vignette) but its permanent negation.

---

[47] *Libri Historiarum*, VIII, 33 (pp. 349–50).

[48] *Liber in Gloria Confessorum*, 2 (p. 750), trans. Van Dam, *Glory of the Confessors*, p. 19. Cf. Brown, *Cult of the Saints*, pp. 125–6, with discussion but mistaken reference.

[49] S. Deyts, *Les Bois sculptés des sources de la Seine* (Paris, 1983); Wallace-Hadrill, *Frankish Church*, ch. 2, esp. p. 29. Cf. G. Traina, *Paludi e Bonifiche del Mondo Antico* (Rome, 1988), pp. 120–4.

I have set out evidence to support the proposal that we envisage some of the monsters infesting the pages of Merovingian and related early medieval hagiography as dragons of epidemic disease, and therefore that we recognise in some feats of dragon-slaying a means of restoring salubrity. This is, I submit, at least a possible interpretation of the sources. To demonstrate that it is a possibility quite clearly capable of being realised in medieval hagiography, whatever our final assessment of the Merovingian evidence, I turn to another corpus of texts not entirely remote from those already reviewed.

IV

'If we take the Celtic world as a whole,' Le Goff noted, 'certain areas are swarming with dragons.'[50] A good many of them are aquatic monsters. They emerge from standing water. A certain amount of what we initially find is, indeed, familiar, particularly in Irish sources (both Latin and vernacular). St Molua saves two young swimmers from a beast pursuing them across a lake, and then, when the monster attempts to climb on to dry land, orders it to return to the lake and stay there – rather as Marcellus despatched his dragon. St Samthanne confronts another lacustrine beast, dangerous to men and animals alike. The Latin *Life* of Abbanus is more detailed than most. Here, the saint first causes a poisonous leonine monster that is terrorising the area literally to lie down and die. He is then besought by the people to deal with the equally poisonous beasts living in the lake that have already killed one hundred men and as many animals. Much like Marcellus he goes forward with the people to the place of danger. He then enters the water alone. The beasts are overcome by the sight of his angelic countenance. He orders them to go with him deep into the lake, and establishes a particular habitat for them there, binding them that they remain in it until the end of the world. It is no surprise, then, that the saint should subsequently chain to the edge of a lake a monstrous and fiery cat that he has 'domesticated'. Such beasts have to be kept within aqueous confines.[51]

The Old Irish *Life* of Colman Ela presents us with a rather unusual, explicitly pestilent, enemy: 'a small pointed gaping appari-

---

[50] Le Goff, 'Marcellus', p. 171. Cf. Graus, *Volk*, pp. 231–2.
[51] *Vita Moluae*, 25, ed. C. Plummer, *Vitae Sanctorum Hiberniae*, 2 vols. (Oxford, 1910), II, p. 213; *Vita Samthanne*, 8 (ed. Plummer, II, p. 255); *Vita Abbani*, 15–16, 18 (ed. Plummer, I, pp. 12–13, 15).

tion in the shape of a woman' with 'short bushy hair, unwashed and unkempt'.[52] And the various *Lives* of Coemgen bring out the connection between the taming or containment of such a beast and the improvement of health. In the Latin *Life*, the saint is found praying at night in the freezing water of a lake, where he is threatened by a horrid beast. One of the Old Irish *Lives* adds some detail:

> There was a horrible and strange monster in the lake, which wrought frequent destruction of dogs and men . . . Coemgen . . . drove the monster from him into the other lake. That is to say, the lesser lake, in which the monster [originally] was, is the place where help of every trouble is wrought both for men and cattle; and they all leave their sicknesses there, and the sicknesses and diseases go into the other lake to the monster, so that it does not injure anyone.

A verse *Life* clarifies this account a little. The saint 'expelled . . . the drop-poison of the monster from the lough', so that, far from being a source of harm, its function was, as it were, reversed, and 'plagues were removed from the kine of the Gaels'.[53]

These examples are all drawn from Plummer's editions of Irish saints' *Lives*. The Latin versions are apparently the earliest, and none of them is very ancient. (One of the first monsters in Celtic hagiography, the seventh-century ancestor of the Loch Ness monster that is subdued by St Columba in Adomnan's *Life* of him, does not belong here, because the monster remains in the water and bites, shark-like, at its victims.[54]) The identifiable individuals who appear in Plummer's texts can generally be dated to the sixth or seventh centuries. But the impulse toward their composition may have been the reconstitution of many monasteries that followed the coming of the English in the twelfth century. Very little can be said about the prior elaboration of the traditions on which they depended, except by adducing parallels and comparisons from other literary genres.[55]

---

[52] *Betha Cholmain Eala*, 1, 2, ed. C. Plummer, *Bethada Náem Nérenn: Lives of the Irish Saints*, 2 vols. (Oxford, 1922), I, pp. 168–9 (text); II, pp. 162–3 (trans.).

[53] *Vita Coemgeni*, 18 (ed. Plummer, *Vitae Sanctorum*, I, p. 243); *Bethada Caoimhgin* (I) 8, (II) 3b (ed. Plummer, *Bethada*, I, pp. 126, 135; II, pp. 122, 131).

[54] *Vita Columbae*, II, 27, ed. A. O. and M. O. Anderson, *Adomnan's Life of Columba* (Edinburgh, 1961), pp. 386–8.

[55] Plummer, *Vitae Sanctorum*, I, p. clxxxvii. Since the above was written, R. Sharpe, *Medieval Irish Saints' Lives* (Oxford, 1991), has shown that base-texts from around 800 may be postulated for some of the Latin hagiography.

(One such comparison is the extraordinary image to be found in the twelfth-century *Vision* attributed to the peasant Tnugdal. A fire-breathing bird-like monster sits on a frozen swamp digesting the souls of sinners and excreting them as dung on the ice.[56]) It seems reasonable, however, to suppose, with Plummer, that the *Lives* contain much earlier, and 'sometimes primitive', materials – dating from the ninth or tenth centuries, if no earlier.[57] The saints may therefore not be quite as remote in time from the world of Marcellus (and Adomnan) as the textual history of their *Lives* would suggest.

Less remote in a geographical sense is a late ninth-century text, the *Life* of St Paul Aurelian (Paul of Léon in Brittany) by the monk Wrmonoc. A monster, described with extraordinary physiological exactitude, is terrorising the coastal area of an island, the Ile de Batz, causing man and beast to expire with, among other attributes, its pestiferous breath. The saint confronts it with the question, 'what are you up to here, you sower of a malign, pestiferous crop?', and then proceeds to harangue it at some length. He subdues the monster by tying his stole around its neck and then, in a phrase strikingly reminiscent of Fortunatus's narrative, banishes it 'to the inaccessible wastes of the sea'.[58] No mere dragon-tamer, moreover, the saint has already proved adept at turning back the forces of nature to appointed confines. His sister planned to establish a religious house on the coast of their native Britain, but the sea continually encroached on the narrow strip of available land. Paul took her to the edge of the water at low tide and told her to dispose pebbles in two rows as a boundary marker. The pebbles immediately grew into huge stone columns – still visible in Wrmonoc's day. The sea never thereafter crossed the boundary. And the land thus reclaimed became the most fertile in the nunnery's possession.[59]

Samson of Dol should also be allowed his contribution at this point. According to his early Breton hagiographer, this saint confines a giant fire-spitting serpent within a circle that he has drawn on

---

[56] *Visio Tnugdali: Lateinisch und Altdeutsch*, ed. A. Wagner (Erlangen, 1882), pp. 27–9 (cf. pp. 16–17); trans. J. M. Picard and Y. de Pontfarcy (Dublin, 1989), p. 130. On the work see H. Spilling, *Die Visio Tnugdali* (Munich, 1975).

[57] Plummer, *Vitae Sanctorum*, I, p. xc.

[58] 'Vie de Saint Paul de Léon en Bretagne', ed. C. Cuissard, *Revue Celtique*, 5 (1881–3), pp. 447–9 (*cap.* 18).

[59] Ed. Cuissard, pp. 434–6 (*cap.* 10). Cf. the parallel anecdote (of St Illtud) on pp. 422–3 (*cap.* 14); also G. H. Doble, *Lives of the Welsh Saints*, 2nd edn (Cardiff, 1971), pp. 146–61, for topographical speculations.

the ground. (The monster gives up its venom as it dies.) He also deals with a poisonous snake that has depopulated two villages and, significantly in the present context, lives beyond a river in a cave. A similar beast, 'afflicting with a severe pestilence' according to a late version of Samson's *Life*, is made to cross the Seine and remain under a stone.[60]

'Possibly some of the many stories of the destruction of monsters are to be explained in this way': Plummer had two grounds for the explanation that he cautiously offered in a footnote.[61] One was the frequency with which monsters such as those now described are said by the hagiographers to be spreading pestilence. The second was the small number of texts in which the apparent implication of the others is made quite explicit and the monster does indeed embody some epidemic. I have already noticed the unprepossessing female apparition in the *Life* of Colman Ela. I now present two other monsters, neither of which, unfortunately, can confidently be said to derive from any early tradition.

The first moves us from Ireland and Brittany to Wales. Among the legends of the death of Maelgwn, the king of Gwynedd so prominent in Gildas, is one that has him hiding from an epidemic in a church not far from his court. 'And Maelgwn Gwynedd beheld the Yellow Plague through the keyhole in the church door and forthwith died.' What he is supposed to have seen is described in the verse attributed to the renowned bard Taliesin in the 'Hanes Taliesin' that Lady Charlotte Guest included in her pioneering translation of the *Mabinogion*: a beast with golden eyes, teeth and hair that has come, again significantly, from a marsh.[62]

[60] *Vita Samsonis*, I, 32, 50, 58, ed. R. Fawtier, *La Vie de Saint Samson*, Bibliothèques de l'Ecole des Hautes Etudes, Sciences Historiques et Philologiques, 197 (1912), pp. 129–31, 145–6, 152–3; *The Text of the Book of Llan Dav*, ed. Evans and Rhys, p. 23. For the various versions of the *Life* see E. R. Henken, *Traditions of the Welsh Saints* (Woodbridge, 1987), ch. 8. On the date of the early version, P. Ó Riain, 'Samson alias San(c)tán', *Peritia*, 3 (1984), pp. 320–3; Wood, 'Forgery', pp. 380–4.

[61] Plummer, *Vitae Sanctorum*, I, p. cxi n. 1. Cf. p. cxxxix.

[62] T. Williams (ed.), *Iolo Manuscripts* (Llandovery, 1848, repr. 1888), pp. 78 (text), 467 (trans.). *Mabinogion*, ed. Lady C. Guest, 3 vols. (London, 1849), III, p. 377. On the legend of Maelgwn, in Gildas's *De Excidio Britanniae* and elsewhere, see *Trioedd Ynys Prydein: The Welsh Triads*, ed. R. Bromwich (Cardiff, 1961), pp. 437–41. On the 'Yellow Plague' see the divergent accounts and diagnoses in Bonser, *Medical Background*, pp. 64ff; J. C. Russell, 'The Earlier Medieval Plague in the British Isles', *Viator*, 7 (1976), pp. 65–78; G. Twigg, *The Black Death: A Biological Reappraisal* (London, 1984), pp. 38–42.

A more extensive account of such a monster of plague is to be found in the *Life* of the somewhat mercenary and unpleasant saint Mac Reiche. The historical existence of this figure is described by Plummer as 'extremely shadowy' and the *Life* of him as 'utterly unhistorical'.[63] First we meet the Crom Conaill, a beast which, one reads, 'is' the plague. Later in the *Life*, however, we learn of a variety of beasts, each of which attacked a different area of Ireland during the pandemic (of the sixth century?). One of these is the Broicsech, the badger monster, that apparently survived in local tradition in the 1920s. Like Columba's beast, it came from a loch:

> a monster most vehement, strong, malignant, unwearied, with its bestial rage upon it; and it wreaked great slaughters throughout the land generally . . . it would open its ravenous raging maw like a mad dog, with its jaws all on fire, and emit a broad terrifying stream of harsh magical breath . . . and every man whom that poisonous breath touched and every animal died a premature and sudden death . . . and this was the extent of their losses, to wit, men and women to the number of sixty every day.

The *Life* goes on to describe an agonised assembly where the people debate what should be done (and which the monster itself infiltrates), the collective fasting and the eventual summoning of the saint who uses his staff to force the monster back into its loch, and then contains it with a skull cap when it reappears.[64]

V

I have relied on the presumed continuities of the various Celtic traditions as a licence to extend the search for pestilent dragons into the central and later Middle Ages. I shall not take the same chronological liberty with other traditions. Instead, I come back to Marcellus. Now that the *ideological* context of his legend has been offered for inspection (principally in the form of hagiographical analogies), I turn to its *material* context, the environs of Merovingian Paris.

[63] *Miscellanea Hagiographica Hibernica, Subsidia Hagiographica* XV, ed. C. Plummer (Brussels, 1925), p. 8.

[64] *Bethe Meic Creiche*, 9, ed. Plummer, *Miscellanea*, pp. 18–19 (text), 58–9 (trans.); 14–18 (pp. 36–51, 75–90); quotation from pp. 36, 76; 'survival' of monster in local tradition, p. 11.

The backdrop against which we should visualise Marcellus's encounter with his dragon can be reconstructed in surprising detail.[65] By the time that Fortunatus wrote, Marcellus's name had come to be associated with the territory of a particular suburban village, later the Faubourg Saint-Marcel. This faubourg covers the lower valley of the Bièvre, a small confluent of the Seine that once joined it in the region of the Gare d'Austerlitz. Something of the area's aboriginal character can still be seen in low-lying parts of the present-day Jardin des Plantes. Because it rests on a base of soft impermeable clay, the soil of Paris has always been poorly drained, and the rivers have, until modern times, easily spilled over into marshes. One of the most frequently flooded and marshy areas of the Left Bank was the confluence of the Seine and the Bièvre. Not far from such marshes lay the edge of the forest, of which the Bois de Boulogne and the Forest of Vincennes are the modern remnants. Pollen analysis reveals the ancient abundance of this forest. In the spaces remaining here for agriculture and settlement, cultivation had to be quite intensive to make the best of limited resources. For marshes that stretched in a barely interrupted arc from the site of the Bastille to the Champ de Mars prevented extensive colonisation of the Right Bank.[66]

There were other reasons why the area that concerns us became important. In Roman and sub-Roman times the main road to Sens and Lyons ran through it, parallel to the Left Bank. Marcellus's suburb, the oldest of those around Paris, grew up beside this road. Along it, stone from the nearby quarries could, of course, easily be transported. (The stone of the public buildings of Roman *Lutecia* is nearly all of local provenance.) Saint-Marcel was, then, in all likelihood a Roman faubourg of masons and artisans. Along its main road, also, came Christianity from the south. This suburb is indeed the oldest area of Christian settlement in Paris. From the end

---

[65] In what follows I have relied on: P.-M. Duval, *Paris antique des origines au troisième siècle* (Paris, 1961); M. Roblin, *Le Terroir de Paris aux époques gallo-romaine et franque*, 2nd edn (Paris, 1971); M.-L. Concasty, 'Le Bourg Saint-Marcel à Paris des origines au XVIe siècle', in *Ecole Nationale des Chartes: position des thèses 1937* (Nogent-le-Rotrou, 1937), pp. 26–37. Cf. Le Goff, 'Marcellus', pp. 162, 172–3. It is not clear what evidence permits Le Goff to assert so confidently (pp. 160–1) that 'the site of [Marcellus's] last miracle was the location of his tomb'.

[66] See A. Lombard-Jourdan, *Paris – genèse de la 'ville': la rive droite de la Seine des origines à 1223* (Paris, 1976).

of the third century, Christian cemeteries spread out on either side of the main road. And during the fifth century, tombs began to cluster around the doubtless modest sanctuary where Marcellus was – or was later thought to be – buried.[67] Such was the area to which the saint lent his name. Its topography corresponds to what we find mentioned in the *Life*. The scene there is suburban. There is a cemetery, but also settlement. Forest, wasteland and water are not far off. But for some conception of the hazards of life in the faubourg we have to turn to evidence of a later date. The floods seem to have posed the greatest clearly identifiable danger. Gregory of Tours records what is perhaps the earliest one of known date in Paris. That of 1196 was, so a seventeenth-century report had it, equal in volume to Noah's. Exactly a century later, the Bièvre flooded so destructively that Philip the Fair had to order the hasty construction of pontoon bridges. And the early fiftccnth-ccntury *Journal d'un Bourgeois de Paris* creates a vivid impression of the terrible impact of recurrent inundation on city life generally.[68]

To read Richard Cobb's *Paris and its Provinces* is to gain the perhaps not wholly misleading impression that the ecology had not changed fundamentally by the time of the Revolution. Eighteenth-century Paris remained encircled by woodland. Trees lined the major roads leading into the city to within two leagues of its centre. The Left Bank was still periodically flooded. Narrower than the Seine, the Bièvre burst its banks more easily, covering wide areas of Saint-Marcel with pestilential mud and adding to the continual stench produced by the Gobelins. In the early nineteenth century, to turn from Cobb to Louis Chevalier, fevers and consumption remained the occupational hazards of the laundrymen and dyers who worked alongside the Bièvre. The pattern of disease had changed so little

[67] Vieillard-Troiekouroff *et al.*, 'Anciennes églises'; M. Vieillard-Troiekouroff, *Les Monuments religieux de la Gaule d'après les œuvres de Grégoire de Tours* (Paris, 1976), pp. 210–11; Lombard-Jourdan, 'Du nouveau sur les origines chrétiennes de Paris'; P. Périn, 'Les Cimetières mérovingiens de Paris', *Paris et Ile-de-France*, 32 (1981), pp. 91–6.
[68] *Libri Historiarum*, VI, 25 (pp. 264–5). The classic work on such matters is M. Champion, *Les Inondations en France depuis le VIe siècle jusqu'à nos jours*, I (Paris, 1858). Flood of 1196: G. Brice, *Description de la ville de Paris* (1752 edn), ed. P. Codet, II (Paris and Geneva, 1971), p. 117. A. Vernet, 'L'Inondation de 1296–1297 à Paris', *Paris et Ile-de-France*, 1 (1949), pp. 49–50. 'Bourgeois de Paris', *A Parisian Journal*, trans. J. Shirley (Oxford, 1968), pp. 165, 275, 323, 347.

that medical topographies could be copied from eighteenth-century classics of the genre without fear of contradiction. Saint-Marcel was deservedly known as 'the sick faubourg'.[69]

It would be rash, of course, to assume that it had always been as insalubrious. And we have no direct evidence from the Middle Ages of the epidemics that might have followed in the wake of the flooding. Of the numerous water-borne diseases that could have been prevalent in such an ecology, malaria is the only one that I shall single out. This is partly for the reason stated at the outset: it is a disease that deserves greater prominence in our historical epidemiologies. But it is also because its presence in the area during the sixth century seems to be attested in the sources. Gregory of Tours records in one of his miracle books that Marcellus once expelled a huge serpent from Paris. Gregory had perhaps learned of the expulsion from Fortunatus's *Life*, which he cites as an authority. He then adds: 'the priest Ragnimodus, who is now bishop of Paris, went to Marcellus's tomb with a quartan fever. He knelt and for an entire day was occupied in fasting and praying; when evening came, he slept. A short while later he awoke from his sleep and rose from the tomb a healthy man.'[70]

References to the miraculous remission of periodic fever – usually of the tertian or quartan variety – provide the best evidence of malaria that we can hope for from this period. Marcellus was hardly the only Merovingian saint to cure malaria. Sufferers from fever are quite common in the miracle books of Gregory of Tours, to look no further afield.[71] Indeed, the account of Marcellus in Gregory's *Glory of the Confessors* is matched by notices of two other holy Parisians. The first of them, the virgin Criscentia, was buried in a suburb not far from what Gregory perplexingly refers to as the senior church (*ecclesia senior*) – which some have identified with the church of Saint Marcellus. 'A man whom the burning of a tertian fever was distressing with severe tremors scratched a bit of dust from the tomb and drank it; soon his tremors were calmed and all was well. The news was published and was of great benefit to many

---

[69] R. Cobb, *Paris and its Provinces 1792–1802* (Oxford, 1975), pp. 40, 63, 81. Cf. A. Sutcliffe, *The Autumn of Central Paris* (London, 1970), pp. 3ff. L. Chevalier, *Labouring Classes and Dangerous Classes* (London, 1973), pp. 86, 340ff.

[70] *Liber in Gloria Confessorum*, 87 (p. 804), trans. Van Dam, pp. 92–3.

[71] M. Weidemann, *Kulturgeschichte der Merowingerzeit nach den Werken Gregors von Tours*, 2 vols. (Mainz, 1982), II, p. 378.

people afflicted with this illness.'[72] The second holy Parisian is the nun Genovefa. She was buried, Gregory tells us, in the church of the Holy Apostles (actually, the construction of the church was undertaken, by Clovis, in order to house her tomb). 'The fevers of people suffering from chills very often are extinguished by her power.'[73]

A few reports of this kind will not, of course, establish the prevalence of malaria in Merovingian Paris. Nor are they evidence of an epidemic. But the direction in which they point is, nonetheless, suggestive. And whatever the diseases involved, the sufferers will probably have attributed them to miasma, the bad air that arose from standing water, such as that left behind after a flood.

VI

I have now proposed that we envisage Marcellus's dragon not only as a dragon of disease but as an animal to be conceived as intimately related to its local environment: a beast with an ecology. Much more than a symbol of epidemic disease, it *is* the epidemic (as the hagiographer of Mac Reiche insisted), or at least the cause of it. By whatever means, in the saint's flood-ridden eponymous faubourg, it spreads pestilence. In confronting the dragon and taming or killing it, the saint is restoring salubrity to the area. Such is the implication that the *Life* of Marcellus could have had for those to whom it was read in the sixth century.

It is tempting to proceed from that conclusion to an obvious question: what did Marcellus (if he existed) and his kind actually do? Just as I have not attempted to translate hagiographical dragon narratives into the terms of modern epidemiology, so I resist the notion that Marcellus's feat can be demythologised. The dragon is an animal that embodies or causes the disease. The corollary is that the saint has genuinely to subdue the monster. Reports of his doing so are not allegories of some other achievement.

It is, of course, conceivable that a historical Marcellus somehow dealt with a historical dragon – a snake perhaps, magnified in the telling to monstrous proportions. Le Goff entertains the possibility,

[72] *Liber in Gloria Confessorum*, 103 (pp. 813–14), trans. Van Dam, p. 104. On the *ecclesia senior* see Vieilliard-Troiekouroff, *Monuments religieux*, pp. 215–16.
[73] *Liber in Gloria Confessorum*, 89 (p. 805), trans. Van Dam, p. 94. On the accuracy and authenticity of the *Life* of Genovefa, see the references in Van Dam, p. 94 n. 100, and Wood, 'Forgery', pp. 376–8.

only to dismiss it. We may, however, recall the observation of a distinguished anthropologist that 'myths are not the creation of unbridled fancy, but in many cases, at least, are sober historical records'. It is also worth remarking that legends of monsters have sometimes been observed to develop from comparatively mundane beginnings. In June 1764, for instance, a large wolf appeared near the little French town of Langogne in Lozère. It had claimed about fifty lives before hunters could despatch it. Since wolves usually attacked humans only surreptitiously and in winter, the local people were unsure of the terrifying beast's identity. Rumours about its form and ancestry multiplied. And its renown was increased by the imaginative depictions sold on broadsheets. It became, within a relatively brief time, the monstrous *Bête de Gévaudan*.[74] A comparable explanation of the origin of Marcellus's dragon would not invalidate my theory of that beast as a monster of epidemics, given the pestilential attributes of snakes in the early Middle Ages. And it would be a kind of explanation that deserves greater intellectual respect than it has customarily been accorded since the demise of positivism. Even so, it could hardly be a satisfactory solution to the problem. A knowledge of the particular origin of the legend of Marcellus – were it attainable – would still leave us with no understanding of why the legend developed as it did, of why one feat of snake-killing should have been elevated to supreme importance in Marcellus's presumed career. The answer to the question of what Marcellus actually did must be something far less specific.

Once again, a sense of context is needed – an awareness of the environment in which representations of dragon-taming might prove 'contagious'. About the historical relationship between the context and the representation we can have no notion. The cast of mind, the interaction of metaphor and metonymy, that linked one to the other are of course irrecoverable. We do not even have an agreed theory to show how we may conceptualise the link. We must be content to describe.

What merits description in this context arose from the progressive weakening of local political leadership in the barbarian West of the

---

[74] Le Goff, 'Marcellus', pp. 163–4; quotation from *Imagination and Proof: Selected Essays of A. M. Hocart*, ed. R. Needham (Tucson, Arizona, 1987), p. 51; J. Devlin, *The Superstitious Mind: French Peasants and the Supernatural in the Nineteenth Century* (New Haven and London, 1987), pp. 75–6, and see also pp. 77–80.

fifth and sixth centuries, the time of Marcellus and Fortunatus. Bishop-saints gradually became far more than spiritual leaders, miraculous healers and fathers of the poor. Partly in default of alternative executants, partly (it may be) in order to enhance their often precarious position in the community, they took on an increasing variety of what had been thought of as secular public functions.[75] One bishop, Nicetius of Trier, of whom Fortunatus has left a verse eulogy, erected fortifications; more than one minted coins.[76] Others busied themselves responding to environmental threat or disaster. Examples are again forthcoming from Fortunatus's poetry. Sidonius of Mainz had dams constructed to contain the flooding of the Rhine. Felix of Nantes deployed earthworks for a similar purpose. Meanwhile, in the letters of Desiderius of Cahors we find a request to a fellow bishop for aid in laying water pipes.[77] Among such practical projects, it is to be expected that measures were taken to combat disease. The most striking example again comes from the correspondence of Bishop Desiderius. He received a letter from Gallus (II) of Clermont about instituting road blocks to prevent the spread of bubonic plague.[78]

Evidence such as this suggests that it is by no means wholly fanciful to envisage some bishops of the period as generally concerned with organising the community to withstand the progress of an epidemic, and more particularly with establishing the sort of drainage schemes necessary for reducing the risk of water-borne infections such as malaria. We have very little idea of the fate of Roman systems of drainage in the early medieval West. But if they

[75] R. Doehaerd, *Le Haut Moyen Age occidental: économies et sociétés* (Paris, 1971), pp. 122ff; F. Prinz, 'Die bischöfliche Stadtherrschaft im Frankenreich vom 5. bis zum 7. Jahrhundert', *Historische Zeitschrift*, 217 (1974), pp. 1–35; Heinzelmann, *Bischofsherrschaft in Gallien*, pp. 98–183; Brown, *Society and the Holy*, pp. 246–7; Geary, *Before France and Germany*, pp. 131–8. Cf. Le Goff, 'Marcellus', p. 173.

[76] Fortunatus, *Carmina*, III, 12, lines 21–2, ed. F. Leo, *MGH, AA*, IV, 1 (1881), p. 64; M. Prou, *Les Monnaies mérovingiennes* (Paris, 1892), pp. 355, 380, cited from I. Wood, 'The Ecclesiastical Politics of Merovingian Clermont', in P. Wormald *et al.* (eds.), *Ideal and Reality in Frankish and Anglo-Saxon Society* (Oxford, 1983), p. 51.

[77] *Carmina*, IX, 9, lines 27–30; III, 10 (pp. 216, 62–3). Desiderius, *Epistulae*, I, 13, ed. W. Arndt, Corpus Christianorum, Latin series CXVII (1957), p. 322. See further J. Durliat, 'Les Attributions civiles des évêques mérovingiens: l'exemple de Didier, évêque de Cahors (630–655)', *Annales du Midi*, 91 (1979), pp. 237–54.

[78] *Epistulae*, II, 20 (p. 341).

were maintained, restored or imitated, bishops would surely have been responsible.[79]

Their (on our estimation) purely practical undertakings could find spiritual counterparts. Thus Bonitus of Clermont achieved the ending of drought through ordering public fasts; indeed, a flood ensued – to end which more fasting was necessary. Gallus (I) instituted Rogations and a pilgrimage to protect Clermont from bubonic plague. The sheer saintly presence of Nicetius, along with that of the relics of two of his predecessors, was apparently enough to avert the same disease from Trier. In less dire circumstances, the relics of the martyr Clement restored to its original point of emergence a spring that (through a system of canals) had been irrigating fields near Limoges until it was mysteriously diverted into a swamp.[80] The slaying or taming of dragons may belong in this context – as another miraculous means of coping with a large ecological problem.

Between the practical and the miraculous approaches to the management of epidemics, then, no discontinuity seems to have been perceived. It is not inappropriate to discuss dragons and drainage in virtually the same breath. It could even be hazarded that traces of the practical approach are discernible in some of the hagiography earlier summarised. Why else do we find saints drawing circles around dragons or confining them under stones, and inscribing boundaries on beaches and islands? These, it was argued over a century ago, are to be interpreted as aspects of construction work on dams and drainage. The bishop marks out the ground before the workmen move in.[81] As before, I would not expect such precise congruences between the legends and their historical origins. It is the broad context that we should rather try to imagine. If these minor touches in the hagiography can be referred to some aspect of that

---

[79] For the classical background see Traina, *Paludi e Bonifiche.* For the early Middle Ages, see Doehaerd, *Haut Moyen Age,* p. 107; G. Bertrand *et al.* (eds.), *Histoire de la France rurale,* 4 vols. (Paris, 1975–6), I, pp. 78ff. A late antique legendary parallel: R. Lane Fox, *Pagans and Christians* (Harmondsworth, 1986), pp. 531–2. Cf. the dykes of St Illtud: Henken, *Welsh Saints,* p. 110.

[80] Wood, 'Merovingian Clermont', p. 52; Gregory of Tours, *Liber Vitae Patrum,* XVII, 4 (p. 731); *Liber in Gloria Martyrum,* 36 (p. 511). On Rogation processions to protect from pestilence, see I. Wood, 'Early Merovingian Devotion in Town and Country', in D. Baker (ed.), *The Church in Town and Countryside,* Studies in Church History XVI (Oxford, 1979), pp. 61–76.

[81] J.-F. Cerquand, 'Taranis et Thor', *Revue Celtique,* 6 (1883–5), pp. 417–56.

context, then I suggest that they reflect what I earlier called the practical but non-technological management of epidemics.

This concept obviously requires elaboration. I derive it, not from the evidence or historiography of Merovingian Gaul, but from the findings of some students of disease and colonialism in sub-Saharan Africa. It has come to be realised that first-world epidemic control may have been as unsuitable in a third-world ecology as first-world economics in a 'developing' economy. Indeed, the insensitive application of first-world techniques may have been positively damaging. Pre-colonial Africa was hardly free of epidemics; one should not attribute all of the continent's disasters to colonial expansion. But in certain areas a delicate ecological equilibrium had been arrived at between diseased waste and healthy settled land. That equilibrium was maintained by local leadership and custom. It required no extraordinary technology. This, for example, is how one leader managed trypanosomiasis:

> Shoshangane of the Gaza ordered his people to congregate around him in the tsetse bush of the Mzilizwe valley. The bush was cleared, the new land cultivated (and thus kept clear), but several large areas were deliberately left uncleared. Wild game was confined to them and outside them the game was hunted. Game guards controlled their movement. The tsetse vanished.[82]

Shoshangane was succeeded by his son in 1885. The latter was driven south by the Portuguese and forced to abandon Gazaland in 1889. The tsetse returned. For the 'ancient ecological equilibrium' had been destroyed.[83] (At about the same time, comparable disruption was being wrought by the arrival of immigrant workers in Manchuria: the third pandemic of bubonic plague ensued.[84]) It is not inordinately hard to visualise Marcellus as a Dark-Age Shoshangane managing epidemics by all the means at his disposal. In the case of my principal example, malaria, these perhaps included initiating drainage schemes or maintaining a corporate sense of purpose in the 'cleaning up' after a flood. But not the least of his skills, I would tentatively propose, was the oversight of the subtle adjustments that had always to be made between settlement on one

---

[82] G. Prins, 'But What Was the Disease? The Present State of Health and Healing in African Studies', *Past and Present*, no. 124 (1989), pp. 170–1.

[83] J. Ford, *The Role of the Trypanosomiases in African Ecology. A Study of the Tsetse Fly Problem* (Oxford, 1971), p. 145.

[84] W. H. McNeill, *Plagues and Peoples* (Harmondsworth, 1977), pp. 146–7.

hand (the settlement of those who observe his taming of the dragon) and water or wasteland (to which he confines the monster) on the other.

'Should a traveller, returning from a far country, bring us an account of men . . . who knew no pleasure but friendship, generosity, and public spirit; we should immediately, from these circumstances detect the falsehood . . . with the same certainty as if he had stuffed his narration with stories of centaurs and dragons, miracles and prodigies.' So thought David Hume.[85] In a narration that has lacked only centaurs among the implausibilities mentioned, I hope to have shown that – in the management of epidemics – dragons, miracles and public spiritedness may have been intimately linked.

[85] *Enquiry Concerning Human Understanding*, VIII, 1, ed. L. A. Selby-Bigge, rev. edn, ed. P. H. Nidditch (Oxford, 1975), p. 84.

4. Epidemic disease in formal and popular thought in early Islamic society

LAWRENCE I. CONRAD

In considering the impact of epidemic disease on a society, historians usually conceive of their task in terms of problems of mortality and such associated discontinuities as the collapse of orderly government, the flight of threatened populations and the disruption of agriculture and trade. Important as these factors are, however, they tend to obscure the fact that, in terms of the perceptions of the peoples at risk, of no less significance is the fact that epidemic disease in the past has held, and today continues to hold, some of its worst terrors in the way it challenges the ideological structures that sustain all societies.

This is not simply a matter of explaining away incomprehensible horrors. The ideological underpinnings of a social system – whether in the form of political ideology, myth or religion – serve to rationalise the physical world in terms of the priorities, agenda and claims of the society generating these structures, and they comprise an ongoing discourse of self-definition that both responds to changes in social perceptions and historical circumstances and figures in the determination of how that society will react to any further changes or new developments. As these structures encompass the very essence and cohesive elements of a society – its sense of origins, identity, purpose and future – threats of the gravest and most disruptive kind are posed by challenges that falsify the assumptions and claims made in these structures.

It is for these reasons that epidemic disease has always posed such a formidable ideological challenge and has consistently provoked a wealth of speculation seeking to harmonise the trauma and suffering experienced in great epidemics with prevailing ideas on a broad range of other issues. Medieval Islamic society was no exception to this, and through the course of medieval Islamic history epidemic disease was the subject of formal and popular discussions which have survived to modern times in abundance. Most particularly, Muslim scholars, like their counterparts in Europe, dealt with the plague in elaborate treatises written in response to the Black Death and other plagues of the mid-fourteenth century and after.[1] But in terms of ideas, these treatises owe most of their conceptual framework to the formulations argued out in a much earlier period, that ranging from about AD 700 to 850, and it is upon these early speculations that I would like to focus in the following remarks.

THE BACKGROUND AND PRIORITIES OF EARLY ISLAMIC DISCUSSIONS

These earlier discussions survive in several types of literature. Of primary importance is the *ḥadîth*, which consists of narratives, usually less than a page long and often only a line or two, reporting what the Prophet (as well as other early figures) said or did or relating other matters in which his (or their) opinion was in some way expressed. These reports have survived in medieval compilations of various kinds.[2] Most of the traditions in these works are later creations projected back from a subsequent era, and they were often used to argue about issues of concern at the time the tradition was created, the point being to claim for one's position the justification that it agreed with what the Prophet or some other esteemed personality said or did or tacitly approved.[3] We also have literary accounts, called *akhbâr*. These too are self-contained narrative units, and can comprise texts of only a few lines or of several pages.[4]

---

[1] On these works, see Manfred Ullmann, *Die Medizin im Islam* (Leiden, 1970), pp. 242–50; Michael W. Dols, *The Black Death in the Middle East* (Princeton, 1977), pp. 320–35; Lawrence I. Conrad, 'Arabic Plague Chronologies and Treatises: Social and Historical Factors in the Formation of a Literary Genre', *Studia Islamica*, 55 (1981), pp. 51–93.

[2] On *ḥadîth* compendia generally, see Fuat Sezgin, *Geschichte der arabischen Schrifttums* (Leiden, 1967– proceeding), I, pp. 50–84.

[3] On the *ḥadîth* literature, see Ignaz Goldziher, *Muhammedanische Studien*, 2 vols. (Halle, 1889–90), II, pp. 1–274 = *Muslim Studies*, ed. and trans. S. M. Stern and C. R. Barber (London, 1967–71), II, pp. 15–251; Joseph Schacht, *The Origins of Muhammadan Jurisprudence* (Oxford, 1950), on legal traditions; and more recently, the fundamental study by G. H. A. Juynboll, *Muslim Tradition. Studies in Chronology, Provenance and Authorship of Early Ḥadîth* (Cambridge, 1983).

[4] The *akhbâr* literature has been examined in a series of important studies by Stefan Leder. See his 'Prosa-Dichtung in der *akhbâr* Überlieferung. Narrative Analyse einer Satire', *Der Islam*, 64 (1987), pp. 6–41; 'Features of the Novel in Early

Some of the *akhbâr* on epidemic disease were very early on drawn together into short collections of narratives, especially concerning the plague, and eventually were incorporated into books intended to offer edifying consolation in time of suffering or bereavement. The two earliest known works in this genre are fortunately still available to us, at least in part: there survives a substantial fragment from the *Kitâb al-taʿâzî*, the 'Book of Condolences', by the Baṣran compiler and historian Abû l-Ḥasan ʿAlî ibn Muḥammad al-Madâʾinî (d. 228/843),[5] and the complete text of the *Kitâb al-taʿâzî wa-l-marâthî*, the 'Book of Condolences and Elegiac Orations', by another Baṣran of the next generation, Abû l-ʿAbbâs Muḥammad ibn Yazîd al-Mubar-rad (d. 285/898), is extant and now in print.[6] A third work known to the bibliographer Ibn al-Nadîm (wr. 377/987), the *Kitâb al-taʿâzî* by his contemporary Abû ʿUbayd Allâh Muḥammad ibn ʿUmrân al-Marzubâni (d. 384/993), was a large work of about 300 folios but is now apparently lost.[7] Notices on the plague also survive in large numbers as reports scattered in later texts: literary works, for example, frequently record reports concerning epidemics and epidemic disease when the author of such a book has found narratives he considers of some edifying or didactic merit, or just general interest, and historians naturally report on epidemics relevant to the times and regions they cover in their own works.

The interest in epidemic disease manifested in these discussions should be viewed in light of the fact that the eighth and ninth centuries marked the era in which the Muslim community was confronted with the task of setting forth, discussing and reaching some sort of consensus on the fundamental questions defining the form, agenda and content of Islamic culture and thought. In about 632, the date traditionally given for the death of the Prophet

Historiography: The Downfall of Khâlid al-Qasrî', *Oriens*, 32 (1990), pp. 72–96; *Das Korpus al-Haitham ibn ʿAdî (st. 207/822). Herkunft – Überlieferung – Gestalt früher akhbâr-Literatur* (Frankfurt, 1991), pp. 1–16; 'The Literary Use of *Khabar*: A Basic Form of Historical Writing', in Averil Cameron and Lawrence I. Conrad (eds.), *The Byzantine and Early Islamic Near East, I: Problems in the Literary Source Material* (Princeton, 1991), pp. 277–315.

5   Al-Madâʾinî, *Kitâb al-taʿâzî*, ed. Ibtisâm Marhûn al-Ṣifâr and Badrî Muḥammad Fahd (Najaf, 1971). The preserved part of the book unfortunately preserves little of the material on epidemic disease quoted from it by later authors.

6   Al-Mubarrad, *Kitâb al-taʿâzî wa-l-marâthî*, ed. Muḥammad al-Dîbâjî (Damascus, 1396/1976), esp. pp. 209–18, on the plague.

7   See Ibn al-Nadîm, *Kitâb al-fihrist*, ed. Riḍâ-Tajaddud (Tehran, 1391/1971), p. 148:8.

Muḥammad, Islam as a religious, social and cultural system of norms and ideas was fairly simple.[8] The faith preached by Muḥammad was, so far as we can tell, a basic message of absolute monotheism in which a broad range of important dogmatic and theological points still remained unconsidered: as historians of religion are fond of pointing out, prophets are not theologians. Further, in socio-cultural terms Islam in its original Arabian milieu held nominal sway over territories which, if of very broad extent, nonetheless shared similar Arabian tribal ideas, norms and traditions. A century later, however, Islam was the spiritual ideology of the Arab masters of an empire that extended from Central Asia and the Indus valley in the east, across the whole of the Middle East south of Anatolia and westward over North Africa to Spain. Within this vast empire Arab Muslims comprised a tiny minority and found themselves confronting subject peoples who, though defeated in military terms, were the bearers of a variety of religious and cultural systems of great antiquity and intellectual sophistication.

As Islam had expanded at a pace far more rapid than that of its own intellectual, social and cultural development, and was faced with challenges and influences from the subject peoples on almost all fundamental points, Muslims were confronted with the task of working out precisely of what the faith and culture of their new religion would consist, where the parameters of such categories as the obligatory and the blasphemous should lie, and how external challenges and influences were to be confronted, contained or accommodated. The need to deal with such questions was of the greatest urgency, for if Islam, as a spiritual and cultural entity, was allowed to remain amorphous and ambiguous on even central issues of identity, it would eventually be overwhelmed by the regional cultural and spiritual systems in the various provinces of the empire. It was the debate over this problem of self-definition that eventually served to produce the civilisation now familiar to us as that of classical Islam. But the outcome was for a long time uncertain,[9] and it was only toward the approximate end of the period of interest

---

[8] The question of the message and character of the Islamic faith in its earliest stages is extremely difficult to address and has become an issue of heated controversy in recent years. For an introduction to the problem, see Michael Cook, *Muhammad* (Oxford, 1983).

[9] See, for example, H. A. R. Gibb, 'The Social Significance of the Shuʿūbīya', in *Studia orientalia Ioanni Pedersen septuagenario* A.D. *VII Id. Nov. anno MCMLIII a collegis discipulis amicis* (Copenhagen, 1953), pp. 105–14; reprinted in his *Studies on*

to us here, about 850 and in many respects even later, that the basic intellectual and cultural structures of Islam emerged in stable form.

A close reading of the discussions pertaining to epidemic disease that occurred in this period will reveal that these materials comprise part of this debate. It is clear that the great plague pandemic of 541–749 was the paramount problem of the age so far as epidemic disease was concerned – in fact, few epidemics of other diseases are specifically mentioned for this period. But when the pandemic ended in 749, there was no parallel cessation or even decrease in discussions of the plague among Muslim scholars. Indeed, new formulations and new issues continued to emerge, and interest in the discussions seems to have been at its peak long after the plague had disappeared. That is, these discussions on epidemic disease came to form part of a greater overarching discourse in which epidemic disease itself was not necessarily the issue of primary concern. In fact, when these accounts were collected and systematically arranged in later times, the compilers seem to have recognised that, though the reports were all ostensibly about epidemic disease, the direction and tenor of their discussion suggested larger arguments on other issues. Hence, in the *ḥadīth* collections, one finds that traditions about epidemic disease appear not only in the *Kitāb al-ṭibb* ('Book of Medicine'), but also in the *Kitāb al-anbiyā'* ('Book of the Ancient Prophets'), for example, if the account in question involves appeals to how God had also afflicted the ancient Israelites with epidemics, or the *Kitāb al-qadar* ('Book of Divine Will'), if the account raises the question of epidemics as a manifestation of God's divine decree.

The problem of paramount importance to us here is that of identifying what was really at issue in these discussions. Though the point is in some ways an obvious one, it is worth emphasising in this connection that while our sources offer us a rich corpus of material concerning epidemic disease, they do not, at the same time, convey in any immediate or obvious way the messages that these reports were meant to bear at the time they were set into circulation. That is, the extant sources subject the old material to a thorough reorganisation in which reports are juxtaposed in a single narrative plane to suit the purposes and objectives of the author or compiler collecting them. The fact that such a procedure obstructs a proper appreciation of the intellectual processes that generated this

the Civilization of Islam, ed. Stanford J. Shaw and William R. Polk (Boston, 1962), pp. 62–73.

material, and (perhaps the reverse of the same coin) obscures its true origins, is of course our problem, and not a fault of the author/compiler. It does mean, however, that an understanding of how epidemic disease was perceived and explained in early Islamic times will not be achieved by simply lining up sources and retelling their tale in what would essentially amount to yet another recasting of already reorganised material. The task at hand is not to carry this process further along, but rather to attempt, insofar as this is possible, to 'undo' it.

This task may be pursued by, in the first instance, taking into account the fact that although the subject of thinking on epidemic disease spans numerous disciplines in the traditional Islamic sciences, in its essence and origins it represents an ongoing discourse, one in which the resolution of one question immediately poses another, or evokes a response, so that the conclusion of one stage of discussion simply moves the debate on to a new direction or level of argument. That is, later stages should generally be the more sophisticated ones, in the sense that solutions to the arguments in early stages will comprise the presuppositions of later stages. Hence, while there can be no doubt that what have survived to reach us today are numerous samplings from the various stages in this debate, but with the element of chronology – and hence of intellectual development – no longer in immediate view, this element, obviously crucial to the task at hand, is nevertheless implicit in the character and content of the material itself and thus can be recovered in at least general terms.

EARLY POPULAR PERCEPTIONS OF EPIDEMIC DISEASE

Proceeding on the basis of this mode of analysis, it seems clear that the debate over epidemic disease in early Islamic times arose in arguments over the causes of epidemics. For the pre-Islamic Arabs, as well as for many of the other peoples of the early medieval Near East, the matter was quite simple – epidemics were caused by demons and other spirit beings who spread pestilence among mankind by means of their various weapons,[10] an animistic notion already prominent in ancient thinking for more than a millennium.

[10] Ḥassân ibn Thâbit (d. c. 40/659), Dîwân, ed. Walid N. 'Arafat, 2 vols. (Leiden, 1971), II, p. 172:10–13; al-Jâḥiẓ (d. 255/868), Kitâb al-ḥayawân, ed. 'Abd al-Salâm Muḥammad Hârûn, 2nd edn, 8 vols. (Cairo, 1385–8/1965–9), I, p. 351:5–9; VI, pp. 218–20; Ibn Qutayba, 'Uyûn al-akhbâr, ed. Aḥmad Zakî al-'Adawî, 4 vols. (Cairo, 1343–8/1925–30), II, p. 114:6; al-Mas'ûdî (d. 345/956), Murûj al-dhahab, ed.

These spirits, the *jinn* and *shayâṭîn*, were beings that one could see, bargain with, trick and even defeat, and they were responsible for not only misfortune, but also good luck and prosperity.[11] While linking the spread of epidemic disease to the activities of the *jinn*, the pre-Islamic Arabs also considered it obvious that such maladies were also transmissible directly from one victim to another: that is, they acknowledged 'contagion' (*'adwâ*). In the sense in which they understood such terms,[12] this was clear from the spread of disease among their herds, the most frequently cited example being mange in camels.[13] Among human afflictions, smallpox was regarded with particular dread not only because it was a terrible fatal disease, but also, and especially, because it was 'contagious'. In a particularly

Charles Pellat, 7 vols. (Beirut, 1966–79), III, p. 214:8–12; al-Thaʻâlibî (d. 429/1038), *Thimâr al-qulûb*, ed. Muḥammad Abû l-Faḍl Ibrâhîm (Cairo, 1384/1965), pp. 68:1–69:2; Ibn Abî l-Ḥadîd (d. 656/1258), *Sharḥ nahj al-balâgha*, ed. Muḥammad Abû l-Faḍl Ibrâhîm, 20 vols. (Cairo, 1959–64), XV, p. 240:2–8.

[11] On these spirit beings, see Gerlof van Vloten, 'Dämonen, Geister und Zauber bei den alten Arabern', *Wiener Zeitschrift für die Kunde des Morgenländes*, 7 (1893), pp. 167–87, 233–47; 8 (1894), pp. 59–73, 290–2; Julius Wellhausen, *Reste arabischen Heidentums*, 3rd edn (Berlin, 1927), pp. 148–59; A. S. Tritton, 'Spirits and Demons in Arabia', *Journal of the Royal Asiatic Society* (1934), pp. 715–27; Ernst Zbinden, *Die Djinn des Islams und der altorientalische Geisterglaube* (Bern and Stuttgart, 1953); *Encyclopaedia of Islam*, ed. H. A. R. Gibb *et al.*, 2nd edn, 6 vols. to date (Leiden, 1960–   ), II, pp. 546–8 (Duncan B. MacDonald and Henri Massé); Toufic Fahd, *La Divination arabe: études religeuses, sociologiques et folkloriques sur le milieu natif de l'Islam* (Leiden, 1966), pp. 68–76; *idem*, 'Anges, démons et djinns en Islam', in *Génies, anges et démons*, Sources orientales VIII (Paris, 1971), pp. 153–214.

[12] In the word *'adwâ*, medieval Arabic conveys the sense of a spreading disease, approximately, that it is 'transmissible', and so comprehends the ideas of both 'contagion' and 'infection', with no distinction between the two. In fact, the word *'adwâ*, which I render here as 'contagion', comes from the same root that produces the verb *aʻdâ*, 'to infect', said of a disease. See Ernst Seidel, 'Die Lehre von der Kontagion bei den Arabern', *Archiv für Geschichte der Medizin*, 6 (1913), pp. 81–93; Ullmann, *Die Medizin im Islam*, pp. 242–50; *idem*, *Islamic Medicine* (Edinburgh, 1978), pp. 86–96; Felix Klein-Franke, *Vorlesungen über die Medizin im Islam* (Wiesbaden, 1982), pp. 17–19. Hence, although in some of the cases to be considered in this study either the one sense or the other is clearly more appropriate, it must be borne in mind that the modern epidemiological distinctions between infection and contagion were unknown in those times.

[13] For some examples, see al-Mufaḍḍal al-Ḍabbî (d. *c.* 168/784), *Al-Mufaḍḍalîyât*, ed. Charles James Lyall (Oxford, 1921), p. 752:7–11; al-Nâbigha al-Dhubyânî (d. *c.* AD 604), *Dîwân*, ed. Muḥammad Abû l-Faḍl Ibrâhîm (Cairo, 1977), p. 73, v. 8; al-Ḥumaydî (d. 219/834), *Musnad*, ed. Ḥabîb al-Raḥmân al-Aʻẓamî, 2 vols. (Hyderabad, AH 1381–2), II, pp. 308:9–309:3, no. 705; al-Bukhârî (d. 256/870), *Al-Jâmiʻ al-ṣaḥîḥ*, ed. Ludolf Krehl and T. W. Juynboll, 4 vols. (Leiden, 1862–1908), II, pp. 16pu–17:4, *Buyû* no. 36; Abû l-Faraj al-Iṣfahânî (d. 356/967), *Kitâb al-aghânî*, ed. Naṣr al-Hûrînî, 20 vols. (Cairo, AH 1284–5), IV, p. 155:26–7.

vivid illustration of this attitude, Ibn Isḥâq (d. 151/761) reports that when a certain leader of the tribe of Quraysh in Mecca died of the smallpox, his sons for several days refused to go near the body to prepare it for burial, because 'the Quraysh fear smallpox as [other] folk fear the plague'.[14] When a dreaded disease occurred or threatened to spread, people who could do so quickly fled. The bedouins were particularly wary of infectious and contagious disease and of towns notorious for their pestiferousness, and they would not go near a place where an outbreak of disease had been reported.[15]

Muslims in early Islamic times seem to have considered it perfectly acceptable to continue to speak of epidemic disease in terms of these traditional ideas. The Umayyad poets sang, for example, of 'spreading contagion quickly communicated [to others]', and of how contact 'infects the healthy';[16] indeed, the acceptance of 'contagion' was so pervasive as to become proverbial – a disease, habit, rumour and so forth, which spread very quickly from one person to many others, was said to be a'dâ mina l-jarab, 'more contagious than the mange'.[17] In a ḥadîth which appears to be quite early, the Prophet is

[14] See Ibn Hishâm (d. 218/833), Sîrat Rasûl Allâh, ed. Ferdinand Wüstenfeld, 2 vols. (Göttingen, 1858–60), I.1, p. 461:13–14; Ibn Sa'd (d. 230/844), Kitâb al-ṭabaqât al-kabîr, ed. Eduard Sachau et al., 9 vols. (Leiden, 1904–40), IV.1, p. 52:7–13; al-Ṭabarî (d. 310/923), Ta'rikh al-rusul wa-l-mulûk, ed. Muḥammad Abû l-Faḍl Ibrâhîm, 2nd edn, 10 vols. (Cairo, 1968–9), II, p. 462:16–22; Aghânî, IV, pp. 32ult – 33:6.

[15] See al-Jâḥiẓ (attrib.), 'Risâla fî l-ḥanîn ilâ l-awṭân', in his Rasâ'il, ed. 'Abd al-Salâm Muḥammad Hârûn, 4 vols. (Cairo, 1384–99/1964–79), II, p. 388:5–7; al-Tha'âlibî, Thimâr al-qulûb, pp. 549:12–550:5; Yâqût (d. 626/1229), Mu'jam al-buldân, ed. Ferdinand Wüstenfeld, 6 vols. (Leipzig, 1866–73), II, p. 505:6–15. Cf. the later medieval example of bedouin attitudes in Usâma ibn Munqidh (d. 584/1188), Kitâb al-i'tibâr, ed. Philip K. Hitti (Princeton, 1930), p. 12:8; also the modern cases cited in Carlo Guarmani, Northern Najd: A Journey from Jerusalem to Anaiza in Qasim, trans. Lady Capel-Cure (London, 1938), p. 82; Charles Doughty, Travels in Arabia Deserta, 4th edn, 2 vols. (New York, 1921), I, pp. 143–4, 210; Alois Musil, The Northern Hegaz: A Topographical Itinerary (New York, 1926), pp. 181–2, 186, 192.

[16] For some illustrative passages, see al-Farazdaq (d. c. 112/730), Dîwân, ed. Karam al-Bustânî, 2 vols. (Beirut, 1386/1966), I, p. 367:1; Jarîr (d. c. 115/733), Dîwân, ed. with the commentary of Muḥammad ibn Ḥabîb. (d. 245/860) by Nu'mân Amîn Ṭâhâ, 2 vols. (Cairo, 1969–71), II, p. 894, v. 35; Dhû l-Rumma (d. c. 117/735), Dîwân, ed. C. H. H. Macartney (Cambridge, 1919), p. 455, v. 4; Abû 'Ubayda (d. 207/822), Naqâ'iḍ Jarîr wa-l-Farazdaq, ed. A. A. Bevan, 3 vols. (Leiden, 1905–12), I, pp. 14:10, 124:3, 524:16; II, pp. 554:10, 1029:4; Bashshâr ibn Burd (d. 167/783), Dîwân, ed. Muḥammad Ṭâhir ibn 'A'shûr, 2 vols. (Cairo, 1369–86/1950–66), I, p. 155, v. 6. Cf. also Naqâ'iḍ, II, p. 1026:3 and the commentary on this verse.

[17] Al-Maydânî (d. 518/1124), Majma' al-amthâl, ed. Muḥammad Muḥyî l-Dîn 'Abd al-Ḥamîd, 2 vols. (Cairo, 1374/1955), II, p. 45b:12–13, no. 2612. Cf. also Abû Tammâm (d. 231/845), Dîwân, ed. with the commentary of al-Tibrîzî (d.

said to concede that 'the plague is the stinging of the *jinn*' or 'the stinging of the *jinn* invoked by your enemy'.[18] In another tradition he is made to say: 'Flee from the leper as you would flee from a lion.'[19] In a very early report preserved by lexicographers and collectors of traditions containing rare vocabulary, the caliph 'Umar ibn al-Khaṭṭâb (r. 13–23/634–44), who ruled during the period of the most spectacular of the Arab conquests, travels toward Syria for some unstated purpose. But before he reaches it he is advised that the plague is raging there. 'Those Companions of the Prophet accompanying you are *qurhânûn*', he is told, 'so do not enter Syria'. A *qurhân*, we are told by these same authorities, is a camel or human being which has never been stricken by *qurûh*, or ulcerous swellings, or which lives in a land where diseases of this kind do not occur. Where persons were concerned, the specific disease originally intended by the term was smallpox (some add measles), and by analogy it came eventually to be applied to the plague as well.[20] Though the term was originally more likely related to the Syriac

502/1109) by Muḥammad 'Abduh 'Azzâm, 2 vols. (Cairo, 1964–5), I, p. 57, v. 22, and al-Tibrîzî's note: 'Mange is notorious for its contagiousness' (*wa-l-jarabu yûṣafu bi-l-'adwâ*).

[18] Aḥmad ibn Ḥanbal (d. 242/855), *Musnad*, 6 vols. (Cairo, AH 1311), IV, pp. 395:11–14, 413:25–7; al-Jâḥiẓ, *Ḥayawân*, I. p. 351:8–9; VI, p. 220:5; Ibn Qutayba, *'Uyûn al-akhbâr*, II, p. 114:6; al-Ṭabarânî, *Al-Mu'jam al-ṣaghîr*, ed. 'Abd al-Raḥmân Muḥammad 'Uthmân, 2 vols. (Medina, 1388/1968), I, pp. 50:3–8, 127:8–13; al-Tha' âlibî, *Thimâr al-qulûb*, p. 68:1–2; Ibn Qayyim al-Jawzîya (d. 751/1350), *Al-Ṭibb al-nabawî*, ed. Shu'ayb al-Arna'ûṭ and 'Abd al-Qâdir al-Arna'ûṭ (Beirut, 1402/1982), p. 39:8.

[19] See 'Abd al-Razzâq al-Ṣan'ânî (d. 211/827), *Muṣannaf*, ed. Ḥabîb al-Raḥmân al-A' ẓamî, 12 vols. (Beirut, 1390–2/1970–2), X, p. 405:5–6; XI, p. 204:12–205:1; Aḥmad ibn Ḥanbal, *Musnad*, II, p. 443:24–5; al-Bukhârî, *Al-Jâmi' al-ṣaḥîḥ*, IV, p. 55:8–10, 'Ṭibb no. 19; Ibn Qutayba, *'Uyûn al-akhbâr*, IV, p. 69:5–6; idem, *Ta'wîl mukhtalif al-ḥadîth*, ed. Faraj Allâh Zakî al-Kurdî (Cairo, AH 1326), p. 123:8; al-Sharîf al-Murtaḍâ (d. 436/1034), *Kitâb al-durar wa-l-ghurar* (= *Al-Amâlî*), ed. Muḥammad Abû l-Faḍl Ibrâhîm, 2 vols. (Cairo, 1373/1954), II, p. 200:5.

[20] Al-Harawî (d. 224/838), *Gharîb al-ḥadîth*, ed. Muḥammad 'Aẓîm al-Dîn, 4 vols. (Hyderabad, 1384–7/1964–7), III, pp. 411:2–412:3; al-Azharî (d. 370/980), *Tahdhîb al-lugha*, ed. 'Abd al-SalâmMuḥammad Hârûn et al., 7 vols. (Cairo, 1384–7/1964–7), IV, 39a:5 b:4; al-Jawharî (d. 393/1003), *Tâj al-lugha wa-ṣiḥâḥ al-'arabîya*, ed. Aḥmad 'Abd al-Ghâfûr 'Aṭṭâr, 2 vols. (Cairo, 1376–7/1956–7), I, p. 395b:4–16; al-Zamakhsharî (d. 538/1143), *Al-Fâ'iq fî gharîb al-ḥadîth*, ed. Muḥammad Abû l-Faḍl Ibrâhîm and 'Alî Muḥammad al-Bijâwî, 2 vols. (Cairo, 1364–7/1945–8), II, p. 180:4–6, 12–13; Ibn 'Asâkir (d. 571/1176), *Ta'rîkh madînat Dimashq*, I, ed. Ṣalâḥ al-Dîn al-Munajjid (Damascus, 1371/1951), p. 557:1–9; Ibn al-Jawzî, *Gharîb al-ḥadîth*, ed. 'Abd al-Mu'ṭî Amîn Qal'ajî, 2 vols. (Beirut, 1405/1985), II, p. 229:6–9; Ibn al-Athîr (d. 630/1233), *Al-Nihâya fî gharîb al-ḥadîth*, 4 vols. (Cairo, AH 1311), III, p. 240:2–6; Ibn Manẓûr (d. 711/1311), *Lisân al-'arab*, 15 vols. (Beirut, 1374–6/1955–6), II, pp. 558b:24–559a:17.

kôrhanâ, meaning simply 'a disease', this origin does accord with the applications cited by the Arabic lexicographers. As the epidemic in Syria in the period to which this report is assigned was plague, the persons travelling with 'Umar are apparently being called *qurḥânûn* because they have never before been exposed to this disease in particular: as we have already seen, there was no plague in Arabia until a much later time, probably that of the Black Death in 1348. The issue of 'contagion' is not raised here, but the attitude toward epidemic disease is still an eminently practical one: one avoids areas where epidemics are raging, and those who have never before been exposed to a particular disease feel very much more at risk by reason of this fact.

EARLY RELIGIOUS INFLUENCES FROM ISLAM

As Islam developed as a spiritual system, however, such notions could not remain unopposed. First and foremost, in a religious order dominated by the doctrine of an all-powerful and all-ordaining God, there was no place for the concession of devastating powers to minor spirits, or for a conception of disease causation that allowed for the capricious infection of one individual after another regardless of their good or evil deeds, or that considered it the norm for God's faithful to scatter and flee for their lives as epidemics spread. In sum, a world in which an entire community can be laid waste by mere chance or an offended *jinnî*, or in which one's security from a horrible death depends purely on chance or on one's access to means of flight, is not a world ordered and maintained by an almighty benevolent God.

The early Muslim thinkers could not, however, attack and deny the existence or power of the *jinn*. The belief in these spirits was too deeply entrenched; and in any case, an attack on them from an Islamic perspective (once such a perspective developed) would have been fatally compromised by the fact that the Qur'ân acknowledged their existence, included them in God's Creation, and frequently spoke of their interaction with mankind in the domain of the physical world (the *jinn*, for example, worship God).[21] What they could and did do, however, was to deny that the powers of the *jinn*

---

[21] The following Qur'ânic passages are of interest to present concerns: Sûrat al-An'âm (6), vv. 100, 112, 128, 130; Sûrat al-A'râf (7), vv. 38, 179; Sûrat al-Ḥijr (15), v. 27; Sûrat al-Isrâ' (17), v. 88; Sûrat al-Niml (27), vv. 10, 17, 39; Sûrat al-Qaṣaṣ (28), v.

extended to the spreading of plague. The 'stinging of the *jinn*', as it was called, which was a phrase synonymous with 'plague', was impugned and written off as a foolish bedouin superstition, and in support of this there appeared a report attributed to the time of the great plague of 'Amwâs, which struck Syria in 638–9.[22] In this report the Companion 'Amr ibn al-'Âṣ advises the warriors in the threatened Muslim army that the plague is a 'stinging from the demons' (*shayâṭîn*), and that they should flee for their lives. 'Amr's superior, however, the pious Mu'âdh ibn Jabal, then comes forth and denies that this is the case.[23] These are summaries of what must surely have been a fuller story: they are very similar to more detailed accounts in which the attribution of the plague to stinging demons is replaced by some other explanation which, though still un-Islamic, is less repugnant to religious sensitivities. In these versions 'Amr, or 'the people', warn or speculate that the spreading epidemic will engulf the people like a great fire or flood, or that it is a foul malediction (*rijs*). This proposition is then sharply refuted by Mu'âdh, by some other pious Companion, or by the Prophet himself, who states that the outbreak is a chastisement similar to those by which God has chastised peoples of the past. Of particular note here is the tremendous variation in historical details through which the same didactic message and religious interpretation is conveyed.[24]

31; Sûrat Saba' (34), v. 12; Sûrat Fuṣṣilat (41), vv. 25, 29; Sûrat al-Ahqâf (46), v. 18; Sûrat al-Dhâriyât (51), v. 56; Sûrat al-Raḥmân (55), vv. 15, 33, 39, 56, 74; Sûrat al-Jinn (73), vv. 1, 5–6. Cf. Paul Arno Eichler, *Die Dschinn, Teufel und Engel im Koran* (Leipzig, 1928).

[22] On this epidemic, see M. J. de Goeje, *Mémoire sur la conquête de la Syrie*, 2nd edn (Leiden, 1900), pp. 161–5; Leone Caetani, *Annali dell'Islam*, 10 vols. (Milan, 1905–26), IV, pp. 4–31; Michael W. Dols, 'Plague in Early Islamic History', *Journal of the American Oriental Society*, 94 (1974), pp. 376–8; *idem*, *Black Death in the Middle East*, pp. 21–5; Lawrence I. Conrad, 'The Plague in the Early Medieval Near East' (Princeton University, PhD dissertation, 1981), pp. 167–246. Cf. also Julius Wellhausen, *Prolegomena zur ältesten Geschichte des Islams*, in his *Skizzen und Vorarbeiten*, VI (Berlin, 1899), pp. 65–8.

[23] Al-Jâḥiẓ, *Ḥayawân*, VI, p. 220:5–8; al-Tha'âlibî, *Thimâr al-qulûb*, p. 68:3–6.

[24] Ibn Sa'd, III.2, pp. 124:11–25, 125:4–12; Aḥmad ibn Ḥanbal, *Musnad*, I, p. 196:6–18; IV, pp. 195:28–196:12; V, p. 248:9–17; al-Ṭabarî, *Ta'rîkh*, IV, p. 62:6–12, from Ibn Isḥâq (d. 151/761); Ibn Ḥibbân al-Bustî (d. 354/965), *Ṣaḥîḥ*, in the recension of 'Alî ibn Balbân al-Fârisî (d. 739/1339), *Al-Iḥsân bi-tartîb ṣaḥîḥ Ibn Ḥibbân*, ed. Kamâl Yûsuf al-Ḥût, 10 vols. (Beirut, 1407/1987), IV, p. 264:13–17, no. 2940; al-Ṭabarânî (d. 360/971), *Al-Mu'jam al-kabîr*, ed. Ḥamdî ibn 'Abd al-Majîd al-Salafî, 25 vols. (Baghdad, 1404–8/1983–8), I, pp. 130:6–12, 131ult–133:5, 146pu–147:2, 161:13–18, 165ult–166:4, nos. 267, 274–7, 330, 383–4, 403; VII, p. 305:2–15, nos. 7209–10; Ibn 'Abd al-Barr (d. 463/1071), *Al-Istî'âb fî ma'rifat al-aṣḥâb*, ed. 'Alî Muḥammad al-Bijâwî, 4 vols. (Cairo, n.d.), III, p. 1406:4–9, from al-Zuhrî (d. 124/742); Ibn 'Asâkir, I (Munajjid), pp. 557:21–558:10, from Ibn 'A'idh (d. 233/847).

As for 'contagion', this notion was particularly prominent since it arose not only in connection with epidemic disease, but also with reference to leprosy.[25] From both of these concerns, there emerged a tradition of the Prophet in which Muhammad says: *lâ 'adwâ*, 'No contagion'. That this denial of 'contagion' was based on considerations far beyond those of medicine or the explanation of epidemic disease (or even of leprosy) is proven by the fact that this pronouncement usually occurs in a list of traditional beliefs now repudiated by Islam as baseless superstition: 'No contagion, no omens from birds, no owl, no serpent.' The 'omens from birds' (*ṭiyara*) refers to the old augury custom of foretelling the future from the cries, flight and alighting places of birds; the term for this was eventually generalised to cover all physical phenomena believed to influence or indicate the course of future events. The 'owl' (*hâma*) was believed to represent the spirit of a wrongfully slain man; it would never rest until his death had been properly avenged by the killing of his murderer. The 'serpent' (*ṣafar*) was thought of as a parasite that attacked and afflicted men in their bellies, and was considered more easily transmissible from one person to another than mange spreading among camels. All of these – 'contagion', the omens from birds, the wandering owl and the abdominal 'serpent' – are repudiated because they are regarded as major constituent elements in a system of causation based largely on concepts of pagan animism and simple caprice.[26]

---

[25] See Michael W. Dols, 'The Leper in Medieval Islamic Society', *Speculum*, 58 (1983), pp. 891–916.

[26] See Mâlik ibn Anas (d. 179/795), *Al-Muwaṭṭa'*, ed. Muḥammad Fu'âd 'Abd al-Bâqî, 2 vols. (Cairo, 1370/1951), II, p. 946:4–6, *'Ayn* no. 18; 'Abd al-Razzâq, *Muṣannaf*, X, pp. 404:15–405:3, 405:12–406:3; XI, 205:5–7; al-Ḥumaydî, *Musnad*, II, pp. 308:9–309:3, no. 705; Aḥmad ibn Ḥanbal, *Musnad*, I, pp. 174:21–3, 180:1–5; II, pp. 152ult–153:2, 222:14–16, 397pu, 420:19–21, 487:24–7, 507:1–2; III, pp. 130:18–20, 154:8–10, 173:23–5, 178:2–4, 251:20–2, 275:29–276:1, 277pu–278:1, 293:6–7, 312:23–4, 382:24–8, 449pu–450:1; al-Bukhârî, *Ṣaḥîḥ*, II, pp. 16pu–17:4, *Buyû'* no. 36; IV, pp. 65:7–10, 15–19, 70:6–8, *Ṭibb* nos. 43–5, 54; Muslim (d. 261/874), *Ṣaḥîḥ*, ed. Muḥammad Fu'âd 'Abd al-Bâqî, 5 vols. (1375–6/1955–6), IV, pp. 1742:9–1747pu, *Salâm* nos. 101–16; Ibn Mâja (d. 273/886), *Sunan*, ed. Muḥammad Fu'âd 'Abd al-Bâqî, 2 vols. (Cairo, 1372–3/1952–4), I, p. 34:1–5, *Muqaddima* no. 10; II, pp. 1170:5–6, 1171:1–4, *Ṭibb* no. 43; Ibn Ḥibbân, *Ṣaḥîḥ*, VII, pp. 639:3–5, 641:3–5, 644:1–13, nos. 6081, 6085, 6094–5, 6100; al-Ṭabarânî, *Al-Mu'jam al-kabîr*, VII, p. 149:7–18, nos. 6657–9; VIII, pp. 216:6–14, 230ult–231:4, nos. 7761–2, 7801; XVII, p. 54:2–6, no. 111; al-Sharîf al-Murtaḍâ, *Al-Durar wa-l-ghurar*, II, p. 200:3; al-Khaṭîb al-Baghdâdî (d. 463/1071), *Ta'rîkh Baghdâd*, 14 vols. (Cairo, 1349/1931), IV, pp. 339:19–22, 378:5–9. Cf. also Fahd, *La Divination arabe*,

The counter to the denial of 'contagion' was the obvious one: does not simple manifest experience demonstrate that some diseases are indeed transmissible, and very quickly and easily so? The Islamic thinkers had a response to this point, however, and this stage of the argument is characterised by the following formulation: one mangy camel mixes with a herd and soon the entire herd is mangy, thus suggesting that the introduction of the diseased animal into the herd caused the mange in the others – but who caused the mange in this first one?[27] The answer, of course, is God. The same argument appears in other traditions in a more narrative form: the Prophet says, 'No contagion', and a bedouin replies: 'O Apostle of God, what about my camels? They are like gazelle does on the sand;[28] but let a mangy camel come and mix with them, and soon they are all mangy.' The Prophet counters: 'And who caused the mange in the first one?'[29] By the very skilful formulation of its argument, this presentation not only uses the case of the mangy camels as an illustration, but also, at the same time, refutes the validity of this case as proof of 'contagion'. This is unlikely to be mere coincidence, nor is there much reason to suspect that it reflects an effort deliberately to be archaic or quaint. Rather, the argument presupposes an Islamic community in which a major attack on the transmissibility of disease would be best understood and most effective if formulated in this way: that is, and irrespective of the time at which the saying became a formal tradition cited on the authority of the Prophet, it presumes an audience in which Muslims are still largely tenders of herds, or at least still thoroughly familiar with the problems associated with this vocation. Viewed in this way, the argument must be very early indeed, as compared to other extant materials.

p. 238; G. H. A. Juynboll, *The Authenticity of the Tradition Literature: Discussions in Modern Egypt* (Leiden, 1969), pp. 140–1.

[27] Al-Ḥumaydî, *Musnad*, II, p. 475:10–13, no. 1117; Aḥmad ibn Ḥanbal, *Musnad*, II, p. 434:28–9.

[28] I.e. their unblemished hides are like the tawny pelts of gazelles, which camouflage them against the background of the Arabian steppe.

[29] Aḥmad ibn Ḥanbal, *Musnad*, I, pp. 269:14–17, 328:11–13, 440:24–9; II, pp. 24pu–25:2, 267:2–5, 317:26–30; al-Bukhârî, *Ṣaḥîḥ*, IV, pp. 57:6–11, 69:10–70:6, *Ṭibb* nos. 25, 53–4; Muslim, *Ṣaḥîḥ*, IV, pp. 1742:10–1743:6, *Salâm* nos. 101–2; Ibn Mâja, *Sunan*, II, p. 1171:5–9, *Ṭibb* no. 43; Ibn Qutayba, *Ta'wîl mukhtalif al-ḥadîth*, p. 123:4–7; Ibn Ḥibbân, *Ṣaḥîḥ*, VII, pp. 640:12–641:1, 641:7–11, nos. 6083–4, 6086; al-Ṭabarânî, *Al-Mu'jam al-kabîr*, XI, pp. 238:1–7, 288:12–17, nos. 11605, 11764; al-Sharîf al-Murtaḍâ, *Al-Durar wa-l-ghurar*, II, p. 200:3–4.

There are other cases, however, in which we can see that a solution of the type proposed here was not particularly satisfying or convincing. In accounts of various plagues in al-Baṣra in southern Iraq, we are offered *akhbār* narratives in which, for example, a graverobber exhumes the recently buried corpse of a plague victim and steals the man's robe; but as soon as he touches it he falls dead of the plague.[30] Did he die from contact with the infected robe, or did God strike him down for sacrilege? The tale seems to allow for either interpretation. Similarly, another narrative has it that a man dreamed that twelve dead would be carried out of his house in a forthcoming plague. Sure enough, an epidemic breaks out and quickly kills eleven members of his family, leaving only the dreamer himself alive. Struck with fear for his life, he flees from his house. When he returns in the morning he finds a thief dead on the floor: hoping to plunder the possessions of those who had perished, the thief had broken into the house and had been smitten by the plague. The owner of the house has the thief's body removed, of course, and that completes the twelve, as he had seen in his dream.[31] But had the thief been struck down by the pestiferousness of the house, or by an enraged God punishing him for his sins? An even more equivocal formulation is a *ḥadīth* which attempts to uphold the perfectly sensible precautions founded upon awareness of a disease's transmissibility, while avoiding any specific acknowledgement of this fact. In this tradition, in the circulation of which the Medinan Abū Salama (d. *c*. 94–104/712–22) seems to have played a leading role, the Prophet is made to say: 'Do not mix the diseased [camels] with the healthy', or: 'The owner of diseased [camels] should not water/graze them together with the healthy ones owned by someone else.'[32] In some cases the contradiction can become quite prominent: 'No contagion, but do not mix the diseased [camels] with the

---

[30] Al-Mubarrad, *Al-Taʿāzī wa-l-marāthī*, p. 211:1–2, from al-Madāʾinī.

[31] Al-Mubarrad, *Al-Taʿāzī wa-l-marāthī*, p. 210:12–16; al-Tanūkhī (d. 384/994), *Al-Faraj baʿd al-shidda*, ed. ʿAbbūd al-Shāljī, 5 vols. (Beirut, 1398/1978), II, p. 330:1–11; al-Rāghib al-Iṣfahānī (d. 502/1108), *Muḥāḍarāt al-udabāʾ wa-muḥāwarāt al-shuʿarāʾ wa-l-bulaghāʾ*, 4 vols. (Beirut, n.d.), IV, p. 502:14–16. The first two of these authorities name their source as ʿAlī ibn al-Qāsim, one of Abū ʿUbayda's informants.

[32] Mālik, *Muwaṭṭaʾ*, II, p. 946:4–6, *ʿAyn* no. 6; Aḥmad ibn Ḥanbal, *Musnad*, II, pp. 406:4–5, 434:28–29; al-Bukhārī, *Ṣaḥīḥ*, IV, pp. 69:14–17, 69ult–70:3, *Ṭibb* nos. 53–4; Muslim, *Ṣaḥīḥ*, IV, pp. 1743:11–1744:12, *Salām* nos. 104–5; Ibn Māja, *Sunan*, II, p. 1171:10–12, *Ṭibb* no. 43; Ibn Qutayba, *Taʾwīl mukhtalif al-ḥadīth*, p. 123:7–8; Ibn Ḥibbān, *Ṣaḥīḥ*, VII, pp. 639:9–640:5, no. 6082.

healthy ones',[33] or: 'There is no such thing as *ṣafar*, which is a kind of abdominal disorder.'[34]

THE MATURATION OF THE DEBATE

At this point a new problem arises for consideration. If there is no 'contagion', and if the spirit world has no power to afflict mankind with epidemic disease, then how does epidemic disease arise? The answer of the early thinkers is to drive home the point that had been motivating the earlier discussions all along: epidemic disease – and here the plague is the archetype usually evoked – is an affliction visited upon man by God. There are many formulations pursuing this theme, and it is unlikely that from this mass of material any detailed chronology of development can be recovered. In general, however, the prior arguments seem to be those in which the Prophet or one of his Companions makes the point that God has inflicted pestilence upon other peoples in the past: epidemic disease is a chastisement (*rijz, 'adhâb*) sent by God upon 'a group of the Israelites', 'those who were before you', 'the righteous who were before you', 'certain communities (*umam*) which have gone before you', or even just 'a group'.[35] The old argument illustrated by the mangy camels, while denying 'contagion' and asserting the primal role of God, had contributed nothing to clarify the nature of that role. This new group of traditions now attempts to elaborate on this issue by noting that just as God smites the Muslims with epidemic disease, so also in past times he has smitten other favoured peoples and righteous persons. While a great epidemic is thus a chastisement for failings and shortcomings, it is not a sign of implacable divine wrath or impending universal destruction, as

---

[33] See Mâlik, *Muwaṭṭa'*, II, p. 946:4–6, *'Ayn* no. 6; Aḥmad ibn Ḥanbal, *Musnad*, II, p. 434:28–9; Muslim, *Ṣaḥîḥ*, IV, p. 1744:7–10, *Salâm* no. 105.

[34] Al-Bukhârî, *Ṣaḥîḥ*, IV, p. 57:6, *Ṭibb* no. 19.

[35] See, for example, Mâlik, *Muwaṭṭa'*, II, p. 896:5–9, *Jâmi'* no. 23; 'Abd al-Razzâq, *Muṣannaf*, XI, p. 146:9–13; Ibn Sa'd, III.2, p. 124:9–11; Aḥmad ibn Ḥanbal, *Musnad*, I, pp. 173:22–5, 176ult–177:3, 182:8–11, 196:6–18; V, pp. 202:16–20, 207pu–208:2, 209:6–11, 213:25–8, 240:20–3; al-Bukhârî, *Ṣaḥîḥ*, II, p. 377:10–15, *Anbiyâ'* no. 54; IV, p. 344:9–12, *Ḥiyal* no. 13; Muslim, *Ṣaḥîḥ*, IV, pp. 1737:8–1740:2, *Salâm* nos. 92–7; Ibn Ḥibbân, *Ṣaḥîḥ*, IV, pp. 264ult–265:4, 266:5–8, nos. 2941, 2943; al-Ṭabarânî, *Al-Mu'jam al-kabîr*, XX, pp. 116:10–17, 121:12–122:2, 171:14–19, nos. 230–1, 243, 364; Ibn Qayyim al-Jawzîya, *Al-Ṭibb al-nabawî*, pp. 37:3–7, 38:8, 9.

well may have seemed to be the case during many of the severe plague epidemics of Umayyad times, or from accounts of these outbreaks.

Numerous crucial questions remain unaddressed by these formulations, a situation that reflects the still tentative state of the debate. On the other hand, significant maturation is evident among the circles engaged in this discussion, for the appeal to the experiences of past peoples indicates a clear historical perspective. Islam's connection with past peoples as the culmination of human spiritual experience is in place, and a broadening awareness of tales of epidemics among these people implies progress in the collection and compilation of materials in subjects where such stories would eventually be found: Qur'ânic exegesis (*tafsîr*), lore about the Israelites (the *isrâ'îlîyât*), and tales of the ancient prophets (*qiṣaṣ al-anbiyâ'*).[36] Just as the old *ḥadîth* about the mangy camels – as well as the response to it in terms of mixing diseased with healthy animals – implies an audience at a rather basic level of social development, these traditions surely emanate from, and were addressed to, a far more refined urban milieu in which Muslims were working out a universal historical-religious perspective on the origins of their faith and marshalling various literary endeavours to that end.

The explanation of epidemic disease in terms of the divine activity of God soon leads the discussion further. That is, if epidemic disease is a matter of divine decree, then is there any point to efforts to avoid

---

[36] The leading example of this is the story of Ezekiel. In a tale reminiscent of the story of this prophet and the valley of dry bones in Ezekiel 37:1–14, the Islamic version is largely exegesis of Sûrat al-Baqara (2), v. 243: 'Hast thou not regarded those who went forth from their habitations in thousands, fearful of death? God said to them: "Die!"' The explanation for this verse is that a certain people suffered an epidemic of plague from which some fled while others did not. Those who stayed were devastated by the pestilence, while those who had left remained safe. So the next time an epidemic struck, all of them fled; but before they reached the haven where they expected to be safe, God's angels struck them all dead in one fell swoop. Later, the prophet Ezekiel passed by the place where their bones lay (variants have it that he was of this people and had gone out in search of them), and as a token of mercy God allowed him to recall them to life. The Old Testament version is clearly a metaphor prophesying the restoration of the kingdom of the Israelites (pestilence has nothing to do with this and does not appear in the account), but in the Islamic version the tale teaches the lesson that ancient peoples too discovered that as epidemic disease comes at the bidding of God, flight from it is futile and a sign of weak faith. See Conrad, 'Plague Chronologies and Treatises', pp. 77–9, 88–9.

epidemics, and, indeed, are not such acts defiance of the will of God? In many *ḥadîth* and *akhbâr* reports this issue is specifically addressed. In one of the accounts of the herd of mangy camels, the reader is left in no doubt as to whom the tradition intends as the cause of the mange in the first camel: 'God has created every soul: He has ordained its span of life on earth and the time of its death, the afflictions it will suffer and the benefits it will enjoy.'[37] Other didactic tales drive this point home very clearly where persons threatened with epidemic disease are concerned. The great Umayyad viceroy of the East, Ziyâd ibn Abî Sufyân (d. 53/673), for example, asks the caliph Muʿâwiya ibn Abî Sufyân (r. 41 60/661–80) for control of the Ḥijâz in addition to Iraq, since governing the latter does not require all of his time. As Ziyâd's rule could at times be harsh, the prospect of him governing their lands frightens the Ḥijâzîs, who pray that this might not be allowed to come to pass. Shortly thereafter, Ziyâd is stricken by the swellings of some epidemic disease (plague buboes are most frequently mentioned), and the question arises of whether he should resort to some drastic medical procedure (excising the bubo or swelling, amputating the affected limb) to save his life. The argument against this is that the procedure may not help, in which case Ziyâd will die and meet God with his body bearing proof of his effort to escape his Maker's will: 'Live whole and die whole', as one version has his advisers warning him. He therefore declines treatment and perishes, much to the relief of the Ḥijâzîs.[38] This tradition is essentially anti-Umayyad in origin and becomes increasingly so over time; but its key presupposition of God as the cause and giver of disease is present from the beginning

---

[37] Aḥmad ibn Ḥanbal, *Musnad*, I, p. 440:28–9.
[38] For the various versions of this story, see Abû ʿUbayda, *Naqâ'iḍ Jarîr wa-l-Farazdaq*, II, p. 620:10–18; Ibn Qutayba, *ʿUyûn al-akhbâr*, II, p. 114:1–6, from al-Madâ'inî; al-Balâdhurî (d. 279/892), *Ansâb al-ashrâf*, IV.1, ed. Iḥsân ʿAbbâs (Wiesbaden, 1400/1979), p. 276:3–8, from multiple authorities (*qâlû*); al-Yaʿqûbî, *Ta'rîkh*, 2 vols. (Beirut, 1379/1960), II, p. 236:7–14; al-Ṭabarî, *Ta'rîkh*, V, pp. 288:19–289:21, from ʿAbd Allâh ibn Mubârak (d. 181/797) and al-Madâ'inî; Ibn Aʿtham al-Kûfî (d. *c*.254/858), *Kitâb al-futûḥ*, ed. Muḥammad ʿAbd al-Muʿîd Khân, 8 vols. (Hyderabad, 1388–95/1968–75), IV, p. 203:1–11; Ibn ʿAbd Rabbih (d. 328/940), *Al-ʿIqd al-farîd*, ed. Aḥmad Amîn *et al.*, 8 vols. (Cairo, 1368–84/1949–65), V, p. 12:9–13; al-Masʿûdî, *Murûj al-dhahab*, III, pp. 216:1–9, 216:18–217:4; Ibn ʿAsâkir, *Tahdhîb ta'rîkh Dimashq al-kabîr*, abridged edn, ed. ʿAbd al-Qâdir Badrân and Aḥmad ʿUbayd, 7 vols. (Damascus, AH 1329–51), V, p. 424:9–14. Cf. Ignaz Goldziher, *Abhandlungen zur arabischen Philologie*, 2 vols. (Leiden, 1896–99), I, p. 35.

and remains a constant feature of all versions of the story. As we have seen in other cases above, a variety of shifting historical details tends to cluster around the stable core of a constant didactic message.

There are many reports in which the ultimate point is the futility of flight from the plague, and in accounts of this kind a favoured motif, one that stresses the absurdity of attempts to escape, is that of the man fleeing on his donkey. In one account (in which, again, the different versions bear varying details), a man in al-Baṣra decides to flee when a plague epidemic devastates the city. As a servant boy helps him pack his donkey, the youth suddenly recites these verses:

> By none will God be left behind
> By clutching fast to a donkey's lead,
> Nor from him can one haven find
> By turning to his dashing steed.
> To each a set time God will bind
> When he shall meet his death decreed.
> The night-trod road may well but wind
> To where God waits with writ to heed.

The master agrees that his servant is right, and so stays and is one of those stricken in the epidemic.[39] In another case, the implications of the motif are exploited in vivid fashion. The eminent *ḥadîth* transmitter and scholar Nâfiʿ ibn Jubayr (d. *c.* 120/738) was in al-Baṣra during a plague epidemic, and saw a man leaving the city on a donkey. 'Look!', he cries out in contempt, 'he flees from God on a donkey!'[40]

Where epidemic disease is concerned, however, this stage of the

---

[39] For the various versions of the story, see al-Jâḥiẓ, *Ḥayawân*, III, p. 461:8–12, from al-Aṣmaʿî (d. 213/828); *idem, Al-Bayân wa-l-tabyîn*, ed. ʿAbd al-Salâm Muḥammad Hârûn, 4 vols. (Cairo, 1367–70/1948–50), III, p. 278:7–10; Ibn Qutayba, *Taʾwîl mukhtalif al-ḥadîth*, p. 125:6–10, from al-Aṣmaʿî; *idem, ʿUyûn al-akhbâr*, I, p. 144:17–20, from al-Aṣmaʿî; al-Mubarrad, *Al-Taʿâzî wa-l-marâthî*, pp. 217ult–218:5, from Abû ʿAmr ibn al-ʿAlâ (d. 154/771); al-Ṭabarî, *Taʾrîkh*, IV, p. 63:5–14, from Sayf ibn ʿUmar (d. 180/796); al-Râghib al-Iṣfahânî, *Muḥâḍarât al-udabâ*, IV, p. 503:8–12.

[40] Al-Mubarrad, *Al-Taʿâzî wa-l-marâthî*, p. 213:6–7. Cf. Ibn Saʿd, VII.1, p. 131:15–18, from Ḥammâd ibn Zayd (d. 179/795); al-Balâdhurî, *Ansâb al-ashrâf*, Süleymaniye Kütüphanesi (Istanbul), MS Reisülküttap no. 597, fol. 572r:26–8, from al-Madâʾinî.

discussion has yet to encounter the crucial question of how a merciful and benevolent God could send upon man a scourge which kills the righteous with the wicked, the faithful Muslim with the unbeliever. This problem is addressed in a new set of traditions: epidemic disease is an affliction which God visits upon whomsoever He wills, but while it is a painful chastisement for the unbeliever, it is a martyrdom for the Muslim. That is, a good Muslim who perishes of the plague or, by analogy, certain other diseases, will not have to wait for the balance of his good and evil deeds to be reckoned on the Day of Judgement; he will proceed straight to Paradise. The earliest expression of this notion is probably its simple assertion. In a tradition of the Baṣran scholar ʿÂṣim ibn Sulaymân al-Aḥwal (d. 142/760), the famous Companion Anas ibn Mâlik inquires about the cause of someone's death; when told that he died of the plague, Anas responds: 'The Apostle of God said: "The plague is a martyrdom for every Muslim"'.[41] This is then developed into other traditions in which it is asserted that the plague victim will enjoy status as a martyr equal to that of a warrior slain in God's cause, that if a Muslim remains in his home and does not flee from an epidemic his steadfast faith will gain him a martyr's reward should he be stricken, and that while the plague is a martyrdom for the Muslim it is a painful chastisement for the unbeliever.[42]

Here we can see the argument proceeding on from the consideration of the omnipotence of God to the issue of His justice. That is, to propose that epidemics come from God secures the case (where epidemic disease is concerned) for His all-encompassing dominion; but in Umayyad times the plague was of greatest severity in the towns, where Arab Muslims were concentrated. The ensuing slaughter of believers during these epidemics would thus now call into question any argument for God's justice. A solution is thus found in the proposition that while death in an epidemic simply hastens the unbelieving on their way to Hellfire, it is an act of divine mercy for Muslims, who will as a result proceed directly to Paradise regardless of the measure of their earthly deeds.

The appeal to martyrdom was in fact a much-exercised argument

---

[41] Aḥmad ibn Ḥanbal, *Musnad*, III, pp. 150:20–2, 220:27–9, 223:24–7, 258:18–21, 265ult–266:2; al-Bukhârî, *Ṣaḥîḥ*, II, p. 209:7–8, *Jihâd* no. 30; IV, p. 60:11–14, *Ṭibb* no. 30; Muslim, *Ṣaḥîḥ*, III, p. 1522:1–3, *Imâra* no. 166.

[42] See, for example, Aḥmad ibn Ḥanbal, *Musnad*, IV, pp. 128:14–19, 128pu–129:4, 185:8–11; V, p. 81:16–19; al-Bukhârî, *Ṣaḥîḥ*, IV, pp. 60:16–61:1, *Ṭibb* no. 30.

at the time, and it was frequently used in similar cases. As in medieval Europe, medieval Islam conceived of the Last Judgement as an event in which all men would be called forth in their physical bodies. But what of a person who, for example, had drowned in the sea and thus had probably been eaten by the fish, or someone who had been killed in a fire? This latter case was particularly grave, since fire was believed to consume the soul as well as the body. The answer was that such persons, and others in many similar cases, were martyrs and would proceed directly to Paradise. Discussions similar to those concerning the status of plague as a form of martyrdom were thus producing claims to such standing for a variety of diseases and other non-medical afflictions, and at what must have been a late stage it became possible to compile from these materials lists of the accepted forms of martyrdom, which always included death from the plague.[43]

The late eighth and ninth centuries bring us to an era in which there is a wealth of contemporary documentation, both in terms of historical and literary texts incorporating the old *akhbâr*, and with respect to compilations of traditions ascribed to the Prophet and other early personalities. At this time, then, it becomes far easier to discern how the discussion of epidemic disease is proceeding, and in this connection the case of *ḥadîth* is of particular interest. As *ḥadîth* collections arranged according to subject begin to appear, medical traditions are being collected where they bear on other topics, but in this early stage medicine itself does not form a specific category and is not considered as a distinct subject. Mâlik, for example, discusses

---

[43] The various causes of death that came to be categorised as forms of martyrdom included death by plague, dysentery or pleurisy (? the Arabic is *dhât al-janb*), by drowning, in childbirth, in a fire, in a collapsed house, in the *jihâd* or by accident for the cause of God, in defence of one's property or family, in fighting injustice, from grief or (for women) while yet a virgin or with child. See Mâlik, *Muwaṭṭa'*, I, p. 131:1–6, *Jamâʿa* no. 6, pp. 233:7–234:3, *Janâʾiz* no. 36; ʿAbd al-Razzâq, *Muṣannaf*, III, p. 562:1–15; V, pp. 266:15–272:9; Ibn Abî Shayba (d. 235/849), *Al-Muṣannaf fî l-aḥâdîth wa-l-âthâr*, ed. ʿAbd al-Khâliq al-Afghânî, 15 vols. (Bombay, 1399–1403/ 1979–83), V, pp. 332:2–333:10; Aḥmad ibn Ḥanbal, *Musnad*, II, pp. 310:3–6, 324ult–325:2, 522:3–5, 533:5–10; III, pp. 400:29–31, 401:19–24, 489:13–18; IV, p. 201:24–7; V, pp. 314:26–315:4, 323:10–13, 328pu–329:2, 446:8–14; VI, pp. 465:2–4, 466:2–7; al-Bukhârî, *Ṣaḥîḥ*, I, pp. 170:2–8, 187:14–17, *Adhân* nos. 32, 73; II, p. 209:7–8, *Jihâd* no. 30; IV, p. 60:11–16, *Ṭibb* no. 30; Muslim, *Ṣaḥîḥ*, III, pp. 1521:1– 1522:4, *Imâra* no. 50; Ibn Mâja, *Sunan*, II, pp. 937:9–938:3, *Jihâd* no. 17; al- Balâdhurî, *Ansâb al-ashrâf*, MS 598, fol. 347v:6–8; Ibn Ḥibbân, *Ṣaḥîḥ*, V, pp. 75:8– 77:14, nos. 3176–80; al-Ṭabarânî, *Al-Muʿjam al-kabîr*, VIII, p. 56:5–17, nos. 7328–30.

material about epidemics in a *Bâb mâ jâ'a fî l-ṭâ'ûn*, 'Chapter on What Has Been Handed Down Concerning the Plague', within a larger discussion on Medina (because it had never been stricken by the plague) in his *Kitâb al-jâmi'*,[44] roughly a 'Collective Book' discussing various matters to which no separate book has been devoted; 'Abd al-Razzâq does likewise, placing his material on epidemics in a *Bâb fî l-wabâ' wa-l-ṭâ'ûn*, 'Chapter on Epidemics and Plague', in his *Kitâb al-jâmi'*,[45] which considers such other matters as love of money, mendacity and veracity, suicide and the wives of the Prophet. The earliest collection containing a specific 'Book of Medicine' seems to be that of Ibn Abî Shayba (d. 235/849),[46] but while this long discussion contains over 300 traditions on a wide range of subjects, its concern is primarily to refute a mélange of old pagan customs and beliefs and no attention whatsoever is paid to traditions on epidemics. This subject is discussed elsewhere, in his *Kitâb al-jihâd*, 'Book on Holy Mission', within the context of plague victims as martyrs.[47] It is not until the compilation of the *Ṣaḥîḥ* of al-Bukhârî (d. 256/870), a student of Ibn Abî Shayba who used his collection as one of his own main sources, that there appears a 'Book of Medicine' in which traditions on epidemics and the plague occupy a prominent place.[48]

The emergence of such collections tended to transform the *ḥadîth* into a better-defined corpus, and as the leading ninth-century collections assumed an increasingly authoritative status in the Islamic community at large, discussions on many subjects came to focus on the materials available in these works. Where the discussion of epidemic disease was concerned, the emergence of new ideas dwindles to insignificance at this time, and it can be said that the formulations that had come to prevail by this era were the ones that continued to hold sway thereafter, with such new traditions as did emerge after this time tending to comprise varia on already existing themes rather than explorations of new possibilities. Of these themes, the most prominent and important were two based on the plague as their archetypical example. One must not flee from the plague if one is in a stricken area, but such an area is to be avoided

[44] Mâlik, *Muwaṭṭa'*, II, pp. 894:10–897:9.
[45] 'Abd al-Razzâq, *Muṣannaf*, XI, pp. 146:8–151:8.
[46] Ibn Abî Shayba, *Muṣannaf*, VII, pp. 359:1–457:6.
[47] *Ibid.*, V, pp. 332:2–333:10.   [48] Al-Bukhârî, *Ṣaḥîḥ*, IV, pp. 50:1–72:2.

by those not yet affected. Also, the plague is a martyrdom for believers and a painful chastisement for unbelievers, and hence is to be viewed within the context of divine mercy. The issue of contagion also remained important, but in this case considerable controversy was aroused.[49]

Looking ahead to the theme of the next chapter in this volume, it is worth observing that the positions on epidemic disease which Islamic society reached and settled on as authoritative by the mid-ninth century are precisely the ones that dominate the Arabic plague treatises written in response to the Black Death and subsequent outbreaks of plague through much of the Islamic world. These works have often been characterised as derivative and lacking in originality – indeed, so low is the modern interest in them that not a one of them has yet been fully edited.[50] But this derivativeness – in terms of ideas – is in fact a feature of the genre which bears some concluding comment, for it is surely erroneous to dismiss it as a function of some ubiquitous intellectual impoverishment that had supposedly paralysed Islamic culture by the fourteenth century. New and important advances were being achieved in numerous fields of cultural and scientific endeavour in this era; and where the Black Death is concerned, the fact that such a horrific scourge so seldom motivated authors to question the old-established ideas indicates not a failing on the part of the treatise writers, but rather the strength and continuing validity of these old ideas. That is, while epidemic disease in the form of the plague comprised a tremendous challenge to emergent Islamic thinking in the seventh and eighth centuries, it did not do so in the fourteenth. Indeed, it is fairly clear that it was around the guardians of the traditional faith that threatened Muslim communities rallied and found their greatest solace and strength. The plague condemned untold multitudes to terrible suffering and an agonising death, and often reduced communal life to ruin, but it did not shake the Muslim's faith in the values

---

[49] I would therefore not agree with Michael Dols in including the denial of contagion as one of the normative Islamic views on plague and epidemic disease generally. See his 'Plague in Early Islamic History', p. 377; idem, Black Death in the Middle East, p. 23.

[50] For a discussion of one of the most prominent treatises, see Jacqueline Sublet, 'La Peste prise aux rêts de la jurisprudence: le traité d'Ibn Ḥaǧar al-'Asqalânî sur la peste', Studia Islamica, 33 (1971), pp. 141–9.

and ideals shaped six centuries before his day. The fact that past generations had endured and survived similar terrors played an important role in sustaining the hope among Muslims in the Mamlûk era that they would again weather the storm and pass through to more felicitous times ahead.

5. *Plague and perceptions of the poor in early modern Italy*

BRIAN PULLAN

This chapter is concerned with ways in which outbreaks of pestilence influenced perceptions of the poor. Discussion will focus on the Italian states between the late fifteenth and the mid-seventeenth centuries, making occasional forays into other parts of Europe in search of contrasts and parallels. How did the threat of plague, and of those epidemic fevers that presaged it, ran concurrently with it or were mistaken for it, contribute to the mixture of pity and fear that characterised the attitudes of educated and authoritative people towards the poor in the early modern period? Much of the evidence will be drawn, at first or second hand, from legislative acts, and from chronicles, letters and reports compiled by clergymen and religious, by physicians, by professional men and by administrators. Their authors were generally pillars of urban society, proud that they had not fled from the plague, persons who saw in the countryside both a place of refuge for the less dutiful and stout-hearted, and a force which laid siege to the city, blockading its gates and approach roads, and withholding its supplies.

In 1630, with the onset of a terrible epidemic that was eventually to destroy more than 30 per cent of Venice's population, the Venetian senate passed two decrees intended to clear particular quarters of the city of the beggars infesting them. Issued on 22 June, the first decree seemed wholly dedicated to placating the wrath of God, of which the plague was the unmistakable sign.[1] It strove to

---

The following abbreviations will be used:
ASV   Archivio di Stato, Venice
RRVT *Relazioni dei rettori veneti in Terraferma*, ed. Amelio Tagliaferri *et al.*, 14
      vols. (Milan, 1973–9)
[1] ASV, Senato, Terra, reg. 103, fols. 192r–3r. For plague in Venice generally, see
    Richard Palmer, 'The Control of Plague in Venice and Northern Italy, 1348–1600'

create three regions of special holiness, like powerhouses of piety spaced at intervals across the city: around the doges' chapel, St Mark's; around the church of St Roch (otherwise San Rocco), the healing plague saint of Montpellier whose bones reposed in Venice; and around the cathedral of San Pietro di Castello. Here a prominent feature of the ritual would be a display of the mortal remains (later called the 'holy ashes') of Lorenzo Giustinian, Venice's first patriarch, famous as a healer as far away as Palermo, and shortly, by behest of the state, to become a candidate for canonisation. This Venetian ceremony may have been designed to imitate, if only modestly, the six-hour parade held a few days before in Milan of the body of the sainted archbishop Carlo Borromeo, hero of the last great plague of northern Italy in the mid-1570s.[2] In all three holy places the sacrament was to be exposed for adoration and to be accompanied in procession at intervals round the immediate neighbourhood, as though its effluvia were being sent forth to combat the insidious force of the plague. To appease God by curbing the sins of the citizens two boards of magistrates were solemnly reminded to do their duty. One of these had the task of suppressing blasphemy and related excesses such as gambling and loose living, and the other was concerned with the control of ostentatious expenditure on clothing, jewellery and hospitality.[3] It was then declared to be 'scandalous and indecent' that there should be so many poor people in the first of the three sacred areas – in the doge's palace (where they had probably taken over the open stairways, courtyards and arcades), in St Mark's itself, and in the great square before it. All of them must now be removed.

On the face of it this displacement of the poor was not an act of hygiene in a purely physical sense, or a measure undertaken for aesthetic reasons. Rather, it was an act of propitiation, and a gesture of public piety or charity on the part of the state itself. What was

(Univ. of Kent PhD thesis, 1978), and various authors, *Venezia e la peste, 1348–1797* (Venice, 1979).

[2] ASV, Senato, Terra, reg. 103, fols. 261v–2v, 5 Aug. 1630; Fausto Nicolini, 'La peste del 1629–1632', in Fondazione Treccani degli Alfieri, *Storia di Milano*, X (Milan, 1957), pp. 523–5; cf. Jean Delumeau, *La Peur en occident (XIVe–XVIIIe siècles). Une cité assiégée* (Paris, 1978), pp. 138–40.

[3] For these bodies, see Giulio Bistort, *Il magistrato alle pompe nella Repubblica di Venezia: studio storico* (Venice, 1912); Renzo Derosas, 'Moralità e giustizia a Venezia nel '500–'600: gli Esecutori contro la Bestemmia', in Gaetano Cozzi (ed.), *Stato, società e giustizia nella Repubblica Veneta (sec. XV–XVIII)*, 2 vols. (Rome, 1980–5), I, pp. 431–528.

most 'scandalous and indecent' is not entirely clear. The state may have been reproaching itself for its conspicuous neglect of the poor at the very seat of government, and for allowing the hypocrisy of a supposedly pious republic to be indecently revealed. Alternatively, the scandal might well have arisen from the beggars' own misconduct, for over the last century they had often been described in secular or ecclesiastical legislation as immoral blasphemers, ignorant of the most elementary Christian doctrine.[4] In Venice itself the very poor had been seen in a jubilee year as importunate nuisances who distracted the faithful from their devotions, so that guards had to be posted to keep them out of the most frequented churches.[5] Whatever view it took of them in 1630, the senate vowed money for the support of these abjectly poor people and had it disbursed by the select group of public trustees, the procurators or lay advocates of St Mark's, who were most closely identified with the state itself and its official religion.[6] Like an individual, a state or community could amass merit and cancel sin through an act of charity, and the poor (if confined to their proper spaces) were a means to salvation and to surviving disaster.

Another decree, passed four months later, on 22 October 1630, provided with closer attention to detail for the removal of beggars from another sacred area: this time from the church of San Rocco and from that of the Carmini nearby. However, the context was very different, for although the decree was issued on the same day as the famous vow to build the church of Santa Maria della Salute in thanksgiving for the day when the plague would eventually depart from Venice, the senate was now issuing copious legislation which treated the plague as a natural phenomenon. It was designed to protect the quality of food, to control the movement of infected goods, to separate the sick from the healthy, to guarantee fresh water and oil for the poor and to accumulate firewood against the approaching winter.[7] Another enforcing agency was used: the

---

[4] See Brian Pullan, 'Poveri, mendicanti e vagabondi (secoli XIV–XVII)', in Corrado Vivanti and Ruggiero Romano (eds.), *Storia d'Italia. Annali I. Dal feudalesimo al capitalismo* (Turin, 1978), pp. 1016–20.

[5] ASV, Provveditori alla Sanità, reg. 732, fol. 86r–v, 12 Jan. 1575 Venetian style (i.e. 1576).

[6] See R. C. Mueller, *The Procuratori di San Marco and the Venetian Credit Market* (New York, 1977).

[7] ASV, Senato, Terra, reg. 104, fols. 365v–8r. See fols. 363v–5r for the vow to build the Salute.

governors of the beggars' hospital, San Lazzaro dei Mendicanti, were called to assist in the task of transporting the beggars to the island monastery placed at their disposal by the patriarch. Inevitably this procedure calls to mind what Michel Foucault called 'the great internment', the measures launched in sixteenth-century Italy and seventeenth-century France for a total enclosure of the homeless poor, so that all public begging, with few exceptions, would be eliminated from the land.[8]

There is nothing extraordinary in this account, for descriptions of the plague, whether compiled by eye-witnesses or historians, explore standard themes, report stock incidents and record debates on well-worn issues. Here are two familiar kinds of dualism, the first being the belief that plague was both a divine penalty and a natural phenomenon. As lord of nature, God could work through natural causes, although these, as Defoe was later to argue, might well be so subtle and so far beyond human diagnosis or control that action would best be concentrated on imploring forgiveness and alleviating the terrible poverty inflicted by the plague's economic disruption.[9] Plague could at once be provoked by acts of sacrilege and spread by acts of human greed and stupidity, such as trading in goods purloined from quarantine centres and sequestrated houses.[10] It was not merely, however, as some observers suggested, an act of war between God or the heavens and the human race:[11] its function was corrective, for, as the Venetian legislators had it, 'God is accustomed to show us the scourge of his wrath, to recall us to good and to the better way of his service.' Plague was a call to reformation: not,

---

[8] Michel Foucault, *Folie et déraison: histoire de la folie à l'âge classique* (Paris, 1961); cf. Brian Pullan, 'Support and Redeem: Charity and Poor Relief in Italian Cities from the Fourteenth to the Seventeenth Century', *Continuity and Change*, 3 (1988), pp. 196–201, and on the Venetian beggars' hospital, see Brian Pullan, *Rich and Poor in Renaissance Venice. The Social Institutions of a Catholic State, to 1620* (Oxford, 1971), pp. 362–70.

[9] See especially Daniel Defoe, *A Journal of the Plague Year*, ed. Kenneth Hopkins (London, 1960), pp. 194–7. For the theme in general, see Richard Palmer, 'The Church, Leprosy and Plague in Medieval and Early Modern Europe', in W. J. Sheils (ed.), *The Church and Healing*, Studies in Church History XIX (Oxford, 1982), pp. 79–100, and the physicians' discussions excerpted in Paolo Preto, *Peste e società a Venezia nel 1576* (Vicenza, 1978), pp. 160–86.

[10] E.g. in the Milanese plague which began in 1629: Nicolini, 'La peste', pp. 499, 503–5.

[11] E.g. in G. G. Gerbaldo, 'Memorie della guerra, carestia e peste del Piemonte negli anni 1629, 1630 e 1631', *Miscellanea di Storia Italiana*, 5 (Turin, 1868), pp. 151–2; Danilo Presotto, 'Genova 1656–1657. Cronache di una pestilenza', *Atti della Società Ligure di Storia Patria*, n.s., 5 (1965), p. 386.

perhaps, to the reconstruction of society, but certainly to its moral improvement. In the October decree of the Venetians, the principle was clearly stated that

> After the proper humble recourse to his divine majesty we must, by the rules of wise government, and as a continued act of public charity towards our beloved citizens and subjects, daily apply those human remedies that are likewise enjoined upon us by every divine law, and are invoked by nature itself, that we may daily arrive at some resolution that will minister to the preservation of so many poor people and to the consolation and benefit of the entire community.[12]

In Italian and French cities the domains of faith and reason, and the jurisdictions of clergy and laity, were not always as harmoniously related as this passage implies. As theories of contagion gained ground, from the mid-fifteenth century onwards, harsh conflicts could well arise between clerical and popular faith in collective rituals and churchgoing as the most effective means of appeasing God's wrath, and the contrasting determination of physicians and sanitary officers to prevent the assembly of crowds.[13] Tensions may have been less acute in countries where, as Paul Slack puts it, religious responses to plague had been 'driven off the streets by the Reformation', or where fasting was preferred to processing;[14] but conflict was latent wherever religion called for public acts of worship. However, there were bridges between faith and reason, and the poor made one of them. Relieving the poor could at once be an act of placation addressed to God and a practical measure for containing an epidemic. Conspicuous in accounts of plague in most parts of continental Europe are descriptions of votive churches, solemn masses, parades of relics and (in Barcelona in 1482) the confection of a candle whose coils measured 4 miles – as thick as a finger, and as long as the circumference of the town walls. Modest equivalents to the Venetian votive churches, Palladio's Redentore and Longhena's Salute, were the three silver statues vowed *c.* 1630 to the patron saint of the subject town of Treviso, and the 50-ounce

---

12 ASV, Senato, Terra, reg. 103, fol. 192r; reg. 104, fol. 365v.
13 See especially C. M. Cipolla, *Faith, Reason and the Plague in Seventeenth Century Tuscany* (Ithaca, 1979); also J. N. Biraben, *Les Hommes et la peste en France et dans les pays européens et méditerranéens*, 2 vols. (Paris, 1975–6), II, pp. 63–8.
14 Paul Slack, *The Impact of Plague in Tudor and Stuart England* (London, 1985), p. 37; Delumeau, *La Peur*, pp. 138–9.

silver lamp destined for the Madonna at Pordenone in Friuli.[15] However, acts of charity, either communal or personal, could equally well form part of a city's expiatory ritual. In the plague-ridden August of 1576, the patriarch of Venice had exhorted his flock to the sacrifice of almsgiving, citing texts from Tobias, 'Alms bring freedom from death; it is alms that purge away sin', and from Daniel, 'Redeem your sins by almsgiving and your wickedness by mercy to the poor.' In September the patrician Antonio Bragadin combined two forms of propitiatory piety by voting 500 ducats to the promised church of the Redentore and another 500 to the poor of the city.[16] On occasion, organised charities were founded or promised in times of pestilence, not merely for down-to-earth practical reasons, but for the purpose of tempering God's anger. An isolation hospital planned in Florence in 1464 was intended to 'placate almighty God and persuade him to be merciful to this people and preserve them from such pestilential disease'. Much later, on 7 September 1720, the échevins of Marseilles made a solemn vow to assign 2,000 livres a year in perpetuity to the foundation of Notre Dame de Bon Secours, for the care of poor girls in the city and territory. 'Such a sacrifice', wrote Dr Bertrand, chronicler of the epidemic, 'could not fail to be acceptable to the Most High; and was more proper to appease his anger than what was made by the antient Marseillois on similar occasions.'[17]

Implicit in the Venetian decrees and in many of the strategies adopted in plague years was another kind of dualism, familiar to historians and suggested by the antithetical titles of recent works, such as 'Fear and Charity' or 'Pity and the Gallows'.[18] Epidemics heightened the conflicting roles of the poor as subjects of pity and objects of fear. As objects of fear, the poor were the incubators and

[15] See W. A. Christian, Jr, *Apparitions in Late Medieval and Renaissance Spain* (Princeton, 1981), pp. 132–3; Biraben, *Les Hommes*, II, pp. 71–2; *RRVT*, III, p. 193; Michele Gottardi, 'La situazione socio-sanitaria nel Friuli occidentale durante la peste del 1630', *Studi Veneziani*, n.s., 6 (1982), p. 178.

[16] From the compilation by Cornelio Morello, clerk to the office of public health in Venice, 'Monumenti della peste di Venezia nel 1575', Biblioteca Correr, Venice, Cicogna MSS no. 1547, under date.

[17] A. G. Carmichael, *Plague and the Poor in Renaissance Florence* (Cambridge, 1986), p. 102; J. B. Bertrand, *A Historical Relation of the Plague at Marseilles in the Year 1720* (London, 1805, repr. 1973), p. 174.

[18] Giorgio Politi, Mario Rosa and Franco Della Peruta (eds.), *Timore e carità: i poveri nell' Italia moderna. Atti del convegno 'Pauperismo e assistenza negli antichi stati italiani'* (Cremona, 1982); Bronislaw Geremek, *La pietà e la forca. Storia della miseria e della carità in Europa* (Italian translation from the Polish, Bari, 1986).

spreaders of disease, the gateway through which the plague might enter and fatally weaken society. They were also a force for rebellion which might well take possession of the half-deserted towns from which their masters had fled. At the same time they were the most numerous and pathetic victims both of the sickness itself and of the social disruption caused by the measures adopted to control it. As subjects of pity, as receivers of God sent among mankind, the poor extended to the faithful the means of liberation from the pestilence through divine acceptance of the sacrifice of charity. In this discussion, therefore, it seems reasonable to consider the poor in three contrasting roles: as bearers of the plague, as victims of the plague and as beneficiaries of the plague – as those deemed capable of extracting profit from the extraordinary change of circumstances it created. It is logical, too, to ask the question whether epidemics made any lasting contribution to the treatment of the poor whether they deposited any institutional structures that continued to function between epidemics or had some application outside the context of a crisis. Here the term 'poor' will be used elastically and stretched from beggars, vagrants and the permanent inmates of hospitals upwards through the hidden mass of the house-poor, the 'shamefaced' or *vergognosi* who shrank from disclosing their distress.[19] It will extend to all those who 'get their daily bread in this city by their labour, whether artificers or mere workmen',[20] and to all who had accumulated only the scantiest reserves: to them, and to all their dependants, forming at least two-thirds of the city's population.

It was axiomatic for many observers that plague was a lethal sickness that flourished chiefly among the poor. Plague was a consequence of malnutrition, overcrowding, polluted water and carelessness. It might even be a form of food poisoning, an inward putrescence caused by eating herbs, fruits and roots, the left-overs of fish and meat markets, and worst of all, bread made of mixed and impure flour and badly cooked. Such was the opinion of the physician Donzellini, who published at Venice in 1577. He perhaps did less than justice to the Venetian people's well-known preference

---

[19] For definitions of poverty and categories of poor, see Pullan, 'Poveri', and Paola Lanaro Sartori, 'Radiografia della soglia di povertà in una città della Terraferma Veneta: Verona alla metà del XVI secolo', *Studi Veneziani*, n.s., 6 (1982), pp. 45–85.

[20] Defoe, *Journal*, pp. 102–3.

for pure wheaten bread, but it was true that, despite their strong feelings, a noxious millet flour had been forced upon them a few years earlier, and some of them had almost desecrated the corpse of the doge they held responsible.[21]

However, there were plagues and plagues. Insofar as they were ascribed to natural causes, some seemed to be transmitted by contagion, others by corruption of the air and water and some again by both. Where infection through close proximity was the culprit, the rich – or so Fracastoro argued in the mid-sixteenth century – had a better chance of escaping through flight and through avoidance of overcrowding.[22] Reinforced by observation, the tradition persisted. 'The streets are wide, the houses large, and inhabited chiefly by persons in a state of opulence', wrote Dr Bertrand of the St Ferréol quarter of Marseilles in 1720, 'and such are always the last attacked by a contagion, on account of the means they have to place themselves out of its reach.'[23] In Europe generally it was not just the rich who left the cities: the urban poor of Spain and Portugal ran for the woods, and some French towns, including Angers, and Apt in Provence, despaired of supporting their poor and despatched them into the countryside, with or without a tiny subsidy, in the last years of the sixteenth century.[24] But the chances of survival in a hostile, suspicious environment were greatly enhanced by the possession of money and a country house. In the words of Hooper, an English bishop expressing a European truth, the poor 'have no friends, nor place to flee unto, more than the poor house they dwell in'.[25] Those social reformers who, like John Howard at the close of the eighteenth century, placed their faith in cleanliness and a good, plain, but ample diet as general prophylactics against sickness, found little difficulty in explaining why plague should fall more heavily upon the poor than upon the rich.[26]

---

[21] Preto, *Peste e società*, pp. 62, 66, 120, 170–2, 174–7, 182; for the episode of the 'millet doge', Pietro Loredan, see the 'Cronaca Agostini', Biblioteca Correr, Venice, Cicogna MSS no. 2853, fols. 164r–8r, 183r, 187r–8r. For similar themes, see Defoe, *Journal*, pp. 223–4; Bertrand, *Historical Relation*, pp. 26–8, 55, 57, 59.

[22] See Carmichael, *Plague and the Poor*, p. 131.

[23] Bertrand, *Historical Relation*, pp. 208–9.

[24] Bartolomé Bennassar, *Recherches sur les grandes épidémies dans le Nord de l'Espagne à la fin du XVIe siècle: problèmes de documentation et de méthode* (Paris, 1969), p. 52; Biraben, *Les Hommes*, II, pp. 145–6.

[25] Slack, *Impact of Plague*, p. 43.

[26] John Howard, *An Account of the Principal Lazarettos in Europe*, 2nd edn (London, 1791), p. 25.

More subtly, others believed that a kind of improvidence, a deep-seated recklessness, characterised the culture or mentality of poverty: the insouciance that made the poor poor also exposed them to the plague, and itself precluded them from taking precautions.

> It must be confessed that though the plague was chiefly among the poor, yet were the poor the most adventurous and fearless of it, and went about their employment with a sort of brutal courage; I must call it so, for it was founded neither on religion nor prudence; scarce did they use any caution, but ran into any business which they could get employment in, though it was the most hazardous.[27]

The theory was thus most eloquently stated by Defoe, but there was Italian evidence to support it. Giulia Calvi's researches on the judicial records of Florence in the 1630s suggest an extraordinary indifference to the risk of infection on the part of labouring folk: a surprising readiness to enter stricken houses, handle objects supposedly impregnated with the plague and even (when working as gravediggers, traditionally recompensed with the clothing of the deceased) to strip shirts off corpses and put them on themselves.[28] Notions of the plague as a divine penalty for the poor's thoughtlessness were elaborated, in somewhat different terms, during the savage epidemic in Genoa in 1656. Sister Maria Francesca, an articulate and censorious nun who witnessed the epidemic from her convent in the poor quarter of Pre, depicted the poor in her letters as obstinate, self-deluding creatures, unable to face reality and sadly in need of discipline.[29] In the same dreadful years Father Antero Maria di San Bonaventura, warden of the Genoese pesthouse, saw the plague as a consequence of poor people's fecundity, and of their failure to follow the example of the rich by restricting marriages: hence the plague was necessary, as a divine instrument for thinning out the surplus population.[30] Plague might, as Defoe later implied, drive poverty to the point of desperation, but plague mortality acted as a control upon it, decimating and enfeebling the poor to the point at

[27] Defoe, *Journal*, pp. 95–6; cf. also pp. 211–12.

[28] Giulia Calvi, *Histories of a Plague Year. The Social and the Imaginary in Baroque Florence* (Berkeley, 1989), pp. 141–2, 148.

[29] See her letters of 25 Nov. 1656 and 12 May 1657, in Presotto, 'Genova', pp. 375, 389.

[30] C. M. Cipolla, 'The Plague and the Pre-Malthus Malthusians', *Journal of European Economic History*, 3 (1974), pp. 277–84. For other examples of 'pre-Malthusian' sentiments, see Preto, *Peste e società*, pp. 61, 71–2.

which they could not really cause a sustained and dangerous tumult.[31]

To Alessandro Righi, a Florentine physician writing in the 1630s, the city poor, like glands or ignoble peripheral organs of the body, far from the heart and brain, were a depository for noxious substances expelled by the nobler parts: they retained the poison, but could not transmit it to others. It was true that in Tuscany in those years, or at least in Florence and Prato, few noblemen had suffered, even as in the Spanish town of Sepúlveda in 1599 'by the mercy of God the plague has smitten no one in easy circumstances'.[32] But had the plague been safely confined to the poor, or had it been generally recognised as a device of God and nature for reducing their numbers and restoring demographic balance, it would not have seemed so terrible. True, the performance of the disease was variable, but its most frightening attribute was its potential for spreading from the poor quarters of the town and striking at persons of every social rank, although it seldom killed members of different social orders in equal proportions. Plague could be defined as plague in terms of its broad social impact as well as of its clinical signs and symptoms. Some physicians, partly for pragmatic reasons (for no one would thank them for starting a panic or getting a city banned by its neighbours) refused to diagnose malignant fevers as pestilential until they saw evidence that all levels of the population were affected.[33] Where disease spread through poisoned air rather than contagion, opined Fracastoro, the rich man's luxurious habits might easily tell against him, his resistance proving lower than that of the tough and frugal poor.[34]

During the 1570s the plague in Padua seemed to descend with equal violence on persons of every social rank, even, with a kind of perversity, sparing the beggars and cripples who were normally its

---

[31] Defoe, *Journal*, pp. 104, 134–5.

[32] Calvi, *Histories*, pp. 65, 255; C. M. Cipolla, *Cristofano and the Plague. A Study in the History of Public Health in the Age of Galileo* (London, 1973), pp. 107–8. For Spanish evidence, see Bennassar, *Recherches*, p. 53.

[33] For the famous case of the Paduan physicians in Venice in 1576, see Preto, *Peste e società*, pp. 48–50; for other examples, see Biraben, *Les Hommes*, II, p. 92; Bertrand, *Historical Relation*, pp. 55, 57; J. T. Alexander, *Bubonic Plague in Early Modern Russia. Public Health and Urban Disaster* (Baltimore, 1980), pp. 130, 133, 143; Giovanni Restifo, *Peste al confine: l'epidemia di Messina del 1743* (Palermo, 1984), pp. 213–14.

[34] Carmichael, *Plague and the Poor*, p. 131; cf. C. M. Cipolla, *Fighting the Plague in Seventeenth-Century Italy* (Madison, 1981), p. 106.

first victims. Pasquale Cicogna, the Venetian governor, reported the deaths of some twenty members of his own entourage, who had perhaps been restrained from flight (unlike the local commissioners of public health) by a strong sense of public obligation – the 'judge of evil deeds', the 'judge over victuals', the chancellor of the town, a knight and so forth. One of his successors, Vincenzo Capello, in 1632, in the aftermath of an epidemic which had wiped out more than half the population, lamented the deaths of nineteen distinguished doctors who had lectured at the university.[35] Noblemen of the Venetian Great Council (admittedly a social order which comprised enormous differences in wealth and included some abjectly poor creatures) fell in number from 2,000 in 1620 to 1,660 by the end of the plague of 1630–1. Their loss of 17 per cent compared with an overall descent of over 30 per cent in the city's population.[36] 'The plague begins to take on noble rank', drily observed the nun of Genoa in 1656. Indeed, over 40 per cent of the town's elite, concentrated in the Greater and Lesser Councils, died during that epidemic, though overall mortality in the city, much of it from starvation, proved even higher; assessments made immediately after the disaster suggested that three-quarters of the inhabitants of Genoa had been swept away by this unparalleled disaster.[37] Discourses on the plague as social leveller were sometimes found in witnesses' accounts of epidemics. In 1598 the Venetian governor of Cividale in the province of Friuli resisted the pleas of the well-to-do locals to be allowed to depart, exhorting them to stay, as he was doing, and not to spread the infection. Canon Jacopo Strazzolini, chronicler of the outbreak, reported that even noblemen had been carried off to the pesthouse and seen naked, without badges of rank, by the physicians who attended the victims of plague.[38] Poverty was feared as an incubator of disease that might easily spread to more delicate and refined sectors of the population, even to those who enjoyed a much more pleasant and spacious environment and greater possibilities of escape.

---

[35] Preto, *Peste e società*, pp. 74–5; *RRVT*, IV, pp. 73, 254.

[36] J. C. Davis, *The Decline of the Venetian Nobility as a Ruling Class* (Baltimore, 1962), p. 57; Paolo Preto, 'Peste e demografia', in various authors, *Venezia e la peste*, pp. 97–8.

[37] Presotto, 'Genova', pp. 336–7, 361, 433–4.

[38] See *RRVT*, V, p. 44; Mario Brozzi, *Peste, fede e sanità in una cronaca cividalese del 1598* (Milan, 1982), pp. 33–4, 40.

Tracing the origins of particular plagues, chroniclers and other witnesses were prone to ascribe them to invaders from outside the community: to soldiers, whether down-at-heel deserters or defeated armies retreating in disarray; to vagabonds; or to infected merchandise eluding the vigilance of corrupt or somnolent sanitary officers in the quarantine stations. Sometimes the culprits were named, immortalised in the annals of disaster, as were Lucia, daughter of Giacomo Cadorino, and her lover Matteo Farcinatore, who allegedly brought the plague from the Trento region to Venice in 1575; or Pietro Antonio Lovato, the Milanese soldier who had been trading in garments with German troops and brought the plague to Milan in 1629.[39] But observers were equally capable of tracing the origins of disease to the permanent conditions of the physical environment within the city, as if the plague was always lurking there. From Florence and Genoa came horrendous accounts of polluted water supplies; of damp; of overcrowding; of the stench proceeding from the silk-worms that provided (at a heavy price) a useful by-employment for the poor; of houses so tall and served by such narrow and rickety wooden staircases that it proved almost impossible to extract dead bodies from them. Such phenomena could easily be reconciled with theories both of contagion and of poisonous miasma. Certainly Sister Maria Francesca, the nun of Genoa, held that a pestilence was always present in the dwellings of the poor, contained in a filthy cloud of infected air, even in times when the city officially enjoyed good health: these dreadful houses, as she portrayed them, call to mind Tom-all-Alone's in *Bleak House*, the slum of Dickensian London whose 'pestilential gas' blows forth and menaces the entire social order: 'There is not a drop of Tom's corrupted blood but propagates infection and contagion somewhere.'[40]

Theories of contagion, which saw the plague transported through human movement from infected to uninfected regions, gained

---

[39] Preto, *Peste e società*, p. 1, and Nicolini, 'La peste', pp. 504–5. Cf. especially Giulia Calvi, 'L'oro, il fuoco, le forche: la peste napoletana del 1656', *Archivio Storico Italiano*, 139 (1981), pp. 408–9, 418–20; Calvi, *Histories of a Plague Year*, pp. 21–58; *RRVT*, XI, p. 344.

[40] For Florence, see C. M. Cipolla, *I pidocchi e il Granduca. Crisi economica e problemi sanitari nella Firenze del '600* (Bologna, 1979), pp. 12–14, 60–6, 74–5; Daniela Lombardi, '1629–1631: crisi e peste a Firenze', *Archivio Storico Italiano*, 137 (1979), pp. 33–7. For Genoa, see Presotto, 'Genova', p. 385 (letter of 24 March 1657). See *Bleak House*, Chapter XLVI.

ground from the mid-fifteenth century onwards among administrators and perhaps from the mid-sixteenth century among physicians, until the terms 'plague' and 'contagion' became almost synonymous.[41] They did not so much displace theories of miasma as take their place beside them, accentuating the tendency to blame epidemics on strangers. Fear of them was one of the forces that drove vagrants, and perhaps prostitutes also, to a marginal position that allowed them the lowest possible claims on society's compassion; they became prominent candidates for expulsion, or at least for isolation and imprisonment, while an epidemic lasted. Brothels were attacked in Italy and France as potential foci of plague infection before they were blamed for disseminating the pox; it was not always clear whether they supposedly endangered society by indiscriminately entertaining strangers, or whether they did so by provoking divine retribution on a community which tolerated fornication.[42] Only a thin line separated the wanderer who carried the plague stupidly and irresponsibly but without malevolence from the evil outsider who might well be the agent of a foreign power, sent to spread the disease by poisons and noxious substances. Prime targets for suspicion in Tuscany in the 1630s were a character 'dressed as a priest and talking Neapolitan', who was charged by the villagers of San Martino a Gangalandi near Florence, and Bastiano, the travelling pedlar-cum-charlatan accused of poisoning stoups of holy water in a church at Volterra.[43] Suspicion tended to spread from casual or seasonal migrants to refugee populations: in Venice it clung to Slavs and Albanians in the mid-fifteenth century, and a century later to Marranos or Portuguese New Christians from the Low Countries. The expulsion of the Marranos by the senate in 1550 was prompted, not only by the argument that they were bearers of heresy, mingling Christianity and Judaism or moving at will between the two faiths, but also by the fear that their squalid and overcrowded lodgings would breed disease. Hence the metaphorical plague of heresy would

---

[41] Cf. Carmichael, *Plague and the Poor*, pp. 90–107; Biraben, *Les Hommes*, II, pp. 25–7.

[42] Carmichael, *Plague and the Poor*, p. 98; cf. L. L. Otis, *Prostitution in Medieval Society. The History of an Urban Institution in Languedoc* (Chicago and London, 1985), p. 41.

[43] See Daniela Lombardi, *Povertà maschile, povertà femminile. L'Ospedale dei Mendicanti nella Firenze dei Medici* (Bologna, 1988), pp. 55–6; Calvi, *Histories of a Plague Year*, pp. 25–7.

combine with a clinical pestilence to undermine both the physical health and the orthodoxy of Venice.[44]

Scarcely less dangerous in the eyes of authority were the panic migrants from the surrounding subject territories of the city, who invaded during famine years in the frantic hope of finding bread and charity. Here, it was said, there were two agencies, smell and terror, which threatened to impart fatal illness to the citizens. The stink of starvation and impending death, a 'filthy odour and infected air', clung to exhausted peasants as they urged their skeletal bodies into the town. No one, wrote Dr Benaglio, who recorded the disaster years of 1629–31 in the hospitable city of Bergamo, could live with 'a stench that infects, with the continuous spectacle of the dead and dying'.[45] As he implied there was a strain of medical opinion which held that lethal disease could be rooted in fear alone: that the terror of death engendered by the spectacle of others' misfortunes, by the horror of extreme destitution, could be as bad as the plague itself. Describing similar invasions of the cities by the poor more than a century earlier, Luigi Da Porto, a nobleman of Vicenza, had speculated: 'I think there is no contagion in the air, but only a sickness in the souls of men, caused by pity for these things, which breeds poisonous humours in the body.' If this was more than a literary conceit, it suggested that compassion, far from giving rise to the saving virtue of mercy, might well become fatal to those who experienced it in too acute and painful a form.[46] The only solution to these evils, as Benaglio suggested, was to decentralise charity in such a way as to curb these terrifying convergences on the towns.

If the poor were often depicted as the means by which the whole social order was exposed to assault and depletion by fatal sickness, it was equally clear that the poor were the favoured victims of that sickness: not just because of their own improvidence or the plague's predilection for persons of a certain constitution, but because of the immediate social and economic consequences of measures taken to

[44] Carmichael, *Plague and the Poor*, pp. 117–18; letters of Hieronymo Feruffino, ambassador of the duke of Ferrara, in David Kaufmann, 'A Contribution to the History of the Venetian Jews', *Jewish Quarterly Review*, 2 (1890), pp. 304–5.

[45] Marc'Antonio Benaglio, 'Relazione della carestia e della peste di Bergamo e suo territorio negli anni 1629 e 1630', ed. Giovanni Finazzi in *Miscellanea di Storia Italiana*, 6 (Turin, 1865), pp. 419–25.

[46] Delumeau, *La Peur*, p. 117; Luigi Da Porto, *Lettere storiche dall' anno 1509 al 1528*, ed. Bartolomeo Bressan (Florence, 1857), pp. 327–8.

contain it. News that plague had been discovered, the reluctant pronouncement of the terrible word, would inevitably cause a collapse of employment and a suspension of vital supplies to the city. These developments had at least four causes: in the flight of employers and prosperous inhabitants to country retreats; in the banning of the city by its neighbours and the creation of an encircling sanitary cordon; in quarantine regulations applied within the city itself, especially the confinement of suspect persons to their own houses; and in the extreme reluctance of villagers and peasants to approach the city gates and sell their produce to the imprisoned townspeople. 'Such evil things were believed', remembered Canon Strazzolini of Cividale, 'that the peasants did not dare to bring so much as a bundle of firewood to sell, or even to give to friends or brothers beyond the gates . . . you could truthfully say that we were under siege, since even for money you could not get the most essential things.'[47] In Treviso province in 1631 the villagers of Cartigliano passed formal resolutions, and had them proclaimed in church on Sunday, that they were not to approach the town of Bassano.[48] Yet these country people were not just a besieging force, suddenly more privileged than their betters in the town, for any suspension of normal relations between town and country threatened the well-being of rural society. To the Florentine authorities in 1631 the representatives of the village of Santo Stefano in Pane described with foreboding the likely effect of strict quarantine regulations upon poor people, especially country women who did odd jobs: laundresses, or load-carriers, or those who went into Florence to weave and had to be where the looms were, or simply trudged into the city to beg.[49] Strict regulation of human movement, often enforced by the threat of hanging, opened up the prospect of a slower and scarcely less agonising death by starvation to vulnerable persons without reserves. Within the towns, the most prominent victims were 'numerous people who live by manual labour in a city founded entirely on commerce, that expects to get everything from abroad', especially if they worked in textiles or other high-risk trades such as papermaking.[50] But all were

[47] Brozzi, *Peste*, p. 31.
[48] Giuliano Galletti, 'Peste e reazioni della società in una provincia della Terraferma Veneta: il Trevigiano nel 1630–31', *Studi Veneziani*, n.s., 8 (1984), p. 177.
[49] Lombardi, '1629–1631', pp. 22–4.
[50] Presotto, 'Genova', pp. 340, 367, 385.

threatened by the breakdown of supplies, and especially perhaps by the collapse of the bakers' trade, even where (as in Genoa) grain – itself a dangerous substance – was plentiful enough. Agostino Bembo, governor of Brescia in 1630–1, found himself left with only six bakers to serve a big city. He had a task force sent out to him from Venice, but many were understandably detained at Verona on the outward journey. Five of them arrived safely in Brescia, but three promptly died, and he was able to solve the problem only by commandeering wagon-loads of bread, already baked, from eight to ten neighbouring villages.[51]

Yet there was a sense in which the plague, while suspending certain forms of employment, created others through heavy public spending that was partly intended to enforce hygienic measures and partly to forestall the danger of 'tumult'. On occasions witnesses spoke of the poor as beneficiaries rather than victims of the plague, which had created sinister opportunities for them. The deserted city, with the houses of the well-to-do locked up and abandoned, became the province of the poor. In the wake of popular disturbances, such as the rising of the textile workers in Florence in 1378 or Masaniello's revolt in Naples in 1647, the connection between epidemics and rebellion was heavily stressed by some observers. Indeed, it was suggested that plague had been imported into the poor quarters of Naples in 1656 by a former officer of the people in the 1647 rising, who now died of the plague himself. It was as though a deadly medical contagion was treading on the heels of a political corruption, and both were located among the dangerous people.[52] Epidemics may not have created the most sustained and organised forms of class conflict, although the poor directed much resentment and some violence against barber-surgeons and sanitary personnel, as well as against authorities who tried to interfere with religious rites.[53] And if class conflict arises out of a simple binary opposition between the more and the less fortunate, the plague undoubtedly threatened for a time to divide society into the two camps of those who fled and those who stayed – which often, though not invariably, meant an opposition of rich and poor. In the sudden absence of the

---

[51] *RRVT*, X, pp. 345–6. For the dangers of the grain trade, see L. F. Hirst, *The Conquest of Plague. A Study of the Evolution of Epidemiology* (Oxford, 1953), pp. 311–15.

[52] Carmichael, *Plague and the Poor*, pp. 99–100; Calvi, 'L'oro', pp. 421–5.

[53] See Alexander, *Bubonic Plague*, pp. 177–80, 186–200; Calvi, *Histories of a Plague Year*, pp. 195–6.

merchant entrepreneurs who gave out work, the artisans of Bassano rose in 'tumult' in 1631, saying that 'rather than let themselves die of hunger, they would go and pick up whatever they could find'.[54] Epidemics, and reactions to them, threatened to destroy the illusion of paternalistic care on the part of the rich for the poor, particularly that of employers for servants; they threatened to dissolve reciprocal relations between the almsgiver and the recipient. In Naples in 1656 rumours circulated to the effect that the rich, unafflicted by plague, were trying to poison the poor wholesale out of revenge for the revolt of Masaniello.

Like carnival, plague inverted the normal world. It did so in its own way, by creating a temporary dependence on the unrespectable poor, especially vagrants and criminals, for the performance of essential services. Plague seemed to offer extraordinary gains to the ghoulish figures of undertakers, fumigators, cleaners and clearers of plague-stricken houses: *monatti, beccamorti, picigamorti, nettezini*, often characterised as scavenging birds, as the 'kites' of Florence and the 'crows' of France.[55] Such functionaries were heavily recruited from prisoners, vagrants and galley slaves; but seemingly generous incentives, in the form of high advance payments to members of the ordinary labouring poor, were frequently offered by city governments.[56] Occasionally, as in Florence in the 1630s, there occurs a suggestion that the poor actually welcomed the plague because it released them from dependence on the uncertain fortunes of the textile industry. 'It seemed', wrote one Settimanni, 'that out of greed for the gain [from becoming bearers of the dead] they thought nothing of death and of the great danger in which they were clearly placing themselves.' Much the same sentiments were to be repeated in Defoe's *Journal* many years later.[57] 'I hear it was as good as a play', wrote Sister Maria Francesca in Genoa, repeating reports from Rome in 1657, 'to see these creatures feasting and clowning over the corpses, and playing tricks on whores with ribbons in their

---

[54] Galletti, 'Peste', p. 173.

[55] For the terms, see Biraben, *Les Hommes*, II, pp. 120–1; Preto, *Peste e società*, pp. 38–41; Calvi, *Histories of a Plague Year*, pp. 155–6.

[56] For Venetian examples of the use of vagabonds and prisoners, see Morello, 'Monumenti' under date 3 Aug. 1576; ASV, Senato, Terra, reg. 104, fols. 391, 415r–v, 2 and 15 Nov. 1630; *RRVT*, XI, p. 345. For the recruitment of galley slaves in Genoa and Marseilles, see Presotto, 'Genova', pp. 399, 400, 417; Bertrand, *Historical Relation*, pp. 164–6, 171–9.

[57] Lombardi, '1629–1631', p. 39; Defoe, *Journal*, pp. 95–6, 211–12.

hats.'[58] Sometimes there was a grudging admiration for the courage of these graveyard workers; surprisingly, a contingent sent from Venice was praised for its skill and care by the chronicler of Cividale, and Dr Bertrand expressed a touching gratitude to the galley convicts who had served Marseilles.[59] Equally often, however, the criminal strain in their natures seemed to predominate, emerging in foul conspiracies and plots to prolong the epidemics which brought them unlooked-for gains. Hence they assumed, in a different form, the role of bearers of the sickness. In Savoy–Piedmont and the Milanese province especially it was they, rather than Jews or alleged witches, who offered the most conspicuous targets for accusations of plague-spreading. They had ready access, not to unguents endowed by the Devil with supernatural powers of destruction, but rather to toxic matter extracted from corpses, to the foam from dead men's mouths, and to infected materials that could be tossed out of carts or dropped from windows at strategic points.[60]

Mild forms of social revolution seemed to have occurred at the close of plague epidemics, both through a redistribution of wealth and through the emergence of those who had survived an attack of plague as a privileged body insolently sure of their own invulnerability.

> Priests and friars who have survived the plague, and persons of low condition who have recovered from it, are both grown very rich, the first by burying, administering the sacraments, and helping the sick, and the second by physicking and serving infected persons – for people in these extreme needs were forced to spend lavishly and without restraint ... The fumigators, bearers of the dead, police constables, quacks, thieves and other such people did very well for themselves.'

So testified Dr Benaglio of Bergamo.[61] Like usurers, these persons of low condition had allegedly grown fat on the misfortunes of others, and their being public employees exposed to high risk was no excuse for their offences. A carnival poem of Florence in 1631 celebrated the 'cunning man of the people (*furbo plebo*)', an uppity character sporting gloves and silk stockings and bedecked with

[58] Presotto, 'Genova', p. 385.
[59] Brozzi, 'Peste', p. 34; Bertrand, *Historical Relation*, pp. 236–7.
[60] For this theme see Paolo Preto, *Epidemia, paura e politica nell' Italia moderna* (Bari, 1988), pp. 25, 28–9, 31, 46–7; Calvi, *Histories of a Plague Year*, pp. 151–2.
[61] Benaglio, 'Relazione', pp. 469–70.

flowers: one fit for carnival satire, but more lasting than carnival itself.[62] Reports of the aftermath of plague were punctuated by complaints of insolent domestic servants, artisans and country labourers fully aware of their own scarcity value and demanding exorbitant wages.[63] This was the price of disproportionately high losses among the labouring poor; the contraction of demand through the fall of population was offset by the high spending power of those who had become unexpectedly rich by inheritance.

Did recognition of these links between poverty and plague result in changes of strategy on the part of rich people and public authorities towards the poor? They undoubtedly established the principle that defence of subjects from disease, as from human enemies, was a fundamental duty of government. A large population was the richest treasure of a state: 'the greatness of princes lies in having populous cities and a populous dominion, and they may be called poor who rule over untilled and unpeopled lands', as the governor of Bergamo spelled it out in 1542.[64] A reduced population meant a reduced yield from taxes and excise duties; the labour force, compelled to be idle during an epidemic, must be protected from starvation against the day of economic recovery, by public action as well as by voluntary charity. The importance of such charity could never be denied; it was far too important as a tactic for placating heavenly wrath. But the restriction of personal contacts demanded by the plague regulations, the termination of personal almsgiving by the removal of beggars from churches and public squares, the terror of infection which inhibited neighbours, friends and relatives from performing the personal services inspired by ordinary human sentiments: all these things contributed to the establishment of more impersonal and bureaucratic schemes for poor relief, financed at least in part by taxation, rather than by voluntary donations.[65] Large sums of money were sometimes borrowed from the municipal pawnshops or Monti di Pietà, which now functioned as disaster banks, and plans were laid to repay them over the years by increasing the interest on the small loans they made on pledge. In Padua in the early 1630s

[62] See Marisa Brogi Ciofi, 'La peste del 1630 a Firenze con particolare riferimento ai provvedimenti igienico-sanitari e sociali', *Archivio Storico Italiano*, 142 (1984), pp. 60–1.

[63] E.g. Presotto, 'Genova', pp. 422, 427; *RRVT*, XI, pp. 358–9.

[64] *RRVT*, XII, p. 13.

[65] See, for example, Pullan, *Rich and Poor*, pp. 320–1.

public funding devoted 57,000 ducats to maintaining the pesthouses and 'meeting many other essential needs', 12,000 ducats to assisting the poor.[66] Should general quarantines be introduced to check the infection, confining a large proportion of the remaining population to their houses, something like 44 per cent of the Florentine people in 1630–1 would require relief from public funds.[67]

It is probably true, however, that the contributions of plague were very largely in the field of crisis management and emergency planning; epidemics seldom if ever gave rise to long-term or radical solutions to the problems of the ordinary poor, although they did provide added incentives to the control of begging, vagrancy and prostitution. Even here they generally resulted in temporary enclosures of some or all of the beggars, rather than in the permanent segregation of the whole mendicant body.[68] In this, however, they rather resembled the 'great internment' itself, which in reality probably consisted of a series of temporary measures designed to enclose beggars as comprehensively as possible in years of acute distress, after which most of them, in the absence of sufficient resources for their support, were allowed to go free.[69] Like famine, plague made its contribution to these spasmodic actions, but it did not create a new generation of lepers, permanently and shamefully withdrawn from society.

There is always a temptation to portray the campaigns against plague as a futile struggle against a disease whose real causes, in vermin and fleas rather than contagion and miasma, were to remain unknown until the late nineteenth century. In fact Italian cities, however unaware of rats and however much inclined to kill off their dogs and cats instead, came close to diagnosing plague in general terms as a 'disease of the dwelling-house'. Some of them endeavoured to control it by evacuating plague contacts from their houses and installing them in hutted or tented encampments far removed from the foci of infection. In one week, between July and August 1576, the Venetian government veered between two drastic solutions: a mass confinement of the people in their own houses, in an endeavour to stop contagion by virtually suspending all human interaction; and a mass evacuation of those most at risk from their

---

[66] *RRVT*, IV, p. 255.   [67] Lombardi, '1629–1631', pp. 43–5, 48–9.
[68] E.g. *RRVT*, III, pp. 191–2 (relating to Treviso).
[69] See especially Lombardi, *Povertà maschile*; cf. Pullan, 'Support and Redeem', pp. 198–9.

own homes, in an attempt to find more salubrious quarters in huts on the lagoon island of Sant' Erasmo. About 1,200 huts were used for this purpose on the island, although a more ambitious evacuation proposal, to settle up to 10,000 people on a site on the river Brenta, probably came to nothing.[70] Canon Strazzolini of Cividale was sure of the efficacy of the method of removing potential victims to a 'clean house' when he saw this employed in his town at the turn of the sixteenth century, and claimed that it had saved more than 500 persons, including a number mortally imperilled by eating, sleeping and having close contact with those who had caught the plague.[71] A Milanese chronicler recorded large sums spent on maintaining the poor in cabins of straw or wood during the great plague of the mid-1570s, and John Howard observed the use of hutted camps in the Venetian possession of Spalato, on the Dalmatian coastline, towards the close of the eighteenth century.[72]

It is unlikely, though, that plague ever inspired systematic assaults on the problem of squalid housing, out of a wish to forestall the next disaster. Swings of mood, from depression to elation, from fear and penitence to a kind of antinomianism, sometimes characterised plague epidemics and their aftermath.[73] These may well have contributed to the failure of plague to make a more lasting impact on social policies, together with the belief that as well as creating unparalleled distress it also controlled the dimensions of poverty. There were, as Carlo Cipolla has argued, Malthusians before Malthus.[74]

Not all the institutional creations of plague, however, were ephemeral, or mere pieces of machinery stored away for occasional use in emergencies. Founded in the fifteenth century, the Venetian board of health functioned continuously between epidemics and acquired broad and lasting responsibilities. By 1540 its competence had extended to the general supervision of a system of parochial poor relief, to the suppression of begging and to the control of prostitution.[75] Pesthouses, too, had their uses in the intervals

---

[70] Pullan, *Rich and Poor*, p. 322; Preto, *Peste e società*, pp. 128, 158–9.
[71] Brozzi, *Peste*, p. 46.
[72] Paolo Morigia, *Historia dell' antichità di Milano* (Venice, 1592), p. 127; Howard, *An Account*, pp. 45–7.
[73] E.g. *RRVT*, XII, p. 480 (Bergamo); Bertrand, *Historical Relation*, pp. 242–3.
[74] See n. 30 above.
[75] Pullan, *Rich and Poor*, pp. 252–4, 380.

between epidemics; not all of them became unused plant, or mere quarantine centres for ships' crews. They were convenient places of seclusion that could be used to accommodate the very poor in times of distress; they were substitutes for, or even precursors of, the hospices for beggars. After 1580 the pesthouse of Genoa was used for many years as a refuge for the homeless poor, and sustained this role until it was superseded by the vast and ambitious Albergo dei Poveri in the third quarter of the seventeenth century.[76] While the authorities in Bergamo were chary of sending their starving peasants to the pesthouse, for fear of starting rumours that the plague was at large in the city, those of Udine in Friuli had fewer misgivings. Indeed, the lieutenant of Friuli, Giovanni Mocenigo, claimed in 1629 to have sheltered and fed 2,000 poor creatures in the Lazaretto di San Gottardo.[77] Isolation of the sick and suspect in time of plague provided a framework for concentration of the very poor in the intervals between epidemics, lest they contaminate the health of society in general by their presence in normal surroundings.

Witnesses, chroniclers and physicians were well accustomed to explaining outbreaks of disease in terms of a variety of causes, material and metaphysical, natural and supernatural, mundane and astrological. Plague, to them, was not merely an impersonal natural force. Its incidence was not determined solely by the prudence, administrative competence and medical skill prevailing within a community, but also by its moral qualities. Was it devout, upright, orderly, merciful and compassionate towards the poor? Dr Benaglio of Bergamo and his contemporary, Giovanni Giovenale Gerbaldo, a priest of Fossano near Turin, found plenty of explanations between them. They attributed the plague, not only to the wrath of God and the influence of the heavens, but also to deficiencies in diet caused by shortages of salt and by corn of poor quality; to the movements of troops; to the poisonous miasma which hung visibly over Bergamo in the two fatal months of June and July 1630; to the greed of dyers and traders doing illicit deals in infected clothing and bedding; and to the spread of manufactured strains of lethal disease by anointers,

---

[76] See Edoardo Grendi, 'Pauperismo e Albergo dei Poveri nella Genova del Seicento', *Rivista Storica Italiana*, 87 (1975), pp. 630–40; Rodolfo Savelli, 'Dalle confraternite allo stato: il sistema assistenziale genovese nel Cinquecento', *Atti della Società Ligure di Storia Patria*, n.s., 24 (1984), pp. 196–9.

[77] Benaglio, 'Relazione', pp. 421–2; *RRVT*, I, p. 191; Gottardi, 'La situazione', p. 167.

poisoners or witches in league with the Devil.[78] As incubators, disseminators and victims of the plague, and yet in some sense its ghoulish and insolent beneficiaries, the poor had a role to play in most of these causes. Was it their sins that offended God, or was it the neglect of the poor that helped to bring his wrath on the community? Plague seemed bred in the stench of starvation, in the foetor of airless, humid lodgings and contaminated water supplies. It appeared to travel with the vagrant on the road to the town, with the refugee in retreat from oppression and foreign conquest. Fear, disgust and contempt often threatened to drown compassion. But it was partly through pity for the poor, and through the generosity of the city towards them, as well as through acts of devotion and the invocation of saints old and new, that the anger of God might be appeased.

[78] Benaglio, 'Relazione', especially pp. 463 4, 470–1; Gerbaldo, 'Memorie', *passim*.

6. *Dearth, dirt and fever epidemics: rewriting the history of British 'public health', 1780–1850*

JOHN V. PICKSTONE

TWO VIEWS OF PUBLIC HEALTH

What you see depends on where you look and on what you are looking for. So historians maintain when analysing the beliefs and actions of previous generations, whether in matters of health and disease or in other aspects of social life. But, of course, the same point can be made about historians themselves. Their conclusions also depend heavily on the sites they have chosen for study, on the time-frames used and on the ways in which the range of subject matter has been limited. There can be no general remedy, for no one can write about everything. We can only try new ways of cutting across our material, so producing new perspectives which may serve new purposes.

In this chapter I want to suggest a range of new perspectives, not just by drawing attention to some little-studied areas, but by drawing together a series of historical discourses which are usually conducted separately. The results can only be suggestive and tentative, but they may be helpful for readers who wish to take a broad view of medicine in Britain in the decades of the industrial revolution, and who may be wondering how certain kinds of historiography

I am grateful to Christopher Hamlin and to my colleagues Mary Fissell, Roger Cooter, Bill Luckin and Steven Sturdy for comments on the pre-conference draft.

Since I wrote the present version Chris Hamlin has completed a very useful, complementary paper, 'Predisposing Causes and Public Health in Early Nineteenth Century Medical Thought' (*Social History of Medicine,* forthcoming). He elaborates the theory of causation behind what I have called the broad or eclectic view of fever, and he discusses the Chadwickian 'reduction' – the concentration on filth as the exciting cause, the neglect of more 'social' dimensions. The two papers seem to me mutually reinforcing. In extending the seminal work of Pelling they argue for a major reorientation of the historiography of 'public health' in Britain.

are supposed to hang together. We can begin with two views of 'public health'.

I shall discuss first the model which was used by Edwin Chadwick and other 'ultra-sanitarians' in the 1840s, and which is familiar from popular histories. Epidemic disease was primarily the product of dirt and decomposing matter; it was concentrated in towns and especially in their least sanitary districts; it could be remedied primarily by public health engineering. Note the elements of such descriptions: physical causes are distributed across environments; where they are concentrated, human bodies will be poisoned more commonly and more intensively. The discourse is spatial and physical; it is political inasmuch as these inequalities are projected as undesirable and preventable. High death rates should alert local authorities to the need for action, or central government should compel such public health schemes as would remove the concentrations of disease causes. The model is familiar and powerful; we cling to it for its social justice, and in the knowledge that public health measures did indeed help reduce the rate of death of the Victorian poor.[1]

But there is another model, rehearsed by 'sociologists' from the later nineteenth century. It is familiar to historians of pre-industrial societies, often because it was indeed used by doctors and concerned laymen in such societies. This model was temporal rather than spatial, economic rather than 'physical' (in that sense 'moral' rather than physical). It was, of course, the model of dearth – of agricultural failures and high corn prices, of food shortages and consequent *fever*.[2]

---

[1] The best general survey of nineteenth-century public health is now Anthony S. Wohl, *Endangered Lives. Public Health in Victorian Britain* (London, 1983). See also the ever-useful biographies: S. E. Finer, *The Life and Times of Sir Edwin Chadwick* (London, 1952); R. A. Lewis, *Edwin Chadwick and the Public Health Movement 1832–1854* (London, 1952); and the comprehensive and penetrating Introduction by Michael Flinn to the Edinburgh University reprint (1965) of Edwin Chadwick's *Sanitary Conditions* ... (1842). In the mid-1950s E. P. Hennock stressed the Chadwickian initiatives of the 1840s by contrasting the failure of earlier sanitary programmes, especially the Manchester Board of Health, as described by B. Keith Lucas. Here I stress the *different intentions* between the fever campaigns of the 1790s and Chadwickian sanitation. B. Keith Lucas, 'Some Influences Affecting the Development of Sanitary Legislation in England', *Economic History Review*, 2nd ser., 6 (1953–4), pp. 290–6, and E. P. Hennock, 'Urban Sanitary Reform a Generation before Chadwick', *Economic History Review*, 2nd ser., 10 (1957–8), pp. 113–20.

[2] The indispensable recent work on the understanding of fever in nineteenth-century Britain is Margaret Pelling, *Cholera, Fever and English Medicine, 1825–1865*

As is usually the case in the history of ideas, there are no intrinsic reasons why these two models cannot be combined. We often tell ourselves that diseases are multicausal, but historians, at least, seem to have operated with one model or the other, to an extent which can surprise. Consider, for example, the historical demographer, D. V. Glass, commenting on a dispute in 1839 between Edwin Chadwick and William Farr, a doctor newly appointed to the office of the Registrar General. In 1839 Farr had recorded that sixty-three deaths in six months were due to starvation. Chadwick objected, claiming that no one starved in England and Wales except as a result of specific pathologies, such as gastro-intestinal obstructions. Chadwick, Glass tells us, was correct on the detail, but Farr was right, indeed he was ahead of his time, in recognising the connection between deprivation and disease which would only be clarified and quantified in later decades. Though Glass had written on eighteenth-century demography and especially on Malthus, he here seems to forget all that the eighteenth century knew of the connection of dearth and disease. Because he is discussing Victorian urban England, his own perspective is Chadwickian and old commonplaces become precocious elaborations of the Chadwickian model.[3]

The problem is not peculiar to Glass, but it is often hidden. Most relevant histories are of 'pre-industrial' *or* 'industrial' England, so the mismatch goes unnoticed. Where historians have studied both

(Oxford, 1978). The classic older accounts of the fever epidemics are: C. Murchison, *A Treatise on the Continued Fevers of Great Britain* (London, 1862); C. Creighton, *A History of Epidemics in Great Britain* (London, 1894). For a very useful review of 'famine' in Georgian England, and for data on prices and mortality rates in the fever years of 1794–6 and 1800–1, see Roger Wells, *Wretched Faces. Famine in Wartime England, 1793–1801* (Gloucester, 1988), esp. ch. 4. Ann Hardy uses the London outbreak in 1860s to argue that typhus was a disease of social disruption and thereby often consequent on dearth. Her account of its real causes, emphasising economic depression and *local* crises, is profoundly non-Chadwickian. So social history (now) stands with 'social medicine' (then) in opposition to polemical reductions: 'Urban Famine or Urban Crises? Typhus in the Victorian City', *Medical History*, 32 (1988), pp. 401–25. Luckin, in an earlier paper, is also sceptical of Chadwickian explanations, stressing the importance of Irish immigration: 'Typhus and Typhoid in London', in R. Wood and J. Woodward (eds.), *Urban Disease and Mortality in Nineteenth-Century England* (London, 1984).

[3] D. V. Glass, *Numbering the People* (Farnborough, 1973), p. 146. See also John M. Eyler, *Victorian Social Medicine. The Ideas and Methods of William Farr* (Baltimore, 1979).

periods, they have shifted gear, from temporal dearth to spatial dirt, usually without analysis. This is true even where there was no such discontinuity in the chief primary sources. In Scotland, as we shall discuss, the major Edinburgh authority on epidemic disease maintained in the 1840s a position which was not so different from that of his late eighteenth-century forbears. Even so, historians of early industrial Scotland have generally failed to take this perspective seriously, even as an actor's view. They have silently shifted into the Chadwickian mode, even for discussion of the 1847 fever epidemic in Glasgow, which, one imagines, could plausibly be seen as the knock-on effect of modern Britain's greatest subsistence crisis – the Irish famine.[4]

So one purpose of this chapter is to bring together these two perspectives to gain a deeper, more stereoscopic view of 'public health' in Britain in the decades of the industrial revolution. And this conjunction will involve others, at various levels. As I have already hinted, the 'public health' histories of Scotland and of Ireland need to be included with the English (and Welsh) histories – not just for comparison and rectification, but because the three were interlinked in all manner of ways. So too across this broader canvas, we need to link ideas to institutions, so that we can see the connected ways in which both changed. Specifically, by discussing 'fever' I want to connect ideas about epidemics with the forms of response to epidemics, and with changes in medical men's understanding of disease in general; to argue that the changes in ideas about epidemics need to be understood in terms of political theory and medical theory, and that these can only be fully understood via an historical sociology of knowledge which roots ideas in changing social structures.

FEVER IN LATE EIGHTEENTH-CENTURY ENGLAND

As Riley has recently reminded us, 'public health' was an invention of the Enlightenment inasmuch as medical writers then set out to

---

[4]   See M. W. Flinn (ed.), *Scottish Population History from the Seventeenth Century to 1930s* (Cambridge, 1977); p. 371 stresses the 'public health' failures in Chadwickian terms; the more detailed account of the 1840s (p. 375) acknowledges the role of the trade cycles and unemployment. But note the comments in T. C. Smout, 'Famine and Famine-Relief in Scotland', in L. M. Cullen and T. C. Smout (eds.), *Comparative Aspects of Scottish and Irish Economic and Social History* (Edinburgh, 1977), esp. p. 28.

show how the old canons of hygiene and health maintenance could be applied and adapted to populations rather than individuals.[5] The movement was European (and colonial), often mercantilist in inspiration, varying with forms of government. Health policy or 'medical police' was most formal and detailed in continental despotisms and bureaucracies. In Britain, medical police was initially and primarily a matter for the governance of military and criminal populations. But the problems extended to civilians, sometimes because disease spread from prisons to the surrounding populations; sometimes because the civilian poor, at work or at home, were perceived as crowded, dirty, underventilated, underfed and depressed – all factors which seemed to encourage fevers in ships, camps or jails. Civilian physicians could then advise cleanliness, whitewashing, ventilation and the boiling of clothes. They might even help provide food, at least in the 1790s when soup kitchens had been invented as a way of feeding the poor without interfering in the grain economy. But to understand the civilian responses and the medical theory we need briefly to characterise eighteenth-century medicine and the society in which the relevant medical practitioners moved. The theory one might describe as neo-classical; the society as urban, face-to-face, and 'polite'.

To describe eighteenth-century medicine as neo-classical is to underline its continuities with that of ancient Greece and Rome – the continued importance of the great tradition of western medicine which medical men shared with their educated clientele. The body was a system in balance and in balance with its surroundings. The 'constitutions' of individuals and of places could be characterised in terms of the opposition of primary qualities (hot/cold; wet/dry). Illness was constitutional disturbance, to be rectified by changes of regimen or of place, by medicines to raise or depress, by bleeding, by warmth or cold, feeding or starving, vomiting or purging, etc., etc. The common 'generic' disturbances had names, based on symptoms, and a crude correspondence of disturbance and remedy could be utilised in medicine for the poor. But proper doctoring required a discrimination which depended on knowing individual biographies, constitutions and circumstances. As Jewson has emphasised, the

[5] James C. Riley, *The Eighteenth-Century Campaign to Avoid Disease* (London, 1987); George Rosen, *A History of Public Health* (New York, 1958).

patron who paid for such medicine expected a doctor to meet his particular wishes and inclinations.[6]

Epidemic diseases were understood in much the same way as all others. Some, for example smallpox, were rather specific and appeared to result from a material contagion, passed from person to person. Most, including continuous fevers, varied much more between places and people. But where the poor were underfed, underworked, crowded and underventilated, there they would become feverish, with 'nervous' symptoms such as headaches or delirium, and with small red spots like flea-bites. This low, nervous or typhus fever seemed a peculiarly British problem, one on which British doctors wrote an increasing number of pamphlets and books from the 1720s onwards, and especially in the 1780s and 1790s.[7]

For the leading British authorities – teachers or products of the Edinburgh medical school – such fevers were primarily due to debility and depression of the nervous system. By the 1780s, the disciples of William Cullen were generally agreed that *typhus* fever was a general, constitutional disease for which undernutrition and anxiety were predisposing causes. Rebreathing expired air seemed to be the major exciting cause, especially if the air was expired by a patient already fevered. But close confinement, even of a single non-fevered individual, could cause fever to be generated. The model explained why such fevers were characteristic of ships and jails and why the new cotton spinning factories might also produce fever. It explained why the rich rarely suffered and why fever could spread from a single victim to a whole dwelling-place. There was no mystery as to why years of high corn prices were usually years of fever.[8]

The remedies, individual and social, seemed equally obvious.

---

[6] For a model of eighteenth-century medicine see N. Jewson, 'Medical Knowledge and the Patronage System in Eighteenth Century England', *Sociology*, 8 (1974), pp. 369–85. For an alternative account of ordinary doctors see I. S. L. Loudon, *Medical Care and the General Practitioner 1750–1850* (Oxford, 1986). For a rich depiction of healers and patients alike see the volumes of Roy Porter, most recently: Roy Porter and Dorothy Porter, *In Sickness and in Health. The British Experience 1650–1850* (London 1988).

[7] W. F. Bynum and V. Nutton (eds.), *Theories of Fever from Antiquity to the Enlightenment*, *Medical History*, Supplement No. 1 (London, 1981), esp. the articles by Dale Smith and W. F. Bynum; Margaret De Lacy, 'Social Medicine and Social Institutions in Eighteenth Century Lancashire' (unpublished) and 'Puerperal Fever in Eighteenth Century Britain', *Bulletin of the History of Medicine*, 13 (1989), pp. 521–56.

[8] J. V. Pickstone, 'Ferriar's Fever to Kay's Cholera; Disease and Social Structure in Cottonopolis', *History of Science*, 22 (1984), pp. 401–19.

Since typhus was a condition of debility one did *not* bleed; bleeding was for general or local inflammations. If you wanted to reduce the risk of others becoming fevered, you *ventilated* the space in which the fevered patients breathed, and you kept clean the neighbours, their houses and their clothes. Such cleansing might be advised and encouraged by magistrates, especially in smaller towns. In larger communities, the magistrate and doctors often worked through that characteristic agency of eighteenth-century Britain – the voluntary, subscription society. Thus the concerned middle classes could subscribe to Dispensaries, from which doctors would visit the fevered in their homes; or to relief programmes to aid the destitute, including, perhaps especially, the fevered poor. The fever hospitals, in a sense, grew from such agencies.

Fever patients were not taken into the main body of general hospitals; indeed they often needed to be removed from them, so separate fever wards were one possible solution, pioneered by Haygarth at Chester Infirmary. Better still was a separate fever hospital where victims could be cleansed and ventilated so that fever was dispersed. The Manchester 'House of Recovery', founded in 1796, served as a model for many more. To such fever hospitals one could bring those of the fevered poor whose conditions were so dire that they could not be cleansed or ventilated at home. Thus one could reduce the generative power of 'fever nests', without creating new centres for the propagation of the infection.[9]

THE CONTINUED CENTRALITY OF 'FEVER'

This early history of fever hospitals in Britain is well known. M. C. Buer's still useful volume shows how the Manchester example was taken up in Liverpool, in London and elsewhere.[10] But historians have failed to recognise the continued significance of the 'fever

[9] See M. C. Buer, *Health, Wealth and Population in the Early Days of the Industrial Revolution* (London, 1926), esp. ch. 15. For the Manchester Fever Hospital see J. V. Pickstone, *Medicine and Industrial Society. A History of Hospital Development in Manchester and its Region, 1752–1946* (Manchester, 1985), and Peter Povey, 'Aspects of Public Health in Manchester and District in the Late Eighteenth and Early Nineteenth Centuries' (Department of Community Medicine, Manchester University, MSc thesis, 1982).

[10] Buer, *Health, Wealth and Population.* The Liverpool Fever Hospital was supported out of the poor rates. On London, see W. F. Bynum, 'Hospital, Disease and the Community: The London Fever Hospital, 1801–1850', in C. Rosenberg (ed.), *Healing and History Essays for George Rosen* (Folkestone, 1978).

hospital movement'. One key purpose of this chapter is to show the institutional and ideological continuities which linked fever hospitals and fever theories from the 1790s to about the middle of the nineteenth century, and to show how widespread was their influence. Though historians seem scarcely to have noticed, it was essentially the English fever-charity model which was taken up in Glasgow and Edinburgh in the typhus epidemics which followed the Napoleonic wars. Before these wars, fever patients in Scottish cities had been taken into the general infirmaries: hence, one might argue, there seemed less need of new, specific, provision. But as the cities grew, more facilities seemed necessary and additional premises were taken over on an emergency basis (e.g. the Queensberry House barracks in Edinburgh). More interestingly, voluntary societies began to help find fever cases, and to help support the families of fever victims (so encouraging their hospitalisation), in ways pioneered in England.[11]

As mentioned above, the Irish experience also needs to be integrated, not just because Ireland was part of the British Isles and an important laboratory or model for mainland doctors and political economists, but because Irish epidemics had major consequences for mainland Britain, especially the large west-coast ports. In the most obvious sense, fever hospitals in Ireland were part of the British story; the initial impetus came from the evangelical lobby behind the London Fever Hospital – the Society for Bettering the Conditions of the Poor. In Ireland as in mainland Britain, the majority of the reports of fever came from doctors attached to fever hospitals.[12]

These institutional continuities also point to continuities in medical theory and practice through to mid-century, and because I shall go on to emphasise and try to explain some major *dis*continuities, it is important here to emphasise the extent to which the eighteenth-

---

[11] J. H. F. Brotherston, *Observations on the Early Public Health Movement in Edinburgh* (London, 1952), esp. pp. 59–67. See also Thomas Ferguson, *The Dawn of Scottish Welfare* (London, 1948), pp. 116–23. For medical police and Scottish voluntarism, see Brenda M. White, 'Medical Police. Politics and Police: The Fate of John Roberton', *Medical History*, 27 (1983), pp. 407–22.

[12] For example, J. M. Barry, *Report of the State of Fever and other Infectious Diseases in the City of Cork, Drawn up and Published at the Request of the Society for Bettering the Conditions of the Poor, Introduction to the Establishment of a House of Recovery* (Cork, 1801). See also the reports of the Cork Fever Hospital (consulted at the Wellcome Institute for the History of Medicine, London); E. M. Crawford (ed.), *Famine: The Irish Experience 900–1900* (Edinburgh, 1989), esp. ch. 6: Peter Froggatt, 'The Response of the Medical Profession to the Great Famine'.

century tradition of 'fever' did in fact persist (or was redeveloped) through the 1830s and 40s. The key authority was W. P. Alison, who, from about 1820 to mid-century, instructed generations of Edinburgh medical students.

Significantly, Alison was closely associated with the foundation of Edinburgh New Town Dispensary in 1815, a contentious addition to the range of eighteenth-century services in that it was independent of the Royal Infirmary. Like the Dispensaries in England, on which it was modelled, it provided a 'home-patient' service for fever victims. Inasmuch as medical students attended this service, they gained important insights into the home-conditions of the sick poor. From 1822, Alison was a physician at the Infirmary and was thus closely associated with the emergency fever hospitals already discussed.

In politics and religion, Alison was a conservative, a Tory member of the Episcopalian church, when Edinburgh politics were dominated by Whigs schooled in the new political economy. Against them, Alison campaigned for *statutory* poor relief. Fever, he maintained, was associated primarily with destitution – the poor suffered in times of shortage. His view of fever was not greatly different from that of Cullen, though the political and medical contexts had changed greatly meanwhile, and hence the political import of a then-old disease theory.[13]

That Alison was suspicious of Chadwickian sanitation and maintained a very different model of fever and its causation has been noted in three excellent studies.[14] But here I would emphasise diachronic patterns – the extent to which Alison and the fever institutions through which he worked may be seen as part of a tradition rooted in the 1790s, or earlier. As to the extent of this tradition, much more historical exploration is required, but we have enough examples to make a case even for England, even from among associates of Chadwick.

[13] 'The Late Dr Alison', *Edinburgh Medical Journal*, 4 (Nov. 1859), pp. 469–86; W. P. Alison, *Observations on the Management of the Poor* (Edinburgh, 1840). Alison's archive at the Royal College of Physicians, Edinburgh, has recently been listed by Ms Joy Pitman, to whom I am indebted, as I am to Dr Michael Barfoot of Edinburgh University Medical Archive Centre.

[14] Pelling, *Cholera, Fever and English Medicine*, pp. 41–6; Graeme Davison, 'The City as a Natural System', in D. Fraser and A. Sutcliffe (eds.), *The Pursuit of Urban History* (London, 1983), pp. 349–70; Chadwick, *Sanitary Conditions*, ed. Flinn, pp. 63–5. On Alison and Chalmers see Boyd Hilton, *The Age of Atonement. The Influence of Evangelicalism on Social and Economic Thought* (Oxford, 1988), esp. pp. 55–63.

Our key secondary source is Margaret Pelling's immaculate *Cholera, Fever and English Medicine*, which shows quite decisively how 'fever' dominated discussions of epidemic disease in early Victorian England, and how eclectic (compared to Chadwick) were the majority of doctors who ventured explanations of fever. The reductive, physicalist, Chadwickian account of fever was never accepted beyond a small, but influential, grouping of 'ultra-sanitarians'. From Pelling we may at least conclude that most doctors *could* have maintained the elements of late eighteenth-century theory. And from my own research on Manchester it is clear that major medical figures did indeed do so. Two key figures, at least, seem to show major continuities with the 'broad' tradition. R. B. Howard wrote a report on Manchester for Chadwick's 1842 survey, but he was not Chadwickian in the specific sense here used. He referred fever not to animal or vegetable matter but to 'human miasma', by which he meant body effluvia which infected when breathed in. He was particularly concerned with the effects of underfeeding among the Manchester poor. The physician Daniel Noble offers supporting evidence from about 1850. In discussing the reasons for high mortality among the poor, he ran through a long and traditional list including food, fresh air and recreation. Dirt and decomposing matter was indeed one cause of disease, but too much was expected by the 'ultra-sanitarians' who concentrated exclusively thereon.[15]

Much more investigation is needed, but heuristically at least, we can now advance a model to counter the excessively 'Chadwickian' emphasis of most historical writing on 'public health'. We should not see late eighteenth-century 'fever' measures as (just) an ineffective, voluntary precursor of (statutory) Chadwickian programmes. Rather we should recognise the continuities between later eighteenth-century 'public health' and the fever measures which continued to 1850 or so, in England, Scotland and Ireland. We should be alert to the continued importance, and perceived importance, of poverty, dearth and economic cycles as determinants of fever, and to the broad, complex view of fever causation then maintained by most doctors. We may even see this breadth and these measures as

[15] Pelling, *Cholera, Fever and English Medicine*; R. B. Howard, 'Report on the Prevalence of Diseases Arising from Contagion and Certain Other Physical Causes among the Labouring Classes in Manchester', *Local Reports, England and Wales* (1842), pp. 294–326, and published separately; D. Noble, 'On Some of the Vices of the Poor Law Medical Relief System', *Transactions of the Manchester Statistical Society* (1855–6).

extending chronologically into the 'diversified' public health programmes which were pursued by central government under John
Simon, Medical Officer to the Privy Council after about 1850.[16]
Against this background, one can then see the Chadwickian programme as a reductionist alternative, popular and prominent in the
1840s, but never dominant, though it too had consequences for
'fever hospitals'.

The isolation hospitals which became common in Britain from
about 1870, are usually depicted as an extension of 'environmental'
public health schemes, but we might also see them as replacing
older-style 'fever hospitals', after a generation or so in which fever
hospitals had been undermined by the attempt to make 'pauper
medicine' subsidiary to the Poor Law, rather than voluntary or
quasi-civic. In most British towns in the 1840s, it was indeed the
workhouse fever wards which were customarily used for desperate
fever cases. That such facilities were seen as emergency care rather
than measures to aid public health may perhaps be explained in part
by the prominence then of the Chadwickian view, in which fever
patients were not themselves a direct threat to others. It is to the
construction of that view that we now turn.[17]

RADICAL RECONSTRUCTIONS

For many historians and most commentators, the construction of
the Chadwickian creed has scarcely seemed a problem. The industrial revolution and rapid urbanisation produced vast insanitary
areas in new towns and cities. The consequent epidemic diseases
were investigated and described by reformers, led by Chadwick, who
prescribed environmental remedies, drew up legislation and pushed
for its implementation. For more sophisticated historians, discussion has centred on the construction of a public issue, for no
situation is inherently problematic; problems have to be defined in
terms of interests and expectations. In such perspectives, excess
mortality rates in poor districts may have been an affront to notions
of justice derived from some religious or secular philosophical

[16] Royston Lambert, *Sir John Simon 1816–1904 and English Social Administration*
(London, 1963).
[17] The role of workhouses in fever epidemics is still largely unexplored, but see my
*Medicine and Industrial Society. A History of Hospital Development in Manchester
and its Region, 1752–1946* (Manchester, 1985), pp. 160–1.

position; more commonly and plausibly, the pressure felt or used by reformers seems to have derived from the threats of public unrest or disorder.[18]

Discussion of the medical aspects of the Chadwickian programme has focussed on anti-contagionism – the doctrine that epidemic diseases were, in general, not transmitted from person to person but derived from local conditions. The classic paper by Ackerknecht argued that anti-contagionism became common because of its consonance with 'advanced', physiological, accounts of disease process, and especially because it provided a means by which liberals could undermine quarantine measures and other military or quasi-military intervention by traditional states. Cooter improved on this argument by showing that anti-contagionism in Britain had characteristics of a social movement, a campaign instigated by Charles Maclean, a virulent critic of British policy over plague, etc.[19] Here I want to concentrate on the relationships between the Chadwickian position and the broad view of fever which I outlined in the first half of this chapter. More especially, I want to relate the revisionist account of fever to much more general shifts in English politics and English medicine at the opening of the nineteenth century.

To do so in brief compass we can concentrate on two documents by 'Chadwickians': the medical text on fever produced by Thomas Southwood Smith in 1830 and the report on fever in the metropolis (1837) which Chadwick sponsored and which was written by Southwood Smith in association with two other doctors, James Phillips Kay and Neil Arnott. All three authors were Edinburgh educated. Southwood Smith was Chadwick's chief medical ally. Kay had become known for 'public health' writings while a dispensary physician in Manchester; from 1834 he had been employed as an Assistant Poor Law Commissioner. Arnott was an expert on

---

[18] See n. 1. For an introduction to the historiographical debates, see Valerie Cromwell, *Revolution or Evolution. British Goverment in the Nineteenth Century* (London, 1977).

[19] E. Ackerknecht, 'Anticontagionism between 1821 and 1867', *Bulletin of the History of Medicine*, 22 (1948), pp. 562–93; Roger Cooter, 'Anticontagionism and History's Medical Record', in P. Wright and A. Treacher (eds.), *The Problem of Medical Knowledge. Examining the Social Construction of Medicine* (Edinburgh, 1982), pp. 87–108. For a discussion of French medicine and epidemics see François Delaporte, *Disease and Civilization. The Cholera in Paris, 1832* (Cambridge, Mass., 1986), esp. ch. 7.

ventilation. It is useful to take the 1837 report first, before going on to consider its relation to the 1830 text.[20]

In the report on fever in London we find a long series of responses from relieving officers and Poor Law guardians about fever and its causes. These were then selected and focussed in a way which was surely characteristic of the Chadwickian programme. Many of the reported causes were seen as aspects of 'private' behaviour, and thus inappropriate objects for political action. For example, the over-crowding and intemperance of the poor were seen as 'originating to a considerable extent in their habits'. But drains, cess pools, refuse, burial grounds and slaughter houses arose independently of these habits; these were public matters, hence they could be targeted for political action.[21]

Here, it would seem, we are dealing with a document which was not meant to be inclusive. Individual observers, medical or lay, might wish to include all the plausible causes of fever they could think of, all the causes to which particular observations seemed to correspond; but our Poor Law doctors were focussing in order to produce political action through central government. In this respect, the bureaucratic context of this report is absolutely central. It was produced within the Poor Law machinery and by protagonists of the 1834 Poor Law reform. For them, poverty was no longer an official problem, for it had been officially solved by the New Poor Law. There was no point in discussing poverty as a possible cause of fever – the really destitute would go to institutions, the rest would take care of themselves. The next problem on the agenda was the causes of poverty and among these fever might plausibly be numbered. Typhus killed adults and left dependent families; what then were the independent causes of typhus which were open to political action?[22] The economical and the moral causes were deliberately excluded to allow a concentration on the physical – on the public dirt and decomposition which infected the poor. But, as I hope to show, the

---

[20] Thomas Southwood Smith, *A Treatise on Fever* (London, 1830); *Report on Fever in the Metropolis (1837), Appendix A to the Fourth Report of the Poor Law Commission 1838*; F. N. L. Poynter, 'Southwood Smith – the Man (1788–1861)', *Proceedings of the Royal Society of Medicine*, 55 (1962), pp. 381–92. On Kay, see Frank Smith, *The Life and Work of Sir James Kay-Shuttleworth* (London, 1923). On Arnott, see *DNB*.

[21] 1837 report, esp. pp. 70–1 and 83.

[22] See Flinn's 'Introduction', to Chadwick, *Sanitary Conditions*.

adoption here of physicalist causes needs to be seen not just as politics but as developing a revisionist account of fever which had been under discussion since the opening of the new century and to which Southwood Smith had already contributed very significantly in his book of 1830.

The new view is easily summarised in its full form, not all of which was accepted by all adherents. Fever was primarily a local disturbance, not a general disease of the whole constitution; it was inflammatory, not a matter of debility; it was caused by gaseous products, decomposing matter which infected the patient (other fever patients could here count as a special case of decomposing matter); because fever was a matter of inflammation, bleeding was the appropriate response. For doctors to espouse part or all of this new account was usually to reject the Cullenian account of fever, and to reverse the treatment preferred in the late eighteenth century. The new view of fever *could* also involve a concentration on environmental sanitation and a rejection of fever hospitals as preventive agencies. But the place of typhus fever in debates over contagion was often unclear: no one claimed that typhus was contagious in the strict sense which applied to smallpox (highly specific disease, material contact, no second attack); almost everyone agreed that fever patients were a major cause of other people taking the disease; opinions differed as to whether rebreathing and/or decomposing matter were alone sufficient causes of infection. As far as typhus was concerned, the most obvious novel feature of the revisionist account was therapeutic rather than aetiological. Bleeding was emblematic. But from where then had this new view appeared, and how shall we explain the rejection (by some) of the Cullenian position which had been institutionalised in fever hospitals?[23]

We here approach a general question of central importance for the development of modern medicine – the move from eighteenth-century neo-classical medicine, which Jewson labelled bedside medicine, *towards* what he labelled hospital medicine – a concentration on disease as localised, anatomical changes, detected by physical examinations, illuminated by post-mortem examination. In its full-

---

[23] The best secondary source is P. Niebyl, 'The English Blood Letting Revolution, or Modern Medicine before 1850', *Bulletin of the History of Medicine*, 51 (1977), pp. 464–83.

blown French form from *c.* 1825, this was a medicine practised on paupers in hospitals; patients here had no power of patronage, even their testimony was unimportant; they were objects, carrying local lesions which were to be understood by the procedures of newly professional doctors, who themselves gained status and perhaps patronage by reporting and teaching about lesions rather than patients. Though historians continue to question the degree to which this model is applicable, even to France, two results are clear. Rather than seeing hospital medicine following bedside medicine as one period follows another, we might better see them as corresponding to different power relations and thus as likely to occur (and maybe co-exist) wherever, after *c.* 1820, such power relations were found. (Thus, elements of 'bedside' medicine would continue to be found in private practice, though doctors in such practice would draw on the experience of hospital medicine.) Secondly, one can find in Britain between 1800 and 1830 an interest in anatomical lesions (and a degree of medical specialisation), which in some ways corresponds to French developments, though it would appear to be often independent of French examples. It is not clear to what extent such practice is to be regarded as 'hospital medicine', rather than, say, 'the medicine of anatomy schools'. It is clear, however, that such medicine often involved a rejection of Cullen and neo-classical medicine.[24]

Before we can fully understand these shifts we shall need much more detailed studies of several key medical milieux. Edinburgh is one such site, and there is evidence to suggest that Bristol and Bath would repay careful study (old Whigs like Haygarth retired there; radical Beddoes bled patients there and so did Prichard; old battles from colonial and military medics continued to be fought out there). It is not clear how the northern English provinces were involved, except that while some doctors continued the older tradition, some less known medical men seem to have espoused revisionist accounts. But the key British locale is London, especially the new anatomy

---

[24] The basic texts are E. Ackerknecht, *Medicine at the Paris Hospital, 1794–1948* (Baltimore, 1967), and M. Foucault, *The Birth of the Clinic* (London, 1973). See also T. Gelfand, *Professionalising Modern Medicine: Paris Surgeons and Medical Science and Institutions in the Eighteenth Century* (Westport, Conn., 1980); O. Keel, *La Généalogie de l'histopathologie* (Paris, 1979), and the essays by Keel and others in W. F. Bynum and R. Porter (eds.), *William Hunter and the Eighteenth-Century Medical World* (Cambridge, 1985).

schools and the new 'hospital schools'. For fever in particular, the London Fever Hospital was crucial.[25]

London advocates of the 'fever is local' view included Henry Clutterbuck and John Armstrong, both significant and representative figures for much that was novel in London medicine between 1800 and 1820. Both were from fairly poor non-medical backgrounds, both had been apprenticed before gaining medical degrees (in Glasgow and Edinburgh respectively). Both became known as lecturers and medical writers; indeed, Clutterbuck was enormously prolific in the rapidly expanding world of medical journalism. In a book of 1807 Clutterbuck argued that typhus was indeed a 'nervous' disease, but not a 'general' one; it resulted from a local inflammation of the brain. Other revisionists would disagree about the site of local lesion – for Beddoes it was intestinal – but usually the remedy was clear: inflammation indicated bleeding. Such was the view of John Armstrong, a north-eastern physician who had published on puerperal fever and the uses of bleeding. On the strength of this work he had gone to London, where in 1816 he published his *Practical Illustrations of Typhus and Other Febrile Diseases*. The book became well known and helped to popularise bleeding for typhus.[26]

It seems fairly clear that Clutterbuck and Armstrong represented a deliberate rejection of older forms of medical authority – both of Cullen and of London's 'aristocratic' practice. They moved among medical reformers who were coming to recognise 'general practitioners' as the main body of medical men. One is dealing, it would seem, with a shifting and fragmentation of medical authority. Aristocratic patronage was becoming less important; the values of

[25] On Edinburgh: C. J. Lawrence, 'The Edinburgh Medical School and the End of the "Old Thing", 1790–1830', *History of Universities*, 7 (1988), pp. 259–86. On Bristol, see the various articles on fever, etc., published in the *Edinburgh Medical and Surgical Journal*, e.g. Prichard, 1814, 1817; and review in 1820 volume; Chisholm, 1805, 1810, 1812, 1825; Dickson, 1819. Beddoes, review in 1808 volume. On Haygarth see *DNB* and 'Dr Haygarth on infectious fevers', *Edinburgh Review*, 1 (1802), pp. 245–52. In Manchester, Henry Gaulter represented the radical anti-contagionist position: see his *The Origins and Progress of the Malignant Cholera in Manchester* (London, 1833).

[26] On Clutterbuck: *DNB*; *An Enquiry into the Seat and Nature of Fever* (London, 1807); and *Observations on the Prevention and Treatment of Epidemic Fever . . .* (London, 1819); Francis Boott, *Memoirs of the Life and Opinions of John Armstrong* (London, 1833); J. Armstrong, *Practical Illustrations of Typhus and Other Febrile Diseases* (London, 1816 and successive editions). These authors were championed by Irish as well as English 'bleeders': see *Edinburgh Medical and Surgical Journal*, 9 (1813), pp. 451–62.

the old schools were in question; dissenting groups could have their own values and own systems of patronage; medical schools, societies, journals, special hospitals and dispensaries proliferated (and died off) outside the older hierarchies; through these new institutions medical men would attract support (and patients).[27] And when we examine these changes we must be aware that, for a generation, Britain was at war. We have hardly begun to work out the consequences for British medicine.

The war was certainly good for the teaching business, not least for London medical schools. Young practitioners, trained in the anatomy schools and the hospitals, then went on to army or navy service in Europe, the Mediterranean or the West Indies, and this experience was strongly reflected in the medical periodical literature. Alongside case reports and tables from civilian dispensaries and infirmaries, we now find reports on fever outbreaks in ships, camps or exotic sites, with notes on how they were handled. Dissection of the dead, it would appear, was not a problem; many of these reports carried anatomical detail. Surgeons were keen to dissect; in the services, as in civilian medical schools, mastery of the corpse was becoming a hallmark of the investigative doctor; the geography of the corpse was coming to rival the taxonomic spaces of nosologies, as the major means of 'placing' a disease.[28]

For the fever debates, the war-time reports had an additional, peculiar significance. Between 1802 and 1816 there was, by common observation, very little typhus fever in mainland Britain. The reasons are obscure, but the fact that the journal articles on fever were chiefly about exotic and military experience may go some way to explain the acceptability of 'the revised view'. Military and colonial doctors were dealing chiefly with populations of young men, typically envisaged as physically strong. Fever might still be

---

[27] For clues about London medicine in the early nineteenth century see Adrian Desmond, *The Politics of Evolution. Morphology, Medicine and Reform in Radical London* (Chicago, 1989); R. Maulitz, *Morbid Appearances. The Anatomy of Pathology in the Early Nineteenth Century* (Cambridge, 1987); and see the forthcoming paper of my colleague L. S. Jacyna, 'Mr Scott's Case: A Patient's View of London Medicine in 1825' (to appear in Roy Porter, ed. *The Popularization of Medicine*). British medicine in the French wars would repay research by historians well-read in the literature on later wars and the studies of French military medicine. One way into 'fever and the military' would be via the careers of James McGrigor (see *DNB*) and Robert Jackson: *DNB* and *Edinburgh Medical and Surgical Journal*, 1809, 1810, 1820 and 1823.

[28] See *Edinburgh Medical and Surgical Journal*; and n. 25 above.

generated by overcrowding, but when you were dealing with strong constitutions, bleeding was a more plausible remedy. And if the deceased soldier-patients were dissected, inflammation was more easily found than was debility; or so we may guess.

Further, the contact with new environments and less-analysed forms of fever may have tended to extend the discussion beyond the familiar categories used for urban Britain. Was continued fever more or less the same as yellow fever; was yellow fever confined to marshy areas in much the same way as malarial fever? In such ways, the fever debate in Britain came to draw on and reflect the American and French experience and contentions. Colin Chisholm, for example, a Bristol physician who wrote repeatedly to the *Edinburgh Medical and Surgical Journal*, kept reflecting on his experience in 1790 as an army surgeon in Grenada. He maintained that the fever there had been contagious, at least in the sense that typhus was contagious. He maintained a more or less Cullenian account, and he claimed as an ally Dr Husack of Boston, a 'federalist' who in 1793 had opposed Benjamin Rush and the republicans when they maintained that the epidemic fever in Philadelphia was not contagious and was to be dealt with by sanitary improvement.[29]

During the war, then, debate was renewed about the epidemiology and aetiology of typhus fever; in terms of pathology and treatment, local inflammation and bleeding became increasingly popular. The post-war typhus epidemics of 1816–17 confirmed the vogue for bleeding; even Alison was persuaded to try bleeding, though he soon reverted to more Cullenian remedies.[30] Armstrong was the authority of the day, and in 1819 he succeeded Thomas Bateman as physician to the London Fever Hospital. It is to that institution that we now turn for a final perspective on the constructions of the Chadwickian fever.

Bateman had been physician since the hospital was opened in 1802; he had remained respectful towards the Cullenian position, though increasingly convinced of the uses of purgatives, emetics and

---

[29] On Rush, see Martin Pernick, 'Politics, Parties and Pestilence: Epidemic Yellow Fever in Philadelphia and the Rise of the First Party System', in J. Leavitt and R. Numbers (eds.), *Sickness and Health in America* (Madison, Wisconsin, 1985). On another radical ex-student of Cullen, see W. F. Bynum and R. Porter (eds.), *Brunonianism in Britain and Europe, Medical History*, Supplement 8, 1988.

[30] W. P. Alison, 'Observations of the Epidemic Fever now Prevailing among the Lower Orders in Edinburgh', *Edinburgh Medical and Surgical Journal*, 28 (1827), pp. 233–63.

bleeding and cold water. Armstrong's tune was more radical. He came to reject Cullen's authority and the late eighteenth-century classification of disease (nosologies). He advocated bleeding; he drew on anatomical findings of inflammation; eventually, in 1824, he came to argue that continued fevers were caused by local miasmatic poisons – not by rebreathing or overcrowding; he was now far from convinced that fever could 'spread'. By 1824 he had resigned from the fever hospital which, he felt, was useless in preventing fever. But it is with Armstrong's successor there that we see the full extent of the shift from Bateman's position. With Thomas Southwood Smith we reach the acme of the radical alternative.[31]

Like his predecessors, Southwood Smith was a dissenter, a Calvinist who had early converted to an optimistic, meliorist brand of Unitarianism. When most divines preached judgement Southwood Smith maintained that the task of God's servants was to improve the world. He was active as a Unitarian minister, as a doctor and as a social reformer. And though these modes overlapped, each was organised in a systematic, disciplined manner. Smith moved in professional and 'devotee' associations which were serious about doctrine. The utilitarian circles around Bentham were devoted to legal reform and moral philosophy; on theology, Southwood Smith was a recognised authority; in medicine, he was a radical proponent of a programme which, in its appreciation of experimental physiology, microscopy, clinical examinations and post-mortem dissections, can surely be called 'French medicine'.

To an extent which was then remarkable, Southwood Smith's text on fever separated two levels of description: the symptomatic and the morbid-anatomical. His accounts of symptoms were fuller, more detailed, and included much more of the patients' feelings than was common. His account of dissection findings was presented as exploratory and preliminary, as bound to no hypothesis; he claimed to be systematically searching all the body systems to see how they might be affected in fever. It was presumed that if 'fevers' could be separated and characterised, it would be primarily at the level of morbid anatomy. The London Fever Hospital seems to have been

---

[31] For Armstrong's repudiation of the London Fever Hospital's preventive role see his *Lectures on the Morbid Anatomy, Nature and Treatment of Acute and Chronic Diseases*, ed. Joseph Rix (London, 1834). One notices with interest that Alison now stressed the preventive role of fever hospitals, while doubting the therapeutic effects of ventilation: 'Observations' pp. 250–1.

crucial for this 'research'. It is certainly significant that Southwood Smith's appointment there was rapidly followed by the appointment of his friend R. O. Granger as surgeon to the hospital, so as to carry out dissections. When one recalls the public outcry and high profile of dissection as a political issue around 1830, and when one reflects on the prominence of the fever hospital as a medical agency in the East End, then the institution's involvement with a systematic programme of post-mortem investigations is indeed revealing.[32]

How then, for Southwood Smith, did the London poor come to be affected with the fever for which they were brought to the fever hospital, and perhaps to the dissection table? Smith discussed and dismissed Cullen and the debility theory, he identified himself with Clutterbuck and the French radical Broussais, the new champion of inflammation.[33] But he still agreed (in 1830) with the common old argument that the exhalations of fevered bodies were the major means of propagation. This claim had been standard among proponents of fever hospitals from the 1790s onwards, but Smith wore this view with a difference. He saw these exhalations not as specific poisons (as in smallpox), or as specifically human products, but as direct analogues of marsh miasma – as poisons arising from the decomposition of animal matter.

Here, in Southwood Smith's 1830 text, we approach the heart of the Chadwickian movement with which he came to be so closely associated. He did not deny the observations from which Alison and others had argued for their broad theory of fever causation. Unlike Armstrong, he did not argue that fever districts produced more fever cases simply because they were more afflicted with vegetable poisons or animal waste. Rather, he ignored the difference, for this purpose, between the humans and their surroundings. A fevered patient in a closed heated room was the same as a pool of dead locusts under the tropical sun. 'The room of a fever patient in a small and heated apartment in London, with no perflation of fresh air, is perfectly analogous to a stagnant pool in Ethiopia, full of the bodies of dead locusts'.[34] The sun was of 'nature'; the rags, and filth and the

[32] On Granger's appointment, see MS minutes of London Fever Hospital, 29 July 1825. The minutes are in the care of Dr Edith Gilchrist in the Archive of the Royal Free Hospital, Hampstead, London. Ruth Richardson, *Death, Dissection and the Destitute* (London, 1987), gives an excellent analysis of the contemporary politics of dissection but does not mention the Fever Hospital.

[33] Southwood Smith, *Treatise on Fever*.   [34] *Ibid.*, p. 364.

attempts to keep warm were of poverty. The passage seems to me of crucial importance. Poverty (about which Alison would argue so extensively) was here literally 'naturalised', made a context for a physical process which imitated malign aspects of non-human nature.[35]

That Southwood Smith could make this move can be explained, I would argue, by three features of his background and beliefs. First, his immersion in what we have called the revisionist accounts of fever. His examples of animal or vegetable poisons causing fever were drawn largely from writers on military and warm-climate fever, including yellow fever. Here was a model he could develop, especially by concentrating on animal poisons which, he claimed, Cullen had neglected, so misleading his followers. Secondly, and on this point his concentration on *animal* poisons is suggestive, Southwood Smith may have been influenced by Charles Maclean's strenuous assertion of the anti-contagionist position for *plague*. Maclean, a political radical and ferocious critic of military medical organisations, was then lecturing in London; for most doctors, it would seem, Maclean had gone overboard in his critique of 'contagionism', but Southwood Smith may have been sympathetic.[36] Thirdly, and here again we note Southwood Smith's break with previous authors on fever, he adopted an explicitly materialist physiology, which was meant to underpin the felicific principles of utilitarianism.

The point here is that Southwood Smith relied, in principle, on physical and chemical processes to explain the transformation of material in a human body, including the interactions of body constituents with external agents such as air. But if both the process productive of that poison and the process by which it may affect

---

[35] Anna F. La Berge has shown that much of Chadwick's evidence was taken from French authorities, whose data on disease and poverty was neglected in favour of correlations of disease and dirt: 'Edwin Chadwick and the French Connection', *Bulletin of the History of Medicine*, 62 (1988), pp. 23–41. German reformers *c.* 1848 took a broad, economic view; see E. Ackerknecht, *Rudolph Virchow, Doctor, Statesman, Anthropologist* (Madison, 1953). George Rosen has discussed this tradition of 'social medicine' in his *From Medical Police to Social Medicine. Essays on the History of Health Care* (New York, 1974). In a recent conference paper, my colleagues Michael Worboys and Michael Sigsworth have suggested that 'economic' perceptions dominated the view of health taken by the British working classes: 'Relaundering the "Great Unwashed": Public Health and the Working Class in Victorian Britain'. Historians who want to explore working-class attitudes to 'public health' should not be too Chadwickian in drafting their questions.

[36] Pelling, *Cholera, Fever and English Medicine*, p. 28.

another body were envisaged as physico-chemical, then it was not surprising that Smith was able to abolish the distinction between the human body and external agents, and so present a fevered patient as merely a form of decomposition. Here, in a radical and peculiar sense, we do indeed see the 'disappearance of the patient' in nineteenth-century medicine.

And if we now reconsider the 1837 report, we again see the removal of the active subject, here the exclusion of the socio-economic dimension of fever so that attention could be focussed on political action. Paradoxically perhaps, the entry of the New Poor Law machinery meant that socio-economic aspects were now excluded, and the physicalist, medical account of fever was brought to the fore. We can here see how Southwood Smith represented the convergence of three 'sectarian' positions: the revisionist, anti-contagionist medicine, the Benthamite confidence that one could move on from 'poverty', the Unitarian and materialist de-emphasis on individual moral culpability and the corresponding stress on the need for public action in accord with nature's laws.[37]

CONCLUSION

In the perspective I have tried to develop here, the connections between ultra-sanitary doctrines and the industrial revolution would lie as much in the structures of knowledge as in the structures of cities. Fevers might have continued to be treated and theorised on the basis of Whig medicine and civic (often voluntary) action, as Scotland would seem to show. In the Scottish debates reductive ultra-sanitarianism would seem to have been a rather alien presence, at least when continued fever was under discussion.

The sanitary idea, *sensu stricto*, appears to be a product of London. Whiggish medical men had never been dominant in the capital, and during the war decades they were not 'reproducing themselves'. Though medical conservatives such as Bancroft continued to be a significant force, the running was made by 'new men'

---

[37] See Robert M. Young, 'Natural Theology, Victorian Periodicals and the Fragmentation of a Common Context', reprinted with other relevant and seminal essays in his *Darwin's Metaphor. Nature's Place in Victorian Culture* (Cambridge, 1985). Ruth Hodgkinson edited a collection of extracts: *Victorian Social Conscience. Public Health in the Victorian Age*, 2 vols. (Farnborough, Hants., 1973). R. J. Morris, *Cholera 1832. The Social Response to an Epidemic* (London, 1976), contains a stimulating discussion of disease theory and religious denominations.

who conducted empiricist, often specialist, critiques of enlighten-ment medicine, perhaps using Brown's simplistic alternatives, or his American and continental equivalents: Rush and Broussais.[38] Sur-geons and general practitioners, then, sought to ground a new medicine in dissection, so effecting the kind of shift we can see also in the associated field of political economy – a move to technical discipline and laws. Poor, dissectible patients became the key to medical knowledge. One might have sympathy with the patients' predicaments, but their fates were determined by organic changes to which doctors had privileged access. One might pity the poor, even when they were not sick, but the economic fate of the worker was predictable from the doctrines of political economy. To pity was indeed morally sound, but the fate of pity's object would follow from the laws of economics and/or medicine. These 'semi-disci-plines' were forming in opposition to older, less differentiated forms of knowledge, including easy providentialism; they would function as the basis of quasi-professional expertise and status. In its radical, Chadwickian form, as we have seen, the sanitary idea advanced 'lawfulness' and expertise by presenting a reductive, physicalist account of disease.

But by mid-century the political climate was changing and with it the structure of ideas. Theology (surely), medicine (probably) and economics (possibly) were becoming less sectarian, less concerned with party conflict. The readiness of churchmen to engage in common fronts on 'secular' questions (e.g. elementary education) was one such aspect. The softening of natural law theology among evangelicals, and the move of Unitarians away from Priestleyan positions may be seen as aspects of the same shift.[39] In medicine, accounts of disease causes seem to have become more generally eclectic, partly as a result of increased differentiation between epidemic species. The self-sufficiency of medicine, the determinism of its phenomena, did not need to be asserted in simple catch-all

---

[38] On Bancroft see Edward Bancroft, *An Essay on the Disease Called Yellow Fever* (London, 1811); on Rush, n. 29; on Broussais see E. H. Ackerknecht, 'Broussais or a Forgotton Medical Revolution', *Bulletin of the History of Medicine*, 27 (1953), pp. 320–43, and J. F. Braunstein, *Broussais et le matérialisme* (Paris, 1986).

[39] See the subtle and comprehensive discussion in Part 3 of Hilton, *Age of Atonement*, esp. pp. 267–70; also J. V. Pickstone, 'Establishment and Dissent in Nineteenth Century Medicine: An Exploration of Some Correspondence and Connections between Religious and Medical Belief-Systems in Early Industrial England', in W. J. Sheils (ed.), *The Church and Healing*, Studies in Church History XIX (Oxford, 1982), pp. 165–89.

doctrines that made nearly all epidemic diseases into forms of poisoning; and for the Poor Laws too, 'less-eligibility' would seem to have been weakening as a general remedy, as the paupers began to be 'classified' and treated accordingly. New voluntary groups, like the Manchester and Salford Sanitary Association, founded in the 1850s, nicely exhibited both the catholicity of personnel and the increasing range of sanitary concerns – including the need for new 'fever hospitals' (infectious disease hospitals), not least for children. So died the great simplicities, in medicine, economics and theology. So passed the peculiarities of ultra-sanitarianism, that remarkable conjunction of radical sectarian positions, which continues to attract analysts as it once attracted publicists, by its uncommon single-mindedness.

But, as I have tried to show, there is another history of 'public health' which does not centre on, nor originate from, these doctrines. It is a history of fever theories and fever hospitals which extended from the relative stability of Britain in the 1780s, across the industrial revolution, the French wars and the Chartist years, to the renewed stability of the mid-Victorian decades. These traditions need to be explored further, especially at local level, where the concerns of doctors and of philanthropists may well appear less exclusive than were those of pressure groups focussed on central government. We need to find out the importance of fever hospitals in Scotland and Ireland, as well as in England and Wales, and to see how they articulated with the Poor Law, especially after 1834; we need to see how local doctors theorised poverty as well as pathology, temporal causes as well as spatial differences. We need to include military experience, and we also need to explore lay experience and the views of patients. Who knows to what extent the view of fever which I have here described as 'broad' or Cullenian was rooted in common perceptions of the social causes of disease? Such research would surely reveal the centrality of 'fever' to medical discourse and to lay accounts of illness and epidemics in the period here covered. It would probably underline both continuity and breadth in medical and popular views of the causes of fever. It should enable us to explore the diffuse and varying linkages of disease and 'social theory' – whether formal or implicit. Only against such a background will we be able properly to assess the roots and effects of the 'reductionist' views which have so often dominated the historiography of British public health.

7. *Epidemics and revolutions: cholera in nineteenth-century Europe*

RICHARD J. EVANS

The fall of the Duvalier regime in Haiti, it has recently been claimed, is the first revolution to have been caused by AIDS. In July 1982 the *New York Times* reported that the killer disease not only affected gays but was endemic, for reasons that seemed frighteningly obscure, in Haiti as well. The publicity subsequently accorded to this revelation ensured that the number of American tourists visiting Haiti fell from 70,000 in the winter of 1981–2 to a mere 10,000 the following season, with worse to come in the subsequent three years. Tourism was the second biggest source of income for the impoverished Haitian state, and the collapse of the industry sparked off an economic crisis with mounting unrest met by growing repression, and ending with the ousting of the president-for-life, 'Baby Doc' Jean-Claude Duvalier (himself by this time rumoured to be suffering from AIDS) early in 1986.[1] AIDS is not the first epidemic disease to have been credited with overthrowing a regime. In *Plagues and Peoples*, his panoramic survey of the impact of disease on human history, William H. McNeill has put forward a whole range of examples of the ways in which micro-organisms have destroyed or transformed state structures in the past, from the Roman Empire to the pre-Columbian Incas and Aztecs, whose civilisation was destroyed not so much by the small bands of *conquistadores* under leaders such as Cortez and Pizarro as by the diseases, new to the Americas and therefore devastating in their impact, which the Spaniards brought with them.[2]

---

[1] David Black, *The Plague Years. A Chronicle of AIDS, the Epidemic of our Times* (London, 1986), pp. 41–2.

[2] William H. McNeill, *Plagues and Peoples* (Oxford, 1977). See also Alfred W. Crosby, *The Columbian Exchange. Biological and Cultural Consequences of 1492* (Westport, Conn., 1972).

As a growing number of historians have recognised, epidemics have played an important role in modern European history as well. Epidemics of plague, smallpox and similar diseases only visited their affflictions on society intermittently; but when they did, it was often with all the force of a natural disaster, killing large numbers of people in a geographically limited area or areas in a very short space of time. Because of the severity of their impact, epidemic diseases could seldom be accommodated in the emotional structures by which societies lived, in the way that was possible, for example, with the largest single source of (normal) mortality up to the beginning of the twentieth century, the deaths of infants. Society evolved ways of coping with constantly recurring aspects of death and disease, but it was far harder to come to terms with sudden and violent visitations of mass epidemics.[3] Moreover, unlike natural disasters like earthquakes or floods, epidemic diseases were often influenced in their spread and impact by social and political factors and affected different groups of people – men and women, adults and children, rich and poor, town- and country-dwellers – in different ways and to different degrees. Thus they opened up the possibility, the likelihood even, of widely varying responses by different groups in society, and of strongly diverging theories of where the blame for their arrival and spread in the community lay. This in turn meant that they were likely to bring out latent social tensions, and to lead to conflict, violence and even, ultimately, revolt and revolution.[4]

Epidemic diseases, as the example of AIDS reminds us, are no mere relic of the pre-industrial age. On the contrary, they have been a frequently repeated feature of human history up to the present day. Some indeed may be said to be creations of the industrial age itself. The classic example of such a disease, as many historians have pointed out, is cholera.[5] Unknown in Europe, this terrible affliction was spread from its home in India across to Afghanistan and Russia as trade began to increase with the combined effects of British industrialisation and the creation of the British raj. Once in

[3] Philippe Ariès, *The Hour of our Death* (Harmondsworth, 1981), pp. 409–72.
[4] Paul Slack, *The Impact of Plague in Tudor and Stuart England* (London, 1985), pp. 3–7; Roderick E. McGrew, 'The First Cholera Epidemic and Social History', *Bulletin of the History of Medicine*, 24 (1960), pp. 61–73; Charles Rosenberg, 'Cholera in Nineteenth-Century Europe: A Tool for Social and Economic Analysis', *Comparative Studies in Society and History*, 8 (1965–6), pp. 452–63.
[5] Louis Chevalier (ed.), *Le choléra: la première épidémie du XIXe siècle* (La Roche-sur-Yon, 1958).

Europe, it moved rapidly along the waterways and, later, railways, which were the main arteries of the rapidly expanding commerce of the nineteenth century. As it arrived in the mushrooming towns and cities of a society in the throes of rapid urbanisation, it took advantage of overcrowded housing conditions, poor hygiene and insanitary water supplies with a vigour that suggested that these conditions might almost have been designed for it.

The disease spread in a series of waves or pandemics. The first, beginning in India in 1817, reached China, Japan, parts of South-East Asia, Madagascar and the East African coast opposite Zanzibar, but petered out in Anatolia and the Caucasus in 1823 before it had a chance to afflict Europe. It was the second pandemic, lasting from 1826 to 1837, that saw cholera sweep across Europe and North Africa and over the Atlantic to the eastern seaboard of North America, while the third, conventionally dated 1841–59, took the same route and affected much the same areas, with the addition of parts of South and Central America. The fourth pandemic (1863–75) once more affected the whole of Europe and large parts of north-eastern, Central and South America, Africa, China, Japan and South-East Asia. In geographical terms it was probably the greatest of the cholera pandemics. The fifth wave (1881–96) had a more limited effect, but again much of continental Europe, the whole of the North African coast and a number of areas in Asia and the Americas were hit. The sixth pandemic (1899–1923), by contrast, had virtually no impact on western Europe, failed to reach the Americas and confined its really serious impact to Asia. The disease has subsequently only made isolated appearances in Europe, and although more serious outbreaks have occurred elsewhere in the world from time to time, these have mainly been caused by a milder variant of the micro-organism that causes the symptoms – the so-called El Tor vibrio, named after the Egyptian site of its first observed appearance around the turn of the century.[6]

Thus Asiatic cholera has a good claim to be regarded as the classic

---

[6] Michael Durey, *The Return of the Plague. British Society and the Cholera, 1831–32* (Dublin, 1979), pp. 7–18; R. J. Morris, *Cholera 1832. The Social Response to an Epidemic* (London, 1976), pp. 21–4. For the transmission of cholera, see P. Bourdelais and J.-Y. Raulot, 'Sur le rôle des contacts interhumains dans la transmission du choléra, épidémies de 1832 et 1854', *Bulletin de la Société de Pathologie Exotique*, 71 (1978), pp. 119–30. For an easily accessible series of maps illustrating the pandemics, see P. Bourdelais and A. Dodin, *Visages du choléra* (Paris, 1987), pp. 35–6, 40, 48, 50.

epidemic disease of the nineteenth century, above all of Europe in the age of industrialisation. Here the novelty of its first impact and the severity of its subsequent visitations stimulated governments, administrators, politicians, caricaturists, doctors, statisticians and private individuals to pour out a vast mass of writings on the subject which historians in the last two decades have not been slow to exploit. Studies of cholera in France, Spain, Russia, Britain, Germany and Sweden have appeared, and while there is a growing literature on cholera in the rest of the world, the documentation and scholarly discussion are more detailed and more advanced in Europe than for nineteenth-century Africa, Asia or America.[7] Over a quarter of a century ago Asa Briggs, in a seminal article published in this journal,[8] called for the comparative study of cholera and its impact on European society, and enough research would now seem to have been carried out to warrant a first, preliminary attempt to meet his demand.

Most historians who have dealt with cholera have been drawn to the subject because they have seen in the impact of the disease 'a test of social cohesion', as R. J. Morris has put it; 'to follow the cholera track', he claimed, 'was to watch the trust and co-operation between different parts of the society strained to the utmost'. In another recent study of cholera in Britain in 1832, Michael Durey has concurred in this view, noting that it 'unsettled the normal functioning of society, and brought to the surface latent social antagonisms'. Nor has this perception been confined to historians of the British experience. Roderick McGrew, author of a fine study of the impact

[7] Chevalier (ed.), *Choléra*; P. Bourdelais and J.-Y. Raulot, *Une peur bleue* (Paris, 1987); Esteban Rodríguez Ocaña, *El cólera de 1834 en Granada* (Granada, 1983); M. V. Ortiz, *Epidemias de cólera en Vizcaya en el siglo xix* (Bilbao, 1978); Roderick E. McGrew, *Russia and the Cholera, 1823–1832* (Madison, 1965); Morris, *Cholera 1832*; Durey, *Return of the Plague*; Richard J. Evans, *Death in Hamburg. Society and Politics in the Cholera Years, 1830–1910* (Oxford, 1987); Brita Zacke, *Koleraepidemien i Stockholm, 1834: En socialhistorisk Studie* (Stockholm, 1971) and further references below. For studies of cholera outside Europe, see Charles Rosenberg, *The Cholera Years. The United States in 1832, 1849 and 1866* (Chicago, 1962; 2nd edn, with new Afterword, 1987); Louis Dechêne and Jean-Claude Robert, 'Le Choléra de 1832 dans le Bas-Canada: mesure des inégalités devant la mort', in H. Charbonneau and A. Larose (eds.), *The Great Mortalities* (Liège, 1979), pp. 229–56; Geoffrey Bilson, *A Darkened House. Cholera in Nineteenth-Century Canada* (Toronto, 1980); Francis L. K. Hsu, *Religion, Science and Human Crises* (London, 1952); Charles M. Godfrey, *The Cholera Epidemics in Upper Canada, 1832–1866* (Toronto, 1968).

[8] Asa Briggs, 'Cholera and Society in the Nineteenth Century', *Past and Present*, no. 19 (1961), pp. 76–96.

of cholera in Russia, also noted that 'cholera scored the European social consciousness, exacerbated contemporary tensions, intensified the impact of current social problems'.[9] Yet there have been dissenting voices too. Margaret Pelling, for example, in a study of nineteenth-century theories of cholera and fever in Britain, has suggested that the impact of cholera was far less significant than that of tuberculosis or the fevers, and concluded that cholera had almost no effect on political, administrative or medical history. Similarly, Charles Rosenberg noted that cholera had no permanent effect on political and administrative structures.[10] Sufficient work has now been done in the area, however, to attempt to bring this conflict of opinion at least to a provisional resolution.

Three major questions need to be asked. First, was the psychological and social impact of cholera powerful enough to enable us to discount the fact that – as Pelling rightly points out – in terms of the absolute numbers of people affected, its impact was relatively minor compared to that of tuberculosis or the various forms of infant mortality? Secondly, did cholera epidemics play a part in the major political upheavals of the nineteenth century – for example, the revolutions of 1830 and 1848? Thirdly, did people blame the state for outbreaks of cholera, and did this lead to any changes in state policy or variations of approach from country to country? In other words, even if cholera did not cause political revolutions, did it perhaps lead to administrative or sanitary revolutions? Does the differing experience of the various European countries which it affected tell us anything about the abilities of their state structures to adapt to the challenge posed by disease and its associated discontents?

I

The cholera bacillus, which thrives in warm water, is passed on in the excreta of victims and carriers, and enters the body through the mouth and the digestive system. The nature of its symptoms – massive vomiting and diarrhoea, in which a quarter of the body's fluids along with essential body salts may be lost within a few hours, reducing the victim to a comatose, apathetic state, with sunken eyes

---

[9] Morris, *Cholera, 1832*, p. 17; Durey, *Return of the Plague*, p. 1; McGrew, *Russia and the Cholera*, p. 3.
[10] Margaret Pelling, *Cholera, Fever and English Medicine, 1825–1865* (Oxford, 1978), pp. 3–6; Rosenberg, 'Cholera in Nineteenth-Century Europe', p. 98.

and blue-grey skin – might almost have been designed to achieve the maximum shock effect on a society that, perhaps more than any other, was concerned to conceal bodily functions from public view. There could be few more violent affronts to Victorian prudery than the grossly physical symptoms of a cholera attack.[11] Cholera was shocking to the nineteenth-century sensibility – above all, to the bourgeois sensibility of the towns where it had its maximum impact – in other ways too. At the height of a self-confident era of economic growth, material progress, scientific achievement and expanding European dominion over the world, here was a disease that came from the 'uncivilised' East and challenged common assumptions of European cultural and biological superiority by demonstrating the vulnerability of even the most civilised people to a disease associated mainly with oriental backwardness.[12] At a time when European literature and culture were celebrating the 'age of the beautiful death', with diseases like typhoid or tuberculosis being accorded a transforming, almost beatifying influence on their victims, here was an affliction that killed rapidly, remorselessly and with symptoms that could not be seen as anything other than degrading.[13] Half of all victims died from the disease. A period as short as twelve hours could elapse between the onset of symptoms and death, giving the victims no chance to make preparations or reconcile themselves to their fate. And cholera seemed to affect healthy adults just as much as, or even more than, it affected the young and old, the sickly and the weak. All this made it into an object of peculiar terror and revulsion to the contemporary imagination, and further contributed to the shock effect it had on nineteenth-century society.

Cholera also undermined bourgeois optimism by revealing the existence in the great towns and cities of nineteenth-century Europe of whole areas of miserable poverty and degradation. Virtually all commentators were agreed from the start that cholera affected the poor more than the well-off or the rich, and the widespread middle-class view that the poor only had themselves to blame was hardly calculated to mollify the apprehensions of the poor. Early writers on

---

[11] Norbert Elias, *Über den Prozess der Zivilisation*, 2 vols. (Frankfurt-on-Main, 1969), for the classic analysis of the development of these attitudes.

[12] François Delaporte, *Disease and Civilization. The Cholera in Paris, 1832* (Cambridge, Mass., 1986).

[13] Susan Sontag, *Illness as Metaphor* (Harmondsworth, 1983), p. 41; Ariès, *Hour of our Death*, pp. 409–72. For a splendid compilation of graphic images inspired by cholera, see Bourdelais and Dodin, *Visages du choléra*.

the disease constantly reiterated the common bourgeois belief that drunkards, layabouts, vagabonds and the idle, 'undeserving' poor were those most affected, and echoes of this view continued to surface in the literature right up to the end of the century. In this way, confidence in bourgeois society as the epitome of progress and civilisation was precariously maintained by ascribing the ravages of the disease to the uncivilised nature of the poverty-stricken masses.[14] By contrast, the poor could easily interpret the relative immunity of the bourgeoisie as evidence of exploitation, injustice or even a positive desire on the part of the rich to reduce the burden of poverty by killing off its main victims.

Clear evidence of the social distribution of the disease is hard to come by, especially for earlier epidemics, and in an age when water supplies, one of the main vehicles of transmission for cholera, were still mainly local in character, the distribution of cholera obviously to some extent reflected whether or not a local water supply had been contaminated (as John Snow showed in his classic study of the Broad Street pump in 1854).[15] However, proximity to infected water was itself at least in part socially determined, especially in the case of manual labourers in an age when canals and waterways were still the main arteries of internal transport for industrial goods and bulk produce. Throughout the century, sailors, boatmen, fishermen and quayside workers were among the worst-affected groups. Similarly, occupations which involved dealing with water, food, toilets and other sources of infection were particularly vulnerable. Prominent among these were domestic service, washing and cleaning, and inn-keeping.[16] An occupational analysis of victims in Aix en-Provence during the epidemic of 1835 has shown that workers, day-labourers, beggars, paupers, artisans, small traders and small peasant farmers caught cholera in higher numbers than their proportion in the working population.[17] In the majority of *arrondissements* in the department of Seine-et-Oise during the epidemic of 1832, artisans and workers accounted for about 70 per cent of cholera

[14] Delaporte, *Disease and Civilization*; Evans, *Death in Hamburg*, pp. 234–6.

[15] Briggs, 'Cholera and Society', p. 78; Durey, *Return of the Plague*, pp. 47–9. For a general survey of the secondary literature, see Hartmut Kaelble, *Industrialisation and Social Inequality in 19th-Century Europe* (Leamington Spa, 1986), pp. 135–42.

[16] Evans, *Death in Hamburg*, pp. 433–45. Hamburg in 1892 drew its water from a single, central supply system.

[17] Daniel Panzac, 'Aix-en-Provence et le choléra en 1835', *Annales du Midi*, 86 (1974), pp. 419–44.

deaths, but only for just over 30 per cent of occupied persons in the first available census, from 1851.[18] In Hamburg in 1892 there was a positive correlation between the proportion of wage-earning manual labourers in 1895 and the cholera morbidity (0.62) and mortality (0.70) rates across the twenty residential urban districts north of the Elbe, and weaker but still suggestive negative correlations between cholera rates and white-collar workers (-0.56 morbidity, -0.56 mortality) and economically independent persons (-0.53 morbidity, -0.66 mortality) in the occupied population of each district.[19] In the same epidemic the occupations most seriously affected were domestic service (23.6 per thousand mortality, compared with an average of 14.8 per thousand for all occupations) and transport workers (mainly longshoremen, stevedores, boatmen and the like), whose mortality rate worked out at 22.5 per thousand.[20]

Poverty in a general sense also heightened the risk of infection. In the North German town of Brunswick in 1850, the cholera death rate in streets with an average per capita income of under 75 marks was 5.3 per thousand, while the corresponding rate for the higher income group of 75–100 marks was 3.0 per thousand, for 100–200 marks 1.4 per thousand, and over 200 marks 0.3 per thousand.[21] In London in 1849 and 1853–4, cholera mortality rates in the poor districts of Bermondsey or Rotherhithe were between six and twelve times as high as they were in better-off areas such as Kensington or St James and Westminster.[22] The poor suffered because of over-crowding and poor sanitation, and because they could not employ servants to take the necessary hygienic precautions (and cleanliness was advised by many commentators even before the bacillus and its

[18] C. Rollet and A. Souriac, 'Le Choléra de 1832 en Seine-et-Oise', *Annales: Economies, Sociétés, Civilisations*, 29 (1974), pp. 935–65.

[19] Evans, *Death in Hamburg*, Table 15 (p. 593).

[20] *Ibid.*, Fig. 19 (p. 435). The figures in Zacke, *Koleraepidemien i Stockholm*, p. 165, though not conclusive, suggest that nurses, cleaning-women, sailors, soldiers and artisans were particularly badly affected. Most studies, however, only manage an occupational breakdown of victims without being able to link it to the occupational structure of the population as a whole: for example, M. Dineur and C. Engrand, 'Epidémie et pauperisme: le choléra à Lille en 1832', in M. Gillet (ed.), *L'Homme, la vie et la mort dans le Nord au xixe siècle* (Lille, 1972), pp. 41–78; or Morris, *Cholera, 1832*, pp. 72–92.

[21] [Dr Reck], *Die Gesundheitsverhältnisse der Stadt Braunschweig in den Jahren 1864–1873 und die Verbreitung der Cholera daselbst in den Jahren 1850 und 1855* (Brunswick, 1874).

[22] F. B. Smith, *The People's Health, 1830–1910* (London, 1979), pp. 230–4 (though uncontrolled for factors such as the localisation of water supplies).

mode of operation were discovered in 1884). Across the twenty residential districts of Hamburg in 1892, the correlations between cholera mortality and key social indicators were as follows: average per capita income −0.60, proportion of households with living-in servants −0.72, and proportion of households with own bathrooms −0.69.[23] Among those in accommodation with an average living-space of less than 10 square metres per person, the cholera mortality rate in Hamburg in 1892 was 17.2 per thousand; among those with over 50 square metres per person it was below 10.2 per thousand.[24] These are only the most persuasive of a mass of statistics on the social and occupational distribution of cholera which suggests that while it could and did affect the well-off and the rich, its impact on the poor was disproportionately high in most epidemics. The rich could flee from outbreaks with relative ease, their occupations did not usually bring them into contact with contaminated water, and their employment of servants and ownership of spacious accommodation with separate bathroom and toilet facilities made it easier for them to maintain strict standards of hygiene and cleanliness. The differential impact of cholera on rich and poor was plain for all to see, and would lead us to expect that its power to exacerbate existing social tensions would be very considerable.

II

There can be little doubt that cholera epidemics tended to occur at moments of crisis in European history. The first great epidemic came as the reverberations of the revolutions of 1830 were still echoing across the continent, reaching Britain during the profound political crisis over the Great Reform Bill of 1832, a year which, some historians have argued, saw the only real possibility of a political revolution in modern British history. Cholera next swept across Europe in the revolutionary year of 1848 – probably the greatest and most devastating of all the epidemic years, at least in terms of the sheer number of people affected. After a series of epidemics in the 1850s, including a major one during the Crimean conflict in 1854–5, there was another mass outbreak in 1866, the year when the German Confederation was overthrown and the independence of a number

---

[23] Evans, *Death in Hamburg*, Table 15 (p. 593).
[24] [Georg Gaffky], *Amtliche Denkschrift über die Choleraepidemie, 1892* (Kaiserliches Gesundheitsamt, Berlin, 1895), Appendix, p. 32.

of North German states brought to an end by Bismarck's war with Austria. Further cholera epidemics coincided with the overthrow of the Second Empire in France in 1871 and with disturbances in Russian Poland in 1892. Of all these conjunctures of epidemic and revolution, that of 1848 has perhaps attracted the most attention among historians of the European continent; one of the earliest modern studies, edited by Louis Chevalier in 1958, was published as part of a series of books on the 1848 revolution.[25] But the British case in 1832 has also been intensively studied, and indeed the general coincidence of cholera epidemics with years of upheaval and revolution has proved too obvious to ignore.

The link appears stronger still when we turn to the popular unrest to which cholera almost everywhere gave rise. The progress of the disease across Europe in the early 1830s was marked by a string of riots and disturbances in almost every country it affected. Popular opinion did not accept that cholera was a hitherto unknown disease, but considered instead that an attempt was being made to reduce the numbers of the poor by poisoning them. Riots, massacres and the destruction of property took place across Russia, swept through the Habsburg empire, broke out in Königsberg, Stettin and Memel in 1831 and spread to Britain the next year, affecting cities as far apart as Exeter and Glasgow, London, Manchester and Liverpool.[26] The power of epidemics to stir up popular passions had been known as far back as the Middle Ages, when the Black Death led to a similar wave of unrest in 1348–9; Jean Delumeau, indeed, considers the longevity of this pattern as evidence of the deep-seated nature of such reactions to epidemics in the collective mentality of European society.[27] In the context of 1830–2, 1848 or 1871, however, rioting and unrest of this kind could have a very different political connotation from that which it might have had in less crisis-ridden times.

Cholera did not ravage the European continent at times of revolution and upheaval by chance, but the reasons why it should have done so are not at first sight very obvious. The poverty and malnutrition which played such an important role in preparing the ground for the popular uprisings of the 'Hungry Forties' only had a

[25] Chevalier (ed.), Choléra.   [26] Durey, Return of the Plague, pp. 158–9.
[27] Jean Delumeau, La Peur en occident (XIVe–XVIIIe siècles). Une cité assiégée (Paris, 1978), pp. 129–42.

limited relevance to cholera. There is some evidence to suggest that malnutrition lowers the stomach acid level and therefore weakens resistance to the cholera bacillus once it enters the alimentary canal.[28] But this evidence is far from conclusive and does not seem to be universally accepted, and in any case it does nothing by itself to explain the central feature of cholera epidemics, namely their very rapid spread across the whole of Europe. Cholera epidemics did sometimes follow years of dearth such as 1830, 1847 or 1891 (in Russia) or coincide with economic crises such as the crash of 1873 in Germany or the depression of 1890–3 in Hamburg. But in such years nutritional decline was less than catastrophic at least in the prosperous West, even though cholera still occurred.

Cholera was spread in a variety of ways: by barges and ships travelling on inland waterways and across the seas and discharging the excreta of carriers into rivers, canals and harbour waters as they did so; by railways carrying victims rapidly from a place of infection and depositing them somewhere else before they even knew they had the disease; by road, as travelling salesmen, merchants and the general public went about their business. Often markets and fairs were focal points of distribution for epidemics. Once an epidemic began, it generated its own dynamic of expansion, as thousands fled on its approach to their homes or abandoned their place of domicile once it had broken out there. The mass movement of human beings formed an important means by which the disease was spread. And one of the major forms of mass migration in the nineteenth century, if we understand by this the rapid movement of many thousands of people in large consolidated groups across long distances, was the military campaign. War and combat brought huge numbers of men together in cramped and confined conditions, with makeshift and rudimentary forms of sanitation and few chances of maintaining strict standards of hygiene. In the nineteenth century, as in all previous centuries, war and pestilence went together.

Disease could be transferred from the military to the civilian population by a number of means: through the occupation of towns, through the billeting of troops, through the return of conscripts to their homes after the cessation of hostilities. The greatest smallpox epidemic in nineteenth-century Europe, for example, broke out when troops were demobilised at the end of the Franco-Prussian

---

[28] Jacques M. May, *The Ecology of Human Disease* (New York, 1958), p. 38.

War in 1871.[29] As armies marched across the countryside civilians fled before them. The hygiene and sanitation available to refugees were if possible even less satisfactory than in the army, and mass movements of homeless people in the face of war added fresh possibilities of carrying cholera and other diseases from place to place. Conditions were probably worst of all in the improvised prisoner-of-war camps that were constructed on occasions such as the war of 1870–1, and here too large masses of men were brought together in conditions that were usually dirty, insanitary and grossly overcrowded.

A second cause of mass movements of human beings was indeed famine and deprivation. In 1847–8 in particular, hunger and destitution drove vast numbers of people in central Europe to flee from the countryside to the towns, and from one town to another, in search of poor relief. Governments themselves could make things worse by taking action against unwanted groups of citizens. In 1892, for instance, cholera was spread across Russia, and eventually to Hamburg, not least by a sharp rise in the numbers of Russian Jews emigrating to the United States following the famine of 1891 and the expulsion of Jews from Moscow earlier in the year.[30] Another major cause of mass migration was probably revolution and revolt. In the first place, uprisings and armed struggles once more took thousands of people from their homes and moved them in consolidated groups across the land. Even more important, they were met by the mobilisation, usually, of vastly greater numbers of troops in defence of the status quo; and of all the connections between revolutions and epidemics, the military operations involved in the suppression of uprisings were probably the most important.

Cholera first broke out of its original home when the marquess of Hastings fought a military campaign against the Marathas in 1817, losing 3,000 out of his 10,000 troops to the disease in the process.[31] Trade patterns accounted for the march of the disease across

[29] Bundesarchiv Koblenz, R86/1097, Bd. 1, Tabellen zur Veranschaulichung der Pockensterblichkeit in Deutschland und im Ausland. Smallpox death rates in Prussia also doubled between 1863 and 1866, before being more than halved again in 1868–70. For the Crimea, see Bourdelais and Dodin, *Visages du choléra*, pp. 41–4. For Portugal and Austria, see Bourdelais and Raulot, *Peur bleue*, pp. 47–8.

[30] Richard R. Robbins, *Famine in Russia, 1891–1892* (New York, 1975); Nancy M. Frieden, 'The Russian Cholera Epidemic, 1892–93, and Medical Professionalisation', *Journal of Social History*, 10 (1977), pp. 538–59; Imre Ferenczi (ed.), *International Migrations*, 2 vols. (New York, 1929), I, p. 808.

[31] Morris, *Cholera, 1832*, p. 21.

Afghanistan and Persia to Russia at the end of the 1820s; the autumn fair in Nijhni-Novgorod played a central role in its further diffusion across Russia. In 1831, however, the Russians waged an intensive military campaign against a Polish rebellion, and it was this, together with the flight of thousands of Polish refugees, that ensured the rapid movement of cholera further west.[32] In 1832 British troops carried cholera with them when they sailed for Portugal, while in 1866 cholera was spread by armed conflict between the Austrians and the Italians. In 1854 French troops embarking for Gallipoli and Varna at Marseilles and Toulon carried cholera with them and ensured that a major outbreak occurred when they finally reached the theatre of war in the Crimea – the only known time when the disease travelled the Mediterranean from west to east. Such a combination of forces was present in many of the cholera outbreaks of the nineteenth century, although more research is needed on the neglected post-1832 epidemics in order to delineate them comprehensively. It is vital, however, not to overestimate the importance of war and revolution in the spread of disease, particularly in the nineteenth century when normal means of communication were improving so rapidly. Most cholera epidemics were spread initially and above all by trade, and political or military upheavals only provided an additional boost to their progress. Cholera epidemics were generally well under way before they felt the multiplying effects of political crisis. Cholera was already in Russia in 1829, before the outbreak of the 1830 revolutions, while the epidemic that reached its climax in 1866 had been raging in Europe since the previous year.[33] Sooner or later, the growing volume of international traffic by river, road and rail, by sailing-vessel and (increasingly) by steamship would have brought the disease with it in any case. The most one can say is that revolutions and troop movements tended to accelerate the spread of cholera or to prolong epidemics and make their impact wider and more severe.

In periods of crisis like the early 1830s or the late 1840s, cholera was only one among a number of elements in a complex of social antagonisms. In the 1830s cholera did not reach central and western Europe until the tumult of the 1830 revolution had largely died down. In Britain, as Michael Durey pointed out, 'the crisis periods of reform, October 1831 and May 1832, do not synchronise with the

---

[32] *Ibid.*, p. 23.
[33] For a brief account, see Norman Longmate, *King Cholera* (London, 1966).

crisis periods of cholera in the major towns'; cholera riots were not subsumed into the general popular movements for the extension of the suffrage.[34] In 1848 cholera hit central Europe only in the early summer and did not reach its height until the autumn, while the major revolutionary upheavals had already taken place in March and the impact of the disease was generally more severe in 1849.[35] Epidemics were less causes than consequences of revolutionary upheavals and the government reactions associated with them. Contemporaries were far from unaware of these connections. Reactionaries in France argued in 1849 that cholera was a 'revolutionary infection ... Cholera, like revolution, must be eradicated at the source.'[36] The French political scientist André Siegfried actually wrote a book to demonstrate that epidemics and ideologies spread in the same way.[37] Other, more sceptical voices could also be heard, however. French republicans asserted in 1832 that 'Everyone knows that Moscow, St Petersburg, Vienna, Berlin and London have yielded many victims to this epidemic, and yet none of these cities has toppled a tyrant from his throne.'[38]

III

Arriving as it did in times of heightened social tension, during or after revolutions and insurrections, cholera nonetheless led, as we have seen, to widespread popular unrest, above all in the early 1830s. On whom did popular opinion pin the blame? Collective aggression in the aftermath of epidemics in medieval and early modern Europe was generally directed against Jews, witches and other outcast groups. It hardly ever seems to have been turned on the authorities or even on the wealthy or aristocratic upper echelons of feudal society.[39] By the nineteenth century, however, the objects of aggression had changed. It is rare to find outcast groups being attacked during cholera riots even where a feudal system was still in

---

[34] Durey, *Return of the Plague*, pp. 185–6.
[35] Thus the cholera mortality rate in Berlin more than doubled in 1848–9: E. H. Müller, *Die Cholera-Epidemie zu Berlin im Jahre 1873: Amtlicher Bericht* (Berlin, 1874), copy in Stadtarchiv Berlin (hereafter StAB), Rep. 01 6B 220.
[36] Cited in Delaporte, *Disease and Civilization*, p. 60.
[37] André Siegfried, *Itinéraires de contagion: épidémies et idéologies* (Paris, 1960).
[38] Cited in Delaporte, *Disease and Civilization*, p. 60.
[39] Delumeau, *La Peur*, pp. 129–42.

operation, as it was in much of central Europe up to 1848. Instead popular resentment was focussed in the first place on the authorities, and in the second on the medical profession.[40]

With the growth of the state in the seventeenth and eighteenth centuries, culminating in the age of absolutism, it became possible for widespread and intrusive policing measures to be taken against epidemics. When cholera arrived on the European continent, most regimes dusted off their files on bubonic plague and put what were by now fairly traditional policing measures into operation: military *cordons sanitaires*, quarantine, fumigation, disinfection, isolation.[41] The resources at the state's disposal were far more powerful than they had been even a century before, and their impact on the population was all the greater. At the same time, decades of unrest, the slow decay of central European feudalism, the impact of the French Revolution and the rise of radical democratic political movements and ideas had all left their mark, in varying degrees, on popular consciousness. The coincidence of inexplicable outbreaks of mass mortality with the sudden appearance on the scene of government officials, troops and medical officers readily aroused popular suspicion. It was not cholera by itself so much as the actions taken by the state against it which sparked off popular unrest.

In feudal regimes like Russia and Austria-Hungary, and to some extent also parts of Prussia in the 1830s and 1840s, the nobility were still the main agents of local and regional government, so it is not surprising that they became the object of conspiracy theories among the peasantry. In Hungary, after over 1,000 cholera deaths between June and September 1831, castles were sacked and nobles massacred in an outburst of popular fury against those believed responsible for the deaths. Stockpiles of chlorate of lime were discovered in castle cellars, confirming suspicions that the nobility had been poisoning the wells.[42] Deep-seated resentments against burdensome feudal obligations, to which new rules and regulations, not sanctioned by

---

[40] For some stimulating observations on these points, see Bill Luckin, 'States and Epidemic Threats', *Bulletin of the Social History of Medicine*, 34 (June 1984), pp. 25–7. Anti-Semitic protests were reported in Congress Poland in the course of the 1831 epidemic, however.

[41] Geheimes Staatsarchiv Berlin (hereafter GStAB), Rep. 84a, 4178, for a file containing anti-plague measures at the beginning and anti-cholera measures later on. See also Esteban Rodríguez Ocaña, 'La dependencia social de un comportamiento científico: los medicos españoles y el cólera de 1833–35', *Dynamis*, 1 (1981), pp. 101–30.

[42] Durey, *Return of the Plague*, p. 19.

custom, were now being added in the name of disease control, may well have played a role in this unrest.[43] In Russia military officers – themselves usually noble – bore the brunt of a good deal of popular hostility, as peasants attacked *cordons sanitaires* and murdered those who were trying to set them up.[44] Military cordons and the restriction of movement not only prevented people from escaping the scene of the epidemic, they also interfered with their livelihood by interrupting the flow of goods and produce to and from local markets, and above all they cut off or at least drastically reduced the supply of food and essential goods to urban populations, thus reinforcing popular belief in an official conspiracy to reduce the burden of the poor on the public purse by simply killing them off. In Königsberg in East Prussia in July 1831, disturbances broke out after food prices had jumped following the imposition of quarantine measures and the sealing-off of the city by a military *cordon sanitaire*.[45] Where people's livelihood was affected similar disturbances took place, as in the riots of 4 April 1832, when rag-pickers and rag merchants led a series of popular disturbances in Paris, with barricades erected and property being burned, in reaction to official measures ordaining a centralised collection of garbage. Other, similar instances would not be hard to find.[46]

The medical profession came under attack in such countries mainly because it was medical officials who were usually in charge of the implementation of government measures such as the isolation of victims once an epidemic had actually broken out. Medical officials violated popular customs of mourning and burial when they ordered the rapid disposal of the bodies of those who had succumbed to the disease. In the Baltic port of Memel in 1831, for example, a crowd broke into the cholera hospital and took a patient back to his home, demanded that cholera corpses be buried in the churchyard and claimed 'that the butcher Schadewaldt has been boiled alive in a steam bath by the doctors and this treatment has led to his death'.[47] In Stettin crowds tried to prevent cholera victims being removed

[43] C. A. Macartney, *The Habsburg Empire* (London, 1968), pp. 255–425.
[44] McGrew, *Russia and the Cholera*, pp. 67–74, 107–22, for a detailed account.
[45] Dirk Blasius, 'Sozialprotest und Sozialkriminalität in Deutschland: Eine Problem-studie zum Vormärz', in Heinrich Volkmann and Jürgen Bergmann (eds.), *Sozialer Protest: Studien zu traditioneller Resistenz und kollektiver Gewalt in Deutschland vom Vormärz bis zur Reichsgründung* (Opladen, 1984), pp. 212–27.
[46] Delaporte, *Disease and Civilization*, p. 66.
[47] GStAB, Rep. 84a, 4178, Bl. 185–9, report of 25 July 1831.

from their homes and sacked the house of the responsible official.[48] Popular opinion in Prussia had it that the doctors were being paid up to 3 thalers for every cholera death reported to the king. As late as 1892 medical officials were massacred during a cholera epidemic in Russia.[49]

Where the medical profession had established a more independent role for itself, and where the state was less active in enforcing military cordons, quarantine and isolation, as in Britain, popular resentment was directed much more clearly against the doctors. In numerous cholera riots and disturbances in 1832, British doctors were attacked by crowds who believed they were killing off the poor not at the behest of officialdom, but for their own purposes, to obtain corpses for anatomising in the medical schools. A spate of grave-robbing cases had preceded the epidemic. The notorious case of Burke and Hare, who had actually made a living by murdering people and selling their bodies to the University of Edinburgh medical school, had rekindled long-held popular resentments against the anatomists, and the cholera epidemic was widely held to be another example of the same business. Relatively little popular resentment against the state was displayed in British cholera riots.[50] In France, where state measures were rather tougher in 1832, it was recorded that popular opinion thought the wealthy, who dominated the state under the July Monarchy, were ordering the doctors to rid them of the burden of the poor by poisoning the water supply.[51] Some considered the reactionary, legitimist resistance to the July Monarchy was to blame, but mostly it was thought that the government was responsible, in an attempt to avert an economic crisis or a famine. Here too the medical profession were seen as the primary agents, not least because of the reputation hospitals had as places of medical experimentation on the poor.[52]

Everywhere except Britain, therefore, it seems that popular opinion in 1831–2 blamed the government and its agents the doctors for

[48] GStAB, 4179, Bl. 41, report by Oberlandesgerichts-Präsidium Stettin, 3 Sept. 1831.
[49] Frieden, 'Russian Cholera Epidemic'.
[50] Durey, *Return of the Plague*, ch. 7; Peter Linebaugh, 'The Tyburn Riot against the Surgeons', in Douglas Hay *et al.* (eds.), *Albion's Fatal Tree. Crime and Society in Eighteenth-Century England* (London, 1975), pp. 65–118.
[51] René Baehrel, 'La Haine de classe en temps d'épidémie', *Annales: Economies, Sociétés, Civilisations*, 7 (1952), pp. 351–60; René Baehrel, 'Epidémie et terreur: histoire et sociologie', *Annales historiques de la Révolution Française*, 23 (1951), pp. 113–46.
[52] Delaporte, *Disease and Civilization*, pp. 51–5.

the spread of cholera. There is no doubt that the authorities found the cholera disturbances of the early 1830s alarming. True, cholera riots were generally free from any encouragement by political radicals. As the Königsberg authorities noted in their report of the cholera riot of 1831, the 'tumult originated in neither a political ideology nor widespread dissatisfaction with the government of the state'.[53] Reformers and radicals in most European countries were afraid of the passions of the mob even at this time, and were more inclined to regard fear of cholera as a government ploy to discredit their efforts.[54] Similarly, some French radicals considered that fear of cholera was being sown in an attempt to create confusion preparatory to the restoration of the legitimist monarchy.[55] Oppositional liberals in Germany and Austria shared the bourgeois view of cholera as an affliction of the 'dangerous classes', caused by drunkenness and vice. The idea that poor sanitation, overcrowded housing conditions and lack of pure water supplies were to blame was seldom expressed in the course of the earliest cholera epidemics; still less the belief that it was the responsibility of government to put these things right. Mass medicalisation, as Bill Luckin has pointed out, had not become a reality in Europe at this time, and so few liberal reformers saw any explicit connection between mass mortality and undemocratic state structures.[56]

IV

Most European governments followed the same policy, dealing with cholera in 1831–2 by traditional policing methods. Few emerged from the experience convinced that it had been worth while. The grand duchy of Baden continued to impose *cordons sanitaires* all the way up to the end of 1832 and to adopt strict controls at all its borders, but then cholera did not reach Baden either in 1831 or in 1832, and so the authorities considered the policy had been a success.[57] For most European states, however, military cordons, quarantine and other policing measures had clearly been unsuccessful, and so they were dismantled or at least relaxed. Fear of popular

---

[53] Blasius, 'Sozialprotest und Sozialkriminalität', p. 224.
[54] Durey, *Return of the Plague*, pp. 185–6.
[55] Delaporte, *Disease and Civilization*, pp. 51–5.
[56] Luckin, 'States and Epidemic Threats'.
[57] Badisches Generallandesarchiv Karlsruhe, Abt. 313, 6. 2447, 2448, 2449, *passim.*

disturbances played a major role in this change of tack. Already in 1832, as Michael Durey has noted, the British government abandoned the idea of military cordons and compulsory hospitalisation 'in consequence of the violent opposition raised in various capitals in Europe, to all attempts made to enforce more rigid regulations'.[58] Similarly, the Prussian authorities, who had begun by imposing strict controls on the movement of people and goods, even threatening death to those who violated them, conceded in September 1831 that military cordons were causing economic problems; they ordered police forces not to remove victims from their homes against the wishes of the head of the family, told them to avoid 'unusual gatherings of people' and advised burial of cholera victims only after nightfall.[59] Similarly, the Habsburg monarchy conceded that cordons and quarantine measures had led to 'consequences more mischievous than those resulting from the malady itself', while the Russians abandoned quarantine in August 1831 for similar reasons.[60]

In relaxing their measures, European authorities were to some extent giving way to pressure from merchants, traders and manufacturers. These in turn were not slow to raise the spectre of 'the labouring classes . . . deprived of a living and driven to desperation' so that 'the flames of rebellion' would be 'fanned from the east' as well as from Paris, the traditional home of European revolutions, in the west. Where mercantile interests were paramount, the state withdrew almost entirely from the fight against cholera.[61] In Hamburg, for example, no official announcements were made of cholera cases in 1832,[62] while the senate file on the 1848 epidemic in the city archives is entitled 'File Concerning the Epidemic of So-Called Asiatic Cholera which Took Place in Hamburg in 1848, against which No Quarantines, Hospitals or Otherwise Important Preventive Measures Were Taken'.[63] The city authorities were supported in this by the local medical profession, whose representatives

[58] Durey, *Return of the Plague*, p. 21.
[59] GStAB, Rep. 84a, 4178, Bl. 233; 4179, Bl. 81, 215, 229; StAB, Rep. 01 6B, 217, 218, 257, for successive instructions.
[60] Durey, *Return of the Plague*, p. 19.
[61] Anon., *Stimme aus Danzig über die Cholera: Zur Beruhigung Aller, die sie fürchten* (Danzig, 1831), pp. 5, 11.
[62] See the account in *Hamburger Fremdenblatt*, 27 Oct. 1892, copy in Staatsarchiv Hamburg, Senat, Cl. VII, Lit. Ta, Pars 2, XI, Fasc. 17, Inv. la.
[63] Staatsarchiv Hamburg, Senat, Cl. VII, Lit. Ta, Pars 2, I.

declared in July 1848 that 'the first thing we feel impelled to express, before anything else, is the wish that the public be alarmed and disturbed as little as possible', and backed this up by denouncing the release of public notices about cholera as alarmist and advising people that remaining calm was the best prophylactic against infection.[64] A similar policy of total inaction was followed by the authorities in Lübeck in 1832, 1848, 1850, 1853 and 1856–9, as in Hamburg not only because of the damage quarantine and publicity would do to trade, but also because of the threat which strong measures posed to public order.[65] In Britain, too, administrative and policy changes that had occurred since 1832 meant that, as Durey has noted, 'The General Board of Health was forced to watch cholera march unopposed through the country in 1849.'[66] The medical profession throughout Europe had spent much of the intervening period arguing about the causes of cholera, and by 1849 the weight of opinion was firmly against contagion, thus reinforcing the decision of many governments to do nothing.[67]

In states where mercantile and manufacturing interests were less influential, bureaucratic inertia ensured that policing methods continued, albeit in a milder form than in 1831. The Prussian regulations of 1835, for instance, declared firmly that cholera was contagious, and provided for isolation, quarantine, fumigation, disinfection and other measures of control. Public order was to be maintained not by silence but by propaganda. In 1866 the authorities in Berlin continued to act on the explicit assumption that the disease was contagious: only with the additional police regulations of 1867 did the emphasis placed by the most influential medical opinion of the time on the role of infected ground-water in creating deadly miasmas find its way into official policy through a number of clauses providing for gutters, cesspools and public lavatories to be cleaned up. Local officials in Prussia frequently imposed measures that went beyond those laid down in 1835. These in turn stayed in force almost until the end of the century.[68] Even though they did little to control

---

[64] Staatsarchiv Hamburg, Medizinalkollegium III A 2, Bd. 1, Bl. 3ff, report of 5 Aug. 1848.
[65] Dietrich Helm, *Die Cholera in Lübeck: Epidemieprophylaxe und -bekämpfung im 19. Jahrhundert* (Neumünster, 1979).
[66] Durey, *Return of the Plague*, p. 207.
[67] Chevalier (ed.), *Choléra*.
[68] StAB, Rep. 01 GB 257, Bl. 157–8, for the 1835 regulations; Bl. 57, for their confirmation in the 1850s; GB 219, Amtsblatt der königlichen Regierung zu

the movement of river traffic or impose quarantines in 1873, the authorities in Berlin remained convinced that the state always had to 'take certain measures and secure their implementation . . . irrespective of whether they correspond to one theory of cholera or another'.[69] Protest meetings of bourgeois citizens angry at the extent of police controls imposed in Berlin in 1871 and at other times seem to have had relatively little effect.[70] By contrast, Hamburg stuck to its now traditional policy of suppression and inaction as late as the outbreak of 1892.[71]

In contrast to 1831–2, the epidemic of 1848, despite its greater extent, aroused relatively little popular unrest. Partly this was because of the almost universal relaxation of the very strict police controls imposed in the first epidemic, even, to a degree, in states such as Prussia and Baden.[72] Partly it was because the general standing of the medical profession had improved (most notably, perhaps, in Britain, where the Burke and Hare outrages were now a distant memory). Partly it was because underlying sources of discontent, most notably feudal obligations in the central European countryside, had been or were in the course of being removed. And partly it was because discontent had been channelled into more direct political action in the course of the revolution itself, so that popular unrest had a different, more political focus than in 1831–2. Finally, the concern of the authorities to avoid inflaming popular passions may also have had an effect, however much the policies to which it gave rise may have differed from place to place.

Only where these conditions were not fulfilled, above all in Russia, did cholera disturbances continue. As late as 1892, the spread of cholera across the tsarist empire, following the previous year's famine, caused the familiar pattern of riot and murder, as crowds of angry peasants attacked government and medical officials. The occasion for the disturbances was the usual combination of strict and harshly enforced government quarantine, isolation and disinfection

Potsdam und der Stadt Berlin, 21, 26 June 1866; GB 220, E. H. Müller, 'Die Cholera-Erkrankungen zu Berlin im Jahre 1871', p. 121.

[69] *Stenographische Berichte über die Verhandlungen des Deutschen Reichstags*, col. 1954, 21 Apr. 1873 (Secretary Boetticher).

[70] GStAB, Rep. 84a, Bl. 280, *Allgemeine Zeitung*, 17 Aug. 1831; StAB, Rep. 01 GB 257, Stadtverordnetenversammlung to Magistrat, 22 Sept. 1831, and following documents.

[71] Evans, *Death in Hamburg*, pp. 285–92, 310–14.

[72] For anti-contagionist opinion in Baden in the 1840s and 1850s, see Badisches Generallandesarchiv Karlsruhe, Abt. 236 Nos. 16054, 16055, 16056, 16057.

measures, popular impoverishment and indebtedness (this time in the form of long-term arrears in payments redeeming the peasants from serfdom), official assaults on traditional burial customs, and the inability either of the medical profession or the state to persuade what was by now one of Europe's most illiterate populations of the validity of medical theories of the disease. Brutal repression quelled the disturbances; but the weakness and inefficiency of the tsarist state made it not unlikely that similar events would occur again, long after the disappearance of cholera from the rest of Europe, despite the growing effectiveness of the medical profession in educating the peasants in preventive measures after 1892.[73]

V

In the end, it is perhaps asking too much of an epidemic disease such as cholera if one expects it to lead directly to social upheaval and revolution. Morris and Durey, in their studies of the 1832 epidemic in Britain, have taken such an expectation as their starting-point, but their conclusion – that cholera proved the essential stability of British society – is foreordained by their assumption that only a revolution along the lines of 1789 in France could have demonstrated the opposite.[74] Paul Slack, in his study of the impact of plague in Tudor and Stuart England, has noted that very high mortality indeed had to occur before a breakdown of the social order became evident.[75] Such was the case, for example, in many parts of Europe with the Black Death of 1348–9, where mortality seems to have reached levels as extreme as 40 per cent or more.[76] But even in the severest known visitations of cholera, the death rate was less than half this level, and reached 15–20 per cent only on the most localised basis.[77] Cholera did not after all cause, or even

---

[73] Frieden, 'Russian Cholera Epidemic'.

[74] Morris, *Cholera, 1832*, p. 17; Durey, *Return of the Plague*, p. 215.

[75] Slack, *Impact of Plague*, pp. 5–6, 17–21.

[76] Jean-Noël Biraben, *Les Hommes et la peste en France et dans les pays européens et méditerranéens*, 2 vols. (Paris, 1975–6); E. Carpentier, *Une ville devant la peste: Orvieto et la peste noire de 1348* (Paris, 1962); P. Slack *et al.*, *The Plague Reconsidered* (Local Population Studies Supplement, Matlock, 1977); Johannes Nohl, *The Black Death. A Chronicle of the Plague* (London, 1926).

[77] In some remote mountain communities in the Ariège in 1854 cholera mortality reached levels of 19 per cent (Alsen, Miglos); but the overall cholera mortality in the department was only 4 per cent, and the absolute numbers involved in these communities were very small: A. Armengaud, *Les Populations de l'Est-Aquitain au*

precipitate, major social and political upheavals such as those which swept across Europe in the early 1830s and late 1840s.

Its effects were more limited. From the beginning, contemporaries associated cholera with dirt, and so epidemics were frequently followed by attempts at sanitary reform. But these seem to have been relatively short-lived in their effect, at least in the 1830s. The measures taken to clean up Paris in 1832, for example, seem to have made little difference to the city's sanitation in the longer term.[78] If urban authorities tried to improve the situation, their efforts were quickly outpaced by the rapid growth of the urban population. In Britain, as Morris noted in 1976, cholera seems to have had little real impact on sanitary improvement.[79] In Prussia the cholera epidemics of 1831–2 and 1848–9 did not lead to major state intervention in the health-related infrastructure; rather, as we have seen, the reverse. In Hamburg the central water supply and sewerage systems which for a time made the city into a pioneer of sanitary reform on the continent owed their existence not to the cholera epidemic of 1832 but to the devastating effects of the Great Fire of 1842. The epidemic of 1873 did lead to an attempt to filtrate the water supply and extend the sewerage system in the town, but these ran into opposition which was not overcome for another two decades. The improvements proposed after the epidemic of 1892 in Hamburg were mostly abandoned until the dock strike of 1896–7 led to their revival in modified form as instruments of social control.[80] The rise of the sanitary movement in Germany in the late 1860s and early 1870s owed more to the tendency to found nation-wide conferences and organisations during the wave of national feeling that accompanied and followed the establishment of the North German Confederation and the German empire than to any autonomous impact of the epidemics of 1866, 1871 or 1873. Similarly the great clean-up of

---

début de l'époque contemporaine (Paris, 1961), pp. 204–5. The highest-known cholera mortality rate in a large-scale epidemic seems to have been 7 per cent in Montreal in 1832: Dechêne and Robert, 'Choléra de 1832 dans le Bas-Canada'.

[78] Alain Corbin, *The Foul and the Fragrant. Odour and the French Social Imagination* (Leamington Spa, 1986), pp. 142–60.

[79] Morris, *Cholera, 1832*, p. 197.

[80] Clemens Wischermann, *Wohnen in Hamburg vor dem Ersten Weltkrieg* (Münster, 1983), pp. 333–5, points out the connection between the 1873 epidemic and the Sewage Law of 1875, but overestimates the importance of the latter. Even in 1890 some 5,000 privies in the inner city were still not connected to the sewage-disposal system: Evans, *Death in Hamburg*, pp. 139, 476.

Berlin in the 1870s has to be seen primarily as part of an attempt to establish the city as a worthy capital for the newly founded Reich.[81]

The general, if uneven, withdrawal of the state from the policing of epidemics that characterised the half-century after the arrival of cholera on the European continent ended with the rise of bacteriology and the discovery of the agent of the disease, the 'comma bacillus', by Robert Koch in 1884. Under Koch's influence, European governments, drawing on previous administrative practice but now acting under precise medical instructions, instituted massive preventive campaigns of quarantine, disinfection and the isolation of victims. Resistance to the new interventionism, such as was offered in Hamburg up to the epidemic of 1892, was quickly swept aside. The creation of professional police forces in the aftermath of the 1848 revolutions, the general process of centralisation that had taken place over the nineteenth century, the growth of rapid communications in the form of railway networks, and the general increase in the resources available to the European state, meant that such measures were infinitely more effective in the 1890s than they had been sixty years earlier. Cholera epidemics still swept across Russia in the last decade of the nineteenth century, but now they were successfully stopped at the German frontier. At the same time, mass public education ensured the adoption of higher standards of personal hygiene and contributed to the process of the 'medicalisation' of the European population that was taking place at this time.[82]

By the end of the century, not least thanks to this process of 'medicalisation', medicine and health had become political issues in most western and central European countries. In Hamburg, for instance, the cholera epidemic of 1892 was blamed on the determination of the city's dominant mercantile class to take no precautions for fear of damaging trade. It was widely believed that such narrowly selfish policies could be avoided if the electorate for the city council was broadened, and strong pressure from internal and external forces led to precisely this occurring four years later, in

---

[81] Gerd Göckenjan, *Kurieren und Staat machen: Gesundheit und Medizin in der bürgerlichen Welt* (Frankfurt-on-Main, 1985), p. 109.
[82] Ute Frevert, *Krankheit als politisches Problem, 1770–1880: Soziale Unterschichten in Preussen zwischen medizinischer Polizei und staatlicher Sozialversicherung* (Göttingen, 1984).

1896.[83] Yet this was perhaps a rare instance of a political reform directly following on an epidemic. For by the time that health had become a political issue in this way, the age of epidemics in western Europe was largely over. Sanitary reform, the construction of pure water supplies and efficient sewerage systems in the great European cities, undertaken in the previous quarter of a century for a wide variety of reasons, had done more than anything else to reduce the spread of water-borne diseases. Comprehensive programmes of smallpox vaccination had long been in place. Cholera, smallpox and typhoid gave way to tuberculosis and infant mortality as the major focuses of health politics, and the shock effect of epidemics, for the time being at least, was a thing of the past.

[83] Hans Wilhelm Eckardt, *Privilegien und Parlament: Die Auseinandersetzungen um das allgemeine und gleiche Wahlrecht in Hamburg* (Hamburg, 1980), pp. 35–6.

8. Hawaiian depopulation as a model for the Amerindian experience[1]

A. W. CROSBY

We are at the final frayed finish of the age of Europe's territorial expansion, which stimulates curiosity about its beginnings. The Social Darwinists were sure that white people were genetically superior to the other strains of humanity, and that was why they were such successful imperialists; at the end of the twentieth century that explanation seems as antiquated as a whalebone corset. Technological and managerial superiority are probably adequate to explain the brief subjugation of such lands as Algeria and Burma, but meagre when matched to the Europeans' much more thorough and seemingly permanent takeovers of the temperate regions of the Americas. The new right-off-the-shelf-and-ready-for-instant-use explanation is that the Amerindians, unlike Africans or Asians, died in huge numbers of Old World diseases carried for the first time across the Atlantic by Columbus and his emulators, and therefore were easily displaced and replaced by the invaders.

There is a large body of documentary evidence in support of this theory, but much of the evidence was collected in the pre-scientific and pre-statistical centuries and almost always by soldiers, missionaries, trappers and traders, rather than by physicians and demographers: i.e. it is no better than impressionistic. Furthermore, the enormous extent of the Americas, the number and variety of their aboriginal peoples and the length of time since the first contacts between the Old World invaders and the New World aborigines bring into question even the most obvious interpretations of what accounts we do have of the impact of exotic diseases on Amerindians.

[1] I must thank Eleanor C. Nordyke, Robert C. Schmitt, David E. Stannard and Alan Frost for having given me the benefit of their criticisms. Their advice was

Take, for example, the Huron of the eastern corner of Georgian Bay: they were drastically reduced by smallpox in the 1630s, then ravaged by the Iroquois – and then we hear little of them. What proportion survived the smallpox? How many did the Iroquois kill and how many did they adopt into their tribes, as was their custom? How many fled and joined the Neutral, the Petun and the Ottowa? What percentage of the Wyandot of the Upper Great Lakes area in the nineteenth century were descendants of Hurons who escaped both smallpox and Iroquois and fled west?[2]

We need a model, a case-study with the same advantages for us as the Galápagos finches provided Charles Darwin. We need a case-study narrowly limited in time and space and in the number of factors at work. I nominate the Hawaii Islands and the Hawaiian Polynesians.

In 1778, when Captain James Cook happened upon the Hawaiian archipelago, its Polynesian population numbered from 242,000 (the lowest contemporary estimate) to 800,000 (a recent assessment: startlingly large, yet the product of exhaustive scholarship and analysis). A hundred years later there were only 48,000 native Hawaiians, including even those of only part Hawaiian parentage.[3] The steepness of the Hawaiians' decline recommends them as a model for the post-Columbian demographic history of the Amerindians, but first let us consider whether they and their islands qualify as a laboratory case.

First, the matter of isolation from unaccountable influences: the Hawaiian Islands are among the most isolated in the world, over 2,000 miles from the nearest continent, North America, and hundreds of miles from the nearest islands capable of supporting more than a handful of inhabitants. The archipelago lies north of the latitudes of the most dependable easterly trade winds and to the

invaluable (though not always heeded, so they cannot be blamed for my mistakes and misinterpretations).

[2] Conrad E. Heidenreich, 'Huron', in *Handbook of North American Indians*, XV, *Northeast*, ed. Bruce G. Trigger (Washington DC, 1978), pp. 369, 387, 789–92; Elisabeth Tooker, 'Wyandot', in *Handbook of North American Indians*, XV, p. 398.

[3] Robert C. Schmitt, *Demographic Statistics of Hawaii, 1778–1965* (Honolulu, 1968), pp. 10–12; Robert C. Schmitt, 'New Estimates of the Pre-Censal Population of Hawaii', *Journal of the Polynesian Society*, 80 (1971), pp. 240–2; David E. Stannard, *Before the Horror. The Population of Hawai'i on the Eve of Western Contact* (Honolulu, 1989), pp. 45, 49, 56, and *passim*.

The population of Hawaii: 1778–1878[4]

Year	Population	Percentage of annual change
1778	242,000–800,000	—
1823	134,925	—
1831–2	124,449	−0.9
1835–6	107,954	−3.6
1850	84,165	−1.8
1853[5]	73,138	−3.5
1860	69,800	−0.7
1866	62,959	−1.7
1872	56,897	−1.7
1878[6]	57,985	+0.3

Notes: The 1778 total is, of necessity, the most speculative. The numbers from 1823 through to 1835–6 are estimates by well-informed missionaries living in Hawaii. From 1850 onwards the numbers are the products of official censuses. Note that the number of Hawaiians of all or part Polynesian ancestry continued to drop for the rest of the nineteenth century, although the total of people living in the Hawaiian Islands grew after 1872.

south of the prevailing westerlies.[7] For two and a half centuries the Manila galleon passed to the south of the islands on its voyage to the Philippines and far to the north on its return to Acapulco. A Spaniard or two may have made a one-way voyage and wrecked on Hawaii's shores, but even that is doubtful. Captain Cook came upon Hawaii because he was doing what only an explorer would do intentionally in the eighteenth century: sailing *north* across the Pacific.

The isolation of the Hawaiian Islands was so extreme for so long that about 96 per cent of its native flowering plants occur naturally nowhere else in the world.[8] Its only native land mammal when the

---

[4] Schmitt, *Demographic Statistics*, p. 10; Schmitt, 'New Estimates for the Pre-Censal Population of Hawaii', pp. 240–2; Eleanor C. Nordyke, *The Peopling of Hawai'i*, 2nd edn (Honolulu, 1977), pp. 17–19; Stannard, *Before the Horror*, pp. 45, 49, 56, and *passim*.

[5] 97.5 per cent of population born in Hawaii.

[6] Only 83.6 per cent of population born in Hawaii.

[7] *Atlas of Hawaii*, ed. R. Warwick Armstrong (Honolulu, 1973), pp. 9, 48, 59; National Oceanic and Atmospheric Administration, US Department of Commerce, *Climates of the States*, 2 vols. (Port Washington, NY, 1974), II, p. 615.

[8] *Atlas of Hawaii*, p. 63.

Polynesians arrived a thousand years and more before Cook was a species of bat, a *very* distant relative indeed of *Homo sapiens*. When Cook landed, the only land mammals were the bat, plus what had come in the Polynesian canoes: the dog, pig, rat (probably a stowaway) and, of course, the Hawaiians themselves.[9] The Islands had, we may safely surmise, no micro-organisms or parasites pre-adapted to preying on humans when the Polynesians debarked, and no more than a few when Cook stepped ashore.

The Polynesians arrived 1,500 to 2,000 years ago, after which there may have been contacts with other Polynesians islands but for no more than a few hundred years.[10] It is unlikely that the Polynesians brought many kinds of pathogens with them. They came to these islands by a series of voyages in open-decked vessels, voyages linked backward through several millennia and across the broadest ocean on the planet to the Asian mainland. Acute diseases that kill swiftly or produce long-lasting immunity would have used up their fuel (i.e. the susceptible passengers on these vessels) and burned out during the long voyages. People with chronic diseases like tuberculosis would probably not have volunteered and would not have been chosen for such voyages; or, if they embarked anyway, would probably have died on the high seas and have been thrown overboard, taking their germs with them. In other words, the founders of the Hawaiian people in all probability deserved a clean bill of health.[11]

The archaeological record supports the hypothesis that the pre-Cook Hawaiians had few infectious diseases. Examination of 864 prehistoric skeletons dug out of the sand dunes at Mokapu, Oahu, reveals that the ancient Hawaiians commonly suffered from traumatic arthritis, dental caries and possibly such diseases as usually affect

[9] Raymond J. Kramer, *Hawaiian Land Mammals* (Rutland, Vt., 1971), p. 17.
[10] Patrick Vinton Kirch, *Feathered Gods and Fishhooks. An Introduction to Hawaiian Archeology and Prehistory* (Honolulu, 1985), pp. 65–8.
[11] A note in Darwin's *Origin of Species* hints at the degree of the Hawaiians' isolation from the disease pool in which most continental humans were immersed. 'The surgeon of a whaling ship in the Pacific assured me that when the Peduculi [lice], with which some Sandwich Islanders on board swarmed, strayed on to the bodies of the English sailors, they died in the course of three or four days. These Peduculi were darker coloured, and appeared different from those proper to the natives of Chiloe in South America': Charles Darwin, *The Origin of Species and the Descent of Man* (New York, n.d.), p. 532.

only soft tissue, such as yaws, but otherwise were just as Captain Cook described them in 1778: a hearty lot.[12]

Fortunately for historians, the myriad infections of the mainland populations did not arrive in Hawaii until after the spread of scientific and statistical habits of thought in Europe and her colonies. Captains Cook, La Pérouse, Vancouver, Krusenstern and their officers were much more apt to describe disease in terms of symptomatology and epidemiology than had their sixteenth- and seventeenth-century counterparts coasting the shores of America. The estimations of Captain Cook *et al.* of Hawaiian population size, while sometimes based on no more than a glance at coastal settlements, were the products of minds familiar with the techniques of quantification. When an Hernán Cortés said 'a hundred thousand', he may have meant nothing more precise than 'a lot'. When a James Cook said 'a hundred thousand', he meant just that.

The first consecutive records of the Hawaiian experience we have were written by missionaries, whom the Christian resurgence of the nineteenth century, called the Second Awakening in the United States, dispatched into the Pacific. Many of the earliest to reach Hawaii were New England Protestants of considerable education, some of it in science and mathematics, and of a post-Newtonian frame of mind. They kept good records, and their estimations of the number of Hawaiians, based on first hand or at worst second hand observations, between 1823 and the first official census a generation later, are quite respectable. We know more about the demographic history of the Hawaiians from 1823 on than we do about all but a few peoples in the world.[13]

The charge of direct and conscious genocide often filed against the European invaders of the Americas complicates analysis of the impact of the imported diseases they carried with them. There was some genocide, probably a lot, but just how much? There was no

---

[12] Warner F. Bowers, 'Pathological and Functional Changes Found in 864 Pre-Captain Cook Contact Polynesian Burials from the Sand Dunes at Mokapu, Oahu, Hawaii', *International Surgery*, 45 (1966), p. 217; Charles E. Snow, *Early Hawaiians, an Initial Study of Skeletal Remains from Mokapu, Oahu* (Lexington, Ky., 1974), pp. 60–75; Peter Pirie, 'The Effects of Treponematosis and Gonorrhoea on the Populations of the Pacific Islands', *Human Biology in Oceania*, 1 (1972), pp. 191, 193–4. See also Stannard, *Before the Horror*, pp. 73–8.

[13] Ralph S. Kuykendall, *The Hawaiian Kingdom, 1778–1854, Foundation and Transformation* (Honolulu, 1947), pp. 100–13, 335–6; Nordyke, *Peopling of Hawai'i*, *passim*.

omnipresent census-taker to declare authoritatively what percentage of Amerindians were murdered and what percentage were victims of infection. The role played by disease in the Hawaiian population crash was not so obscure simply because the *haole* (the native Hawaiian word for Caucasians) rarely slaughtered Hawaiians. The *haole* were not guiltless – in 1790 the *Eleanora*, under Captain Simon Metcalfe, destroyed more than a hundred unsuspecting Hawaiians with a single broadside[14] – but this massacre was an aberration and quantitatively insignificant compared, for example, to the English slaughter of the Pequots in 1637 or the Argentinian search-and-destroy campaigns against the Amerindians of the pampa and Patagonia in the nineteenth century.[15] We can omit the elusive and volatile factor of direct genocide from our analysis of Hawaiian demographic history.

What about the wars between Hawaiians, wars possibly stimulated by *haole* influence and certainly made deadlier by imported firearms than the wars of old? When Captain George Vancouver anchored in Hawaiian waters in 1792 he found firearms 'solicited with the greatest ardency, by every native of the least consequence'. King Kamehameha tabooed all trade with the Vancouver expedition 'for any commodity whatever than *arms and ammunition*'. A number of Kamehameha's subjects were already using these weapons 'with an adroitness that would not disgrace the generality of European soldiers'. By 1804 he had a quantity of muskets, small guns, swivels and fifty Europeans competent to utilise them in his service. He used this military power to unite the islands for the first time, and many died in his wars of unification. However, the wars lasted less than a generation, and the population decline went on for a century.[16]

What about murderous exploitation of aboriginal labour, which was certainly a factor in the depopulation of parts of Latin America? Neither Kamehameha I nor any of the Hawaiian monarchs who reigned in the nineteenth century had silver or gold mines where thousands of natives went to their deaths. The Islands' plantations were never administered with the disregard for life common in West Indian plantations; and even if it be claimed that they were,

[14] Kuykendall, *Hawaiian Kingdom, 1778–1854*, p. 24.
[15] Bert Salwen, 'Indians of Southern New England and Long Island: Early Period', in *Handbook of North American Indians*, XV, p. 173; Ricardo Levene, *A History of Argentine*, trans. William S. Robertson (New York, 1963), pp. 406–7, 483.
[16] Stannard, *Before the Horror*, p. 62.

plantations only began to figure importantly in the Islands' economy *after* the years of steepest decline of the indigenous population.

Hawaii's monarchy and aristocracy were corrupted by contact with the outside world, which had an undeniably dire effect on the native population. The rulers, keen for European-style clothing, firearms, sailing vessels, etc. (whole houses were broken down, shipped around the Horn and reconstructed in the Islands), fell deeply into debt; and the Islands had only one thing of high value per unit of bulk and weight to pay off the *haole* creditors: sandalwood. North American captains discovered that Hawaiian sandalwood brought high prices at Canton, and by 1817–18 most of the foreign ships dropping anchor in Hawaiian waters were there to take on the sweet-smelling wood and carry it to China. The Hawaiian rulers ordered hundreds, perhaps thousands, of their subjects out of the taro fields and into the rugged highlands to fell and carry down to the shore on their backs ton after ton of the wood. 'Many of the poor wretches', wrote one visitor, 'died in their harness, while many more of them prematurely sank under the corroding effects of exposure and exhaustion.' Can we blame the Hawaiians' population crash on this trade? Probably not, over the long run, because the trade was over and done with before the 1830s. The Hawaiians' decline was underway before the trade waxed and continued long after it waned.[17]

The Hawaiians' decrease in the century following their first contact with Europeans and North Americans provides us with as good a model as we can expect to find anywhere for testing theories about the connection between aboriginal population crash and contact with the West. The documentation is considerable in quantity and respectable in quality, and the influence and number of tangential factors limited.

By the 1840s, Christian missionaries had been living continuously alongside the Hawaiians for two decades and knew a good deal of at

---

[17] Theodore Morgan, *Hawaii, a Century of Economic Change, 1778–1876* (Cambridge, 1948), pp. 62–7; Robert C. Schmitt, 'Famine Mortality in Hawaii', *Journal of Pacific History*, 5 (1970), p. 113; 'The Sandalwood Trade of Early Hawaii', *Hawaiian Almanac and Annual for 1905*, ed. Thos. Thrum, 31 (1905), pp. 43–74; Harold St John, 'The History, Present Distribution, and Abundance of Sandalwood on Oahu, Hawaiian Islands: Hawaiian Plant Studies 14', *Pacific Science*, 1 (1947), pp. 5–9; Ross H. Cordy, 'The Effects of European Contact on Hawaiian Agricultural Systems – 1778–1819', *Ethnohistory*, 19 (1972), pp. 409–10.

least a superficial nature about them. Their guess was that the Hawaiian population had decreased by two-thirds since Cook's first debarkation. The old hands estimated that the decrease in the four years ending in 1836 had been one twelfth: this while missionary families were averaging between six and seven children each.[18] At the Hawaiians' rate of decrease c. 1840 they would be gone from the face of the earth in a half century or so. Their plunge, noted the Reverend Bishop, was similar to that of the aborigines of South and North America, the West Indies, South Africa and of the other islands of the Pacific.[19]

He and other missionaries totted up a list of causes of the plunge: low birth rate, high infant mortality rate, infanticide, sexual licentiousness, venereal disease, alcoholism, inadequate clothing, improvidence, 'the rage for horses' and the consequent neglect of agriculture, the ravaging of croplands by imported and newly feral livestock, the declining quality of native housing, corrupt government, the improper use of European-style clothing, the emigration of young men, poor diet and 'genital impotency'. The missionaries were especially impressed with the evil effects of the collective ownership of land. Like many other *haole*, they were sure that the institution of the fee simple system of landownership would provide a sovereign cure for the Hawaiians' problems.[20]

Let us try to make some sense out of the missionary diagnosis of the Hawaiians' demographic nose-dive. First, let us discard the insignificant. It was true that hundreds of young men were joining the crews of the passing merchantmen and whalers, and that some of them never came back, but their numbers were small relative to the entire population.[21] It was true for a while that Hawaiians would sacrifice nearly anything, including life and limb, to ride the newly imported horses on 'the run, trot, or hobble, helter skelter, whooping and shouting, like so many Cossacks'. The Hawaiian women insisted on riding astride, in spite of the damage that such a practice was certain, according to the principles of Victorian gynaecology, to

---

[18] William F. Blackman, *The Making of Hawaii* (New York, 1899), p. 213.
[19] Artemas Bishop, 'An Inquiry into the Causes of Decrease in the Population of the Sandwich Islands', *Hawaiian Spectator*, 1 (1838), pp. 52–3.
[20] *Ibid.*, pp. 53–61; *Answers to Questions Proposed by His Excellency, R. C. Wyllie, His Hawaiian Minister of Foreign Relations, and Addressed to All the Missionaries in the Hawaiian Islands, May 1846* (n.p., n.d.), pp. 6, 9, 23, 41, 47, 49, 84–5, 92.
[21] Nordyke, *Peopling of Hawai'i*, p. 22.

do to their childbearing capabilities.[22] But the equestrian madness only lasted a few years, and made excellent cowboys out of some of the Hawaiians, which probably increased their incomes. It was true that the locust-like herds of feral Old World livestock were a curse to Hawaiian farmers, but there is little in the record to indicate a widespread or long-lasting famine from this or any other cause. Indeed, one might think that the presence of large quantities of free protein-on-the-hoof would have improved, not degraded, Hawaiian diet. As for who owned the farmland, the traditional system had not prevented the production of plenty of food before the arrival of the aliens.

The other alleged causes were significant. Let us divide them into two categories, anomie and disease. By the word anomie I refer to what has sometimes been called 'culture crunch', i.e. the disorientation – religious, political, culinary and so on – that can overtake an individual or people who suddenly confront others of an alien culture. This disorientation can be especially severe if the others are alien in appearance and behaviour, and are, in one or more ways, perceived as superior or, at least, invincible. Only a few, a very few, people ever die directly of anomie, but it does sap the energies of life; and that may explain the observation of one witness to the Hawaiian condition who remarked in 1848, 'The Hawaiians can lie down and die the easiest of any people with which I am acquainted.'[23] But let us try to be more specific than that.

Surely we may, in this case, construe narcotic addiction, if widespread and carried to outrageous extremes, as an indicator of anomie. In 1815 Otto von Kotzebue (or Otto E. Kotsbu), an explorer sailing in the service of the Tsar, noted that tobacco, an imported plant, was growing in the Islands, that children were smoking before they walked and the adults were using the weed to the point of unconsciousness. He recorded that they, believe it or not, 'frequently die of the stupor'.[24]

---

[22] James J. Jarves, *Scenes and Scenery in the Sandwich Islands* (Boston, 1843), p. 52; W. Hillebrand, 'Report on Labor and Population', *Transactions of the Royal Hawaiian Agricultural Society*, 2 (1855), pp. 73–4.

[23] Andrew W. Lind, *An Island Community. Ecological Succession in Hawaii* (Chicago, 1938), p. 97.

[24] Otto von Kotzebue, *Voyage of Discovery in the South Sea* (London, 1821), Pt I, p. 87. Alonzo Chapin, MD, in his 'Remarks on the Sandwich Islands; their Situation, Climate, Diseases', *Hawaiian Spectator*, 1 (1838), p. 263, also states that individuals, 'have been killed' by the effect of tobacco.

Hawaiians, previously only familiar with one intoxicating beverage, the Polynesian *awa*,[25] swiftly learned and embraced the delights of swift inebriation from the aliens' distilled alcohol. Some time before 1809 William Stevenson, an ex-convict from New South Wales, set up a still in the Islands, got drunk on his own product and stayed that way until Kamehameha seized the still. By 1812 or so every chief had his own still. Kotzebue, a naval officer and, presumably, a man who had seen his share of alcoholism, was appalled at the islanders' drinking habits: 'they empty a bottle of rum at one draught, with the greatest ease, and it is inconceivable how much of it they can drink'. The missionaries wrote of 'periods of general inebriation, when men, women and children are every where met, under all the wild excitement of liquor'. In this matter the Christian men of the cloth were seconded by the clergy of Pele, the Hawaiians' volcano god. When the Reverend Ellis debated with a priestess of Pele, she cited names of several dead chiefs and asked, 'Who destroyed these? Not Pele, but the rum of the foreigners, whose God you are so fond of.' Alcohol, said Henry T. Cheever in 1851, 'has been to Polynesians like firewater to the North American Indians'.[26]

Abortion and infanticide, again if widespread and carried to outrageous extremes, may be also taken as indicators of anomie. These forms of population control can be very injurious to societies under stress because young humans are in general the most adaptable of their species to new challenges, and they are, after the first few years of life, more resistant to exotic infections than are adults. But there are crises during which the immediate interest of individuals, especially mothers, is at cross purposes with the creation of new generations. Indeed, there are times so painful and hopeless that racial suicide seems an agreeable alternative to regeneration: Sarah Winnemucca Hopkins of the Paiutes of the western United States wrote in the 1880s, 'My people have

---

[25] *The Journal of Captain James Cook on His Voyages of Discovery*, ed. J. C. Beaglehole, 4 vols. (Cambridge, 1969), II, pp. 236–7.

[26] Kotzebue, *Voyage of Discovery*, p. 98; Archibald Campbell, *A Voyage around the World from 1806 to 1812* (Edinburgh, 1866), pp. 146, 184–5, 186; C. S. Stewart, *Journal of a Residence in the Sandwich Islands during the Years 1823, 1824, and 1825* (New York, 1828), p. 236; William Ellis, *A Journal of a Tour around Hawaii* (Boston, 1825), p. 179; Henry T. Cheever, *The Island World of the Pacific* (New York, 1851), p. 29.

been so unhappy for so long they wish to *disincrease*, instead of to multiply.'[27]

Many peoples have practised population control, island peoples plausibly more often than many others. One effective means of population control is celibacy, an aberrant behaviour of which no one ever accused the Hawaiians. Another is abortion, which tribal peoples as well as technologically advanced people have resorted to frequently, but probably less often than many of us believe. It is likely that tribal peoples realise that the well-being of the mother and baby are intertwined, and that crude attempts artificially to terminate pregnancy often kill both. The one folk method of birth control that is unquestionably effective and safe for the mother is infanticide. (I define infanticide not only as direct killing of babies, but also as the more common form of elimination by semi-intentional neglect in the first days or months of life.)[28]

Infanticide is not easy to detect unless the executors are caught *in flagrante delicto*. The number of boys and girls is less than it naturally should be, but how is the investigator to discern that? If, however, more of one gender are eliminated than of the other, then the presence of infanticide will stand out sharply in the statistics. Let me explain: it is consistently true across the world that a few more male babies are born than female babies. Among most populations in most years the ratio is something like 103 or 105 boys to 100 girls. The ratio is close to 50/50, and, as a cohort proceeds through life, the male majority usually narrows and eventually disappears because in most places and times more males than females die by violence and by natural causes. Ideally, population records should show a slight majority of boys over girls, a narrower majority in the early decades of adulthood, and then equality and perhaps a majority of women over men in the last part of life.[29] Whenever there is a large majority

[27] Sarah Winnemucca Hopkins, *Life Among the Paiutes. Their Wrongs and Claims* (Boston, 1883), p. 48.
[28] This is a subject of enormous importance and great obscurity; see William L. Langer, 'Infanticide: An Historical View', *History of Childhood Quarterly*, 1 (1974), pp. 353–65; Michael W. Flinn, *The European Demographic System, 1500–1820* (Baltimore, 1981), pp. 39–42; and Lionel Rose, *The Massacre of the Innocents, Infanticide in Britain, 1800–1939* (London, 1968); Thomas R. Forbes, 'Deadly Parents: Child Homicide in Eighteenth- and Nineteenth-Century England', *Journal of the History of Medicine and Allied Sciences*, 41 (1986), pp. 175–99; Maria W. Piers, *Infanticide, Past and Present* (New York, 1978).
[29] Curt Stern, *Principles of Human Genetics*, 3rd edn (San Francisco, 1973), pp. 528–9, 535–6; Edward Novitski, *Human Genetics* (New York, 1977), pp. 302–3.

of males at any age, then we can be sure that some abnormal force has eliminated females.

In many societies males are valued more than females. This is particularly true in periods of severe stress, when warriors, hunters and fishermen may seem more essential than gatherers, farmers and mothers. In such periods limiting the birth rate may seem desirable, even necessary; and it is plain that eliminating girls is a more efficient means of doing so than eliminating boys.

Several of the early Christian missionaries in the Hawaiian archipelago were sure that infanticide, especially female infanticide, was widespread despite decrees against the practice and assurances that it had stopped *c.* 1820. They based their claim on impressions quite probably affected by bigotry, but which were supported by the few contemporary surveys that enable us to compare the ratio of males to females. For instance, a census of the Hawaiians on Oahu taken in 1831 showed nearly 13 per cent more males than females, and almost 15 per cent more boys than girls. (The precise location of the line between adult and child was, unfortunately, not defined.) There was also some data suggesting a correlation between an abundance of living children, a normal percentage of girls as compared with boys, and geographical remoteness from Honolulu and other areas where Hawaiians were in continual contact with *haole*.[30]

Hawaii's population statistics after the 1840s were among the most complete in the world, and are very useful in retrospectively assessing the birth and death rates, and birth- and child-care practices of the previous century. In 1850 there were 10 per cent more males than females, and Hawaiians under eighteen years of age accounted for less than 30 per cent of the population. Among these youngsters there were 25 per cent more boys than girls. By the census of 1884 the Hawaiians were turning away from the brink of extinction, and the number of boys under six years was actually fewer than that of girls, 2,450 as compared to 2,488, but the majority of the older cohorts was unequivocally male. Males between the ages of six and fifteen years inclusive exceeded females by 7 per cent. The

---

[30] Robert C. Schmitt, *The Missionary Censuses of Hawaii*, Bernice P. Bishop Museum, Pacific Anthropological Records, no. 20 (Honolulu, 1973), p. 12. See also John H. R. Plews, 'Charles Darwin and Hawaiian Sex Ratios, or, Genius Is a Capacity for Making Compensating Errors', *Hawaiian Journal of History*, 14 (1980), pp. 34–6, 39–41.

edge for Hawaiian males from sixteen to thirty years of age was 8 per cent, for thirty-one years to fifty years 27 per cent and for those over fifty years of age 43 per cent.[31] These figures suggest that *c.* 1880 the Hawaiians, in thousands of individual choices by mothers, midwives and relatives, voted to survive as a people.

The extreme skewing of the sex ratio among Hawaiians in the nineteenth century is open to many explanations, of course, but few pass examination. The ratio was not carried forward into the twentieth century, and so we can be sure it had little or nothing to do with Polynesian genetics. Female Hawaiians were in the minority from the earliest ages of life, so the sex ratio cannot be blamed on infections or injuries associated with pregnancy or delivery. Adult women might have acquired venereal disease, widespread in the Islands, earlier than the men, but soon would have transmitted it to the males, to whom it would have proved no more nor less fatal than to females. Venereal disease certainly affected the organs of reproduction of many women, but there is no sexually transmitted disease that blocks the initiation of female embryos or kills female fetuses preferentially. There is nothing in the record to suggest that census-takers tended to overlook females, especially older females. There is nothing in the record about the departure of large numbers of

---

[31] Hiram Bingham, *A Residence of Twenty-One Years in the Sandwich Islands* (Canandaigua, NY, 1855), p. 368; Ellis, *A Journal of a Tour Around Hawaii*, p. 16; Daniel Tyerman and George Bennet, *Journal of Voyages and Travels*, 2 vols. (London, 1831), I, p. 449; Schmitt, *Demographic Statistics*, pp. 31, 43; Plews, 'Charles Darwin', pp. 30–6, 39–41; *The Hawaiian Almanac and Annual for 1890*, ed. Thos. G. Thrum, p. 9. The latter is the source for my discussion of the 1884 census, which I reproduce in exact copy:

The Census of 1884 . . . Hawaiians	
Under 6 years,	
males	2,450
females	2,488
Between 6 and 15 years,	
males	3,742
females	3,490
Between 15 and 30 years,	
males	5,552
females	5,123
Between 30 and 50 years,	
males	6,860
females	5,387
Over 50 years,	
males	2,900
females	2,022
Total	40,014

women from the Islands, voluntarily or involuntarily. Emigration was a male, not a female, behaviour. Hundreds, even thousands, of Hawaiian males were at sea or abroad in every year from at least as early as the 1820s onward. If the censuses had covered all Polynesians of Hawaiian birth, no matter where they were, then the male majority would have been even greater.

Some concealed factor or factors were blocking the births of or killing more Hawaiian females than males. The mystery attracted the attention of even Darwin, who could offer no better explanation than a reference to 'some unknown law'.[32] Overwork and general exploitation may well have erased more adult women than men, but the likeliest candidate as the chief killer of females was infanticide, either by direct intention or, as is much more common, indirectly and semi-intentionally. In 1846 the *haole* missionaries blamed the deaths of so many Hawaiian children on the lack of proper food, clothing, shelter, medical care and 'unskilful management'. I suspect that in Hawaii conventional Christian morality held overt infanticide to a minimum, and, as is true among the poor and desperate across the world today, hunger, dehydration, exposure and a turning away – a 'want of solicitude', as one of the medical missionaries called it – did the actual deed.[33]

Anomie is an effect as well as a cause. What did the Hawaiians suffer that was so horrible that they fell into such confusion and despair and were driven to behaviours that endangered their very survival? They did find themselves confronted with aliens more powerful than they were, but that is an experience through which, one might guess, all peoples have passed at one time or another, usually without skirting extinction. Radical population declines – 50, 75 and 90 per cent – do not necessarily follow upon culture shock. But the Hawaiians did suffer a population crash so severe that many *haole* and at least some of the Hawaiians themselves believed their extinction was inevitable. The chief killer, one who recruited anomie as a lieutenant, was imported disease.

The Hawaiians in 1778 had only a few kinds of communicable

[32] Plews, 'Charles Darwin', p. 29.
[33] Schmitt, *Demographic Statistics*, p. 39; Schmitt, *Missionary Censuses of Hawaii*, p. 15; Plews, 'Charles Darwin', pp. 30–3. I have found Forbes, 'Deadly Parents', and Nancy Scheper-Hughes, 'Death without Weeping', *Natural History*, 98 (1989), pp. 8–16, very helpful in my consideration of semi-intentional infanticide.

disease, as one would expect of an isolated population of less than a million. In contrast, the disease environment of the continental peoples who came to the Hawaiians' home islands in and after 1778 contained numerous kinds of infectious diseases, including many of the most dangerous known to humanity. We can usefully picture the Hawaiian disease environment as a briar patch, and the continental equivalent as a jungle.

Events provided proofs and illustrations of the difference. King Liholiho and Queen Kamamalu of Hawaii sailed for England in November of 1823 'to visit his Majesty the King [George IV], to receive friendly counsel and advice . . . , to increase their acquaintance with the world, enlarge their views of human society', and so on. They arrived in mid-May, 1824, took up residence in Osborne's Caledonian Hotel, London, were entertained by the Secretary of State for Foreign Affairs, Mr Canning, and visited the theatres, where they occupied the royal boxes. While arrangements were being made for their reception at court, they contracted measles, one of the commoner childhood infections in Europe, but as yet unknown in the Hawaiian Islands. Both died in July 1824.[34]

In the case of King Liholiho and Queen Kamamalu, to coin a phrase, Mohammed went to the mountain, the mountain of disease, in this instance. In the case of the majority of Hawaiians, the mountain came to them. After 1778 the Hawaiians were subjected to an influx of alien human beings teeming with dangerous germs, as they, the Hawaiians, realised. In October of 1806 the chief at Anahooroo [Honolulu?] Bay refused to permit a trader to enter the harbour upon hearing there was a sick man on board. The chief feared the introduction of disease, 'which calamity had happened on a former occasion, from an American ship'. In the 1820s a missionary recorded scornfully that the natives were blaming the foreigners for most diseases.[35] They knew more about the matter than he did.

Let me cite a few of the most salient of the epidemics that swept

---

[34] Kuykendall, *Hawaiian Kingdom, 1778–1854*, pp. 76–8. Many Hawaiians who shipped out on *haole* vessels met similar fates. Captain Amasa Delano in *A Narrative of Voyages and Travels* (Boston, 1817), p. 392, tells the horrific tale of Hawaiian sailors contracting smallpox in Canton, 'which most generally proves fatal to them, and the distress and sufferings of the poor creatures have been beyond description; many scenes of which I have been an eye witness to, that would excite the compassion of any man possessed of the least particle of humanity'.

[35] John Martin, *An Account of the Natives of the Tonga Islands* (London, 1818), pp. 1, 36–7; Stewart, *Journal of a Residence*, p. 114.

over Hawaii. The semi-mythic *oku'u*, perhaps the worst single onslaught of disease in the history of the Islands, struck in approximately 1804 just as Kamehameha was gathering his forces to invade Kauai. He fell ill and recovered, but perhaps two-thirds of his men died, though 3 humans and 400 hogs were sacrificed to appease the gods. Nothing much was written down about *oku'u* for many years after the event, and we cannot even be sure whether it was restricted to Oahu or spread throughout the archipelago. It seems to have been some sort of a diarrhoeal infection, like the approximately contemporary *rewa-rewa* in New Zealand, and may have, *may have*, swept off the majority of Hawaiians. If the epidemiologist's rule of thumb that an isolated people's earliest epidemics are apt to be their worst is valid, then *oku'u* may have been as bad as oral tradition claimed.[36]

In 1848–9 three epidemics rolled through the Islands at once: measles, whooping cough (both for the first time, apparently) and a strain of influenza. California, where gold had just been discovered and with which contacts were increasing, was identified as the source of the first two. The death rate for the sick was judged as 10 per cent, and the total mortality at no less than 10,000.[37]

The infection whose arrival from the mainland was feared the most was smallpox. The missionary doctors vaccinated some Hawaiians in the first half of the nineteenth century, but to what avail we cannot be sure because the vaccine often lost its efficacy during long sea voyages. On 10 February 1853, the *Charles Mallory* arrived from California with a yellow flag flying from her foremast: she had smallpox on board. The disease did not appear among the Hawaiians for four months, a long time for an epidemic of a disease like smallpox to hang fire, and so perhaps the *Mallory*'s arrival was no more than coincidental. Perhaps the infection really came, for instance, in a chest of old clothing from San Francisco. It was certain to come ashore from some vessel some time. Before this epidemic burned itself out early the next year, there were officially

[36] Robert C. Schmitt, 'The *Okuu* – Hawaii's Greatest Epidemic', *Hawaiian Medical Journal*, 29 (1970), pp. 359–64; Sheldon Dibble, *A History of the Sandwich Islands* (Honolulu, 1909), pp. 38, 58; James Jackson Jarves, *History of the Hawaiian Islands* (Honolulu, 1847), p. 97; Tyerman and Bennet, *Journal of Voyages and Travels*, I, pp. 423–4.

[37] *The Friend*, 7, no. 3 (1849), p. 20; Laura Fish Judd, *Honolulu, Sketches of the Life, Social, Political and Religious, in the Hawaiian Islands from 1828 to 1861* (Honolulu, 1928), p. 138; Schmitt, *Demographic Statistics*, pp. 10, 37.

6,405 cases and 2,485 deaths. The real numbers were probably higher. The deaths, at the lowest estimate, help considerably to account for the decrease of the Islands' population from about 84,000 in 1850 to about 73,000 at the end of 1853, a steep decline even by Hawaii's grim standards. The death rate and birth rate were 105 per 1,000 and 20 per 1,000 respectively in 1853.[38] (I should note here the inappropriateness of Polynesian therapies, and the lethal lack of even minimal care that followed upon the simultaneous prostration of adults and children alike, all defenceless against smallpox, as well as the rest of what continental peoples fobbed off as 'childhood sicknesses'.)[39]

The depressing effect of this disease upon the Hawaiian morale may have been even greater than the number of deaths suggests. Twenty years later Samuel M. Kamakau recalled the look and smell of the victims:

A person would be full of pimples from the crown of his head to the soles of the feet – no spot had respite. His mouth was full of them; they were in the nostrils, on the face, in the ears – only the teeth and nails had none. The house stank like poison gourds.[40]

No challenge to Hawaiian survival seemed lacking in the middle decades of the century. Hansen's Disease (leprosy), according to European tradition the most repugnant of all maladies, arrived some time before mid-century, probably from Asia, and spread more freely among Hawaiians than resident foreigners.[41] Although not a significant factor in the depopulation, it provided one more source of bewilderment for native Hawaiians and one more excuse for *haole* racism. The Hawaiians had one piece of luck, possibly the only one in the century after Cook. Human malaria did not gain a foothold though Hawaii is tropical and in areas quite humid. Bird malaria did, and may be the chief cause of the extinction of several species of

---

[38] Richard A. Green, 'Oahu's Ordeal – the Smallpox Epidemic of 1853', *Hawaii Historical Review*, 1 (1965), pp. 221–42; Kuykendall, *Hawaiian Kingdom, 1778–1854*, p. 412; Schmitt, *Demographic Statistics*, pp. 10, 12.

[39] Judd, *Honolulu*, pp. 138–9; Gerrit P. Judd, 'Remarks on the Climate of the Sandwich Islands', *Hawaiian Spectator*, 1 (1838), p. 22; Chapin, 'Remarks on the Sandwich Islands', pp. 261–2. For further remarks on such matters, see my article, 'Virgin Soil Epidemics as a Factor in the Aboriginal Depopulation in America', *William and Mary Quarterly*, 3rd ser., 33 (1976), pp. 289–99.

[40] Samuel M. Kamakau, *Ka Po'e Kahiko; the People of Old*, trans. Mary K. Pukui (Honolulu, 1964), p. 105.

[41] Ralph S. Kuykendall, *The Hawaiian Kingdom, 1854–1874* (Honolulu, 1953), pp. 72–5.

birds endemic to the Islands. Anopheles mosquitoes are a prerequisite for the spread of human malaria, and they did not exist in the archipelago.[42]

The epidemics of newly introduced and highly infectious maladies – *oku'u*, measles, whooping cough, influenza, smallpox – were spectacular in their mortality. We should not, however, let ourselves be hypnotised by them. They were the obvious factor in the depopulation of the Islands, but the decisive factor was whatever prevented the Hawaiians from rebuilding their numbers between these epidemics. What was it that *kept* killing them between epidemics, and what was it that suppressed the birth rate?

We must recognise the importance of the less spectacular diseases, the infections that carried off a constant percentage of babes in arms and toddlers year in and year out, and elbowed adults into the grave ten or twenty years short of their normal span of life. The journal of Francisco de Paula Marin, an early *haole* resident, which runs from 1809 to 1826, is shot through with references to sickness: '11 Jany. [1820] All the people ill of coughs', '20 May [1824] Many deaths & many coughs', '1 February [1825] There are many sick of fevers & colds, & many dying'; and so on and so on.[43] There was nothing bad enough to call an epidemic, just a steady corrosive flow of infection. A generation later Drs Andrews and Chapin judged that half of the native infants died before the age of two, most often of something they vaguely referred to as 'fevers'. Dr Chapin noted that these childhood infections were 'the seeds of numerous future diseases'.[44]

The scanty medical records of the Islands in the first half of the 1800s included a continual refrain of references to such vague ailments as 'fevers', 'itches', 'catarrhs', 'eye infections' and 'dysenteries'.[45] *Haole* visitors to the Hawaiian villages always remarked about the dirt and blowing dust, which help account for the eye problems.[46] The influx of new pathogens and unwholesome foods

[42] Joseph E. Alicata, *Parasites of Man and Animals in Hawaii* (Basel, 1969), pp. 32, 72.

[43] Ross H. Gast, *Don Francisco de Paula Marin; a Biography*, ed. Agnes C. Conrad (Honolulu, 1973), pp. 237, 288, 292.

[44] Chapin, 'Remarks on the Sandwich Islands', p. 261; Cheever, *Island World of the Pacific*, p. 233.

[45] Chapin, 'Remarks on the Sandwich Islands', p. 252; Judd, 'Remarks on the Climate of the Sandwich Islands', p. 22; Jarves, *History of the Hawaiian Islands*, p. 13; Cheever, *Island World of the Pacific*, pp. 224–5.

[46] William Shainline Middleton, 'Early Medical Experiences in Hawaii', *Bulletin of the History of Medicine*, 45 (1971), p. 450.

from abroad, plus poor sanitation, provide plausible explanations for the dysenteries. As for most of the 'catarrhs', the ships from the mainlands were doubtless always bringing to the Islands new strains of the rapidly evolving cold and influenza viruses.

One *haole* wit noted that the standard dress of the Hawaiian was 'a smile, a malo [a sort of girdle or sarong], and a cutaneous eruption'. Itches, scurf, pustules and ulcers were ubiquitous. Dr Chapin attributed the prevalence of skin infections among the Hawaiians to the filth of their clothing and sleeping mats, an explanation which he undermined by also referring to their fondness for water and bathing. Venereal pathogens, which often signal their presence by skin lesions, accounted for some of the examples of 'cutaneous eruption'. In the category of cutaneous disease Dr Chapin also included scrofula, a tubercular infection of the lymphatic system, signs of which often show up in the skin. '*Scrofula*', he wrote, 'is not only frequent but extremely malignant.' If the tubercule bacillus was as widespread as Dr Chapin and others indicated, then that might account for many of the illnesses vaguely diagnosed as 'catarrh' and 'asthma'. It might also provide a partial explanation for Dr Gerrit P. Judd's statement: 'The mortality of the natives does not, however, appear to be owing to the ravages of any particular disease, but they die off suddenly and unexpectedly with any disease that seizes them.'[47] Immune systems taxed by smouldering tubercular infections might well collapse under additional stress.

Tuberculosis may have arrived as early as 1778 because it was present among the crew of Captain Cook's command. It unquestionably stepped ashore with the first missionaries, several of whom were tubercular when they arrived. If it were half as deadly among the Hawaiians as among the Amerindians of the Qu-Appelle reservation in western Canada in the 1890s, it was deadly indeed: as high as 9 per cent of these native Americans died in a year of tuberculosis, and in the space of three generations more than half their families died out.[48]

The Hawaiians may have had some venereal infections before 1778, although the liberality of their sexual mores suggests that they

---

[47] Judd, 'Remarks on the Climate of the Sandwich Islands', pp. 22, 26; Chapin, 'Remarks on the Sandwich Islands', pp. 252, 255–6, 258–9; Middleton, 'Early Medical Experiences in Hawaii', pp. 445, 450.
[48] James Bordley and A. McGehee Harvey, *Two Centuries of American Medicine* (Philadelphia, 1976), p. 202.

were subject to none which were painful, disfiguring or fatal. These may have arrived first with the Cook expedition when it visited the archipelago at the beginning of 1778.[49] Captain Cook tried to prevent sexual contacts between members of his crew with active cases of these infections and the Hawaiians, but when he returned to the Islands that same year some of the Hawaiians already appeared to have lesions of venereal illnesses. When the French explorer, La Pérouse, touched at the Islands in 1785 he found the women unattractive: 'their dress suffered us to perceive that the syphilis had committed ravages on the greater number'. When Captain Urey Lisiansky anchored off the shore of the island of Hawaii in 1804, he made every effort to prevent sexual contacts between his men and the Hawaiian women, not for fear that the men would infect the women, but vice versa.[50]

Most of the early *haole* visitors were men without women, and possessed of items of mainland origin which the Hawaiians quickly learned to covet. The latter were a people with what the anthropologist Marshall Sahlins has called an Aphrodisian culture, which included a tradition of sexual generosity that *haole* almost universally misinterpreted as prostitution, and soon, by their expectations, made into just that.[51]

One of the few to try to understand was the latter-day pagan, Robert Louis Stevenson, who visited Hawaii and spent his final years in Polynesia. He pointed to the tradition of sexual generosity as a possible explanation for the more rapid spread of Hansen's Disease among the Hawaiians than other peoples:

> To refuse a male is still considered in most parts of Polynesia a rather unlovely rigour in the female; and if a man be disfigured, I believe it would be held a sort of charity to console his solitude. A kind island girl might thus go to the leper's bed in something of

---

[49] The matter of which venereal disease existed where and when in the Pacific is controversial and has a considerable literature. See, for instance, Pirie, 'The Effects of Treponematosis'; and Stannard, *Before the Horror*, pp. 69–77.

[50] J. C. Beaglehole, *The Life of Captain James Cook* (Stanford, 1974), pp. clix–clxi, 575, 577, 638–9, 709; *The Voyage of La Pérouse Round the World in the Years 1785, 1786, 1787, and 1788*, 2 vols. (London, 1798), I, p. 98; Urey Lisiansky, *A Voyage Round the World in the Years 1803, 4, 5, and 6* (London, 1814), p. 103; Marshall Sahlins, *Islands of History* (Chicago, 1985), pp. 1–5. This subject is controversial and the evidence ambiguous, as the reader can learn from Pirie, 'The Effects of Treponematosis', pp. 187–206.

[51] Sahlins, *Islands of History*, pp. 9–26.

the same spirit as we visit the sick at home with tracts and pounds of tea.[52]

The perversion of the Hawaiian tradition of sexual hospitality to important strangers was already underway when Captain George Vancouver, who had first gone to the Islands as one of Cook's officers, returned in 1792. On this occasion the licentiousness of the Hawaiians struck him as 'a perfectly new acquirement, taught, perhaps, by the different civilised voluptuaries, who, for some years past, have been their constant visitors'.[53]

The spread of venereal infection accelerated as more and more strangers found their way to the archipelago. For four decades starting in 1819 the Islands were the most important crossroads in the central Pacific for victualling, repairs and shore leave for the whalers rushing into that ocean in pursuit of sperm whales. In 1855 William Hillebrand, MD, stated flatly that his opinion was that there was no place on earth where venereal infection was as common as in Hawaii. It is, he said, 'no random assertion, but one based on experience and approximative calculation, that in 10 natives 9 have been infected with this disease at one time or another in their life'. The archipelago had become 'one great brothel', said David Malo, the missionaries' favourite among the Christianised and de-cultured Hawaiians. 'For this cause God is angry, and he is diminishing the people, and they are nigh unto desolation.'[54] (By 'people' he meant, of course, not the *haole* but the Hawaiians.)

The Hawaiians' low birth rate appalled and fascinated the *haole*. Victorian moralists blamed it on 'the premature ripening and exhaustion of the reproductive powers', i.e. too much too soon. They believed that sexual generosity *per se* diminished fertility, 'as the history of prostitution shows that it everywhere does, – though *why*, is by no means entirely clear'.[55] Sir Paul Edmund Strzelecki, famed explorer of Australia and pillar of the British Empire, had a theory about the low rate of reproduction of the Hawaiians and the

[52] Robert Louis Stevenson, *Travels in Hawaii*, ed. A. Grove (Honolulu, 1973), p. 81.
[53] George Vancouver, *A Voyage of Discovery to the North Pacific Ocean and Round the World*, 4 vols. (London, 1801), I, pp. 377–8.
[54] Kuykendall, *The Hawaiian Kingdom, 1778–1854*, pp. 305–13; Hillebrand, 'Report on Labor and Population', p. 75; David Malo, 'Decrease of Population', *Hawaiian Spectator*, 2 (1839), p. 128. Even Herman Melville, who was present in Hawaii in this period and who cannot be accused of looking at the scene with a missionary's eyes, was appalled: see Herman Melville, *Typee, a Peep at Polynesian Life* (Evanston, Ill., 1968), pp. 256–8.
[55] Blackman, *Making of Hawaii*, pp. 213–14.

other indigenous peoples he had seen on his travels in the Pacific and North and South America. According to the Strzelecki Law (as he modestly called it) once a native woman bears a white man's child, she will ever after be sterile when she mates with a man of her own race. He did not explain how this worked, but claimed that it 'follows laws as cogent, though as mysterious, as the rest of those connected with generation'.[56]

The Strzelecki Law was an augustly self-serving interpretation of the evidence that white men were spreading venereal diseases among aboriginal women in the New World and Oceania. These infections killed many women, plus children in the womb and others in the first years of life. Mr Rollins, surgeon-major on board La Pérouse's ship in 1786, claimed that he saw Hawaiian children of seven and eight years with the lesions of congenital venereal disease.[57] Endemic venereal infections probably were in part the explanation for the often cited general debility of the population, and, as well, for the Hawaiians with 'eyes rendered blind – noses entirely destroyed – mouths monstrously drawn aside from their natural position' picking their way through the alleys of Honolulu long before Hansen's Disease spread in the Islands. Most subtly pernicious of all was the damage the venereal infections wreaked on the reproductive systems of the Hawaiian women, preventing the conception and birth of thousands. James J. Jarves, one of Hawaii's very earliest historians, wrote in 1847 that venereal infections were poisoning 'the very fountains of life'.[58]

Captain Cook came to the Hawaiian archipelago in 1778, where he encountered a population in robust health, if we are to trust eye-witness accounts. In the century that followed the population plunged steeply, almost irreversibly, in number. It is a Gothic tale worth studying in and of itself, but that is not my objective. How useful is it as a model for what happened to the Amerindians?

It supports the validity of the hundreds of exasperatingly brief and undetailed reports of devastating disease and population crashes on the expanding frontiers of Europe's colonial empires in the New

---

[56] *Ibid.*, p. 214; H. M. E. Heney, *In a Dark Glass; the Story of Paul Edmond Strzelecki* (Sydney, 1961), p. 164.

[57] *Voyage of La Pérouse*, p. 98.

[58] Chapin, 'Remarks on the Sandwich Islands', pp. 257–8, 263; Hillebrand, 'Report on Labor and Population', pp. 73, 75; Jarves, *History of the Hawaiian Islands*, p. 232.

World, from the Greater Antilles in the sixteenth century to the Amazonian hinterlands in the twentieth. We should look for similar events on the frontiers of people of similar pathological and expansionistic characteristics: the Chinese, for instance.

The Hawaiian record also suggests that we need to look at birth rates of the aboriginal casualties of western expansion more carefully than we have. There is no denying that death rates soared as communicable diseases spread in advance of and along with western imperialists. But birth rates often plunged, too, and we are not so sure why.

Let us compare the demographic histories of the Hawaiians and of Europe's city dwellers. My guess is that the latter in the Renaissance and seventeenth and eighteenth centuries had death rates not tremendously lower than those of the nineteenth-century Hawaiians in all but their worst years. The continental urban populations made up their losses by replacement from two sources: births within the cities and, more important, immigration from the countryside. Children exposed to urban infections from birth were more resistant to them than immigrants from the countryside, but were not numerous. Without the immigrants, the cities would have been no more than large villages, given the nature of the diseases in circulation and the primitive hygiene of the urbanites.[59]

Like Europe's cities, the Hawaiian Islands were rescued from depopulation by immigration. Chinese coolies began arriving in the 1850s, to be followed by waves of labourers from Japan, the Philippines, Portugal and elsewhere. That influx saved the Islands from the kind of demographic and economic decline that afflicted sixteenth-century Mexico, but did the native Hawaiians no good whatsoever. By 1878 the total population of Hawaii had hit bottom and was at last rising, but the number of Hawaiians continued to fall until the next century.[60]

In the cities of Europe of the *ancien régime* spates of new marriages and births between the hard times also helped to compensate for the plunges of the birth rate associated with crises such as epidemics, wars and famines. Graphs of the birth rate through time

[59] Flinn, *European Demographic System*, pp. 22–3.
[60] Kuykendall, *The Hawaiian Kingdom, 1778–1854*, pp. 328–31; Kuykendall, *The Hawaiian Kingdom, 1854–1876*, pp. 178–96; Woodrow W. Borah, *New Spain's Century of Depression* (Berkeley, 1951), *passim*; Schmitt, *Demographic Statistics*, p. 10; Nordyke, *Peopling of Hawai'i*, p. 19.

have a sawtooth profile, up and down, up and down.[61] A graph of the Hawaiian birth rate in the post-Cook century is similar, *but includes only the downs*.

Sir Paul Strzelecki asked the right question, though he produced a worthless answer. We must ask the question again. What was wrong with the reproductive capacities of the peoples he encountered on the frontiers of European expansion? What we have learned about the Hawaiians suggests that we should look for indications of the infanticide-by-neglect, and, possibly of greater importance, venereal disease. Sexually transmitted disease circulated through European populations, also, but not to the extent that was common among nearly all classes of the Hawaiians, a sexually exploited population with a lethally obsolete set of sexual mores. William F. Blackman, a nineteenth-century historian of Hawaii, found in the affairs of North American Indians a story he considered relevant to what had happened to the Hawaiians. An 1895 report from the United States Bureau of Indian Affairs told of two groups of Amerindians: the first consisting of four tribes with limited contact with Euro-Americans, of chaste habits, and no venereal diseases; and the second of seven tribes in continual contact with Euro-Americans, of unchaste habits, and 'saturated with venereal disease'. The former group was actually increasing in number. The latter was in steep decline, having suffered a diminution of 43 per cent in the previous thirteen years.[62]

We need to know more about the sexual mores of the many and various Amerindian peoples.[63] Was there a correlation between the restrictive or liberal attitudes toward sexuality of the various groups and their survival or extinction? We also need to know more about the sexual attitudes of the white chroniclers through whose some-times averted eyes we see the Amerindians of the past. How more or less frank about sexuality were, for instance, Spaniards *c.* 1500 than Anglo-Americans of the nineteenth century? Michele de Cuneo began his letter describing his adventures on Columbus's 1493 voyage to the New World with a dedication to 'Jesus and His Glorious Mother Mary, from whom all blessings proceed', but had

[61] Flinn, *European Demographic System*, p. 54.
[62] Blackman, *Making of Hawaii*, p. 216.
[63] Two places to start the search are John D'Emilio and Estelle B. Freedman, *Intimate Matters; a History of Sexuality in America* (New York, 1988), pp. 6–9, 87–8, and Walter L. Williams, *The Spirit and the Flesh. Sexual Diversity in American Indian Culture* (Boston, 1986), *passim*.

no compunction about including a vignette about the Carib woman he thrashed with a rope until she submitted 'in such a manner that I can tell you that she seemed to have been brought up in a school of harlots'. Anglo-Americans were much more restrained than that, but was it in behaviour or frankness? Sarah Winnemucca Hopkins of the Paiutes tells of Amerindian mothers 'afraid to have more children, for fear they shall have daughters, who are not safe even in their mother's presence'.[64]

How common among a given group of Amerindians was the custom of greeting powerful strangers with sexual hospitality? Were some groups, to use the Sahlins word again, Aphrodisian? The Chinook who lived around the mouth of Oregon's Columbia river may have been so. When the Meriwether Lewis and William Clark expedition crossed the continent and reached that part of the coast in 1805 the local Amerindian traders welcomed the travellers with sexual satisfactions. 'Among these people,' wrote Lewis, fumbling to understand a culture not his own,

> as indeed among all Indians, the prostitution of unmarried women is so far from being considered criminal or improper, that females themselves solicit the favors of the other sex, with the entire approbation of their friends and connections. Her person is, in fact, often the only property of a young female, and is therefore the medium of trade, the return for presents, and the reward for service.[65]

Lewis and Clark and their men were by no means the first whites the Chinook women had seen. Whites, come round the Horn, had been frequenting that coast to trade for sea-otter skins ever since Captain Cook obtained such pelts there in 1778 and discovered that the Chinese would pay a fortune for them. For example, a man named J. Bowman had preceded Lewis and Clark, and left his name for the explorers to see tattooed on the arm of one of the women. Several members of the Lewis and Clark expedition contracted venereal disease from the Chinook, rotten with such infections already. In time Amerindians as far away as Alaska learned to call venereal disease 'Chinook'. The usual succession of Amerindian

[64] *Journals and Other Documents on the Life and Voyages of Christopher Columbus*, trans. Samuel Eliot Morison (New York, 1963), p. 212; Winnemucca Hopkins, *Life Among the Paiutes*, p. 48.
[65] Meriwether Lewis and William Clark, *The History of the Lewis and Clark Expedition*, ed. Elliott Coues, 3 vols. (New York, n.d.), II, p. 779.

troubles, most conspicuously a crushing epidemic of the 'cold sick' (probably malaria) in the early 1830s, reduced the once numerous Chinook, already weakened and diseased at the beginning of the century, to a paltry residuum of 112 in 1885.[66]

Lewis's pronouncement that 'prostitution' was common 'among all Indians' was certainly coloured by cultural misunderstanding, and indeed was wholly wrong, but we should not reject it totally just because we think it originated in bigotry. People without long experience with venereal disease – the Hawaiians, for instance – perhaps had sexual mores very unlike people of long experience: the ancient Hebrews and the Christians, for instance. We should not be surprised if we find that people unfearful of venereal disease have used sexual favours as a currency in diplomacy and commerce just as they did and we do food and drink.

What are the implications for the history of early Virginia of Captain John Smith's story of having been received by women of Powhatan's people in the following fashion in 1608? They formed a circle and danced around their visitor for an hour, 'oft falling into their infernall passions', and then 'Having reaccomodated themselves, they solemnly invited him [Smith] to their lodgings, where he was no sooner within the house, but all these Nymphes more tormented him then ever, with crowding, pressing, and hanging about him, most tediously crying, Loue you not me? loue not me?'[67] Was Smith, pen in hand and middle-aged, indulging himself in a lubricious fiction about his swashbuckling prime, or had Powhatan made an extravagantly friendly gesture – a gesture by which he may have innocently poisoned 'the very fountains of life' of his people? Europe was in the midst of a pandemic of syphilis in this era, and if Smith did not carry the infection, it is likely that several of his comrades did.[68]

The native peoples of Virginia and bordering colonies suffered epidemics in the next two centuries comparable to those endured by the Hawaiians. These Amerindians, however, were not (according to

[66] *Ibid.*, pp. 778–80; Robert H. Ruby and John A. Brown, *The Chinook Indians, Traders on the Lower Columbia River* (Norman, Oklahoma, 1976), pp. 64–5, 127, 156, 188–200, 232–3; John R. Swanton, *The Indian Tribes of North America* (Washington, DC, 1952), pp. 418–19.

[67] *Travels and Works of Captain John Smith*, ed. Edward Arber, 2 vols. (New York, 1967), II, p. 436.

[68] Alfred W. Crosby, *The Columbian Exchange. Biological and Cultural Consequences of 1492* (Westport, Conn., 1972), pp. 156–60.

Euro-American sources) similarly Aphrodisian, which may explain why their numbers *may* not have plunged as steeply as the Hawaiians'. But these Amerindians, too, acquired venereal disease, and were, said John Heckewelder, a missionary who lived among them in the eighteenth century, 'greatly infected with it'.

The Comte de Buffon, author of the immense *L'Histoire Naturelle*, one of the monumental works of the Enlightenment, offered a fanciful explanation for the mysterious plunge in the numbers of the native peoples of the Americas. He announced in 1778 in volume 5 of his *Histoire* that Amerindian males had meagre genitalia, lacked sexual drive, fathered few children and ignored those they did father. Nature had 'treated them rather like a stepmother than a parent, by denying them the invigorating sentiment of love and the strong desire of multiplying their species'. Thomas Jefferson, an American patriot with first-hand knowledge of the Amerindians of Virginia, countered that in sexual ardour and love for their children they were certainly the equal of Europeans. He did grant, however, that the Amerindians had comparatively few children; he blamed this on birth control of some sort, abortion, hunger and overexertion.[69] An examination of the Hawaiian experience suggests a broader and even grimmer interpretation.

As we examine the histories of the decline of Amerindian peoples, we must, of course, take into account the familiar factors of massacre, alcoholism, extinction of game animals and expropriation of farm land. In addition, we must attend to the less familiar calamities of exotic water- and breath-borne diseases; and, finally, to the secret blights of abortion, infanticide and infanticidally negligent child care, venereal infection, sterility and despair.

---

[69] Robert Beverley, *The History and Present State of Virginia* (Chapel Hill, NC, 1947), pp. 170–1; John Heckewelder, *History, Manners, and Customs of the Indian Nations who Once Inhabited Pennsylvania and the Neighbouring States* (Philadelphia, 1876), pp. 261–2; Henry Steele Commager and Elmo Giordanetti (eds.), *Was America a Mistake? An Eighteenth-Century Controversy* (Columbia, SC, 1967), pp. 60–1, 233; Merrill D. Peterson (ed.), *The Portable Thomas Jefferson* (New York, 1975), pp. 93–8.

9. *Plague panic and epidemic politics in India, 1896–1914*[1]

RAJNARAYAN CHANDAVARKAR

Between 1896 and 1914, bubonic plague killed over 8 million people,[2] a modest estimate which does not allow for cases which were concealed, misdiagnosed or wrongly classified. Of all the various epidemics which afflicted India in the late nineteenth and early twentieth centuries, a Kaliyuga, a period of very high mortality, stagnant, even falling population and declining life expectancy,[3] the plague was not the most destructive. Malaria and tuberculosis killed more than twice as many people over a similar period;[4] in barely four months, the influenza epidemic of 1918–19 accounted for twice as many;[5] smallpox and cholera counted their

[1] I am grateful to Jennifer Davis, Larry Epstein and Sheilagh Ogilvie for their comments on an earlier draft of this chapter and to the participants at the Past and Present Conference in September 1989, and seminars at St Antony's College, Oxford, the Centre of South Asian Studies, Cambridge, and the Wellcome Unit for the History of Medicine, Cambridge, where versions of this paper were presented.
[2] *Annual Reports on Sanitary Measures in India, Parliamentary Papers* (henceforth, *PP*), *passim*; R. Pollitzer, *Plague* (Geneva, 1954), p. 26; L. Fabian Hirst, *The Conquest of Plague. A Study of the Evolution of Epidemiology* (Oxford, 1953), pp. 296–301.
[3] The population of Bombay Presidency declined in three of the five decennial periods between 1871 and 1921. See L. Visaria and P. Visaria, 'Population, 1757–1947', in D. Kumar (ed.), *The Cambridge Economic History of India*, II *1757–1947* (Cambridge, 1982), pp. 463–532, especially Tables 5.7 and 5.12; Kingsley Davis, *The Population of India and Pakistan* (Princeton, NJ, 1951), pp. 33–66, especially, on life expectancy, Tables 16 and 17, p. 63.
[4] I. Klein, 'Death in India', *Journal of Asian Studies* (henceforth, *JAS*), 32, 4 (1973), pp. 642–3; *idem*, 'Malaria and Mortality in Bengal', *Indian Economic and Social History Review* (henceforth, *IESHR*), 9, 2 (1972), pp. 132–60; Davis, *Population*, pp. 53–7.
[5] I. D. Mills, 'Influenza in India during 1918–19', *IESHR*, 23, 1 (1986), pp. 1–40; Davis, *Population*, Appendix B, p. 237.

death toll in millions.[6] Yet no other epidemic evoked the fear and panic generated by the plague.

The plague epidemic prompted massive state intervention to control its spread. It also sometimes provoked fierce resistance, riots, occasionally mob attacks on Europeans and even the assassination of British officials. The vigorous and energetic intervention of the state, in itself prompted by the general panic, bore no direct relation to the virulence of the epidemic. The focus of the state's most vigorous measures was Bombay city and its Presidency between 1896 and about 1902. But plague mortality continued to rise thereafter, reached its peak between 1903 and 1907, exceeding the levels of the late 1890s by twelvefold, and proved far more lethal in the Punjab. Yet neither plague policy nor plague riots in the Punjab appear to have displayed the zeal or acquired the political prominence they achieved in Bombay.[7]

Underlying the nature of this response is a further paradox. The late nineteenth century was a period of enormous self-confidence in medical science and, particularly, in its newly founded and burgeoning branch of tropical medicine.[8] The plague epidemic in India became the occasion for the most intensive international research on bubonic plague and its eventual findings largely laid the foundations for, indeed established much of, what is now known about the disease.[9] Yet the measures adopted by the colonial state at the turn of the twentieth century remained highly

[6]   D. Arnold, 'Smallpox and Colonial Medicine in Nineteenth Century India', in D. Arnold (ed.), *Imperial Medicine and Indigenous Societies* (Manchester, 1988), pp. 45–65; *idem*, 'Cholera Mortality in British India, 1817–1947', in T. Dyson (ed.), *India's Historical Demography. Studies in Famine, Disease and Society* (London, 1989), pp. 261–84; *idem*, 'Cholera and Colonialism in British India', *Past and Present*, no. 113 (1986), pp. 118–51.

[7]   Over 354,000 died of the plague between 1896 and 1900. This figure rose to slightly under 4.5 million for the period 1903–7. Between 1903 and 1907, Punjab alone accounted for between one quarter and one half of the plague deaths each year. *Annual Reports on Sanitary Measures in India, PP, passim.*

[8]   M. Worboys, 'The Emergence of Tropical Medicine: A Study in the Establishment of a Scientific Speciality', in G. Lemaine, R. Macleod, M. Mulkay and P. Weingart (eds.), *Perspectives on the Emergence of Scientific Disciplines* (The Hague, 1976), pp. 75–98; H. H. Scott, *A History of Tropical Medicine*, 2 vols. (London, 1939).

[9]   Hirst, *Conquest of Plague*; I. J. Catanach, 'Plague and the Tensions of Empire, 1896–1918', in Arnold (ed.), *Imperial Medicine*, pp. 149–71; Scott, *Tropical Medicine*, II, pp. 702–67.

reminiscent of the Black Death or the epidemic in seventeenth-century England.[10]

The intensity of the panic which gripped colonial officials and humble subjects alike suggests the need to examine how the epidemic came to be constructed. Studies of epidemics in India have ranged widely, examining their demographic implications, or tracing their course and their attendant social and political effects. They have examined the administrative problems posed by epidemics,[11] the conflicts and rivalries which they opened up within government,[12] how the state and elites exploited the chaos they caused to extend their control,[13] how political factions within the Congress arranged themselves around the event[14] and even the 'indigenous' cultural response to western science and colonial policies.[15] These studies have been illuminating but they have often proceeded piecemeal. This chapter is predicated on the assumption that epidemics do not represent a single, integrated phenomenon but signify different things to different people. It argues that their inherent interest lies less in the discrete events which occur in their wake, than in the manner of their construction. The historical process of their construction not only illuminates wider relationships between social groups and between state and society, but it can also be argued that the constituent events of an epidemic upon which historians focus might be grasped most firmly when they are acknowledged to be, separately and discretely, a function of the very process of its

---

[10] P. Slack, 'The Response to Plague in Early Modern England: Public Policies and their Consequences', in J. Walter and R. Schofield (eds.), *Famine, Disease and the Social Order in Early Modern Society* (Cambridge, 1989), pp. 167–87.

[11] Arnold, 'Cholera and Colonialism'; *idem*, 'Smallpox and Colonial Medicine'; *idem*, 'Touching the Body: Perspectives on the Indian Plague, 1896–1900', in R. Guha (ed.), *Subaltern Studies*, V (New Delhi, 1987), pp. 55–90; I. J. Catanach, 'Plague and the Indian Village, 1896–1914', in P. Robb (ed.), *Rural India. Land, Power and Society under British Rule* (London, 1983), pp. 216–43; *idem*, 'Plague and the Tensions of Empire'; I. Klein, 'Urban Development and Death: Bombay City, 1870–1914', *Modern Asian Studies* (henceforth, *MAS*), 20, 4 (1986), pp. 725–54; *idem*, 'Plague, Policy and Popular Unrest in British India', *MAS*, 22, 4 (1988), pp. 723–55.

[12] See, especially, Catanach, 'Plague and the Tensions of Empire'.

[13] Arnold, 'Touching the Body'; *idem*, 'Cholera and Colonialism'.

[14] I. J. Catanach, 'Poona Politicians and the Plague', in J. Masselos (ed.), *Struggling and Ruling. The Indian National Congress, 1885–1985* (New Delhi, 1987), pp. 198–215.

[15] Arnold, 'Touching the Body'; *idem*, 'Cholera and Colonialism'; and Klein, 'Plague, Policy and Popular Unrest'.

construction. This chapter will, therefore, try to explore how the plague epidemic was put together and the interplay between some of the numerous elements which made it up: colonial perceptions of Indian society, medical and scientific rivalries, the interaction between the plague administrators and the people upon whom their attentions focussed. These perceptions, ideologies and political processes were not created for the first time by the plague epidemic; they were indeed endemic to colonial India. However, the significance of these relationships, and of the tensions and antagonisms they generated during the epidemic, lies in the ways in which their interplay helped to construct the panic of the late 1890s.

The policies of the state and the popular response to them have been frequently portrayed in terms of the inexorable conflict between 'Western anti-plague measures and popular culture',[16] the unavoidable clash of 'two different, often antagonistic value-systems, the one Indian, the other European'.[17] Indian responses, it is suggested, served as 'a reminder of the great cultural gulf which divided the colonizers and the colonized'.[18] There was, we are told, an 'Indian view of disease and its treatment' which called for 'family involvement and religious ministration, not secular segregation'.[19] I will be arguing, however, that there was neither a uniform nor a homogeneous, culturally specific Indian response, and further that the response of the populace, like that of the state, was integral to, and the product of, the generalised panic from which none escaped. While antipathy to the plague measures was often shared by disparate social groups who might have nothing else in common, it arose less from the stirrings of an autonomous realm of popular culture than from the political conjuncture in which the plague was constructed.

I

On 23 September 1896, Dr A. C. Viegas, medical practitioner and local politician, declared before the Bombay Municipal Corporation, and thereby to the world, that bubonic plague had broken out in the city.[20] Thus, the plague acquired the character of an epidemic.

---

[16] Klein, 'Plague, Policy and Popular Unrest', p. 739.
[17] Arnold, 'Cholera and Colonialism', p. 119.   [18] *Ibid.*, p. 134.
[19] *Ibid.*, p. 137.   [20] *Times of India*, 24 September 1896, pp. 4, 5.

The colonial state was, at first, reluctant to lend its authority to a panic which might cripple trade and threaten the social order. The Health Officer conceded that 'the peculiar type of fever referred to by Dr Viegas . . . was of a suspicious character' and 'appeared to be in some respects of a bubonic character'.[21] In the following weeks, as the death toll mounted, officials referred to the disease as the 'fever plague' or 'bubonic fever' but never 'bubonic plague'.[22] It was only in early October when the Viceroy provided London with confirmation of 'true bubonic plague'[23] that the epidemic finally received official sanction.

But the mere suspicion of the plague was always likely to wrest the situation out of their control. Viegas's announcement had set the alarm bells ringing across the world. The Calcutta Corporation, fearing that Bombay's fate today might be Bengal's tomorrow, began to discuss precautionary measures on the following day.[24] By early October, ports in South-East Asia, the Persian Gulf and East Africa had applied plague regulations to all vessels arriving from Bombay.[25] The French feared the prospect of riots at Marseilles[26] and pressures mounted for 'restrictive measures to prevent passage of [*sic*] plague to Europe'.[27]

Once the colonial state was compelled to act, it initiated a vigorous, indeed draconian, programme of measures. The plague measures, as W. C. Rand described them from Poona, 'were perhaps the most drastic that had ever been taken to stamp out an epidemic'.[28] They were, indeed, to cost Rand his life. Their primary objective was to identify and isolate the sick, remove them swiftly to hospital and segregate their contacts in 'health camps'. Their houses were to be disinfected, their floors dug up, for they were believed to

---

[21] *Ibid.*, p. 5.

[22] Hirst, *Conquest of Plague*, p. 77.

[23] Viceroy to Secretary of State for India, 2 Oct. 1896, 'Papers Relating to the Outbreak of Bubonic Plague in India with Statement Showing the Quarantine and Other Restrictions Recently Placed upon Indian Trade, up to March 1897', p. 3, *PP*, 1897, LXIII.

[24] *Times of India*, 25 September 1896, p. 5.

[25] Government of Bombay (henceforth, GOB), General Department (henceforth, General), Vol. 131, Compilation no. 178, Part I, and Vol. 132, Compilation no. 178, Part II. Maharashtra State Archives (henceforth, MSA).

[26] Catanach, 'Plague and the Tensions of Empire', pp. 151–2.

[27] Secretary of State for India to Governor of Bombay, 18 January 1897, 'Papers Relating to the Outbreak of Bubonic Plague', p. 5, *PP*, 1897, LXIII.

[28] *Draft of Report to Government of Bombay by the Late Mr W. C. Rand, I.C.S., Chairman, Poona Plague Committee* (n.p, n.d [1897?]), p. 3. MSA.

harbour the offending microbes, and their personal effects fumigated and sometimes burnt. Physicians and families were required by law to notify all cases of sickness and 'all cases of fever were treated as "suspects"'.[29] The sick were to be isolated in hospitals, where most died, and their relatives segregated in special camps. Corpses had to be compulsorily inspected before disposal and the procedures for the registration of deaths were tightened. Vigorous steps were taken to disinfect the whole environment. Houses and gullies 'under any suspicion were at once flushed and disinfected'; buildings were limewashed or cleansed, usually at the owners' expense; and the drains and sewers were flushed every day with 3 million gallons of a dilution of carbolic acid and sea water. The city was literally drenched in disinfectant solution. Hankin, a bacteriologist with the Plague Research Committee, reported that he 'had to put up an umbrella before entering some plague houses in order to protect himself against the deluge of carbolic acid solution descending from the upper stories into which the disinfectant was pumped by a fire engine for spraying on the walls and floors of the premises'.[30] In addition, a system of surveillance was instituted to examine cargo and passengers at the ports,[31] and inspection checkpoints and detention camps became a common feature of the railway system as the movement of people into or out of the city was severely restricted. As plague began to spread, similar measures were extended across a wider area and were sometimes enforced by British soldiers.

This forceful and aggressive intrusion of the colonial state into the private domain was not simply dramatic and brutal but also novel and unprecedented. Its effect was often to intensify and quicken the panic occasioned by the disease. As the epidemic spread across the sub-continent, the severity of the plague measures was matched only by their desperation and it is not surprising that they met with fierce, if sporadic, resistance.

Then, almost as suddenly as the disease had appeared, the stringency of the plague measures was relaxed. In October 1906, the *Times of India* observed that no notice was taken of the revival and

[29] *The Bombay Plague Being A History of the Progress of Plague in the Bombay Presidency from September 1896 to June 1899*, compiled by Capt. J. K. Condon (Bombay, 1900), p. 125.
[30] Hirst, *Conquest of Plague*, p. 117.
[31] Port Health Officer quoted in Condon, *The Bombay Plague*, p. 136.

increase of plague in Poona, 'whereas a few years ago it would have caused a panic'.[32] This was not simply a reaction to popular hostility and violence. Although plague riots had often been heeded by the state as a warning that it should proceed with caution, the recrudescence of the epidemic frequently 'compelled us to attempt more drastic and comprehensive measures'.[33] Nor can this change of heart be attributed to the decreasing virulence of the epidemic since plague mortality rose as the panic subsided.

It was perhaps more important to the changing direction of plague policy that the disease had begun to acquire a specific social character. If at the outset, Viegas had failed to find any poor people among the afflicted, it became increasingly obvious, as the epidemic worked its way through the sub-continent, that 'the poorer classes suffered most severely'.[34] In the memorable phrase of Surgeon-General Harvey, Director-General of the Indian Medical Department, bubonic plague was 'a disease of filth, a disease of dirt, and a disease of poverty'.[35] As the disease took on the character of a plague of the poor, it came to be seen as endemic. 'We Europeans are indifferent', declared one of their number as the plague revived yet again, in its annual cycle, in March 1902: 'for the statistics show that fewer Europeans have died from plague than die each year from cholera, so we can chance plague as we chance cholera.'[36] Bubonic plague had become simply another disease in the formidable pantheon of plagues which flourished in India's malignant climate and integral to the burden which the white man carried dutifully.

II

The pattern of state intervention in the plague epidemic was unique in the history of colonial India. It cannot be taken to exemplify 'the interventionist ambitions and capacity of India's mature colonial

---

[32] *Times of India*, 13 October 1906, quoted in Catanach, 'Plague and the Tensions of Empire', p. 169 fn. 82.

[33] Lord Sandhurst and others, Government of Bombay, Judicial, to Her Majesty's Principal Private Secretary of State for India in Council, London, 9 April 1898, in GOB, General (Plague), Vol. 389, Compilation no. 298, 1898. MSA.

[34] Condon, *The Bombay Plague*, p. 132.

[35] Quoted in the *Report of the Indian Plague Commission, 1898–99, with Appendices and Summary*, V, p. 170, *PP*, 1902, LXXII.

[36] *Pioneer*, 15 March, 1902, quoted in Catanach, 'Plague and the Tensions of Empire', p. 159.

state'.[37] The scale and consistency of state intervention, as it entered homes, meddled with caste and religious practices, regulated the disposal of the dead and restricted the free movement of people, was unprecedented. And the colonial state would never again orchestrate such a penetrative programme of government, intrude so remorselessly upon the private domain, or attempt to exert such ambitious and extensive measures of social control. The frenzied zeal with which the colonial state launched itself at its subjects was integral, as both symptom and cause, to the panic which accompanied the epidemic. It played a determining, perhaps creative, role in the political construction of the plague epidemic.

The severity and desperation of the government's response may be explained partly in terms of folk memories of the Black Death and partly in terms of the possible imperial consequences of the plague. An international embargo on Indian shipping not only threatened to close an important market and source of raw materials for Britain but also disturb the intricate system for the multilateral settlement of its balance of payments, in which India played a large and vital part.[38] The extensive commercial and financial connections centred on Bombay made it seem highly improbable that the epidemic could be contained within the city.[39] If it spread through the subcontinent, it might devastate India's social order and economic base, flatten the pivot of empire and undermine the foundation of Britain's influence between the Yellow and the Red Seas.

These were powerful pressures but they do not provide a sufficient explanation. The European powers were quickly impressed by the stringency of the plague measures and by 1897 there was little evidence that the scourge was about to engulf the West. Nor was the threat to trade insuperable. The International Sanitary Convention which met at Venice in 1897 to discuss the plague favoured the medical inspection of people and their personal effects over embargoes on the import or movement of merchandise.[40] Moreover,

[37] Arnold, 'Touching the Body', p. 56.
[38] S. B. Saul, *Studies in British Overseas Trade* (Liverpool, 1960), pp. 188–207; B. R. Tomlinson, 'India and the British Empire, 1880–1935', *IESHR*, 12, 4 (1975), pp. 339–80.
[39] For an account of Bombay's relationship with its hinterland and its role in the Indian economy, see R. Chandavarkar, *The Origins of Industrial Capitalism in India. Business Strategies and the Working Classes in Bombay, 1900–1940* (Cambridge, 1992), ch. 1.
[40] Hirst, *Conquest of Plague*, pp. 389–90.

plague mortality in the first three years of the epidemic did not distort the ordinary death rate for the sub-continent. Although the threat to trade and empire seemed less grave in the late 1890s, the vigour of the plague administration did not slacken.

So the immoderate, perhaps irrational, severity of the state's response requires that we dig at a deeper level. The official construction of the plague epidemic was shaped by its assumptions about its own statecraft as well as its perceptions of the governed. In the course of the epidemic, colonial officials not only expressed these assumptions with unusual freedom, but also developed them to their logical extreme and further were able to manifest them in practice. The plague, it would appear, became the focus of the most terrible anxieties which India evoked in the British imagination. India appeared to be a land of potential, sometimes hidden, dangers, political and corporeal, moral and cultural. The defence of the 'thin red line' could not be left to the redcoats alone. The struggle to maintain it had to be waged individually against moral and physical sickness, collectively against intrigue, conspiracy and rebellion.

Among the most awesome and compelling dangers represented by India, because it was both intimate and insidious, was the threat of disease. If, in the British perception, India was a repository of infectious diseases, there were two possible remedies. Since most diseases were caused by filth, one obvious solution lay in a massive programme of sanitary measures undertaken by the state. Alternatively, a minimalist answer might be found in segregation and the rigorous maintenance of a substantial social distance from the native town and its inhabitants.

Neither proved to be practicable. The British in India, as the Sanitary Commissioner reported in 1894, would 'never be safe so long as the native population and its towns and villages are left uncleansed to act as a reservoir of dirt and disease'.[41] But the task of cleaning the sub-continent was too gigantic to contemplate. Despite the prominence of the threat of disease in British perceptions of India, sanitation and sewers, town planning and public health occupied a low place in the imperial order of priorities. The colonial state was unwilling to incur the cost and averse to bearing the political risks of sanitising India. For such a project would require

---

[41] *Annual Report of the Sanitary Commissioner with the Government of India, 1894* (Calcutta, 1896), p. 27.

the British to meddle deeply and dangerously in the habits and customs of the natives. Yet as they knew only too well the key to the enjoyment of their political kingdom lay not in social engineering but in salutary neglect. If the problem of public health was thus conceived in terms which could not possibly allow its resolution, the insanitary and unhygienic conditions of India's towns and villages, however dangerous, were increasingly portrayed as innate and natural to the sub-continent. Colonial officials, as the Sanitary Commissioner for the North-Western Provinces observed in 1885, did not hold themselves 'to blame for this condition of things. Plainly, indeed, the view was expressed that if the natives chose to live amidst such insanitary surroundings, it was their own concern. And how they managed to do it without greater penalty of death than seemed apparent, was a frequent cause of expressed surprise.'[42]

It was no more viable for the British to segregate themselves in hygienic, native-free, sanitary enclaves. Indian society was too complex and too turbulent to be managed from afar. It was unrealistic to expect that the army, which employed the overwhelming majority of British residents in India, would function effectively if it was segregated along racial lines. Segregation in India remained more a conceptual than a physical reality. Thus, army cantonments were inhabited predominantly by poor, low caste Indians – prostitutes, hawkers and halalkhores – whose proximity the British so feared and whose habits they so deeply deplored.[43] Similarly, in the larger urban settlements of Europeans, segregation was even more fervently imagined and even more ineffectually maintained. At various times in the nineteenth century, town planners in Bombay city envisaged residential segregation as an integral part of its future development. But as an architect told one such committee: 'A good many middle class Europeans live in Tarwadi and Byculla. Poor Europeans live in the same class of houses as poor Natives.' Moreover, he added, 'the rich and poor have always lived together –

---

[42] *Eighteenth Annual Report of the Sanitary Commissioner of the North-Western Provinces, 1885* (Allahabad, 1886), p. 60.

[43] *Report of the Sanitary Commissioner for Bombay, 1867* (Bombay, 1868), Report on Colaba, Inspection Report, no. 1, pp. 10–11. See also the excellent article by J. W. Cell, 'Anglo-Indian Medical Theory and the Origins of Segregation in West Africa', *American Historical Review*, 91, 2 (1986), pp. 307–35.

the former in the principal, the latter in the back streets – and always will'.[44]

As the possibility of treating the cause of their anxieties grew more remote, so these anxieties grew more entrenched and their social and political implications seemed more menacing. Increasingly, the British became fatalistic, though never sanguine, about the threat of disease. The outbreak of bubonic plague challenged this fatalism. The plague represented the apotheosis of the threat of disease. Moreover, its threat was highly personalised; it attacked scores of Europeans in the first few months.[45] Immediate and summary action now seemed imperative. Policy initiatives which had once seemed impolitic now seemed indispensable; those which seemed to lie beyond the capacity of the state suddenly fell within its grasp and no effort or expense was to be spared. Intervention in a style which was considered unthinkable before was now seriously pursued.

Bombay city had grown prodigiously in the second half of the nineteenth century, but it had lacked the most basic infrastructure to accommodate this growth. Its most densely populated areas in 1900 had only decades earlier been lying beneath the sea. Health Officers in the city had regularly predicted impending doom and devastating epidemics. In 1875, T. S. Weir, observing 'the low standard of living and the insufficient diet of the majority of the people' and 'their weak and puny constitutions', predicted the periodic and recurrent 'outbreak of one or other of the epidemic diseases; it may not be Cholera; it may not be Small Pox, but some disease will arise, and sweep off the most effete of the population'.[46] In the early 1890s, the inadequacy of the city's drainage system suggested that 'there will surely come a time when the population of each district will not be able to live in health'.[47] With the plague, it seemed that the time had come. The apocalypse which the Health Officers had long anticipated was now firmly in their midst. To many colonial officials, the

---

[44] Proceedings of the Committee on the Extension of the City of Bombay, 1887, Evidence, Mr D. Gostling, p. 2. GOB, Public Works Department (henceforth, PWD) (General), Vol. 1162, Compilation no. 4133 W, 1868–89. MSA.

[45] Report by T. S. Weir, Executive Health Officer, Bombay Municipality, in P. C. H. Snow, *Report on the Outbreak of Bubonic Plague in Bombay, 1896–97* (Bombay, 1897), pp. 144–5. Eighty-eight Europeans died of the plague between September 1896 and May 1897; many others were attacked by the disease.

[46] Tenth Annual Report of the Health Officer, in *Annual Report of the Municipal Commissioner of Bombay for the Year 1875* (Bombay, 1876), pp. 148–9.

[47] Report of the Health Officer in *Administrative Report of the Municipal Commissioner for the City of Bombay for the Year 1892–3* (Bombay, 1893), p. 383.

plague appeared not simply the product of ineffectual or misconceived policies, but, more especially, divine retribution for sanitary
neglect.

III

It was from this psychology of guilt and terror that the official mind
formulated its strategy to combat the plague. Public health policies
had been often conceived as the application of modern, scientific
knowledge among people who were not only ignorant of the
principles of hygiene but whose traditions and modes of life were
violated by them. The British in India sought to tame the dangers of
the sub-continent and impose order upon its chaos with justice,
rationality and science. It was their privileged access to reason, the
superiority of their knowledge and their ability to implement it
with an incorruptible justice which legitimised their harshest, most
vigorous measures. Thus, W. L. Reade, who took over the plague
administration in Poona after Rand's assassination, proclaimed, 'I
consider that plague operations properly undertaken present some
of the best opportunities for riveting our rule in India' and 'also for
showing the superiority of our Western science and thoroughness.'[48]

Sanitary and medical science was as integral and critical to the
official perception of their statecraft as education and justice. Yet the
formulation of an effective plague policy was seriously hindered by
general ignorance about the causes and transmission of the disease
as well as about possible methods of treatment. At the start of the
epidemic, plague authorities still favoured the view that its cause lay
in a localised miasma, which could nonetheless be caught through
contact with infected persons.[49] The identification of the plague
bacillus simultaneously by Yersin and Kitasato in 1894 had not
resolved the problem of causation when the epidemic took root in
Bombay two years later. Unless the aetiology of the disease was
known, it was unclear whether the bacillus was indeed its cause or

[48] W. L. Reade to Arthur Godley, 3 March 1898, quoted in Catanach, 'Plague and
the Tensions of Empire', p. 154.
[49] Hirst, *Conquest of Plague*, p. 41. According to Hirst, this 'miasmatico-contagious
point of view' was 'favoured until the end of the nineteenth century by many
writers on plague' and indeed, as late as the 1920s, there was 'a vigorous reaction
on the part of an influential group of British epidemiologists against current
conceptions of the role of microbes in the causation of disease': *ibid.*, p. 89.

simply its consequence. Thus, with the advent of plague in Bombay, several official teams of scientists, sponsored by their national governments, 'hastened to the affected city, charged with the task of studying the disease. Probably never before or since has such an imposing array of epidemiological talent assembled in one place for research into a specific disease.'[50] Their findings were to throw as much darkness as light on the subject while thousands continued to die. At times, their investigations proceeded along lines determined less by scientific evidence than by social assumptions.

The initial consensus which had emerged out of the Hong Kong epidemic was that the plague bacilli entered the body through the alimentary canal. This hypothesis had been developed by analogy with cholera and other food- and water-borne infections, which had recently occupied the attention of bacteriologists and sanitary commissioners in India. It was swiftly replaced, following feeding experiments in Bombay which produced negative results, by the suggestion that human beings became infected when cuts and abrasions on their bare feet came into contact with bacilli in the excreta of rats, who it was still assumed acquired it through ingestion. This notion coincided with the recognition that 'patients mostly belonged to the lower classes who commonly go bare-footed and bare-legged'.[51] Circumstantial evidence that 'halalcores who remove the night-soil from the houses, and who form probably the dirtiest portion of the population, were notably free from plague' cast some doubt on this hypothesis. But this difficulty was briskly overcome with the suggestion that 'they are a strong, well-nourished class, of whom only the fittest have survived, and they are highly paid and live well'.[52] Tests on plague patients showed only a tiny proportion of cases in which the bacillus was found in skin abrasions. By 1898, the studies of Hankin and Simond demonstrated that the plague bacillus survived only briefly outside the body and was only rarely, if ever, recovered from supposedly infected objects, including the surface of the soil, foodstuffs, the floors of houses or other articles in areas of infection.[53]

The major breakthrough in the aetiology of bubonic plague occurred when the French bacteriologist, P. L. Simond, published a

[50] *Ibid.*, p. 105.
[51] Condon, *The Bombay Plague*, p. 104; Hirst, *Conquest of Plague*, pp. 111–19.
[52] Condon, *The Bombay Plague*, p. 70.
[53] Hirst, *Conquest of Plague*, p. 117.

paper in 1898 identifying it as a rat disease and postulating that its transmission to man occurred through rat fleas. The case was not experimentally proven to the satisfaction of his fellow bacteriologists and least of all the Indian Plague Commission. To them, it seemed to rely too heavily upon the imagination. The Plague Commission preferred the theory of bare-foot Indians. It was convinced that if rats were involved in the initial outbreak of the disease, the infection was primarily spread through human agency. It poured scorn on Simond's hypothesis that transmission was effected by a blood-sucking insect and although it acknowledged that plague bacilli in rat corpses rapidly died, it adhered to the notion of infection through microbes on the surface of the ground.[54] The rat flea theory provoked such vigorous scepticism primarily because it undermined the assumptions, connecting hypotheses about the nature of the disease to notions of social behaviour and cultural characteristics in India, upon which epidemiological research had been proceeding. Significantly, it was from Sydney, where the cholera analogy and the bare-foot theory were somewhat less obviously sustained, and where images of proliferating microbes and metaphors of contagion strained credulity, that some of the early confirmation of Simond's hypothesis came forth.[55]

In India, medical and official opinion adhered to the view, attractive in this repository of disease, that the plague was spread by contact between human beings. Consequently, the emphasis of policy was placed primarily on early detection and diagnosis, segregation, hospitalisation, disinfection and the close inspection of travellers and merchandise in transit. These policies had been frequently implemented to control infectious diseases. But in the case of the plague, they were carried to their extreme. Since the 1860s, the response to outbreaks of cholera in the army was to move soldiers out of their barracks and house them in temporary camps;[56] now whole villages and even small towns were evacuated. Isolation in a contagious diseases hospital might appear a reasonable precaution; now it was effected under an armed military guard.

[54] *Report of the Indian Plague Commission, 1898–99*, V, pp. 68–71, 75–7, 101–2, 108–11, 122–7, *PP*, 1902, LXXII; Cell, 'Anglo-Indian Medical Theory', pp. 326–7; Catanach, 'Plague and the Tensions of Empire', pp. 158–9.

[55] Hirst, *Conquest of Plague*, pp. 160–9, 144–8; Cell, 'Anglo-Indian Medical Theory', pp. 325–8; Catanach, 'Plague and the Tensions of Empire', pp. 162–3.

[56] Cell, 'Anglo-Indian Medical Theory', p. 322.

Disinfection was another common recourse in times of smallpox or diphtheria; now cities were flooded and incessantly sprayed with mercuric chloride solution. Fantasies about cleaning up the sub-continent now took on a new and substantive meaning. No form of executive action, it seemed, was too extravagant in the frenzy and panic of the epidemic.

The medical and scientific experts did not always privilege the claims of evidence over their own preconceptions about Indian society and they were eventually ensnared within them. Sometimes they overlooked or neglected the evidence; sometimes, they simply could not read its signs. Thus, it was clear, at the outset of the epidemic, that 'the contagion of the prevailing fever is very slight',[57] and it was soon demonstrated that 'the quickest possible isolation of the sick had no effect on the march of the malady'.[58] As early as 1897, 'discerning observers in Bombay' knew, as Hirst pointed out, that bubonic plague was not 'infectious in the ordinary sense'.[59]

Nonetheless, policies, formulated on the assumption that the plague was a virulently infectious disease, proved at best oppressive and at worst fatal. Thus, the stringent inspections along the railway lines and at ports yielded a minute number of plague cases, although many tens of thousands were detained under 'suspicion'.[60] When roofs were removed, floors dug up, houses flooded with disinfectant, the rats simply moved away and spread the infection. By pumping the sewers with disinfectants, rats were driven into houses and carried the fleas with them to infect the inhabitants.[61] Had the scientists and medical experts given the rat flea theory more serious consideration, they may have resolved some of the conundrums – for instance, the erratic and spasmodic pattern of its dissemination – posed at the time by the epidemiology of the plague. Moreover, its implications for changing the direction of plague policy, swiftly seen as ineffectual, were substantial. For it suggested the need to switch the emphasis from the inspection and control of human beings to

[57] *Times of India*, 25 September, 1896, p. 4.
[58] Hirst, *Conquest of Plague*, p. 116.   [59] *Ibid.*, p. 119.
[60] Condon, *The Bombay Plague*, p. 146.
[61] *A Monograph on Evacuation as a Protective and Combative Plague Measure, Compiled Under the Orders of Sir A. Wingate, KCIE, Acting Chief Secretary to Government by Lt. J. K. Condon, Under-Secretary to Government (Plague Department) for the Use of the Indian Plague Commission, 30 March 1899* (Bombay, 1899), p. 1.

that of merchandise and from disinfection to disinfestation. As it was, plague policies put forward as rational measures to control the epidemic among traditional, ignorant people fell prey to the superstitions of science, derived from preconceptions about Indian society and generated by a wider discourse in which the experts shared.

IV

From the onset of the epidemic, officials readily acknowledged that plague measures were likely to have 'undesirable consequences' but the only alternative was to endure a growing incidence of sickness and a rising death toll. To them, it seemed imperative to do whatever was necessary to stamp out the plague. Yet it was by no means clear how far they could go in asserting the virtues of science over the traditional sentiments and religious susceptibilities of the people. The riots which occurred at the Arthur Road Hospital in Bombay as early as October 1896 suggested to the provincial government 'that it was extremely doubtful whether we could enforce in Bombay City all the measures which high medical authority commended to us as desirable to combat the epidemic'.[62] The annual revival of the plague and its dissemination came increasingly to be explained not in terms of misconceived and misdirected policies but of 'the failure of the people to comprehend its characteristics and the value of the measures'.[63] Popular resistance was perceived as irrational and dysfunctional, a product of the pre-scientific attitudes, the sacred traditions and customary prejudices of the Indian people, a view which later historians have sometimes unwittingly endorsed.

Contemporary officials tended to homogenise the Indian response to the epidemic. In fact, it was extremely uneven. Resistance was not the only response to the plague measures and collaboration was by no means confined to the elites. When the Government of Bombay drew up a list of the city's inhabitants who merited rewards and commendations for their assistance in carrying out plague measures, Demos was strongly represented, including street corner bosses like Hashim Dada of Nagpada.[64] 'In every street row', British officials

[62] Lord Sandhurst, Governor of Bombay and Others, GOB, Judicial, to Her Majesty's Principal Private Secretary of State for India in Council, London, 9 April 1898, GOB, General (Plague), Vol. 389, Compilation no. 298. MSA.
[63] Condon, *The Bombay Plague*, p. 11.
[64] GOB, General (Plague), Vol. 8, Compilation no. 712 P/11 Confidential, 1899. MSA.

were relieved to discover, 'some were found to stand beside the executive and calm the mob.'[65] The epidemic yielded neither a homogeneous popular response to the epidemic nor a simple and consistent opposition between the colonial state and the Indian people as a whole. Nor should we postulate a natural affinity between the colonial state and 'Indian elites', to be neatly distinguished from the mass of the population. To W. C. Rand in Poona, it appeared, 'some of the most influential men in the City . . . were more likely than not to work against any operations that might be set on foot by Government'.[66] In Hubli, where the local Muslim population had 'given trouble ever since Plague operations began', the Collector of Dharwar reported, 'the list of ringleaders' included 'a prominent Kazi and an ex-Municipal Commissioner', who, he believed, had thereby betrayed a pact he had made with the town's elites.[67]

Forms of resistance also varied. Perhaps the most common response to the frenzied plague measures, and indeed the scourge itself, was flight. From most large towns, a substantial proportion of the population simply ran away. This was why the evacuation of whole settlements met with the least resistance and in some places, like Bassein, it was 'in high favour with the people'.[68] Concealment and evasion were also extensively practised. 'Incredible shifts were resorted to', reported Rand from Poona, 'to prevent the authorities from becoming aware of the occurrence of cases. Plague patients were hidden in lofts, cupboards and gardens – anywhere in fact, where their presence was least likely to be suspected.'[69] In Surat city, where 'the virulence of the disease was never great' in 1897 and 1898, patients were moved from house to house to avoid search parties with the effect, it was erroneously supposed, of spreading the germs more quickly.[70] Various stratagems were adopted by travellers to avoid the inspection at ports and along railway lines.[71]

Popular violence and riot provided the least frequent manifestation of such resistance, but they were also, of course, the most

---

[65] Snow, *Report on the Outbreak of Bubonic Plague*, p. 19.

[66] *Draft of Report . . . by the Late Mr W. C. Rand*, p. 4. MSA.

[67] Collector, Dharwar, to Commissioner, Southern Division, 13 March 1898, GOB, General (Plague), Vol. 389 of 1898, Compilation no. 298. MSA.

[68] Condon, *The Bombay Plague*, p. 192.

[69] *Draft of Report . . . by the Late Mr W. C. Rand*, p. 7. MSA.

[70] Condon, *The Bombay Plague*, p. 177.   [71] *Ibid.*, pp. 138, 146.

dramatic. In view of the zeal with which the plague administrators invaded the homes and the physical and social privacy of the people, riots appear to be remarkably rare occurrences. But the colonial state often took careful note of local skirmishes which it might otherwise have simply overlooked. In part, this was because these 'riots' did sometimes exercise a check on what the official mind grasped with certitude as necessary measures. In addition, these moments of collective action often exposed the weakness and vulnerability of local administrations, at a time when they were parading their power and exerting control and in an atmosphere governed by perceptions of physical danger. Finally, these riots often displayed what colonial officials charmingly described as 'racial characteristics and innate prejudices'.[72] Thus, in the Bombay riots of March 1898, the 'mob' chased Inspector Coady shouting 'Mardalo goreku, mardalo goreku' or kill the white man. At the statue of the Standing Parsi, 'it was impossible for any European to pass with safety. No distinction was made; . . . the principle the rioters acted upon was to hit a solah topee wherever they saw it and it mattered not whether the victim had ever had any participation in the plague administration.'[73] Numerous Europeans were attacked in the streets and at least two soldiers were lynched. The only shop to remain open on Abdul Rahman Street sold revolvers and 'the owner of this establishment was much sought after by Europeans during the afternoon'.[74]

It might be supposed that to understand popular hostility to the plague measures we need to look no further than their character and the style of their implementation. If the plague measures were harsh, it might appear that popular resistance to them was wholly rational. It would be tempting to suggest that while the most extravagant fantasy seemed credible and the wildest speculation highly plausible to the boffins of the government bacteriological laboratories and the learned practitioners of the medical sciences, Demos alone took a steady view. This is a useful corrective to the supposition that the idiom of popular thinking was based on rumour and religion rather than fact or reason. But, of course, nobody was exempt from the 'unreasoning panic'. Popular responses, no less than elite reactions,

---

[72] *Ibid.*, p. 131.
[73] 'An Account of the Riots in Bombay on 9 March 1898', in GOB, Judicial, 1898, Vol. 217, Compilation no. 669, Part I. MSA.
[74] *Ibid.* MSA.

the frenzied exertions of the state or the brittle and sometimes destructive certainties of medical and scientific experts, were shaped by the political conjuncture of the plague.

The most prominent feature of the plague operations, because of the stress laid on 'detection', were the search parties. In Poona, but less intensively elsewhere, the chosen agents for search were British soldiers and the searches were conducted like a military operation. The locality was surrounded by cavalry which paraded the streets, while soldiers moved from house to house, accompanied ideally by 'a native gentleman' and at least a hospital assistant to adjudicate upon suspicious cases. But inevitably resources were overstretched. There were too few doctors to accompany every search party[75] and while there was no shortage of 'native gentlemen', they were not always willing to assist: some, according to Rand, 'worked steadily and well ... , others irregularly, others not at all'.[76]

The 'detection' of sickness was a sensitive and intimate operation. 'To eliminate the suspicious cases', as one official report put it, 'a careful individual examination of each native was necessary' which involved in particular 'a careful exploration of his body for glandular enlargement'.[77] Not surprisingly, there were complaints that 'all the females are compelled to come out of their houses and stand before the public gaze in the open street and be there subjected to inspection by soldiers'.[78] Soldiers were said to 'behave disgracefully with native ladies'[79] and the tenor of the official response that they had merely 'joked with a Marathi woman' suggests that sexual harassment probably did occur.[80] Shripat Gopal Kulkarni, an octogenarian, complained that ten or twelve soldiers had burst into his house, forced him to undress, 'felt ... the whole of my body and then made me sit and rise [several times] and, sitting around me, went on clapping their hands and dancing'.[81] In addition, there were complaints that while conducting their house searches, soldiers

[75] In Bombay, in 1898–9, only five doctors were available for 'plague duty'. See Condon, *The Bombay Plague*, pp. 131–2.
[76] Note by Chairman, Poona Plague Committee, 7 July 1897, in GOB, General (Plague), Vol. I, Compilation no. 70/P, 1897, p. 157. MSA.
[77] Condon, *The Bombay Plague*, p. 136.
[78] V. M. Bhide *et al.* to Chairman, Poona Plague Committee, 7 April 1897, in GOB, General (Plague), Vol. I, Compilation no. 70/P, 1897, p. 8. MSA.
[79] *Idem* to *idem*, 20 April 1897, *ibid.*, p. 15. MSA.
[80] Chairman, Poona Plague Committee, to Secretary, GOB, General, 20 July 1897, *ibid.*, p. 179. MSA.
[81] Petition by Shripat Gopal Kulkarni, *ibid.*, pp. 306–7. MSA.

'put into their mouths whatever eatables they find', 'insist upon being supplied with milk and other drinks' or 'put into their pockets such things as come into their fancy'.[82] Petitioners were often aggrieved that there was a wanton and indiscriminate destruction of property during searches. Officials knew only too well that the 'concealment of cases is also practised in order to avoid the inconvenience and petty expenses of disinfection, destruction of clothing etc.'[83]

Those who had the misfortune of being placed under suspicion, however wrongly, by any one plague agency, it was said, could suffer the attention of several others. The suspicion of the search party brought in its train the disinfection gangs and limewashing parties. It could also result in the hospitalisation of suspects, the segregation of their relatives, the loss of their property, perhaps the destruction of their homes.[84] Sometimes, it was said, 'their neighbours and in many cases even the passers by are indiscriminately seized and sent to segregation camp'.[85]

The most common complaint concerned false diagnosis which resulted in 'perfectly healthy persons' being 'seized and forcibly taken away by the search parties'.[86] There was some considerable uncertainty in the diagnosis of the plague, particularly by the search parties. The Chairman of the Poona Plague Committee conceded that the Medical Officer in charge of the Plague Hospital had been 'complaining of the excessive number of cases sent to him which were not plague'.[87] It is probable that before September 1896, bubonic plague had long gone undiagnosed[88] but once the panic gathered force, doctors as well as the lay search parties found plague everywhere.[89]

[82] V. M. Bhide, Chairman, Deccan Sabha, Poona, to Chairman Poona Plague Committee, 20 April 1897, *ibid.*, p. 15. MSA.

[83] Condon, *The Bombay Plague*, pp. 51–2.

[84] Petition of Bhiku-bin-Tatya Shimpi to President, Deccan Sabha, 1 August 1897, GOB, General (Plague), Vol. I, Compilation no. 70/P, 1897, pp. 245–7. MSA.

[85] V. M. Bhide, Chairman, Deccan Sabha, *et al.*, to Chairman, Poona Plague Committee, 20 April 1897, *ibid.*, p. 13. MSA.

[86] *Ibid.* MSA.

[87] Note by Chairman, Poona Plague Committee, 7 July 1897, *ibid.*, pp. 154–5. MSA.

[88] Snow, *Report on the Outbreak of Bubonic Plague*, pp. 1–3; see also, Condon, *The Bombay Plague*, p. 68.

[89] A dispute over the misplaced suspicions of a search party culminated in the Bombay riot of March 1898. See GOB, Judicial, Vol. 217, Compilation no. 669, Part I. MSA. On Dr W. J. Simpson's diagnosis of a case of syphilis as the plague, which caused a panic in Calcutta in 1896, see 'Papers Relating to the Outbreak of

The Government of Bombay vociferously denied the allegations made by petitioners and the press and few of them could be proved. Sometimes, the author of the petition could not be traced which in the prevailing terror is neither surprising nor significant. Of course, the truth of these allegations matters less than the fact that, as their collector was subsequently to point out, 'they were rife in the City'.[90] It is unlikely that the truth would dramatically alter the significance of their narratives.

Historians of India have recently paid considerable attention to rumours about epidemics and especially the plague. In particular, David Arnold has characterised them 'as a form of popular discourse'[91] which shows 'a significant divergence of outlook between the middle classes and the subordinate population'.[92] There are several problems with this argument. First, the historical source of rumours lies most frequently in official reports, the memoirs of civil servants and newspapers, which created as much as they reported them, and which were compiled largely by the middle classes. Rumours may also be taken, therefore, as an elite discourse about popular attitudes.

Second, the British in India were highly susceptible to rumours. This susceptibility reflected their isolation from, imperfect knowledge of and vulnerability to Indian society. Falsehoods put about in the bazaar might spread discontent and provoke rebellion, which they might not always be in a position to control. In part, this was why colonial officials compiled and reported 'rumours' with such exasperation and dread as they occurred, such bemusement, curiosity and fascination after the event. After the 1898 riots in Bombay, the Commissioner of Police reported, 'Rumours, of course, are flying about in plenty, but I think it is a pity that people are so very anxious to credit even the most absurd stories, the origins of which it is almost impossible to trace.'[93] Sometimes, however, it was his own officers who appeared most anxious to credit them. In the immediate

Bubonic Plague in India ... up to March 1897', *PP*, 1897, LXIII, pp. 41–2; Catanach, 'Plague and the Indian Village', p. 241 fn. 107.

[90] Statement by V. M. Bhide, Chairman, Poona Plague Committee, 1 August 1897, GOB, General (Plague), Vol. I, Compilation no. 70/P, 1897, p. 108. MSA.
[91] Arnold, 'Touching the Body', p. 76.
[92] *Ibid.*, p. 68.
[93] Commissioner of Police, Bombay, to Secretary, GOB, Judicial, 1 April 1898, in GOB, General (Plague), Vol. 389, Compilation no. 298, 1898. MSA.

aftermath of the riot, the Plague Committee peon at Bandra, to the north of the island, reported that some Mohammedan 'roughs' were throwing stones at his shed near Mahim causeway and the Superintendent on duty saw 'a large gang of Mahomedan roughs ... to be collecting near the Railway in the vicinity of the [Bandra Observation] camp'. Superintendent A. H. Bingley telegraphed for reinforcements, as he later explained, because 'I was aware that a persistent rumour had been spread abroad for the last few days that a disturbance might be expected on Friday.'[94] The police reinforcements were rushed from Thana districts only to discover that 'no stone throwing had taken place at the camp and that there was not the slightest cause of alarm'.[95]

Moreover, Indian elites subscribed to rumours about the plague as much as the poor. For instance, one rumour, quoted by Arnold,[96] was recorded when 'a well-disposed Brahmin' asked the epidemiologist Hankin, 'in all seriousness ... whether it was true that an English sahib had put snake-venom into the Bombay water-supply and thus produced the great epidemic in the city'.[97] Similarly, P. C. Snow, the Municipal Commissioner for Bombay, reported, in 1896, that of all the plague measures, segregation and hospitalisation 'caused the most alarm' and 'reports were freely circulated that the authorities merely took them there to make a speedy end of them'.[98] But these were measures which 'the whole people, high and low, viewed with the wildest hostility'. Similarly, diverse social groups subscribed, as we have seen, to the 'stories' about soldiers and segregation, search parties and disinfection gangs, medical diagnoses and hospital treatments contained in the petitions to the Poona Plague Committee and found them highly convincing.

Finally, there can be only the most slender distinction between the rumours of the populace and the superstitions of science. To attribute the causes of the plague, against the evidence, to microbes harboured in the earth seemed to many officials and experts to constitute 'in all seriousness' an immutable fact: real

94 Superintendent of Police, Bandra Observation Camp, to Plague Commissioner, Bombay, 25 March 1898, *ibid*. MSA.
95 District Superintendent of Police, Thana to Secretary, GOB, General (Plague), 27 March 1898, *ibid*. MSA.
96 Arnold, 'Touching the Body', p. 70.   97 Hirst, *Conquest of Plague*, p. 21.
98 Snow, *Report on the Outbreak of Bubonic Plague*, p. 6.

knowledge sanctified by scientific learning. But this was not very far removed from the 'well disposed Brahmin's' theory of snake-venom.

Rumours about the plague need not be understood in terms which are specific to Indian culture alone. They may be profitably read as the expression of a pervasive mood of unreality and mortal danger, shared by many across divisions of class, caste and creed, as the plague raged and retreated around them. Rumours were an earthy, accessible and, in a sense, even tangible way of sustaining hope, expressing anger, of paradoxically keeping in touch with reality. Rumours provided a magical idiom for discussing the most horrible and menacing realities while sometimes providing a means of liberation from them. Rumours cited by Arnold anticipating the collapse of British rule or predicting impending doom are examples of the latter. Moreover, sometimes ordinary, daily anxieties could find an exaggerated and exotic focus. Thus, perhaps, stories of being 'kidnapped' by soldiers, and kept segregated, only to return to discover relatives had died, articulated a deep-seated fear of separation and loss, at a time when both abounded. Stories about the behaviour of soldiers may have borne a considerable measure of truth but they also reflected the nightmarish invasion and violation of privacy – even god-rooms and kitchens – by the most frightening, powerful, uniformed and foreign agent of public authority. Sexual harassment by the soldiers and their 'disgraceful behaviour towards native ladies' almost certainly occurred – and, indeed, physical examination, 'the exploration of the native's body' in the streets or at railway checkpoints may themselves be regarded precisely as that – but reports of them also served as a metaphor for the violent eruption of the state into the privacy of people's lives. Rumours about poisoning and snake-venom which attributed the plague to the conspiracy of officials did not simply represent a popular appreciation of the 'undivided malevolence'[99] of the state. It was rather that by blaming official conspirators it was possible to evade one's own irredeemable vulnerability to the epidemic. For the British, too, it was preferable to blame the spread of the plague on the incomprehension and obscurantism of the native, rather than on the failure of their hopelessly misconceived policies, or to attribute their own continued danger from the disease as well as physical

---

[99] Arnold, 'Touching the Body', p. 76.

assault by riotous mobs to the currency of rumours propagated by trouble makers in the bazaars and the credulity of the simple and illiterate, if sullen and resentful, poor.

Rumours during the plague, or indeed at other times, should not be interpreted literally, either for their foundation in reality or as a text, to 'discern' the 'preoccupations'[100] of the popular mind. Rather, rumours, and stories, even when they circulated fictions more terrifying than the facts, were a means of mediating the unremitting horrors entailed in the actual circumstances of the plague. Nor can rumours be regarded as the exclusive, or even primary, idiom of the poor. Men of science and letters, physicians with formidable reputations, the 'most imposing array of epidemiological talent' in the world, and the hand-picked brilliance of Oxford and Cambridge who filled the ranks of the Indian Civil Service, were all similarly susceptible. If the plague epidemic facilitated the expression of the deepest popular anxieties, it had also become the focus of British anxieties about their inability to control India and their vulnerability to the numerous epidemics, medical as well as political, which it harboured.

V

While the prospect of receiving the attention of the search parties, with their military-style campaigns of detection, filled people with dread and provoked them to anger, the threat of hospitalisation loomed alarmingly large in public anxiety. Indeed, at times it culminated in riots and mob attacks upon hospitals. But this should not be taken to signify an innate, indiscriminate and implacable antipathy to western medicine. Of course, it is not intended to suggest that the Indian people embraced western medicine enthusiastically at the first opportunity, but rather that popular attitudes were too complex and too diverse to be reduced to a simple choice between acceptance and rejection. Indeed, this complexity stemmed precisely from the fact that popular attitudes were not simply and reflexively drawn as frequently assumed from a reservoir of religious and cultural traditions, but were shaped by historical and political contingencies and, in particular, by the experience of various medical cures.

[100] *Ibid.*, pp. 72, 75–7.

In late nineteenth-century India, the 'western' medical presence was extremely thin on the ground. In Bombay city, where its density was greatest, the census returned 555 qualified practitioners in 1901,[101] while in the countryside, outside the district towns, there was generally 'no skilled medical assistance of any kind'.[102] To obtain medical attention, most people had to travel considerable distances, suffer a loss of work and incur considerable expense. Nonetheless, where they existed, rural dispensaries were extensively used.[103] In Bombay city, too, there is little evidence that 'western' medical practitioners were abjured. On the contrary, at the very start of the epidemic, Dr Thomas Blainey, visiting the afflicted district of Mandvi with Dr Viegas, found people eager for medical attention. 'The people around me', he wrote,

> urged me to go and see other similar cases at varying distances and said that many persons in their locality were similarly attacked. Several of them informed their friends that I was a municipal representative deputed to inquire into the present fever outbreak and that every facility should be afforded me to make the inquiry complete. I have no doubt that Dr. Viegas corrected their mistake on my official identity ... The people, though ignorant, are quite alive to the dangerous character of the prevailing fever.[104]

Many of them were, of course, shortly to die. But their response to Dr Blainey was far removed from the response evinced by the plague authorities as the epidemic wore on.

Like the colonial officials before them, historians have sometimes too readily taken for granted that 'western medicine outstripped popular disease comprehension'.[105] In fact, 'western' medicine knew little about the disease and its ability to learn more was inhibited precisely by its perceptions of Indian culture and society. To the

[101] *Census of India, 1901*, XIA, *Bombay Town and Island*, Part VI, Tables, compiled by S. M. Edwardes (Bombay, 1901), Table XV, p. 138. These were listed as 'practitioners with diploma'. Another 398 'practitioners without a diploma' were also returned by the census.

[102] J. K. N. Kabraji, 2nd Assistant Collector, to R. B. Stewart, Ag. Collector, Nasik, 16 August 1897, in GOB, Revenue, Vol. 19, Compilation no. 67, Part IV, 1898. MSA.

[103] R. B. Stewart, Collector, Nasik, to Commissioner, Central Division, 25 September 1897, *ibid*. MSA.

[104] *Times of India*, 25 September 1896, p. 4.

[105] Klein, 'Plague, Policy and Popular Unrest', p. 739.

extent that policies were shaped by its wisdom, their effect was often
to intensify and disseminate the epidemic. The plague was notor-
iously difficult to diagnose. As a result, 'numbers of cases had to be
segregated . . . not because the patients had plague but because they
had suspicious symptoms'.[106] Depending upon which symptoms
predominated in a given case, bubonic plague could resemble
relapsing fever, severe cases of malaria, typhoid, typhus, glandular
fever and even drunkenness. Physicians sometimes misread its
symptoms for another disease or treated rather more benign illnesses
as if they were the plague. The official history of the plague cited the
case of Govind Jeeva who, treated for alcoholic poisoning by the
doctor, was thus speeded on his way to death from bubonic plague.[107]

Nor were there any known remedies for the disease.[108] By 1900,
'western' medical practitioners had discovered 'no specific remedy'
for the plague and none of those which they tried had influenced
'favourably the mortality among those attacked'. The plague hospitals could offer nothing more than 'hygienic and symptomatic
treatment'. Not knowing what else to do, they tried to tide 'the
patient over a certain period' and trusted to 'the natural tendency
to recover'.[109] Medical practice, especially in the 'western' tradition,
was seen to be experimental in its procedure and ineffective in its
results. The descriptions of their own activities by plague officials
suggest that this perception was on the whole justified. To
Bombay's Municipal Commissioner, 'The outbreak of plague in the
House of Correction afforded a particularly good opportunity of
watching the effect of M. Haffkine's prophylactic treatment.'[110]
When Haffkine took a medical team to inoculate the villagers of
Undhera, a village near Baroda, in February 1897, they were able
to report their satisfaction that 'the conditions approached very
nearly the strictness of a laboratory experiment'.[111] It is doubtful
whether the subjects of their experiments shared their satisfaction as
the threat of death loomed over them and it is scarcely surprising,

---

[106] Snow, *Report on the Outbreak of Bubonic Plague*, p. 3.
[107] Condon, *The Bombay Plague*, pp. 78–9.
[108] For a description of some remedies tried at the start of the epidemic, see *Times of India*, 25 September 1896, p. 4.
[109] Condon, *The Bombay Plague*, p. 81.
[110] Snow, *Report on the Outbreak of Bubonic Plague*, p. 17.
[111] Condon, *The Bombay Plague*, pp. 43–4; W. M. Haffkine, *Experiment on the Effect of Protective Inoculation in the Epidemic of Plague at Undhera Taluka, Baroda, February and March, 1898* (Bombay, 1898).

in the light of these attitudes, that medical officers found it hard to win public confidence.

The widespread hostility to hospitalisation, shared by diverse social groups, was not simply a function of caste and religious sensibilities. Indeed, it extended 'even to hospitals established and managed by Hindoos for their own caste fellows'.[112] Hospitalisation represented the culmination of all plague measures, perhaps the most coercive manifestation of a brutally intrusive state, and the end of a terrifying chain of events which began with the search parties. The case mortality rate of plague patients entering hospital averaged over 80 per cent at the height of the first epidemic in Bombay.[113] The overwhelming majority who were admitted to hospital did not return alive. The arrival of the ambulance must, therefore, have seemed like the state's death sign on the patient or the suspect. 'People who thought the poor ... ought to be happy because they had been born to it', reported T. S. Weir from Bombay, 'almost wept when they saw one of the same poor ill from Bubonic Plague, lifted into a municipal ambulance.'[114] 'Peals of screams' from plague patients in the Contagious Diseases Hospital in Bombay 'not only pervaded the whole hospital, but even attracted the notice of passers-by on the road', one of the major thoroughfares through the mill districts.[115] Not surprisingly, hospitals came to be perceived in the public imagination less as a refuge from the ravages of the plague, than as a potent and destructive instrument of terror, as 'places of torture and places intended to provide material for experiments'.[116]

If to the Indian mind, as one historian has recently suggested, hospitals were 'a place of pollution, contaminated by blood and faeces', this was often less because they appeared 'inimical to caste, religion and *purdah*',[117] than because these were the real conditions

---

[112] Condon, *The Bombay Plague*, p. 126; Snow, *Report on the Outbreak of Bubonic Plague*, p. 16.

[113] Snow, *Report on the Outbreak of Bubonic Plague*, p. 17; Condon, *The Bombay Plague*, pp. 132–3.

[114] Report by Executive Health Officer, Bombay, in Snow, *Report on the Outbreak of Bubonic Plague*, p. 81.

[115] 'Report on Bubonic Plague Cases Treated at the Arthur Road Hospital from September 24, 1896 to February 28, 1897', by Khan Bahadur N. H. Choksi, Extra Assistant Health Officer, in charge of the Arthur Road Hospital, *ibid.*, p. 237.

[116] Report by Executive Health Officer, Bombay, *ibid.*, pp. 73–4.

[117] Arnold, 'Touching the Body', p. 62.

to be found there.[118] But this was not simply an 'indigeneous' perception. When his daughter contracted the plague in Poona, Surgeon Major Barry, a British officer of the Indian Medical Service, recognised that she would have a better chance of recovery at home. Rather than entrust her to what should have appeared to his 'western eyes' as 'the sanitized and healing environment of the hospital',[119] he conspired with his colleague, Surgeon Major Baker, who examined the patient, to conceal the fact and break the regulations they were working so vigorously to enforce upon others.[120]

Nonetheless, popular attitudes to the plague hospitals and to western medicine, in general, were by no means inflexible. Some caste and communal hospitals, having created an environment which people felt more able to use, found general favour.[121] As Bombay's inhabitants fled the plague in 1897, the Petit Mills, facing an acute shortage of labour, 'promised to erect a temporary plague hospital' where their workers, 'would be looked after instead of being sent away to the Municipal hospitals'. As a result, it was said, they 'abandoned the idea of going away'.[122] If hospitals were not always hospitable places, they were particularly forbidding to the poor.[123]

By contrast, the occasional glimpses that we have into the domestic treatment of the sick during the epidemic suggest the enormous care often taken by friends and relatives. W. D. Shepherd, the Collector of Poona, complained that 'the inability of the family

[118] For a description of the plague hospital in Poona by one who was taken there on suspicion and later released, see the letter from Sodaji Pundlik More to *Dynanprakash* in GOB, General (Plague), Vol. I, Compilation no. 70/P, 1897, pp. 197– 238. MSA. On conditions in the Arthur Road Hospital in Bombay, see 'Report on Bubonic Plague Cases Treated at . . . ', by N. H. Choksi, in Snow, *Report on the Outbreak of Bubonic Plague*, pp. 210–12, 237.
[119] Arnold, 'Touching the Body', p. 62.
[120] W. L. Harvey, Municipal Commissioner, Bombay, to Plague Commissioner, Bombay, 14 March 1900, in GOB, General (Plague) Vol. 16, Compilation no. 15, 1900, pp. 129–31. MSA.
[121] *Report of the Municipal Commissioner on the Plague in Bombay in the Year Ending 31st May, 1899* (Bombay, 1899), p. 318.
[122] *Ibid.*, pp. 354–6.
[123] This is also suggested by some evidence from the 1920s and 1930s. See, for instance, *Royal Commission on Labour in India, Evidence, Bombay Presidency, 1929–31*, Mr Dattatraya Ramchandra Mayekar and Mr Narayanrao Kulkarni representing the Girni Kamgar Mahamandal, Vol. I, Part ii, p. 387. See also Proceedings of the Textile Labour Inquiry Committee, 1938–40, Main Inquiry, Evidence, Cotton Mill Workers, Spinning Side, File 60–A, pp. 1020–2. MSA.

to refrain from attending on sick relatives ensured that a large number should die where many might have lived'. While they were 'generally very keen to keep plague out of their villages', they refused to allow their own 'separation from their sick relatives'.[124] The official historian of the plague expressed his frustration at those who, sharing rooms with plague patients, contracted the infection from being in constant attendance upon them. 'The poor and ignorant' were said to be more vulnerable to infection than, for instance, nursing staff, because of 'the common custom which exists of friends receiving the sputa of the sick in their hands, and using their hands and clothing to wipe away discharges from the patients' mouth'.[125] It would be folly to idealise the Indian family; not even among kin might we find a single and undifferentiated response. From Surat district, for instance, it was reported that 'the relatives and caste fellows of the Hindu patients often shrank from performing the last offices for their own dead', while those who contracted the disease in private segregation camps 'crawled back to their empty houses to die' and neighbours threw their corpses into the streets before officials marked their houses for special attention.[126]

At the height of the panic, western medicine must have often appeared as nothing less than the theological carapace of an intrusive and oppressive state, and the hospital its most terrifying institutional embodiment. We might under these circumstances expect most people to have turned their backs upon the whole apparatus of western medicine. In fact, the public response to western medicine – if indeed an 'Indian' response may be inferred from the evidence at all – was more nuanced and flexible and many showed a willingness to use both doctors and hospitals. During the epidemic, some people strained to hear the 'western' physician's mantra; others read the shaman's lips; still others turned to the hakims and vaidyas or the folk remedies which the most wizened village elders could recall. Each was as likely to be as effective as the other. There is nothing to suggest that those who sought the intercession of Sitaladevi did not also seek the help of the government-approved physician. In fact, popular attitudes to western medicine in the 1890s, as perhaps more recently, were determined by

[124] Report from Poona District in Condon, *The Bombay Plague*, pp. 234–5.
[125] Condon, *The Bombay Plague*, p. 72.
[126] Report from Surat District, *ibid.*, pp. 178–9.

its efficacy, its accessibility and its cost.[127] Popular resistance to medical intervention and hospitalisation during the plague epidemic is more plausibly explained by the terms on which it was offered to those stricken or threatened by the disease than by some primordial sentiment or cultural essence embedded in the Indian mind.

VI

The plague epidemic did not give rise to a single, homogeneous Indian response. Neither is it possible to identify in it any consistent pattern of social differentiation. The diverse responses to the epidemic reflected in part the various ways in which it was perceived and experienced. People found themselves pitted against each other in the panic more often than they were gathered into large social solidarities. Social tension, competition and antagonisms were heightened not only between but also within classes. The fragile facade of social order was cracked open and whole towns and villages appeared to be on the edge of chaos. In virtually every town, the outbreak of plague paralysed trade and put its inhabitants to flight. From Karad, it was reported, typically, in June 1897, 'The utter disorganization that prevailed in the town could hardly be imagined by one who had not seen it.'[128] In Poona, it was said, 'The state of the city was one of panic.'[129] By February 1897, nearly half the inhabitants of Bombay city had fled, there was 'open bidding for labour at the street corners',[130] and the city's officials grew increasingly apprehensive that the social and political fabric of the city was about to disintegrate.[131]

At anarchy's edge, the panic created fresh opportunities for profit and power for those with the temerity and ruthlessness to seize them. Shortly after the first outbreak of the disease in 1896, the Municipal Commissioner in Bombay reported: 'A gang of scoundrels took to blackmailing by personating the Police and Municipal servants, and increased the general terror, extorting money as they did under

---

[127] Cf. A. R. Beals, 'Strategies of Resort to Curers in South India', in Charles Leslie (ed.), *Asian Medical Systems. A Comparative Study* (Berkeley and Los Angeles, 1976), pp. 195, 192–4, 198.

[128] Report from Satara District, in Condon, *The Bombay Plague*, p. 243.

[129] *Draft of Report . . . by the Late Mr W. C. Rand*, p. 4. MSA.

[130] S. M. Edwardes, *The Rise of Bombay – A Retrospect* (Bombay, 1902), p. 330.

[131] Snow, *Report on the Outbreak of the Bubonic Plague*, pp. 4–5, 7–9; Report by Executive Health Officer, *ibid.*, pp. 70–8.

threats of removal to hospital.'[132] The evacuation of towns and villages, which it was believed had a salutary effect on public health, was accompanied by an increased incidence, and fear, of crime. At the model segregation camp at Anand in Kaira district in Gujarat, the banias having set up general provisions stores, were said to be 'in league with the *badmashes* in the town' to rob the detainees.[133] During the epidemic, the police, whose detectives 'gave us the fullest information',[134] may also have found opportunities for gain.[135] The implementation of the plague measures left much to the discretion of the search parties and in the course of their activities, large informal powers accrued to their 'detectives'. Once a household or a neighbourhood became the object of the search party's suspicion, its members were inextricably pulled into the vortex of the plague's terror. Their only means of escape was to negotiate and bargain these suspicions to rest. Sometimes the official status of the search parties was difficult to ascertain, and some behaved no differently from 'scoundrels'. The Government of Bombay became sufficiently anxious about their conduct to instruct its officers that 'The closest supervision is especially necessary over subordinates and they should be taught to treat people civilly.'[136] If search parties fuelled public anxieties, enterprising spirits exploited the uncertainty they created.

The uncertainties which shrouded medical opinion about the plague and the desperation with which people sought cures wherever they might be found cleared the way for the proliferation of quacks. They were drawn from diverse social groups. As the Bombay Health Officer reported,

> Many good men were spoiled by aspiring to the honours of being Plague Doctors. Mallees and Mahars, and even men employed in the service of the Tramway Company and in the service of the

---

[132] Snow, *Report on the Outbreak of the Bubonic Plague*, p. 6.
[133] Report from Kaira District, in Condon, *The Bombay Plague*, pp. 160–3.
[134] Report from Executive Health Officer, Bombay, in Snow, *Report on the Outbreak of Bubonic Plague*, p. 80.
[135] For a general comment on such opportunities for the police during times of disturbances, see S. M. Edwardes, *The Bombay City Police. An Historical Sketch* (London, 1923), p. 183. See also R. Chandavarkar, 'Police and the Public Order in Bombay City, 1870–1940', unpublished paper presented to the conference on 'Policing the Empire', Birkbeck College, London, June 1988.
[136] Circular from GOB, General (Plague), no. 2551 P-43 Confidential, 6 April 1898, Home, Judicial, June 1898, 228–9 (B). National Archives of India. I am grateful to Gordon Johnson for this reference.

city, persuaded themselves and encouraged others to believe that they had a cure for plague ... Once a man became a Plague Doctor, he was seldom happy or contented in any regular work. If he did not save his followers, he ruined himself for honest toil.[137] Healing and curing, blackmail and extortion did not exhaust the commercial opportunities created by the panic. Evacuation and segregation camps opened up new fields in trade. The collapse of the labour market offered marginal groups the chance to entrench themselves in particular occupations. Those who wielded enough influence in a neighbourhood or a village could try to oust their rivals and establish themselves as jobbers and procurers and suppliers of labour. The growing intervention of the state and its feverish search for collaborators enlivened the factions of the neighbourhood and as existing structures of power were subjected to unprecedented stress, political rivalries were more freely pursued.

The style and methods of the plague administration also enabled, indeed invited, people to prey on each other. It assumed that they would spy on their neighbours. It expected that caste elders and local magnates would report suspicious cases and act as enforcers of the plague regulations. It hoped that, when detainees escaped from segregation camps, the inhabitants of uninfected areas would 'refuse to harbour such fugitives'.[138] These hopes were sometimes fulfilled and at other times frustrated. Some people responded with an enthusiasm which could be readily mistaken for public spiritedness. If suspicion was the defining characteristic of the plague operations, it was also the hallmark of the panic.

The burden of this suspicion fell primarily upon those who could be defined as marginal and isolated as outsiders. With its vocabulary of 'detection' and 'search', 'surveillance' and 'informants', 'suspects' and 'fugitives', the plague administration served to criminalise the disease and its victims. At one level, officials identifying the disease with filth, directed their gaze naturally and primarily towards the poor. In October 1898, the 'Surveillance System' introduced on the railways focussed especially upon 'travellers who ... were suspicious whether by reason of their appearance or symptoms, or the daily conditions of their clothes or effects'.[139] In what can only be assumed

---

[137] Report from Executive Health Officer, Bombay, in Snow, *Report on the Outbreak of Bubonic Plague*, p. 80.
[138] Condon, *The Bombay Plague*, pp. 28–9.   '[139] *Ibid.*, p. 143.

to be an extraordinary slip of the pen, the Bombay Health Officer boasted in 1897: 'From the beginning the greatest attention was paid to the disinfection of houses and to the segregation of the poor.'[140] The Anand detention camp in Kaira district was transformed in May 1898 to 'a Disinfection Camp for dirty persons arriving from infected localities'.[141] But, of course, the whole body of the poor could scarcely be stigmatised with the plague or uniformly defined as criminal or marginal.

While plague officials may have worked with rather crude definitions of marginality, dominant groups and local majorities tried to deflect the impact of the plague measures onto weaker and more peripheral groups. Certainly, those whose rights in the village or the neighbourhood appeared the most tenuous, or who could otherwise be defined as out of the 'community', were the most likely to be reported for 'suspicion' of sickness. It was among untouchables, 'deviants' and outsiders that the disease was first identified in previously unaffected localities. The ill-fated search party which visited the village of Ghori in Nasik district in September 1897 was immediately directed by the village schoolmaster to the 'suspicious cases' in the Teli's quarter.[142] The plague in Ankleshwar was said in August 1898 to have 'originated among the Ghanchis, a very dirty class'.[143] In Rajapur in Ahmednagar district, it was first registered among the Mahars and Chambars, but it was nonetheless concealed by the village officers for over a fortnight. Its origin was attributed locally to an outsider: 'the brother of a Marwari from Sirur, who died of the plague, presented the clothing of the deceased to a family of Mahars, of whom five caught the plague'.[144] The 'infection', in Sirur taluka, Poona district, was said to have been imported 'from prostitutes in the town'.[145] The disease was introduced to Broach, it was claimed, not by rats but by butchers and the quarter 'mostly inhabited by Mohammedans' was 'deeply infected with plague'.[146] In Hubli, too, it was associated with 'the Mussalman community'.

[140] Report by Executive Health Officer, Bombay, in *Report on the Outbreak of Bubonic Plague*, p. 87.
[141] Report from Kaira District, in Condon, *The Bombay Plague*, p. 160.
[142] J. K. Kabraji, Assistant Collector, to Collector, Nasik, 26 November 1897, GOB, General (Plague), Vol. 389, Compilation no. 298, 1898. MSA.
[143] Report from Broach District in Condon, *The Bombay Plague*, p. 155.
[144] Report from Ahmednagar District, *ibid.*, pp. 201–2.
[145] Report from Poona District, *ibid.*, p. 227.
[146] Report from Broach District, *ibid.*, p. 156.

They were regarded as 'turbulent',[147] particularly hostile to the plague measures,[148] and as Fakrudin Budansab, in charge of the local police and himself a Muslim, advised, 'being arrogant and daring, it cannot be known what they would do in course of time'.[149]

In view of the havoc which could be wrought upon a locality or even a whole town, once it fell prey to official suspicion, it is not surprising that a common reflex was simply to keep the plague administration at bay. Even local elites preferred to avert the official gaze altogether. This was in part why those who became suspects simply denied that they were sick while the afflicted refused to believe that it was the plague that had struck. The proximity of the disease, let alone its arrival in the locality, was also so terrifying to contemplate that people often refused to countenance the very idea of it. The progress of the search party in Ghori, for instance, was intercepted by a large crowd armed with sticks whose spokesman was reported to have said that 'they did not want a doctor nor was there any sickness in the village' and added that 'we shall not allow men of other creeds into our houses'.[150] Buboes found on two patients in Jalgaon, as mortality rates rose, seemed to suggest that 'it is plague the people are dying of'. But 'the opinion of the town is that it is not plague, and that the mortality is due to ordinary fever acting on constitutions undermined by fever'.[151] As 10 per cent of Karad's population was 'swept away' in three months, in 1897, the Hospital Assistant insisted that the disease was 'not plague but remittent fever'.[152]

At the start of the epidemic in Bombay, an initial and spontaneous search for medical and official help was swiftly replaced by a general refusal of state intervention. The municipal authorities and the provincial government, who had for decades done next to nothing to alleviate the social and sanitary conditions of the city, found it impossible to persuade its inhabitants that the cause of the

---

[147] Collector, Dharwar, to Commissioner, Southern Division, 13 March 1898, in GOB, General (Plague), Vol. 389, Compilation no. 298, 1898. MSA.

[148] District Magistrate, Dharwar to General Officer Commanding, Belgaum, 13 March 1898, *ibid.* MSA.

[149] 1st Deputy Head Constable, in charge of the town of Hubli, to Assistant Superintendent of Police, Dharwar, 11 March 1898, *ibid.* MSA.

[150] J. K. Kabraji, Assistant Collector, to Collector, Nasik, 26 November 1897, *ibid.* MSA.

[151] Report from Khandesh District, in Condon, *The Bombay Plague*, p. 208.

[152] Report from Satara District, *ibid.*, pp. 243–4.

epidemic lay in 'the hopeless condition of their own dark, damp, filthy, overcrowded houses'. Instead, they 'raved about the sewers' and 'looked to everything except the buildings and the rooms in which they lived for the cause of the disease'.[153] It was preferable by far to flee the city or even simply pray that the plague would pass them by than to place their trust in a government which had shown little real or sustained interest in their welfare, and now intervened in an arbitrary and brutal manner. The Municipal Commissioner found that 'the people refused all medical aid or to listen to any advice'.[154] To the official mind, the popular response sometimes appeared indiscriminately hostile. 'Nearly every hand was against the Municipal Officers', complained the Health Officer.[155] 'Such a pass had we come to, that picking up a few sick pigeons ... nearly led to a riot, and peaceful Bunnias, for 10 sick pigeons threatened to raze the city.'[156] It was almost as if to combat the disease and reorganise their lives around the epidemic people felt it imperative to resist the wise and rational men who came bearing the officially prescribed remedies, like so many satanic gifts.

VII

It is perhaps easier to explain why panics begin than why they end and the plague epidemic in India was no exception. Bubonic plague was after all, *the* plague; it was devastatingly and unremittingly deadly in its effects; it was a new and unfamiliar disease which no one fully comprehended and for which no remedies were known. Official frenzy acted as the catalyst of the panic and the public response. This frenzy was informed by colonial perceptions of the threat which the epidemic posed to Britain's empire and its international trade. It was conditioned and its expression inflected by colonial assumptions about Indian society and its cultural characteristics. In the panic, such economy as may have guided the techniques of colonial rule was quickly spent and these assumptions were expressed with an unusually uninhibited freedom. The excesses and desperation of official policies fed upon and fattened the terror which the epidemic unleashed upon those exposed to the disease.

---

[153] Snow, *Report on the Outbreak of Bubonic Plague*, p. 18.   [154] *Ibid.*, p. 5.
[155] Report from the Executive Health Officer, Bombay, *ibid.*, p. 71.
[156] *Ibid.*, p. 70.

Many responded to the desperation of official measures with an equally desperate resistance to and refusal of official, even medical, intervention. What colonial officials saw as an irrational and obscurantist resistance to the dictates of science and reason only incited them to further, yet more ferocious and despairing executive action. In this way, panic, terror and guilt engorged each other in a seemingly unending spiral.

The spiral was broken only when the frenzied temper of the plague measures relaxed. In part, this was a consequence of the identification of the plague as a disease of the poor. At the same time, while the plague continued to flourish, it was impossible to escape the conclusion that the vigorously enforced policies of the state had achieved very little.[157] They had failed to control the spread of the disease, protect the people or save the lives of the afflicted. Rather, as the plague extended its sway, officials perceived more starkly the political risks inherent in these colonial policies. As early as July 1897, the Lieutenant-Governor of the North-Western Provinces had observed, 'If the plague regulations had been enforced in any city of these provinces in the way in which . . . they were . . . enforced in Poona, there would certainly have been bloodshed here.'[158] The formulation and implementation of the plague measures, indeed the official construction of the panic, had been facilitated in the late 1890s, in two respects, by the prevailing political circumstances. First, in Bombay Presidency, British rule was more firmly anchored and British government more developed than in the old Mughal heartland or the outlying frontier regions of the Punjab. In Bombay, the British often fondly perceived the embodiment of the success of their technique of rule through collaboration. The Punjab, vital to the defence of the Indian Empire and the recruiting ground of the Indian Army, was, however, the home of the 'martial races' rather than the 'scribal classes'. At the height of the panic in 1897, the Bombay Government had felt able to strike decisively at the apparently formidable political base which the 'extremist' Tilak had been building, through his famine campaigns, Ganpati and Shivaji festivals and the recently captured

[157] The first shifts of official thinking in this direction can be seen in *Report of the Indian Plague Commission, 1898–99*, V, pp. 400–4, *PP*, 1902, LXII.

[158] Macdonnell to Elgin, 16 July 1897, Keep-with 5, Home Public A, May 1898, 329–44, NAI, cited by G. Johnson, *Provincial Politics and Indian Nationalism. Bombay and the Indian National Congress, 1880–1915* (Cambridge, 1973), p. 97 fn. 1.

Poona Sarvajanik Sabha.[159] By contrast, to officials in the Punjab, it seemed extravagant to antagonise merely in the name of science or in the interests of public health. It was here that the British rediscovered the fatalism with which they had long regarded questions of public health and social conditions before the outbreak of plague. Second, colonial plague policies had also been facilitated by the decline of the Congress as an all-India focus of political opposition. By the mid-1890s, the Indian National Congress had settled into torpor. It was only after 1903, while the plague continued unabated and even reached its peak, that the Congress coincidentally began to revive and in this revival the contribution of Punjab and the North-Western Provinces was to be substantial.[160] As they emerged from the whirligig of the plague panic, the British could reassure themselves about the resilience of their systems of collaboration in Bombay; but more crucially, they had relearnt an old lesson: that the price of political intervention was liable to be the destruction of these systems and, with it, the brittle and unsteady foundations of their rule.

The plague epidemic of the late 1890s in India carries many resonances of the AIDS epidemic of the 1980s in the United States. In the case of AIDS, state intervention and public interest were limited by the belief that only marginal, deviant groups were likely to be affected. But this was not a function of calm. It was accompanied by anxiety that this was Armageddon and rumours circulated about catching the virus from toilet seats, tea cups and toothbrushes. Vested interests from the homosexual bathhouse-owners to the blood banks, at times impeded and deflected measures to control its spread. Rumours, rife at every stage of the epidemic, explained its causes in terms of African initiation rites, the use of 'poppers' and a creation of germ warfare experiments gone wrong. A San Diego Coroner, undoubtedly trained at the best American medical schools, argued that the virus was in fact 'King Tut's curse',

[159] R. I. Cashman, *The Myth of the Lokamanya. Tilak and Mass Politics in Maharashtra* (Berkeley and Los Angeles, 1975); Johnson, *Provincial Politics and Indian Nationalism*, especially, chs. 2 and 3; Catanach, 'Poona Politicians and the Plague'.

[160] N. G. Barrier, 'The Punjab Disturbances of 1907: The Response of the British Government in India to Agrarian Unrest', *MAS*, 1, 4 (1967), pp. 353–83; *idem*, 'The Arya Samaj and Congress Politics in Punjab, 1894–1908', *JAS*, 26, 3 (1967), pp. 363–79; C. A. Bayly, *The Local Roots of Indian Politics. Allahabad, 1870–1920* (Oxford, 1973).

'placed in the tomb to punish those who might later defile his grave'. The legendary 'Orange County Connection' alone was widely believed to be responsible for the first hundred cases in the United States. He visited sex palaces specially to spread the virus as an act of revenge but was so irresistible that the person who went to confront him about his behaviour finished up having sex with him. In May 1985, Burke's Peerage, compiled, of course, by literate and rational people, announced that to preserve 'the purity of the human race', it would omit all families in which somebody was known to have AIDS. Their reason, they declared, was that 'AIDS may not be a simple infection, even if conveyed in an unusual way, but an indication of a genetic defect.' American gays, often prosperous professionals, secular and modern in their outlook and highly educated, rather than pre-scientific, superstitious and illiterate, showed at numerous points an antipathy to medical and policy initiatives as possible infringements on their civil liberties, when 'objectively' they might have been seen as necessary and non-threatening, and developed a whole vocabulary of euphemisms to maintain this position. As Randy Shilts, from whose excellent book these instances are quoted, observed: 'Humans who have been subjected to a life-time of irrational bigotry on the part of mainstream society can be excused for harbouring unreasonable fears.'[161] Perhaps this may provide a better clue to popular resistance to the plague measures in India than sacred traditions or religious susceptibilities.

[161] Randy Shilts, *And the Band Played On. Politics, People and the Aids Epidemic* (London, 1988), pp. 541–3 and *passim*.

10. *Plagues of beasts and men: prophetic responses to epidemic in eastern and southern Africa*

TERENCE RANGER

INTRODUCTION

In his chapter in this book and in his splendid monographs Alfred Crosby describes how epidemic and endemic diseases, introduced by Europeans, wiped out whole aboriginal populations and decimated and demoralised others. The victims lost confidence in their own culture and in their capacity to respond. This chapter also describes a crisis of human and animal epidemic, this time in eastern and southern Africa during the late nineteenth and early twentieth centuries when diseases from Europe and from imperial India ravaged Africa. One African people – the so-called 'Hottentots' of Cape Colony – *were* destroyed as a culture by disease, expropriation and settler violence. But in general my story is different from Crosby's. It deals with societies which biologically were not undermined and which in the end survived the crisis of disease to commence vigorous population growth. Above all, it deals with societies which had *not* lost cultural self-confidence and which retained the capacity to respond intellectually. It is with these intellectual – and particularly religious – responses to epidemic that this chapter is concerned.

The chapter deals with two human diseases – smallpox and influenza; and two cattle diseases – lungsickness and rinderpest. Its argument is that study of response to these diseases allows us to understand something of the dynamics of all three of the major ideological systems of eastern and southern Africa. In the period under study such ideological systems were inevitably religious. The European colonisers brought with them a bio-medical understanding of disease but they did not communicate this effectively to Africans. Africans had available so-called 'traditional' African religion (which in its response to epidemic revealed itself to be dynamic and innovative), Islam and Christianity.

A good deal has been written about the tensions *between* these three systems of ideology. But a study of response to epidemic shows that equally important have been tensions *within* each of them. In their own very different ways African religion, Islam and Christianity each were able to erect 'official' structures of public health, of 'orthodox' medical theory and practice. Such structures sought to control and domesticate disease and in each the power to control disease significantly legitimated wider claims for religious authority. On the other hand, within each of these contending traditions there existed counter-tendencies. Challenges to the official orthodoxies arose where effective medical protection was offered only to an elite and the impoverished majority was regularly exposed to misery and affliction. They also arose when orthodoxies of public health broke down in periods of social, economic and political disorder, or when new diseases – or old diseases in intensified form – overrode all control systems and devastating epidemics broke out.

Typically, in all three of the religious traditions, counter-tendencies expressed themselves in prophetic movements, opposing inspiration to 'clerical' authority and popular enthusiasm to elite wisdom. Prophets – arising outside the official and orthodox structures, claiming an authority from God, calling for a restoration of legitimacy, or for theocratic rule, or for a millennium – are familiar figures, of course, in Islamic and Christian history. But the late nineteenth and early twentieth centuries were a prime period for 'traditional' African prophets too. I shall argue that these arose – like their counterparts within African Islam and African Christianity – at least partly in response to the crisis of epidemic.

Thus the tensions *within* the three religious traditions of eastern and southern Africa are the major theme of this chapter. Yet one must not overstress the point. Even if the most significant tensions were within each religious tradition, conflict *between* them often did express itself particularly clearly at times of epidemic dislocation. Thus while almost all recent work on prophetic movements disputes the older view that they were essentially anti-colonial and proto-nationalist, it remains true that on occasion the prophetic endeavour to cleanse society extended to an attempt to cleanse it of alien and intrusive beliefs and their adherents. While prophets usually identified sins within African societies as the root cause of epidemic, strangers were sometimes blamed and one can often see in anti-colonial protest what William Beinart has recently called 'the medical metaphor'. This also has to be a theme of this chapter.

In seeking to explore and expound these themes I shall follow a simple sequence of argument. First I shall briefly set out what is known of the periodisation and spread of the human and cattle diseases with which the chapter is concerned. Then I shall take each of the religious/ideological traditions in turn and discuss the responses to epidemic within each, starting with African religion, moving to Islam and finishing with Christianity. In doing this, however, I shall try not to isolate each tradition from the others since in response to epidemic (as in many other matters) there was extensive borrowing of ideas. I shall conclude with some brief comparative remarks.

PLAGUES OF BEASTS AND MEN: A BRIEF CHRONOLOGY

According to Donald Hopkins smallpox may even have originated in Africa, as an adaptation to man of domestic animal pox viruses.[1] However that may be, it seems clear that the disease in virulent form was introduced into southern and eastern Africa in recent times. Its first appearance was apparently at the Cape in 1713 when smallpox sufferers landed from a Dutch fleet. The disease spread to the slaves at the Cape and then to their masters; from the town it spread to the countryside; from slaves and whites it spread to the 'Hottentots' or Khoikhoi. Mortality among them was heavy. A contemporary observer recorded dying 'Hottentots' lying along the roads, 'cursing at the Dutchmen, who they said had bewitched them'. By the 1720s smallpox had reached the Bantu-speaking peoples to the north. As Richard Elphick writes: 'Smallpox viruses continued to circulate among southern African peoples for a century, causing disruption whose scale and historical significance may never be fully known.'[2]

There was an especially violent smallpox epidemic in Xhosaland around 1770 which caused the sort of moral and structural disruption out of which prophetic movements emerged. J. B. Peires writes:

The view of death as evil and unnatural was greatly reinforced in

---

[1] D. Hopkins, *Princes and Peasants. Smallpox in History* (Chicago, 1983).
[2] R. Elphick, *Khoikhoi and the Founding of White South Africa* (Johannesburg, 1985), p. 232.

the middle of the eighteenth century by a terrible smallpox epidemic ... Before the epidemic, the Xhosa had buried their dead, but from that time they shrank from touching dead bodies and, as a result, the dying were carried outside and left to expire in the bush. People fled from the sight or sound of death, and in most cases the corpses were not recovered but left to the dogs and the hyenas. With the collapse of ordinary funeral rituals, any comforting thought the Xhosa may have had that death was a normal and natural transition to a more exalted state must have utterly vanished.[3]

Smallpox decimated Ndebele armies in the early 1890s. Thereafter, the disease, having become routinely endemic in most of southern Africa, could take epidemic form whenever extremes of poverty, malnutrition and social dislocation allowed it to do so. In eastern Africa, meanwhile, smallpox certainly became widespread and reached many areas where it had previously been unknown as a result of the great expansion of trade and communication between the coast and the interior in the nineteenth century.[4] In eastern Africa, too, there were links between famine, social dislocation and endemic smallpox which have been explored by Marc Dawson:

Although smallpox has a long history of endemicity in Kenya, the epidemiology of the disease has changed through time. The social and economic changes of the colonial period had significant effects on the way smallpox was spread. In the late nineteenth century, the disease maintained a very low level of endemicity, and at times of ecological stress flared into devastating epidemics. The early colonial periods saw the disease appear more frequently in small local outbreaks with sizeable epidemics becoming uncommon ... As intercommunication increased with the growth of trade, population movements and urban centers, the incidence of smallpox increased, giving rise to many local outbreaks. With the more frequent outbreaks of smallpox in the colonial period, the level of immunity in the population as a whole would rise ... and the disease would tend to appear in a milder form.[5]

[3] J. B. Peires, *The Dead Will Arise. Nongqawuse and the Great Cattle-Killing Movement of 1856–7* (London, 1989), pp. 31–2.
[4] M. Singleton, 'Smallpox in Person or Personification Personalization (Africa)?', *Anthropos*, 71 (1976).
[5] M. Dawson, 'Smallpox in Kenya, 1880–1920', *Social Science and Medicine*, 13B (1979), pp. 239, 249.

Dawson discusses the smallpox epidemics among the Kamba, Kikuyu and other Kenyan peoples in the years 1897 to 1900 in ways which help to set up our later discussion of prophetic response. He shows that the epidemics were preceded by famine and by cattle losses through rinderpest. These set in train large-scale migrations in search of food and after the eruption of smallpox among the Kamba in early 1899 the disease spread rapidly to demoralised populations facing a total ecological crisis. A 'further reason for the massive smallpox epidemics was the breakdown during famines of the traditional means of dealing with the endemic form of the disease', and in particular of the practices of isolation and inoculation.[6]

The periodisation of smallpox means that its epidemics offered a challenge to mission Christianity and colonial medicine in Cape Colony but mostly to African religion and to Islam further north. It was very different with the great influenza pandemic of 1918 which struck at a time when missionary Christianity and colonial medicine had become established almost everywhere and were beginning to make triumphalist claims. There had been many 'influenza' epidemics in Europe and America during the nineteenth century and in southern Africa several much milder outbreaks had been described as influenza prior to the calamity of late 1918.[7] What distinguished the 1918 outbreak everywhere, of course, was its intensity, its rapidity and its unresponsiveness to any form of medication. This deadly variant of influenza reached South Africa by ship in September 1918 and spread along lines of communication and migrant labour, arriving in Southern Rhodesia by October. Those congregated in towns and mining compounds were first, and most severely, affected. Thereafter the disease spread into the rural areas as men fled from the towns. There its impact was uneven, some kraals being devastated and others unaffected. Some people died suddenly, with no preceding symptoms; others languished for days with severe pulmonary and other symptoms. In its novelty, its generality, its capriciousness, its immunity to treatment, the pandemic was bound to give rise to intense speculation and to challenges to established systems of medical thought and practice, not least those of the missions and of the colonial administrations. Then the pandemic was over as suddenly as it had struck, though there was a sharp

6 *Ibid.*, pp. 246–7.
7 Zvidzai Ndava, 'A Study of the 1918–1919 Spanish Influenza Pandemic in Southern Rhodesia' (Univ. of Zimbabwe, BA thesis, 1987).

recrudescence in 1919 and much less severe 'influenza' outbreaks regularly thereafter. On such occasions the colonial administrations hastened to reassure their African subjects that these did *not* represent a return of the pandemic of 1918.

The two cattle epidemics with which this chapter is concerned were earlier in their impact, overlapping with smallpox rather than with influenza, and so forming part of that general nineteenth-century ecological crisis to which African religion had above all to respond. Lungsickness arrived at the Cape aboard a ship carrying Friesian bulls in 1853. By 1854 it had reached Xhosaland where it not only caused the deaths of thousands of cattle but combined with military defeat, land alienation and drought to produce a general crisis. As Peires has written:

> Starting off as little more than a dry, husky cough, lungsickness slowly tightened its grip on the hapless beasts it destroyed, bringing them to a lingering and uniquely horrible death. The cough gradually increased in severity, forcing the animals to stretch forward with their front legs wide apart, their heads extended and their tongues protruding, gasping for air. Yellowish fluid crept over their lungs which stuck to their ribs, and as the disease spread, the cattle putrefied from the inside out . . . In their final agony, the beasts were unable to move or lie down at all . . . Unable to eat, they wasted away and died mere skeletons.[8]

As Peires remarks, 'one can only imagine the emotional impact of this on the Xhosa owner, whose entire social and economic well being depended on his cattle, and who, moreover, loved each beast individually as no miser ever loved his gold'.[9] The disease manifestly offered a terrible metaphor for the concealed inner rot of society itself. Moreover, it came together with a plague of grubs which destroyed the maize, with excessive rains and flocks of marauding birds. 'It seemed as if nature herself was in league with the enemies of the Xhosa.'[10] It was this context which gave lungsickness so devastating an emotional and ideological impact 'at its very first stop' in Xhosaland, an impact not repeated so intensely as the disease spread all over Africa.

Rinderpest, whose symptoms are almost equally distressing to cattle owners, arrived in Africa in the opening months of 1887,

---

[8] Peires, *The Dead Will Arise*, p. 70.
[9] J. B. Peires, 'The Central Beliefs of the Xhosa Cattle-Killing', MS, n.d., pp. 7–8.
[10] Peires, *The Dead Will Arise*, p. 70.

brought to Eritrea by Italian imports of infected cattle. Unlike lungsickness (or influenza) it spread from north to south. It reached the Kenyan coast in 1889; crossed the Zambesi early in 1896 and within a few months had arrived in South Africa. The disease struck rapidly and dramatically; cattle healthy at the beginning of a journey would collapse and die before it ended. But the greatest impact on African ideas came not from the collapse of beasts but from the threatened collapse of societies. For many southern African peoples cattle provided not only milk and hides and dung for fuel, but also payment for bride-price, power for ploughing and resources for the patronage of great men. Rinderpest seemed to threaten a levelling of society to a uniform impoverishment. Its threat was all the more felt because rinderpest did not strike alone but combined with smallpox and drought to create a general ecological crisis in eastern Africa in the late 1880s and 1890s and in southern Africa after 1896.

Three of these diseases, then, lungsickness, rinderpest and influenza, undeniably entered Africa from without in the nineteenth and early twentieth centuries. Smallpox also affected some African peoples as a result of European activities. Yet the response of African religion was by no means merely to reassert itself against alien ideas.

AFRICAN RELIGION AND EPIDEMICS

The prophetic response within African religion arose out of the collapse or perceived inadequacy of 'traditional' public health control systems. This perhaps requires some explanation for non-Africanist readers since while the notion of 'medical orthodoxies' within Islam and Christianity will be familiar enough, the idea of 'traditional' African public health ideologies and practices may cause some surprise. Steven Feierman has given the most complete account of the operation of such public health control systems, cast in African thought idioms, as they operated in Tanzania before the eco-crisis at the end of the nineteenth century. Writing of the Shambaa of north-eastern Tanzania he says:

> Authority for the control of health was in the hands of a set of leaders which included chiefs, healers and local patriarchs. These controlled the conditions of health in several different ways. First, they were responsible for controlling the kinds of deviance which were thought to threaten communal health. Biomedical health

authorities would no doubt agree with them on some points and not on others. Diviners identified witches, and chiefs eliminated them ... Patriarchs, on the advice of diviners, drove out or killed polluted individuals whose presence threatened the survival of local kinship groups. These included twins, and also people with smallpox who were sent out of the village into isolation. The authorities also regulated land-use to increase chances of survival. The same triad of healing specialists, chiefs and patriarchs regulated the use of irrigation channels, burial of the dead, placement of the villages and the location of sites for human waste ... Those with authority also organized rites for communal well-being, to prevent famine, epidemics and damaging wars.[11]

This, then, was an African 'official' system of 'orthodox' medical theory and practice, though plainly none of the officers involved were medics and what was aimed at was total social order.

Such African public health orthodoxies predated smallpox but could be extended to include various routine protections against it. One such was the isolation of smallpox sufferers. Another was the idiom of personification whereby smallpox was domesticated and combated rather in the manner Peregrine Horden suggests for medieval malaria earlier in this book. Michael Singleton, who has given the fullest account of the personalisation of smallpox – in this case in late nineteenth-century south-west Tanzania – quotes an informant who shows how an encounter with smallpox as a personified force was followed by the establishment of control mechanisms.

Eighty years ago there was no smallpox in the area but it was heard of in surrounding areas and in fact there were epidemics in the surrounding country ... When the people began to fear that *ndui* (something with power) might arrive among them, six young men went to a village about fifteen miles away to get *dawa* (medicine). The night they returned to the village a voice was heard repeating 'wamefika kunichujwa' (they have come to take me). A few days later all the young men were stricken by the disease and all died. They were followed by many others in the village. A *mganga* (medicine man) was called in and he vaccinated them against smallpox. The *dawa* was made from the roots and leaves of the *mlenda* (a spinach-like plant).[12]

[11] Steven Feierman, 'The Social Origins of Health and Healing in Africa', MS, 1984, p. 62.
[12] Singleton, 'Smallpox in Person', p. 177.

Sometimes, indeed, we can see the prophetic idiom itself being used to insert protection against smallpox into the orthodox control system rather than to challenge the very notion of protective orthodoxy. This seems to have been the case, for example, with the nineteenth-century Tswana prophet, Tolonyane, who is remembered preeminently for being able 'to foretell disease and drought'. Tolonyane was critical of other 'doctors' who 'dug' for medicines – i.e. herbalists. He himself arrived at treatments by revelation. 'He is said to have predicted a smallpox epidemic, for which he prescribed inoculation of pus from the pox of a patient who had the disease in a moderate degree.'[13]

But the most dramatic prophetic movements arose when the orthodox control systems were seen to be beyond modification. At many moments during the nineteenth century, and very widely in the 1880s and 1890s, neither smallpox, nor drought, nor cattle disease were being kept at bay, and taken together were creating a general ecological crisis. Feierman describes what happened in Shambaa country, stressing the impact of colonial rule, which was coincident there with the late nineteenth-century eco-crisis:

> German conquest can be interpreted (and quite probably was at the time) as an assault on health. The king, whose body was a symbol of fertility and public health, was executed. Forced labour interfered with farming activities – the source of satiety and well-being. Some healers were arrested and beaten. European planters interfered with irrigation ditches and dug up graves. The government controlled the siting of villages. Missionaries cut down bits of ritually dangerous forest, and gave shelter to lepers. At least one chief was killed for his role in administering communal medicines.[14]

In Feierman's view, the health consequences of these disruptions were disastrous. The years of conquest were

> a time of disastrous population loss over large parts of the continent, especially in Eastern and Equatorial Africa. They were years in which knowledge and power were separated. The local African authorities who had the knowledge necessary for preserving population in their particular environments lost power. And the conquerors, who had sufficient power to change basic living

---

[13] B. A. Pauw, *Religion in a Tswana Chiefdom* (Oxford, 1960), p. 30.
[14] Feierman, 'The Social Origins of Health', p. 63.

conditions, had not yet begun to understand the environment or the nature of local economies.[15]

Yet colonial intervention was not an essential factor in the collapse of public health orthodoxies in nineteenth-century eastern and southern Africa. The divorce of knowledge from power could take place when those Africans with the power were confronted with new diseases of which they were themselves ignorant, or when they abused their position for private profit. In such circumstances, the credibility of the orthodoxies lapsed.

This distinction between external intervention and internal moral crisis is not, of course, a sharp one. In many cases the two processes were simultaneous and interlinked. Still, it is a useful one and especially when we come to discuss the many and famous eastern and southern African prophets of the late nineteenth and early twentieth centuries. A major tradition of historical writing has interpreted these prophets essentially as leaders of anti-colonial and anti-missionary sentiment and resistance. This has been the emphasis, for instance, of African cultural nationalists. Jomo Kenyatta, in *Facing Mount Kenya*, discussed Kikuyu prophecy in these terms.[16] So, too, have subsequent African historians in Kenya. I shall quote only one of them – F. E. Makila's account of the Bukusu prophet, Mutonyi wa Nabukelembe. In Makila's version, Mutonyi foresaw 'a new breed of strangers' who 'would transform the country as no one had ever seen before'. Mutonyi summoned his countrymen to listen to his warnings. Strangers would come with skins the colour of the brown termite, with hair as long as a cow's tail-end, with clothes like a giant white mushroom. 'There is a bull coming which will court your herds and mount your cows . . . and this bull will stay amidst our herds for a long time.' He ended: 'You will cultivate for them, you will build houses for them, and to make it worse, you will even cook for them.'

In Makila's spirited account, Mutonyi's audience grew restless and openly contemptuous. There were murmurs of 'Why should he feed us with this drab fatalism? . . . Impossible. It is all bull-shit.' But Mutonyi won them back with a second prophecy. 'A different generation will breed a black bull amidst us which will compete with the red bull and in the end the black bull will dominate the kraal.'

---

[15] *Ibid.*, p. 66.
[16] Jomo Kenyatta, *Facing Mount Kenyatta. The Tribal Life of the Gikikuyu* (London, 1953).

The prophet declared that he himself wished to die before the new people arrived – and he was indeed soon after killed by cattle-rustlers. But he had prepared his people for colonialism, says Makila. Thereafter the brave ones among them believed in Mutonyi, rather than 'any of the Mongolo-Caucasoid prophets' offered by Christianity and Islam, and later nationalists prayed to Mutonyi to help drive the whites away and to usher in the age of the black bull.[17]

Makila here stresses all the themes which are central to a proto-nationalist account of pre-colonial prophets – the fact that colonial invasion was foreseen in indigenous terms and hence as part of indigenous history; the situating of the Europeans in local compre-hension by environmental and animal metaphors; the promise of the coming of the black bull. In such accounts the defining characteristic of the prophet was prediction. And there are parallel stories throughout eastern and southern Africa. Nor has this stress on resistance been unique to African cultural nationalists. European administrators feared the prophets, and many historians of prophetic movements have seen their fear as justified. Thus the sequence of Xhosa prophets which climaxed in the cattle-killing movement of the 1850s has been seen as anti-white; so have African responses to rinderpest in the 1880s and 1890s; so too has the sequence of Nuer prophets in the southern Sudan, whose ritual pyramids the British colonial administration tried to bomb from the air and dynamite from the ground.

Now, if we take an epidemiological perspective rather than a political one it still seems plausible that prophets arising during smallpox outbreaks, or lungsickness and rinderpest epidemics – all perceived as externally generated – or observing the colonial des-truction of African systems of public health, should focus especially on the intrusion of whites. Yet recent work has increasingly seen the prophets as concerned indeed with epidemics but much more in terms of the need to transform their own societies than in terms of defending the existing institutions of those societies against colonialism.

Scholars have often treated prophetic leadership respectfully when it led to anti-colonial uprisings but have been embarrassed by movements of 'intense religiosity' when directed internally, seeing

[17] F. E. Makila, *An Outline History of the Babukusu* (Nairobi, 1978), pp. 216–20.

these as ways of evading the real issues. Yet 'revolutions' need not be anti-colonial and 'intense religiosity' need not be false consciousness or an escape from social contradictions. Religion was rather the idiom for profound and perhaps 'revolutionary' challenge to the official orthodoxies of African societies themselves. Recent studies have got us much further into the heart of the meaning of such 'intense religiosity'. I want now to focus on two such studies, one on the Nuer prophetic succession, the other on the Xhosa cattle-killing. Both have been seen in the past as charismatic and millenarian incitements to anti-colonial militancy. Yet both, in the treatments of Douglas Johnson and Jeff Peires, are shown as something quite different – as movements arising out of the collapse or inadequacy of indigenous institutions of control; aiming to reconstitute a condition of peace, prosperity and fertility; concerned primarily with internal cleansing and ideological transformation.

I have chosen these two cases because they represent striking prophetic traditions or sequences. I have chosen them also because they represent a prophetic response which goes beyond the norm. We saw above how the Tswana prophet Tolonyane used his gifts chiefly to insert protections against smallpox into the orthodoxy of public health. That represented the minimal prophetic response to epidemic. Next along the spectrum came what might be called the 'normal' prophetic reaction, which has been documented in many studies of African prophecy. This was denunciation in order to restore legitimacy; a critique of corrupt chiefs and fraudulent healers in order to restore purified institutions of chieftainship and healing.[18] In the Nuer and Xhosa sequences, however, prophets went further and preached a more radical dispensation. In the Nuer case they sought to replace elders and diviners with continuous prophetic control of 'public health'. In the Xhosa case they sought to achieve a millennium.

Douglas Johnson's forthcoming magisterial analysis of Nuer prophets, on which he has kindly allowed me to draw, seeks to show that they were not war-leaders or anti-colonial rebels but men who sought peace and fertility in a moral society. For him, the prophetic response to epidemic, if not determinative, was at least as important

---

[18] The 'normal' prophetic response has been described in recent years by many historically conscious anthropologists, in particular by John Janzen and Wyatt MacGaffey for the Bakongo prophetic sequence and Matthew Schoffeleers for the M'bona shrines of southern Malawi.

as (and prior to) the prophetic response to colonial rule. Nineteenth-century Nuer society had been disrupted by slave-raiding, migration, drought and epidemic. The first of the great Nuer prophets, Ngundeng Bong, who was born at the end of the 1830s, reached early manhood in 'a period of drought and scarcity'; Nuer invaders of Anuak territory in the 1850s lost cattle to tsetse and themselves died in large numbers from smallpox. Ngundeng's possession by Spirit gave him powers to ensure fertility, cure barren women and protect society from epidemic:

> His reputation was considerably enhanced by his response to the twin epidemics of smallpox and rinderpest which entered Nuer country from Ethiopia in about 1889–90. He is said to have foreseen these diseases and went out to meet them in bush, sacrificing dozens of oxen in front of the path of the plagues, leaving them to rot, untouched, and sacrificing more cattle in his village ... The smallpox appears to have been halted ... To prevent a recurrence he then built his famous Mound, in which all diseases and bad things were buried.[19]

All evil was enclosed in the mound, 'all diseases and epidemics, all magic.' Ngundeng warred against magicians and false doctors. He became himself the supreme moral authority replacing all previous ritual and political leaders.

Johnson stresses that the prophet was seen as overcoming *all* dimensions of nineteenth-century disorder: 'The peace and welfare the prophet brought came through his prayers for rain, cattle and crops, through his sacrifices to combat infertility, epidemics and illness, and through his prohibitions against fighting. It was, in fact, the overcoming of death, the gift of life.'[20] He did not emerge as a response to 'foreign aggression'. Rather he drew on Dinka religious ideas in order to resolve internal Nuer division and insecurity. By the time of the rinderpest epidemic of 1889–90 'he had already articulated a philosophy of social harmony' and his perceived success in combating epidemic enabled him to mobilise followers into acceptance of that philosophy. He was not a violent opponent of the colonial regime, but 'because of that government's own gratuitous violence Ngundeng could not be reconciled'.

Johnson shows how subsequent prophets worked in this same tradition. They too were expected to halt epidemics of beasts and

[19] D. Johnson, 'Nuer Prophets', MS, 1989, p. 126.   [20] *Ibid.*, p. 161.

men. The prophet Deng Laka 'gave forewarning of plagues . . . and sacrificed cattle against epidemics'. The woman prophet, Nyabuor Yoal, was seized by Spirit at a time of 'the simultaneous death of crops and beasts'; only after her possession did 'the land once again begin to prosper'. The Dok Nuer sought a prophet in the late 1910s and one Buom was possessed. Johnson says that the Dok looked for a prophet because of famine, flooding and cattle epidemic. Once possessed, Buom began 'sacrificing to protect cattle and crops'; in the following year there was an abundant harvest and cattle disease ended. Plainly by this time the prophetic idiom had become in itself an institution of public health.[21]

The Nuer prophets were able to move to the centre of the society partly because the Nuer did not possess powerful chiefs. It was very different with the Xhosa. Here the successive prophets felt even more keenly the need to cleanse a filthy society but they did not aspire to set up continuous prophetic control of fertility and morality. Influenced by the diffusion of Christian ideas, they aimed at millennium. In his remarkable *The Dead Will Arise* Jeff Peires describes the sequence from the smallpox epidemic of 1770 to the lungsickness epidemic of 1854. The collapse of funerary rituals after the smallpox epidemic intensified tensions within Xhosa society, already exacerbated by war, loss of land and the pressures of the white colonial economy. In response to these tensions, and influenced by missionary preaching on the resurrection of the dead, there arose the prophet Nxele. In the 1810s Nxele taught that the Xhosa must cleanse their society and that the dead would return:

'Leave off witchcraft. Leave off blood', Nxele had ordered the Xhosa, 'These are the things that are killing our people. I am sent by the Great Chief of heaven and earth and all other things to say, lay aside these two evils, so that the world can be made right again.' A great day was coming, a day on which the people who had passed away would rise again from the dead and the witches would be cast into damnation under the earth.[22]

Nxele combined this teaching of the need to placate the God of the blacks, Mdalidephu, with the parallel teaching that the whites had mortally sinned against *their* God, Thixo, by slaying his son, Tayi. Hence Nxele's doctrine 'inspired the Xhosa during the Fifth Frontier War' and Nxele himself died by drowning as he sought to

[21] *Ibid.*, pp. 266, 277, 290.
[22] Peires, *The Dead Will Arise* (London, 1989), p. 2.

escape from prison on Robben Island. The subsequent prophet, Mlanjeni, who inspired the war against the British between 1850 and 1853, also combined the ideas of internal corruption and the intolerable affront to the divine constituted by the white presence. Mlanjeni came to believe as a young man that 'the power of evil pervaded the world'; he withdrew from society; purified himself; and emerged with 'a special mission for the reformation of mankind'. Mlanjeni taught that the eco-crisis of 1850 was the result of sin.

Mlanjeni launched what anthropologists call a 'witchcraft eradication movement', detecting witches yet not killing or exiling them but rather curing and cleansing them. By so doing, he superseded the routine orthodoxies of divination and protective charms, which came to be classified as *ubuthi*. He came to achieve a sort of this worldly millennium. 'Freed of tension, suspicion and malicious gossip for the first time in many years, the Xhosa relaxed in an atmosphere of peace and security.' But Mlanjeni went beyond this. Now that the nation itself was cleansed, the next steps could be taken. The intrusive and corrupting whites could be driven out and then the millennium completed by the return of the ancestors. Mlanjeni ordered the slaughter of selected cattle; doctored the regiments; and launched another abortive war.[23]

But the twin notions of profound internal corruption and of the return of the ancestors once society had been cleansed did not necessarily have an anti-colonial emphasis. Peires argues that the notorious cattle-killing of 1856–7 and the prophetic ministry of Nongqawuse should not be seen as anti-colonial resistance. It was a response to the unique experience of the lungsickness epidemic, drawing upon the ideas of the Xhosa prophetic tradition and adding to them to produce its own extraordinary ideology. We have already seen how the disease itself impressed the cattle-loving Xhosa as a terrible metaphor of internal corruption. Peires adds that the epidemic defied all the precautions of orthodox public health:

> The Xhosa could see the disease coming and took all the precautions they could to escape from it. They drove their precious cattle to mountainous and secluded places. They quarantined all strange cattle within their borders and prohibited the introduction of others. They fenced kilometre after kilometre of pasturage, and burnt the grass all round the perimeter until the night sky was

---

[23] *Ibid.*, p. 2.

illuminated by the reflection of the flames. Infected carcasses were buried deep in the ground ... King Sarhili and the other chiefs executed men caught infringing these regulations.[24]

It was all in vain. There were massive cattle losses; the maize was blighted. 'Nothing like this', says Peires, 'had ever happened before.' If nature itself warred on the Xhosa it was time for an internal cleansing more profound than any hitherto attempted.

Peires shows that at the time the Governor, Grey, believed that Nongqawuse's movement was a conspiracy against the whites. By contrast he shows the irrelevance of the whites to what was above all a movement of internal cleansing and regeneration. Nongqawuse extended the idea of uncleanliness to cattle as well as to witches. Witches were to be killed. But all existing cattle, even if they had survived the epidemic, were also tainted and must also be destroyed. She ordered their slaughter; some 85 per cent of all Xhosa men obeyed; some 400,000 cattle were killed. Nongqawuse also extended the idea of resurrection to cattle. When all the tainted beasts were eliminated, they would be replaced with pure, recreated cattle, returning with the ancestors in a recreated universe.

Yet the simple idea of the substitution of pure cattle for tainted ones, of reborn ancestors for witches, was in itself inadequate. When the execution of witches failed to stop the spread of the disease, people began to think in terms of a much wider societal guilt. Society itself had to be made anew. The killing of the cattle became a sacrifice of propitiation. The aim was that the whole nation would arise from the dead. The act of Creation would be repeated; the earth itself would be regenerated; there would be new people; new cattle; eternal youth for all. Nongqawuse's prophetic message was the most totalist of responses to the collapse of a public orthodoxy of health which had been precipitated by one epidemic and rendered intolerable by another.

Now, of course, this totalist response was also a disastrous one. At least 20,000 Xhosa died of starvation; more were uprooted; the nation was at the mercy of colonial social engineering. Here we confront the problem of evaluation of the prophetic responses I have been discussing. In his commentary on the original version of this chapter, Gwyn Prins criticised the idea of prophetic movements as signs of popular cultural vitality. Instead he saw in the cattle-killing

---

[24] *Ibid.*, p. 71.

'not cultural suicide, but something worse', 'the sucking out of the very pith of culture from the shell of its social structure'. The case was all too relevant, he thought, to Africa's present condition: 'We must prepare for a triangular crisis. At one apex, epidemic; at the second, collapse of the internal legitimacy of the inheritor states of modern Africa; at the third, collapse of individual entitlements, leading to famine ... Truly, we must prepare for a politics of despair.'[25] Yet what I hope has emerged is the range and variety of the prophetic response within African religion. Some prophets succeeded in establishing protective measures against smallpox. Others succeeded in revalidating the legitimacy of chiefs and healers. The Nuer prophets gave effective moral leadership. Prins himself stresses that it is important to document 'the range and nature of local responses' to epidemic 'and frequent success, even in the disaster decade of the 1890s'. I should suppose that we need to be alert to the range of local responses – among them prophetic responses and to the possibilities of success as we enter what Prins expects to be the disaster decade of the 1990s; as, in his words, 'Africa is about to pass again behind the curtain of the image of a sick and helpless continent.'[26]

ISLAM AND EPIDEMIC

Prior to the later nineteenth-century context of epidemic and upheaval, Islam in East Africa was confined to the coast and the islands. There was a complex medical orthodoxy, relatively little influenced by the scholarly ban on belief in spirits and insistence on an 'omnipotent and all-ordaining God' which Lawrence Conrad describes in this book. Rather, there was much interaction between popular, oral Islam and local spirit belief, with a slight flavouring of Islamic scholarly ideas. In this relaxed state of compromise, where endemic diseases were dealt with by a variety of practitioners, there was nevertheless a prestige urban healing elite:

> There arose a rough distinction between 'town' learning (*elimu*) and 'bush' learning (*uganga*). Town learning was considered religion, while knowledge which came from non-Islamic regions adjacent to the coast was simply 'medicine' ... Individual *tabibs* (*walimu* who specialised in medicine) were noted for being

[25] Gwyn Prins, 'Commentary', Past and Present Conference, September 1989, p. 4.
[26] *Ibid.*, p. 3.

especially skilful in treating certain conditions ... specialists in treating tuberculosis, dropsy, rheumatism, skin disorders, headaches, eye cataracts, and in mending broken bones ... In some centres where written sources were available on the subject, there was some knowledge of the Greek medical tradition and astrology which had been preserved in Islamic sciences.[27]

This long-established balance changed in the nineteenth century as coastal caravans traversed long-distance routes into the interior and as porters and traders and slaves came to the coast from inland societies. Disease spread along the trade routes. In the Tanzanian south-west, where people came to think of smallpox as a person, the personified disease was remembered as a 'young chap from the coast with a small drum in his hand and a bale of cloth on which he was seated'.[28] On the coast, as the numbers of slaves increased and the plantation economy developed, so fears of contagion and epidemic grew. Ideologies and orthodoxies hardened. The idea of pollution, which had always underlain ideas about disease, now came to be applied systematically to slaves, even those converted to Islam.

Scholars have recently documented the rise of an elite, literate Islamic orthodoxy on the East African coast during the last quarter of the nineteenth century. Pouwels describes 'a new literacy':

> The security of the Sultanate, the increasing availability of religious texts, the appearance of new *ulama* from other parts of the coast and from abroad, and the new contacts established from expanding trade opened up coastal towns to new religious perceptions ... All the most prestigious *ulama* at some time or another performed the *haj* and studied in centres in Arabia which were famous for learning in the written Islamic tradition ... They were trained in at least one of the traditional written sciences.[29]

Ideas about disease, healing and medicine were affected by this new elite literacy.

Fred Cooper has shown how far the new *ulama* gave ideological support to the hierarchies and stratifications of coastal slave society:

> Slaveholders could seek in Islam a framework for a hegemonic ideology ... [There was an] interpenetration of the 'learned classes' with wealthy traders, slaveowning families, and political

---

[27] R. L. Pouwels, *Horn and Crescent. Cultural Change and Traditional Islam on the East African Coast, 800–1900* (Cambridge, 1987), pp. 90–1.

[28] Singleton, 'Smallpox in Person', p. 174.

[29] Pouwels, *Horn and Crescent*, p. 145.

elites ... Some of the wealthiest slaveowning and trading families provided the leading scholars and some families had trading and scholarly connections all along the coast ... The slaveowners of the East African coast claimed to be better Muslims. The Qur'an provided the ultimate basis for such a claim ... This was made vivid in ritual form. In Lamu, slaves and their descendants were relegated to a certain part of the mosque and excluded from certain rituals. Such restrictions sprang from a concept of religious purity. Free Lamuans were symbolically associated with light, with heavenly purity. But the slave was close to nature; his thoughts too were earthy. Too close contact with slaves could contaminate Lamuans; only the most rudimentary forms of Islam could be appreciated by slaves.[30]

But this sort of elitist Islamic ideology was not uncontested. Cooper goes on to describe how slaves on the coast and islands tried to 'combat the slaveholders' ideology on its own terms'. He draws on Abdul Hamid el-Zein's extraordinary study of Lamu. In the 1890s the recently emancipated slaves suffered continued and gross discrimination in Lamu. The leading Islamic spokesmen, the *sharifs*, taught that only free men were proper to Lamu. The ex-slaves were 'the defiled people, the forest people, the people of the bush ... part of nature in the crudest sense of the word', a dangerous source of pollution and threat of disease.[31] In reaction the ex-slaves repudiated the authority of these *sharifs*; began their own Islamic rituals; and asserted their own version 'of many myths and symbols':

Where the slaveowners' view of the Creation stressed the distinct categories of beings that were created, the slaves' version played this down and instead stressed that if Adam – God's own creation – could betray Him, so could a person of any birth, and conversely, the deeper anyone's faith and piety, the greater his religious purity.[32]

A young Islamic scholar, Sharif Saleh, emerged to lead the ex-slaves and to build up a movement of popular Islam in Lamu which challenged the old orthodoxies and the old authorities. This popular Islam focussed on Sharif Saleh as the immediate representative of

---

[30] F. Cooper, 'Islam and Cultural Hegemony: The Ideology of Slaveowners on the East African Coast', in P. Lovejoy (ed.), *The Ideology of Slavery in Africa* (London, 1981), pp. 283, 292.

[31] Abdul Hamid el Zein, *The Sacred Meadows* (Evanston, Ill., 1974), p. 109.

[32] Cooper, 'Islam and Cultural Hegemony', p. 292.

the Prophet Mohammed himself and there is a very real sense in which it can be called a prophetic movement. Cooper shows similar developments in Bagamoyo, Malindi and elsewhere on the coast. Like prophetic movements within African religions the cults of the ex-slaves responded to political, social, ecological and epidemic crises by emphasising purification and the superiority of faith to works.

It was in this context of epidemic and upheaval – and of religious innovation – that Islam spread for the first time from the coast to the societies of the interior. Until recently historians have interpreted the spread of Islam at the end of the nineteenth century as the fruit of 'blind anti-christian or anti-European fanaticism'. The *shaikhs* who went into the interior on behalf of the various Islamic mission- ary brotherhoods have been seen as mini-*mahdis*, revolutionary anti- colonial prophets. But they are better understood, as Constantin has recently argued, as prophetic critics *within* East African Islam. The brotherhoods, he writes, were 'the motor for a kind of reaction against what was perceived as oppression even when exercised by a Muslim authority'. The charismatic *shaikhs*

> who spread the message of the Qadiriya or the Shadhiliyya did not engage in any mystic-military struggle or *jihad* against the colonial power ... Their only weapon was the word ... [Instead] they contributed to an Islamicisation of the indigenous peoples and slaves never contemplated by the ruling Arabs, whose monopoly over the Arab-Islamic culture was a corner-stone of their position of quasi-hegemony.[33]

The *shaikhs* were preeminently miracle workers. *Shaikh* Ramiya made his disciples walk on water; Habib Saleh could stop storms or blazing fires; *Shaikh* Kiponda b. Selemani, on the banks of the Malawi, predicted future events, including the influenza pandemic of 1918. Such feats attracted those longing for 'the reduction of the barriers between the rulers and ruled' within Islamic societies. The *shaikhs* attracted especially slaves and ex-slaves, the deprived, women. These followers became missionaries to the tribesmen of the interior. Above all they offered healing. The brotherhoods 'served both as guilds and as therapeutic centres for psychological dis- orders'; the *shaikh*'s 'therapeutic powers were evidence of his

---

[33] F. Constantin, 'Charism and the Crisis of Power in East Africa', in D. B. C. O'Brien (ed.), *Charisma and Brotherhood in African Islam* (Oxford, 1988), pp. 68, 72.

charisma, resolving personality crises which jeopardised public order. So it is that features of Bantu society (cults of possession and healing) facilitated the spread of Muslim charisma.'[34]

Conversion to Islam took place in the context of epidemic. David Sperling in his 1988 doctoral thesis on the growth of Islam among the Mijikenda of Kenya, writes of the conversion of Kivoyero Mwapodzo, the first elder of Diani to become a Muslim. During the famine of 1884–5 Mwapodzo and his father went to stay with Muslim relatives; both then contracted smallpox. The father died, but Mwapodzo 'was cured and became Abdallah'. 'When he came back after the famine, he was a Muslim and was speaking Swahili.' During the same famine, other Digo went to Muslim immigrants into Digo country in search of food; they were told 'that they had an Arab devil and were sick; that they would get better if they became Muslims'.[35] These conversions took Digo away from their own orthodoxy of public medicine but did *not* take them into any sort of official Islamic orthodoxy of public health. The charismatic brotherhoods were alternative communities, seeking the good not so much by reconstruction of tribal or coastal societies but by withdrawal from them.

CHRISTIANITY AND EPIDEMICS

In much of southern Africa, and parts of eastern Africa, the initial diffusion of Christianity took place in the same troubled setting of epidemic and upheaval which was the context for the rise of African prophets and the spread of Islamic charismatic brotherhoods. I began this chapter with the destruction of the 'Hottentots' or Khoikhoi, undermined by smallpox, enslaved, brutalised. Yet before the disappearance of their culture, the Khoikhoi had responded to missionary Christianity as if it were a prophetic movement and had made use of it to redefine and defend their identity. Elizabeth Elbourne describes this process in a fascinating unpublished research paper, which I have her permission to cite. She shows how the majority of Khoikhoi became Christians in 'a highly emotional period of conversion'; many of those who came to hear the London Missionary Society emissaries were 'curious about the

---

[34] *Ibid.*, pp. 75, 83.
[35] D. C. Sperling, 'The Growth of Islam among the Mijikenda of the Kenya Coast, 1826–1933' (School of Oriental and African Studies PhD thesis, 1988), pp. 119, 147.

latest prophet'; the pioneer missionary, Vanderkemp, made rain and healed on request. His preaching also resonated with the traumatic Khoikhoi experience:

> In the chamber of horrors atmosphere of the early Eastern Cape, Calvinist mission Christianity provided a compelling theology of evil which provided an explanation for the apparently meaningless oppression of the Khoisan ... Isaiah 9, 1–3, is a text that fits perfectly into the missionary world view: 'The people that walked in darkness has seen a great light ... the bar across his shoulders, the rod of the oppressor, those you break as on the day of Midian.' It is also a millenarian text, the next verse of which is 'For all the footgear of battle, every cloak rolled in blood, is burned and consumed by fire.' ... According to the evangelical vision, all people are evil, owing to original sin, and can only be rescued from sin by the grace of Jesus. Christ must act on the soul and rebirth must occur if man is ever to rise above his natural wickedness ... Many Khoisan took up this language of the evil of natural man. On the one hand, the purification of the rebirth experience probably provided an outlet for the deep anxieties pervading Khoisan society; there is a tremendously high level of outward emotion described in services, revivals and conversions ... Some Khoisan preachers and missionaries turned the language of fallen man and the equality of the reborn against the Afrikaners ... The settlers upheld a Christianity of exclusion ... arguing that the Khoisan were constitutively incapable of becoming Christian. The Khoisan upheld a Christianity of equality, arguing for access to the moral community through grace alone.[36]

The parallels with ex-slave popular Islam will be obvious.

And like popular Islam this Khoikhoi Christianity was strongly millenarian. The missionaries Read and Vanderkemp believed that 'the vengeance of God was hovering over South Africa. It would soon be unleashed and the land purified at last if white oppression of the indigenous people did not cease.' There had to be a double purification – of Khoikhoi souls and of white society. The endemic sickness of the Khoikhoi, broken only by recurrent epidemic, was a metaphor for sick souls and a sick society. It all sounds not only like ex-slave Islam but like Xhosa prophetic millenarianism. And there were indeed direct connections with the latter. In the war of 1851

---

[36] Elizabeth Elbourne, 'Khoisan and Missionary in the Eastern Cape', MS, 1990, pp. 35, 37–40.

instigated by the Xhosa prophet Mlanjeni some one third of the Cape Colony's Khoikhoi joined the Xhosa 'rebels'; the Khoikhoi rejected missionary pacificism, allied with Xhosa prophetism, but deployed central concepts of their own popular Christianity, especially its millenarianism. As Peires writes:

A new and revolutionary brand of Christianity was introduced to the Xhosa by the Khoi rebels who fought alongside them during the war of Mlanjeni. Mission products all, the Khoi read their Bibles regularly and they prepared themselves for battle by the devout singing of hymns ... The following letter by one of their leaders displays an unmistakably millenarian turn of mind: 'Trust, therefore, in the Lord (whose character is known to be unfriendly to injustice) and undertake your work ... for it is now the time, yea, the appointed time, and no other.'[37]

Peires shows the many echoes of this radical Christianity in Nongqawuse's prophetic movement. The millenarian cleansing creed of a people who were doomed to disappear linked with the millenarian cleansing creed of a people who narrowly survived.

The Khoikhoi were a special case, but much other work, both by anthropologists and historians, is now under way about the early interactions between southern African societies and Christian evangelists. As a result of this work early southern African Christian history begins to appear much more like the dialectical history of African religion and of African Islam than we might have imagined. Yet by the end of the nineteenth century these earlier informalities were giving way almost everywhere to a Christian 'establishment' controlled by white missionaries less passionate and prophetic than Vanderkemp. Missionary stations had developed their own official orthodoxies of public health, which were based on a mixture of moral hygiene, belief in divine providence and commitment to scientific medicine. Missionaries came to put much emphasis upon the evangelical power of doctors and nurses whose dispensation of bio-medicine was thought of as the modern continuance of the healing mission of Christ.

Missionary response to epidemic at the end of the nineteenth century revealed a characteristic mixture of providentialism and modernising calculation. In missionary responses to rinderpest there were some echoes of Vanderkemp. Thus Methodist missionaries

---

[37] Peires, *The Dead Will Arise*, p. 135.

believed that the plague was a punishment from heaven on the reactionary Boer regime in the Transvaal, though they were concerned with sins against Englishmen rather than Khoikhoi. Other missionaries thought that God's purposes were to advance progressive capitalism by driving Africans into the labour market. They also believed that the epidemic would reveal the superiority of Christian 'science' over African 'superstition'.

The most illuminating work done on missionary Christianity and epidemic, however, relates to the influenza epidemic of 1918. By that time, as Megan Vaughan's chapter in this book shows, missionary medicine was self-confident and widely influential, even if, as her chapter also shows, diagnosis was often mistaken and the consequences of treatment paradoxical. Recent work on the influenza pandemic shows that it offered a most formidable challenge to all the dominant missionary assumptions. It might, indeed, appear as a divine judgement on the system of industrialisation and migrant labour and a divine revelation of the inadequacy of the orthodox medical regimes at the mission stations themselves. As we have seen, the disease spread along the migrant labour routes, struck savagely at African workers in urban locations and mining compounds and sent hundreds of thousands of men back to the countryside in panic flight. As many administrators wryly observed, Africans stood a better chance of survival the further away they were from the centres of western bio-medical provision. In the rural areas the mission stations and boarding schools were themselves the first seats of the disease and there were many deaths. This was certainly an epidemic which revealed the impotence of missionary bio-medicine and gave powerful stimulus to alternative ideas of causation and healing.

Both Afrikaners and Africans reacted by declaring the inadequacy and immorality of the British and missionary establishment. Howard Phillips, in his fascinating doctoral thesis on the influenza pandemic in South Africa, shows that there was a sharp division between the three Afrikaans churches in South Africa – who believed the pandemic to be a punishment from God – and the Anglican church, which held it to be a purely natural calamity. Methodists may have believed that rinderpest was God's judgement on the anti-capitalist Boer regime in the Transvaal but Afrikaner theologians were now certain that influenza was His judgement on British colonial capitalism. They pointed to its materialism and its 'worship of science'. Indeed, one Afrikaans church periodical took the 'scientific' explanations which had been advanced to account for the epidemic as 'classic examples of the vanity and conceit which arose when human beings thought they knew better than God and placed Science above Him'. By contrast, there was a strong strain of the prophetic and millennial in Afrikaner responses to the pandemic. Many theologians believed that influenza heralded the Second Coming. The famous Afrikaner seer, Van Rensburg, was said to have predicted the pandemic; in 1916 the visionary Johanna Brandt had 'predicted a great plague as the prelude to the Millennium' and in 1918 she hailed influenza as incontrovertible proof of the accuracy of her prediction. Those Afrikaners who had found solace from the stresses of an industrialising society in membership of the Watchtower and Bible Tract Society or Apostolic and Pentecostal churches also found the pandemic to be a confirmation of their beliefs. Like Johanna Brandt, Watchtower expected the millennium and Apostolic rejection of bio-medicine seemed abundantly justified by its impotence against influenza.[38]

Phillips himself remarks on the similarity between Afrikaner and African responses, suggesting that this suggests a 'correspondence in their structural position in South African society'. Like Afrikaners, Africans in South Africa blamed the pandemic on an unjust and bloody imperial war; on the pressures of industrial capitalism; and on God's wrath. But the most detailed information we possess concerning African responses to the pandemic comes from the Southern Rhodesian case, which both I and the young Zimbabwean historian, Zvidzai Ndava, have studied.

In Southern Rhodesia there was a rapid and universal realisation among black Christians and non-Christians alike of the inefficacy of bio-medicine and of the dangers of remaining in any centre of European enterprise. The question was what alternative ideologies of explanation and control were available and plausible. As Ndava writes:

> Nothing of its sort had ever appeared before among the African population. It brought a clash of the traditional African systems of wisdom about disease against modern wisdom ... Some elders in Chibi district believed that the influenza came just like a 'wind' from somewhere ... probably it was the 'wind' of blood which had flowed freely in the great war. It was traditional knowledge

[38] Howard Phillips, 'Black October: The Impact of the Spanish Influenza Epidemic of 1918 on South Africa' (Univ. of Cape Town, PhD thesis, 1984), ch. 8.

that in most cases wars' aftermaths were inevitably followed by diseases ... due to upset nature ... upheavals in the socio-economic life would be reflected in environmental upsetting.[39]

But how to restore environmental balance and end the epidemic? Africans sought to draw upon the whole range of available interpretations and remedies – searching out witches; sacrificing to Mwali, the High God of the Matopos hills; spirit possession cults of affliction.[40] In short there was recourse to many 'traditional' ways of responding to epidemic, some of them once part of official, orthodox systems of public health and some of them once part of popular counter systems. Yet the one response which did *not* occur in Southern Rhodesia in 1918 – and which does not seem to have occurred elsewhere in southern Africa either – was the emergence of prophetic figures within the African religious tradition.

After all that has gone before in this chapter this must seem surprising. Influenza was at least as devastating as the scourges to which prophets had so effectively responded in the nineteenth century. The answer is that Africans *did* produce prophets in answer to the problems posed by the pandemic but that these were prophets in the *Christian* tradition. It was, after all, Christian bio-medicine which was most challenged by the pandemic. Influenza discredited mission public health orthodoxies among many African Christians. So just as Africans had sought counters to public health orthodoxies in pre-colonial eastern and southern Africa and responded to 'traditional' prophets; just as Africans in the East African coastal hinterland had sought relief from the exploitative elitism of orthodox Islamic medical ideology and practice and had flocked to the charismatic brotherhoods; so now many African Christians sought their own prophetic response to missionary bio-medical regimes. In this way African response to the pandemic was even closer to the Afrikaner since the new African prophets also arose out of the context of counter-establishment apostolic and pentecostal theology.[41]

In Southern Rhodesia the pandemic gave a powerful impetus to the emergence of indigenous Christian prophetic churches – the *Vapostori* movements of Johana Maranke and Johana Masowe.

---

[39] Ndava, 'A Study of the 1918–1919 Spanish Influenza Pandemic', pp. 12, 13.

[40] Terence Ranger, 'The Influenza Pandemic in Southern Rhodesia: A Crisis of Comprehension', in D. A. Arnold (ed.), *Imperial Medicine and Indigenous Societies* (Manchester, 1988).

[41] *Ibid., passim.*

These men were certainly prophets, who had 'died', seen God and been sent back to earth to cleanse society of the pollutions of witchcraft. Like other prophets they denounced the techniques of medical orthodoxy – medicines of all kinds, both African and European – and also the practitioners, whether bio-medics or traditional diviners. In their prophetic teaching, healing came directly to the purified faithful through the descent of the Holy Spirit. The prophetic leader could also redeem nature, bring rain, ensure fertility. These churches were in part a local expression of the great world-wide anti-ecclesiastical establishment movements of pentecostalism and millennialism. They were in part a true indigenous Christian expression of the dialectic I have been seeking to establish within all of southern and eastern Africa's religious traditions.

Now, these movements did not spring up until after the pandemic – indeed, it was so intense in its effects that it was hardly possible for a prophetic movement to emerge during it. But when the visionary Anglican missionary Arthur Cripps came to reflect on the dreadful experiences of mass burial and terror in 1918 he predicted the emergence of African healing churches of the Holy Spirit; the oral testaments of the *Vapostori* churches themselves refer back the initial visions of their founders to the pandemic; their prophetic commission from God drew logical divine conclusions from the failure of bio-medicine in 1918. In this they were part of an Africa-wide response. The Aladura prophetic healing churches of Nigeria arose out of the memory of the quarter of a million dead in southern Nigeria in 1918. Zulu spirit church members interpreted the pandemic as a sign of impending doom and saw recovery from the disease as prophetic death and rebirth. It was in the midst of the pandemic in lower Zaire that Simon Kimbangu heard the voice of Christ calling him to his prophetic mission. Indeed, the main significance of the influenza pandemic in African medical history was the impetus which it gave to the emergence of anti-medicine movements.[42]

CONCLUSION

In many ways this chapter has been not so much an account of responses to epidemic as an account of epidemic as a trigger to

---

[42] *Ibid.*, p. 186.

movements of prophetic innovation. There is a danger here of overemphasising the cruciality of epidemic. As Douglas Johnson insists, Ngundeng had already adumbrated the essentials of the Nuer prophetic idiom before his reputation was enhanced by his successes against smallpox and rinderpest. Christian anti-medicine movements could have emerged – and in parts of Africa already had emerged – without the influenza crisis. Islamic charismatic brotherhoods would certainly have spread even without their interactions with African healing idioms and without the dislocation of epidemic. I agree with Johnson that we must avoid moving from an interpretation of prophetic religion as a crisis response to colonialism only to see it as a crisis response to epidemic.

Nevertheless, epidemics – especially when there is a coincidence of plagues of both beasts and men – *do* represent imaginative and theological challenges to orthodoxies. They sum up everything that is coercive or implausible in an orthodoxy's relationship both to people and to the natural world. Prophets seek to redeem natural creation as well as society. Epidemics dramatise how much both need to be redeemed.

11. *Syphilis in colonial East and Central Africa: the social construction of an epidemic*

MEGAN VAUGHAN

THE FIRST DEFINITIONS OF THE EPIDEMIC

In 1908 a debate unfolded on the pages of *The Lancet* and of the *British Medical Journal* over the causes of an apparently alarming 'epidemic' of syphilis which had broken out in the Uganda Protectorate. In both journals the debate began with an account of a paper recently presented by an officer of the Royal Army Medical Corps, Colonel Lambkin, entitled 'An Outbreak of Syphilis on Virgin Soil'. Lambkin, known for his work on sleeping sickness in Uganda, had described to his medical audience a situation in which syphilis was so widely spread that an estimated 80 per cent of the population of Buganda was infected, and in which a resulting infant mortality rate of 50 to 60 per cent threatened the very survival of what he referred to as the 'race'. The causes of this outbreak, according to Lambkin, were three: the introduction of Christianity, the abolition of previously severe punishments for sexual offences and the opening up of the country to traders from the East. In his analysis, Lambkin laid great stress on the notion of Uganda as a 'virgin soil' in which an innocent and unsuspecting population had been exposed to a new and devastating disease. But the very vulnerability of the Bagandan people had, according to Lambkin, been created by the disintegration of their traditional social and political system brought about primarily by the introduction of Christianity. The lesson, according to the editor of the *British Medical Journal*, was clear:

> The lesson conveyed is this, that in our dealings with subject races it is very important to go gently, and in the first place to respect their customs, the outcome of their evolution and environment, in the next place to avoid dissociating their ideas, which must fatally lead to the break up of such races. Here, a terrible disease has been

269

let loose on an unsuspecting, and in their own way, contented population, and as always with the best and noblest of intentions. The way to hell, again, by an improved method of paving roads.[1]

The Lancet, also reporting Lambkin's address, took up the question of the increased 'freedom' accorded to Bagandan women since the coming of the Europeans and the consequent disruption of 'traditional' rule:

> The freedom enjoyed by women in civilised countries has gradually been won by them as one of the results of centuries of civilisation, during which they have been educated ... Women whose female ancestors had been kept under surveillance were not fit to be treated in a similar manner. They were, in effect, merely female animals with strong passions, to whom unrestricted opportunities for gratifying these passions were suddenly afforded.[2]

Though there was a general consensus that female sexuality was at the heart of the problem, the underlying causes of the unleashing of this danger were hotly disputed in the pages of both journals in the months to come. The missionary lobby was understandably unhappy with an analysis which placed the blame firmly at the door of Christianity. In a letter to the editor of the *BMJ*, Robert Elliott, Secretary of the Church Missionary Society Medical Committee, and Charles Harford, Physician to the Church Missionary Society, protested at the *BMJ*'s account of events in Uganda and asserted that missionaries there held a rather different view of the causes of the spread of syphilis.[3] Meanwhile, the bishop of Uganda, Albert Tucker, who was visiting Britain at the time, wrote to *The Lancet* to make his views clear. It was, he said, the 'sweeping away of the feudal system' in Buganda, which had brought 'not liberty merely but licence'. Christianity, in his opinion, had 'nothing to do with these lamentable consequences'. Quoting Sir Harry Johnston, he argued further that, far from Christianity bringing about a decline in moral standards, it was, in fact, bound to have the opposite effect. Only through the introduction of Christianity, and the 'appreciation of female chastity', would the Baganda be saved from dying out as a 'race'.[4]

The editors of the *BMJ*, however, were soon to declare that they had found another missionary of long Ugandan experience, the

---

[1] Editorial, *British Medical Journal*, 2 (1908), p. 1037.
[2] Editorial, *The Lancet*, 2 (1908), p. 1022.
[3] Letter to the editor, *British Medical Journal*, 2 (1908), p. 1409.
[4] Letter to the editor, *The Lancet*, 2 (1908), p. 1246.

Reverend Roscoe of the Church Missionary Society (CMS), who held firmly to the view that it was female promiscuity resulting from the removal of formerly severe restrictions which accounted for the spread of syphilis.[5]

Behind the scenes in the CMS offices in London there had been a flurry of activity over this issue. The CMS medical missionary, Albert Cook, had been the first to draw attention to the problem of syphilis in Uganda. Although overshadowed by the dramatic epidemic of sleeping sickness of 1900–1, on which so much international attention had been focussed, Cook had frequently asserted that syphilis was 'rampant' in parts of the Uganda Protectorate and constituted a serious medical problem.[6] Lambkin's commission on syphilis in Uganda had taken evidence from many medical missionaries, as well as from administrative officials and chiefs. Albert Cook was named as one of those missionaries who had given evidence, though there was some confusion over whether he had in fact been present. In any case, at the London headquarters of the CMS alarm was expressed at what was seen as unfavourable publicity and the society's physician wrote anxiously to Cook on this matter: 'You will receive a copy of *The Lancet* with a leader on Colonel Lambkin's article on syphilis in Uganda. It seems to me the statement of the case is most unfortunate and I hope that you and your brother jointly may draft a letter on the subject.'[7]

Albert Cook, under increasing pressure from London, wrote a letter to the *BMJ*, which was amended by Harford and published on 12 December 1908. Citing statistics from the mission dispensary, Cook disputed Lambkin's figures for the prevalence of syphilis, arguing that the infection rate was in the order of 15 per cent rather than the 80 per cent claimed by Lambkin. He also disputed Lambkin's analysis of the causes of the 'epidemic':

> Finally, I must give an emphatic denial to the assumption that Christianity has been the chief cause of this epidemic. It has been all the other way. Read 'Civilization' for 'Christianity' and there may be a certain amount of truth in it ... I venture to assert, Sir, that Christianity from the beginning has acted as a deterring and

[5] Editorial, *British Medical Journal*, 2 (1908), p. 1780.

[6] See D. L. Zeller, 'The Establishment of Western Medicine in Buganda' (Columbia Univ. New York, PhD thesis, 1981); B. O'Brien, *That Good Physician* (London, 1962).

[7] Rhodes House Library, Oxford, MSS Afr. s. 1872: Papers of Prof. W. Forster: Harford to Cook, 9.10.08.

restraining force and is, indeed, when intelligently accepted, the only true prophylaxis to this terrible scourge.[8]

By the middle of December 1908, the debate on syphilis in Uganda appeared to have run its course in the pages of the British medical journals. In Uganda, meanwhile, the consequences of this discussion were only beginning to be felt. Though there were real differences of emphasis between what were represented as the two sides of the debate, in fact their proponents shared a great many assumptions. The most central of these was the assumption that the problem was fundamentally a social and moral one. Differences arose, not over the duty of the medical profession to point to the social causes of the epidemic, but in the diagnosis of those social causes.

Two views of traditional Bagandan society were represented here, and two views of the impact of 'westernisation'. On the one hand, Lambkin represented the views of many British officials when he expressed his admiration for the traditional organisation of Bagandan society and its sophisticated system of political and social control. When collecting evidence for the commission of investigation, Lambkin was continually assured by chiefs and headmen that in the past such an epidemic would have been unthinkable.[9] In pre-colonial Buganda (and to a lesser extent in other parts of Uganda), he was told, women were firmly placed under the control of men. As the Prime Minister of the Baganda, Sir Apolo Kagwa, put it, 'the probable immediate cause of the outbreak is the emancipation of Baganda women from the surveillance to which they have hitherto been subjected'.[10]

Given the evidence for the effectiveness of this 'surveillance', and given that female rather than male sexuality was taken to be the problem, Lambkin had to assume that the cause of the epidemic was to be found in the breakdown of the system of chiefly male control occasioned by the extension of Christianity and 'civilisation'. A powerful consensus around this view is clear from the record of the evidence taken by his commission.[11] Unsurprisingly, there was also

---

[8] Letter to the editor, *British Medical Journal*, 2 (1908), pp. 1780–1.
[9] Public Record Office (PRO), CO 536/7: Uganda Correspondence, 1905 onwards: Colonel Lambkin's mission to the Uganda Protectorate on the prevalence of venereal disease.
[10] F. J. Lambkin, 'An Outbreak of Syphilis in a Virgin Soil', in D'A. Power and K. Murphy (eds.), *A System of Syphilis*, 2 vols. (London, 1908), II, p. 344.
[11] PRO, CO 536/7: summary of evidence.

much chiefly support for Lambkin's prescription, which involved the bolstering of chiefly power in order to re-establish social order and control the disease.

Lambkin was much impressed by the Bagandan aristocracy's reception of his account of the syphilis epidemic and the threat it posed to the survival of the Baganda. In January 1908 he had given an address on the subject before the king and a group of senior chiefs. This address was

> listened to with the greatest interest and attention, but nothing surprised me more than the speeches which were delivered by some of the chiefs, showing the most complete and intelligent grasp of the subject under discussion, as well as a thorough knowledge of the ravages which syphilis had already perpetrated ... Listening to those speeches one could hardly believe that one was learning them from the lips of negroes in the centre of Africa.[12]

The medical missionary view of the problem was bound to be rather different. The CMS medical missionaries in Uganda had not had an easy time justifying their work to their own, non-medical, colleagues. The suspicion that medical work represented a superficial way of attracting converts remained.[13] Medical missionaries like Cook had continually to emphasise, in their writing and in their practice, that their medical work was subordinate to their evangelical role. The essential 'sinfulness' of traditional African society was therefore stressed, and the connection between sin and disease was a central feature of medical missionary ideology. An effective cure to any medical problem could only come about through true conversion. Although Cook and his colleagues also held a certain admiration for the traditional organisation of Bagandan society, they necessarily placed more emphasis on what they saw as its essential evils – polygyny and paganism. The syphilis epidemic, then, was represented rather as evidence for the enduring evils of this society, which could only be remedied through a further and deeper extension of the Christian faith.

In the pages of the CMS journal, *Mercy and Truth*, this analysis was made explicit, though explicitness fell short of naming the disease under consideration. In 1910, for instance, J. H. Cook (Albert Cook's brother) wrote of the 'intimate connection between

---

12 Lambkin, 'An Outbreak of Syphilis', p. 344.
13 See Zeller, 'The Establishment of Western Medicine'.

suffering and sin'. Having analysed the figures for out-patient clinics, Cook had concluded that 22 per cent of their patients 'were suffering from diseases directly produced by the appalling immorality and impurity of their lives'.[14] Syphilis, in this medical missionary discourse, was rarely named, but its ravages came to represent the fundamental evils against which the missions were battling. Addressing a Medical Missionary Association meeting in London in 1915, J. H. Cook said that though this was a medical mission meeting 'I cannot, dare not, speak of the fruits of these diseases.' He could say, however, that they were 'ruining that country and sapping the strength of manhood of the natives'.[15]

In Uganda in the second decade of the century differences in analysis between missionaries and officials were largely downplayed, as the need for cooperation became apparent. Medical missionaries provided the facilities attended by the increasing numbers of patients with syphilis. Concern over the spread of what were now termed in the annual medical reports 'venereal diseases', had apparently spread to the Bunyoro, and to other parts of the country, though discussion continued to be focussed on the fate of the Baganda and the belief that they were a dying 'race'.[16] In 1913, legislation was devised which would ensure the compulsory attendance for treatment of all those suffering from 'contagious venereal diseases'. These laws, which placed great responsibility on the chiefs, were circulated to the Buganda chiefly council, the Lukiko, for comment, and approved by them. There was little doubt in the mind of the Principal Medical Officer, G. J. Keane, that the more powerful chiefs were willing and able to enforce these laws, though he had doubts about the 'minor chiefs'. The Medical Officer appointed in charge of venereal disease measures had also undertaken a tour of Bunyoro where:

The anxiety and interest in the subject of the Native Authorities

[14] J. H. Cook, 'The Highest Work of Medical Missions', *Mercy and Truth*, no. 165 (1910), p. 309.

[15] J. H. Cook, 'Pressing Problems in Uganda', *Mercy and Truth*, no. 225 (1915), p. 300.

[16] Over the border from Buganda in north-western Tanganyika, a similar fear was expressed in the 1920s and 1930s over the fate of the Bahaya, amongst whom there was also a high rate of infection with syphilis. For an account of this history, and the role of missionaries in declaring an 'epidemic', see Birgitta Larsson, 'A Dying People?: Women, Church and Social Change in North-Western Tanzania under British Rule', unpublished paper, 1977. I am indebted to Prof. Marcia Wright for this reference.

can only be described as remarkable. The ravages of venereal disease would appear to be more serious than in Buganda, and the Mukama and the leading Chiefs are evidently deeply concerned with regard to the future of their population. They seemed prepared to offer every inducement within their power to Government to commence an anti-venereal scheme. They were prepared to pass any native law, and to provide free buildings, and went so far as to discuss the offering of the half of all the Chiefs' land rents in order to provide a fund.[17]

The Baganda regents, meanwhile, were providing the tribute labour of their peasant clients for the building of Mulago hospital, which was to include two isolation wards for 'males and females of the better classes' suffering from venereal diseases.[18]

The First World War interfered with the Venereal Diseases campaign in Uganda, though the numbers treated for syphilis by the missionaries in Mulago hospital continued to increase in this period. In the 1921 report on Venereal Disease Measures, written by Major G. J. Keane, it was revealed that the pre-war legislation, which had been made under the Dangerous Diseases Ordinance, the Township Rules and under Native Law, had fallen into abeyance. No legal proceedings of any kind had ever been taken under any of the legislative enactments.[19] In general, the problem was not one of the reluctance of the population to come forward for treatment (though women were less forthcoming than men), but rather the inadequacy of the methods of treatment available within the financial constraints. The doctors would have liked to have treated each patient with ten doses of the arsenical treatment, 'Salvarsan', rather than the two which they were given. But the cost of such a course of treatment would amount to thirty shillings per patient, and the number of such patients attending at Mulago was more than a thousand per annum. Ideally, 'Salvarsan' would be replaced by the newer arsphenamine treatments, for which there was already a vocal African demand, but these drugs were even more costly.

Enthusiasm for forms of state control of the syphilis problem

---

[17] Uganda Protectorate, *Annual Medical and Sanitary Report for the Year 1913* (London, 1914), Appendix II, p. 78. See also Zeller, 'The Establishment of Western Medicine', p. 200.

[18] Uganda Protectorate, *Annual Medical and Sanitary Report 1913*, p. 79.

[19] Uganda Protectorate, *Annual Medical and Sanitary Report for 1921* (Entebbe, 1922), Appendix III, p. 66.

continued to be evident, at least amongst the chiefs of Buganda. In 1921, an English woman doctor sent to Uganda to examine and treat women with venereal diseases had caused something of a furore by resigning in protest against the compulsory examination of women suspected of being infected. In a letter to the Catholic Women's Suffrage Society she had expressed her opposition to compulsory examination: 'The worst feature of all . . . is that large troops of men and women are obliged by English Government officials, and Native Chiefs acting under their influence, to come up at intervals for the most insulting of all forms of medical inspection.'[20] The *Annual Medical and Sanitary Report* somewhat defensively argued that examinations were 'not a prominent feature of this work', and provided evidence for the popularity of the examination procedure, amongst the chiefs, for whom it held clear attractions:

Examinations are undertaken at the request of the chiefs. The examinees set great store by the examination certificates, which are handed to each person found free from infection . . . No great importance can be attached to these examinations because of the uncertainty of the procedure followed by chiefs for gathering persons for examination, that is whether any favouritism exists and whether any exemptions are permitted.[21]

More importance was attached to these examinations by the Native Authorities, claimed Major Keane, than by the Medical Department. Indeed, it had become necessary to restrain the chiefs from excessive enthusiasm for medical control measures. At a baraza (meeting) at the headquarters of the Native Government the chiefs had suggested that every Muganda should be compelled to carry a certificate of examination issued by the Medical Department. Keane had disagreed with this, but added that 'In view of the keenness of the Native Government on the procedure, I think that we ought to be willing to fall in with their views whenever we are asked to conduct these examinations.'[22] In Keane's view, the real success of the anti-venereal policy could be measured by the fact that 'at length an awakening of a sense of shame has begun to appear'. Lately he had been told that attendance at the venereal diseases

[20] Dr Lamont, quoted in Zeller, 'The Establishment of Western Medicine', p. 289. This protest should be seen against the background of the opposition in Britain to the Contagious Diseases Acts of the nineteenth century.
[21] Uganda Protectorate, *Annual Medical and Sanitary Report 1921*, p. 68.
[22] *Ibid.*, p. 69.

hospital had begun to bear a stigma, and this, he suggested, was 'really a great achievement in the educational direction'. Eventually, this 'awakening of a moral or social sense' would indicate the need for a change of policy direction away from compulsion.[23]

Albert Cook, meanwhile, was commissioned by the government to tour remoter parts of Uganda giving lectures on the dangers of venereal diseases, and devising propaganda material in local languages. At Boa, he addressed a group of 200 chiefs who 'listened with close attention while I unfolded the grave danger their country was in from the prevalence of venereal disease'. Dwelling, in particular, on the effects of these diseases in causing sterility, abortion and infant mortality, he predicted the ultimate 'extinction' of their 'nation', and emphasised that 'these diseases differed from all others in affecting the soul as well as the body'. A 'full victory in the hours of temptation', he suggested, 'could only be obtained by those who had taken Christ as their personal Saviour and Friend'.[24]

Up to the 1920s, then, the broad outlines of the history of syphilis in Uganda seemed quite clear. All the authorities agreed that syphilis had been unknown in Uganda (a 'virgin soil', as Lambkin put it) until the middle of the nineteenth century, when it was thought to have been introduced by Arab traders from the east coast. It had only become widespread, however, at the end of the nineteenth century, during a period of unprecedented social and political upheaval. The main feature of this period had been the breakdown of traditional authority (exacerbated, some would have it, by the spread of Christianity), bringing a disastrous weakening of control over female sexuality, resulting in promiscuity, and the spread of syphilis. The disease would only effectively be controlled through one of two means: the strengthening of traditional authority in the form of chiefly powers or the extension of Christian morality, with its emphasis on pre-marital chastity, monogamy and the clear connection it drew between sin and suffering. Some medical officers like Keane clearly favoured a combination of these two approaches.

In the period from 1907 to the early 1920s, then, the existence of an epidemic of syphilis in Uganda was undisputed, and a powerful consensus of opinion had formed around it. The problem of syphilis

---

[23] *Ibid.*, p. 70.
[24] A. R. Cook, 'A Social Purity Campaign in Uganda', *Mercy and Truth*, no. 288 (1921), p. 298.

epitomised the dangers and difficulties of colonial rule and the extension of 'civilisation'. These dangers were apparent, even amongst a group like the Baganda, widely regarded as the most sophisticated of African peoples. They were to be even more apparent amongst other groups, therefore. Though medical solutions were sought and applied to this problem, the real danger was seen to lie in an uncontrolled African sexuality, and particularly in an uncontrolled African female sexuality. This was bringing sterility, depopulation and eventually, 'racial' extinction. It was responsible for the high infant mortality rate and was both cause and consequence of 'racial' degeneracy.

This medicalised discourse on African sexuality was, as we shall see, an enduring and powerful one over a wide area of Africa, and came to express many of the dilemmas of colonial rule. It was not a monolithic discourse, but fractured at various times and places by the divisions within the medical profession, differences in perception between administrators, medics and missionaries, and by the changing indigenous discourses of African societies themselves. Buganda was a very specific and unusual case, but one which demonstrated clearly how a shared language around the supposed dangers of female sexuality could unite chiefs and administrators who, for rather different reasons, were anxious about the loss of social control brought about by the rapid economic and social changes of the late nineteenth and early twentieth centuries. Elsewhere in East and Central Africa such a shared representation of the problem was to become evident later – most notably during the 1930s when the Depression brought home the realities of the colonial economic system for rural and urban populations, a fear of depopulation and an increasing emphasis on the need for effective mechanisms of Indirect Rule to avert social disintegration.

Just as official attention was being drawn to the problem of syphilis elsewhere in East and Central Africa in the mid-1920s, in Uganda this marked the beginning of a period of uncertainty amongst the medical profession regarding this issue. In 1923, the Venereal Diseases campaign, having proved inordinately expensive to an underfunded Medical Department, was integrated with the rest of the medical system. Mulago, up to this point purely a venereal diseases hospital, was opened to all patients. By 1926, it was reported that the anti-venereal campaign was losing much of its impetus:

This has been due to a variety of causes: the ever enlarging activities of Mulago; the high cost of efficient anti-syphilis drugs; the slackening of anti-venereal propaganda amongst native populations, enforced by the shortage of European staff; the loss of popularity of Mulago amongst the Baganda, as a result of the influx of alien Banyaruanda to the hospital, and a sense of false security bred amongst Baganda by the knowledge that efficient anti-syphilitic drugs exist.[25]

That syphilis had become *the* Baganda disease, and so something of a prestigious affliction, was to be remarked upon in later medical reports, but as Mulago attracted patients from a wider geographical area, so its popularity amongst the Baganda declined. But doubts were also being expressed about the very diagnosis of the disease. The confident assertions that 80 to 90 per cent of the population was infected gave way to more cautious estimates as the particular course of the disease in Ugandan patients was more carefully described. As early as 1912, Keane had remarked on the rarity of tertiary syphilis in Uganda and the absence of lesions of the nervous system amongst the patients he had encountered. Patients responded to mercurial treatment with marked and immediate improvement, a response which was 'at variance with recognised views and may be a feature of the disease in these people'.[26] The question posed then was this: did Africans present the disease differently, and often less severely than Europeans? By the late 1920s, however, this question had been somewhat overshadowed in Uganda by the recognition that the very diagnosis of syphilis was more complicated than had previously been assumed. In particular, the differential diagnosis of syphilis and yaws was recognised as a serious problem. The two diseases, when correctly distinguished, appeared to be quite geographically specific in their incidence. Syphilis was common amongst the Baganda, and yaws extremely rare. Yaws was widespread in the Northern and Eastern Provinces, whilst syphilis was very uncommon.[27] As the Medical Officer for Gulu remarked, there had probably been a great many misleading diagnoses: 'Yaws is commonly known in this district as "Native Syphilis" and every case of

[25] Uganda Protectorate, *Annual Medical and Sanitary Report for 1926* (Entebbe, 1927), p. 79.

[26] Keane, 1912, quoted in J. N. P. Davies, 'A History of Syphilis in Uganda', *Bulletin of the World Health Organisation*, 15 (1956), p. 1044.

[27] Uganda Protectorate, *Annual Medical and Sanitary Report for 1927* (Entebbe, 1928), p. 12.

'Ugandan' pattern of the retreat of endemic syphilis (and yaws) in the early twentieth century, and the advance of sexually transmitted syphilis, is one which, though not yet fully researched, appears to have been repeated later in other territories of East, Central and southern Africa. In most of these territories, the rise of official concern over syphilis came in the late 1920s and 1930s, by which time endemic syphilis, where it had existed, was truly in retreat. We are, at this point, therefore, talking for the most part about sexually transmitted syphilis and this disease was often, in official reports and statistics, subsumed under the heading of 'venereal disease'. This poses very real problems for the historian attempting to trace the history of ideas against a background of known epidemiological patterns, since the data on the latter are so heavily influenced by perception.

The incidence of syphilis remained a source of concern to doctors and administrators in Uganda throughout the 1930s and 1940s, but was no longer described in the dramatic vocabulary of the epidemic. The continuing high incidence of syphilis, and, increasingly, of gonorrhoea, was a major spur to the creation of a policy towards mother and child health, and the training of midwives, spearheaded by Albert Cook and his wife in the 1930s. In accounts of those early initiatives there was still a clear emphasis on the problem of low birth rate and infertility, thought to be caused by the prevalence of venereal diseases, but there were also important shifts in the way in which the problem was represented. The emphasis now was less on the direct control of female sexuality through a bolstering of chiefly authority, and more on the moral education of women as mothers. This was, of course, a result of the initiative taken by mission doctors in the field of maternal and child health for, though partly funded by the Protectorate government, these programmes remained very much the mission 'baby'. 'Self-control' was held to be lacking amongst African peoples in general, and this was attributed in part to African child-rearing practices.[39] Mothers, then, held the key to the moral reforms needed if the incidence of venereal diseases was to decline. The panic over the syphilis 'epidemic' receded and was subsumed under the maternalist policies of the 1930s. Fear of

[39] M. Vaughan, *Curing their Ills. Colonial Power and African Illness* (Oxford, 1991).

depopulation and of social disintegration was still present amongst officials and chiefs, but the training of mothers was seen as the route to regeneration.

In other parts of East and Central Africa the evidence for heightened official concern over the incidence of syphilis comes precisely in this inter-war period. It is difficult, if not impossible, to say whether this contrast reflects a real difference in epidemiological patterns, or rather a different chronology of perceptions. In most colonies, the concern, amounting to panic, over low birth rates and sterility was most apparent in the 1930s, a period when a number of factors combined to bring to official attention the low living standards of Africans in rural areas, and a perceived (and no doubt, in some places, real) crisis of social reproduction. As in Uganda earlier in the century, the fear of depopulation brought a focus on venereal diseases and on African sexuality, though in the new context of 'maternalism' and the development of welfarist policies.

In most colonies, however, an earlier underlying concern over the problem of syphilis had been evident at least from the First World War. In Nyasaland, venereal diseases (used as an undifferentiated category in contemporary reports) were noted as a medical problem at the end of the nineteenth century by Robert Laws, the Scottish missionary doctor, and their spread attributed to Arab traders and the disruptions of the Mlozi war.[40] In the course of the First World War, in which large numbers of Nyasa men were used as military porters and soldiers, the reported incidence of these diseases increased alarmingly, concern was expressed in London, and in Nyasaland an internal debate was generated about methods of treatment and control. As elsewhere in colonial Africa, the major problem faced by the authorities was the shortage of funds and of trained personnel to administer treatment. In the course of the First World War a new arsenical treatment, marketed as 'Salvarsan', had become available. It was the first specific chemical treatment for syphilis and was said to be highly effective, but it was expensive, and required to be administered by trained personnel. Since the Protectorate was short of both money and personnel, most African patients continued to be treated by mercurial inunction, but were

---

[40] Vaughan, 'Towards a History of Venereal Disease'; M. Gelfand, *Lakeside Pioneers. A Socio-Medical Study of Nyasaland, 1875–1920* (Oxford, 1964), pp. 26, 297.

vocal in their demands for the more effective 'injections' (or 'Jackson' as they were sometimes termed).[41]

In none of the territories of East and Central Africa was there a problem in persuading Africans to attend for treatment initially, though very few of them returned for the whole, very lengthy treatment. In the parts of Kenya where syphilis was prevalent (notably Central Kavirondo) there was a great popular demand for treatment with another arsenical preparation, Novarsenobillon. Perceptions of the problem on the part of officials in medical departments varied somewhat from territory to territory in this inter-war period. These differences reflected a number of things. First, there were real differences in epidemiological patterns. In some territories there was a clear admixture of endemic and venereally transmitted syphilis, for instance; in others this was not so clear. Representations of the problem were also influenced, however, by the nature of the political economy of each territory, and in particular by the extent of industrialisation and urbanisation. In Southern Rhodesia, the initial concern had been with the existence of syphilis in the south-eastern part of the country. In these districts, mercurial pills were widely distributed by the government, through the missions, in the period 1911–14.[42] There were calls for greater control and for lock hospitals, but in time it became clear that much of the syphilis prevalent in the south-east was in fact the non-venereally transmitted disease known locally as njovera, and that in other places there was a misdiagnosis of yaws.[43] Meanwhile concern was being expressed at the spread of venereally transmitted syphilis in the new mining areas – a concern that by the 1920s had come to dominate over discussions of the endemic syphilis amongst what were termed the 'native aborigines' in more remote parts. The 1915 *Report on the Public Health* expressed the problem in these terms: 'a grave danger undoubtedly exists with natives suffering from this

[41] Malawi National Archives (MNA): S1/438/19. For the symbolic power of the injection, see W. T. C. Berry, *Before the Winds of Change* (Halesworth, Suffolk, 1983), pp. 8–9; T. O. Ranger, 'Godly Medicine: The Ambiguities of Medical Mission in Southeast Tanzania, 1900–1945', *Social Science and Medicine*, 15B (1981), pp. 261–77.

[42] Southern Rhodesia, *Report on the Public Health for 1911* (Salisbury, 1911), p. 16; *Report on the Public Health for 1913* (Salisbury, 1913), p. 21; *Report on the Public Health for 1914* (Salisbury, 1914), p. 21.

[43] Southern Rhodesia, *Report on the Public Health for 1915* (Salisbury, 1915), p. 13. On *njovera* see n. 36 above.

disease being brought into contact with Europeans. Meanwhile, the position could to some extent be combated by legislating for the better supervision and control of native women.'[44]

By 1919, European public concern over the danger posed by syphilis in the African population was being vocally expressed, with calls for greater segregation.[45] In 1923, the Legislative Council debated the issue of the spread of venereal diseases amongst African mine employees. At this stage the medical department started to take a less alarmist and more cautious stand, arguing that it was very difficult, from the evidence available, to gauge whether or not venereal diseases were increasing to any great extent amongst the African population, and warning against exaggeration of the prob-lem.[46] As was the case elsewhere in Africa at this time, the difficulties of establishing any real rate of increase were very great, particularly given that treatment became more popular as it became more effective.

From 1926, the Medical Department organised what it termed a 'crusade' against venereal diseases, setting up special clinics to deal with the problem, and encouraging local authorities in urban areas to take more responsibility for treatments and control.[47] As the European clamour for further measures increased, so the Medical Department reiterated its anti-alarmist stand:

Pressure, of course, continues to be exerted upon the Government to exercise more vigilance in the detection and eradication of venereal disease amongst natives, especially where brought into contact with Europeans, and many fantastic suggestions are advanced, most of them coming from persons who have never studied the conditions existing, nor have they taken the slightest trouble to make themselves conversant with what is being done.[48]

Though the voice of the government Medical Department was one of reasonableness and rationality over the issue of intervention, it is nevertheless the case that the language of medicine, and especially the vocabulary of contagion, used by medical officials was a potent one in the context of a settler colony. The 1930 *Report on the Public Health*, for instance, argued again that the incidence of

---

[44] Southern Rhodesia, *Report on the Public Health for 1915*, p. 16.
[45] Southern Rhodesia, *Report on the Public Health for 1919* (Salisbury, 1919), p. 6.
[46] Southern Rhodesia, *Report on the Public Health for 1922* (Salisbury, 1922), p. 5.
[47] Southern Rhodesia, *Report on the Public Health for 1926* (Salisbury, 1926), p. 23.
[48] Southern Rhodesia, *Report on the Public Health for 1927* (Salisbury, 1927), p. 21.

venereal diseases had probably been exaggerated, but went on to discuss the 'health of the native' in these terms: 'The native is the reservoir of infective tropical disease, from which the European and his family is subject to invasion. Unfortunately, the native carrier is commonly a perfectly healthy looking individual, so that the European may not have the opportunity of realising until too late the danger to which he is being subjected.'[49] As elsewhere in southern Africa, what has been termed the 'sanitation syndrome', provided a clear medical rationale for racial segregation.[50] In Southern Rhodesia, attention became focussed on the problem of the 'African prostitute'. Whilst it was difficult to determine the extent of syphilis infection amongst Africans, it was possible, by the 1930s, to point to convincing figures for an increase in venereal diseases amongst the European population. The 1936 report stated that it was 'a fair inference that a great many of these cases are occurring as a result of intercourse with native women'.[51]

In rural areas of Central Africa, and especially in those supplying migrant labour, the 1930s saw increasing concern over the ability of rural populations to reproduce themselves. In Northern Rhodesia and in parts of Nyasaland, there had been a growing perception of the vulnerability of rural production systems in the context of a labour migrant economy, a vulnerability brought into sharp relief by the Depression. A number of factors combined to make this a period in which an increasing amount of documentation was generated on the living conditions of rural Africans in labour reserve areas. Humanitarian pressure groups in the metropole and the League of Nations voiced their concern over the status of women in British African colonies; the new science of nutrition claimed to be able to measure the levels of poverty and malnutrition amongst rural Africans,[52] and social anthropologists were busy documenting the far-reaching changes which colonialism and industrialisation were bringing to the lives of 'primitive' peoples. Worried circulars from the Secretary of State for the Colonies in the 1930s brought a flurry

[49] Southern Rhodesia, *Report on the Public Health for 1930* (Salisbury, 1930), p. 19.

[50] M. Swanson, 'The Sanitation Syndrome: Bubonic Plague and Urban Native Policy in the Cape Colony, 1900–1919', *Journal of African History*, 18 (1977), pp. 387–410.

[51] Southern Rhodesia, *Report on the Public Health for 1936* (Salisbury, 1936), p. 23.

[52] M. Worboys, 'The Discovery of Colonial Malnutrition between the Wars', in D. Arnold (ed.), *Imperial Medicine and Indigenous Societies* (Manchester, 1988), pp. 189–208; J. Iliffe, *The African Poor. A History* (Cambridge, 1987), p. 160.

of activity and data collection in East and Central African territories.[53] Medical officers were ordered to document the causes of low birth rates and high infant mortality rates in their districts. Amongst other issues which came to the fore in this exercise was the incidence of venereal diseases. In labour migrant areas in particular, these diseases were thought to be contributing substantially to high rates of female infertility.

There is a very clear continuity between the way in which the syphilis 'epidemic' was described and explained in early colonial Uganda and the representation of the problem in other territories in the 1920s and 1930s. By this period, a more distinct scientific discourse on 'the African' and on the problems of colonial government in Africa had been developed. This was the period of the formulation and implementation of policies of Indirect Rule, and of a colonial commitment to governing through what were thought of as distinctive African institutions. The work of anthropologists, which documented the customs, beliefs and kinship systems of African peoples, provided a vocabulary with which the African colonial subject could be defined and discussed. This was a period in which the 'otherness' of the African was emphasised by liberal commentators on colonial rule, and by African actors in the Indirect Rule partnership. African marriage customs and family life became a focus of much attention, as did African sexuality.[54] Echoing earlier concerns in Uganda, the processes of urbanisation, industrialisation and 'modernisation' were identified as being responsible for the disintegration of indigenous moralities, and the unleashing of an uncontrolled sexuality. Colonial governments and chiefly authorities sought new ways in which to reassert the control of male elders over sexuality and marriage, usually by trying, through the colonial courts, to preserve a version of custom in aspic. The very real problem of the spread of venereal diseases provided a focus for this concern. Fears over declining fertility were not new to African societies. Pre-colonial religion and ritual had often focussed on these

---

[53] M. Vaughan, 'Measuring Crisis in Maternal and Child Health: An Historical Perspective', in M. Wright, Z. Stein and J. Scandlyn (eds.), *Women's Health and Apartheid. The Health of Women and Children and the Future of Progressive Primary Health Care in Southern Africa* (New York, 1988), pp. 130–43.

[54] M. Chanock, *Law, Custom and Social Order. The Colonial Experience in Malawi and Zambia* (Cambridge, 1987); M. Vaughan and A. Whitehead (eds.), *Marriage, Sexuality and Colonial Discourse. The Crisis over Marriage in Colonial Africa* (forthcoming, London, 1991).

problems, and there were well-established ways of discussing and diagnosing them. The new medicalised discourse of colonial medical officers and missionaries may not, therefore, have appeared so very remote, but could be absorbed and incorporated into a shared vocabulary of disintegration and decay. For the next declaration of an epidemic of venereal diseases, however, we must turn to the Second World War and its aftermath.

THE EPIDEMIC OF THE SECOND WORLD WAR

The Second World War brought an increase in the reported incidence of syphilis and gonorrhoea throughout East and Central Africa. The recruitment of large numbers of African men into the army, the movement of these troops over very wide areas and the general disruption to normal life which the war occasioned were anticipated by most medical departments to give rise to an increase in the incidence of venereal diseases, following the experience of the First World War. In Kenya, the anticipated epidemic was slow in materialising. In 1942, the Medical Department could offer no evidence for any notable increase in the incidence of venereal diseases, reporting instead that the 'East African labourer and soldier are much more continent and less promiscuous than they were thought to be.'[55] By 1944, however, there was a significant rise in reported cases, and a flourishing black market in the new cure – penicillin.[56]

In Uganda, Southern Rhodesia, Northern Rhodesia, Tanganyika and Nyasaland, a war-time surge in the incidence of both syphilis and gonorrhoea was reported. Throughout the region, a tension was evident between the approaches of the military authorities and of the civilian government's medics over ways of dealing with the problem. In general terms, the military authorities were in favour of greater control, intervention and legislation than was acceptable to Medical Departments. Once again the 'native prostitute' became a focus of great interest and concern. In Nyasaland, the military authorities insisted on the fundamental innocence of their soldiers, and blamed the spread of venereal diseases entirely on African prostitutes. The civil authorities meanwhile objected to the methods used by the

[55] Kenya, *Annual Report of the Medical Department for 1942* (abbreviated), p. 6.
[56] Kenya, *Annual Report of the Medical Department for 1944* (abbreviated), p. 1.

military to prevent the spread of these diseases, especially the enforced examination of women.[57]

Dr W. A. Young, a government Medical Officer who became Venereologist to the East African Command during the war, was gradually converted from an essentially non-interventionist stand to that of a 'military hygienist', for whom it was 'essential to realise the danger of extraordinary epidemics occurring in armies, where are gathered together in unwanted conditions a motley of men from various quarters'.[58] He argued that venereal diseases were already 'epidemic' in the army, and that a 'free exchange of varieties' of the diseases was taking place. He feared a widespread epidemic would occur after the war for 'we are preparing to the full a cornucopia for distribution among the homes of Africa "après la guerre finie"', and are even now spilling seeds as men go home on leave'.

Yet Young's conversion to the viewpoint of the 'military hygienist' was only partial. Like most of his medical colleagues his instincts were very strongly anti-interventionist. In particular, there was a determined resistance on the part of most doctors in government service to the forced examination of women, such as had taken place in Uganda in the 1900s. Young, when asked by the Chief Secretary of Tanganyika Territory to comment on regulations to be incorporated into the emergency powers, had several criticisms to make. First, he was doubtful as to whether any of the measures suggested would actually be effective, given the difficulties of identifying carriers, and so was 'loath that this Government should embark on measures that interfere with the dignity of the individual until it has a fair appreciation of the probable measure of effectiveness'. He was also greatly worried by the suggested compulsory examination of women, pointing out that it was doubtful if such a measure would ever be generally acceptable. Given that the War Office had objected to the swabbing of the naso-pharynx of large numbers of people in an attempt to control a recent outbreak of cerebro-spinal meningitis, the 'swabbing of the vagina of any large number of women', he argued, 'is likely to prove even more unfruitful'. In conclusion, he offered the following general observation: 'The draft regulations at present under consideration step out of the (British) fairly consolidated public health position and propose to compel the medical examination of persons who by

[57] MNA: M2/5/56: Director of Medical Services to Brigadier Gormack, 10 June 1944.
[58] Rhodes House Library, Oxford: MSS Afr.s.1519: W. A. Young papers.

reason of their loitering in certain places are suspected of sexual adventure. We thus embark on a law to prohibit promiscuous intercourse.'[59]

Young was posing the question that hovered at the back of much of the discussion of this period: how far should or could the colonial state intervene to control sexual relations? Most medics were, like Young, deeply suspicious of such intervention, though they recognised that they had no purely 'medical' answers to the problem of venereal diseases. Young, in an address to the Imperial Congress on Social Hygiene, had been critical of the process of 'blind, general bismuthization of the population', as he characterised campaigns against both yaws and syphilis. Others were equally critical of the 'needle mentality' of African patients, but continued to see it as being essential that Africans should not be dissuaded by the moralising of missionaries or government from coming forward for treatment. W. H. Watson, a Medical Officer in Nyasaland at this time, had this to say about the Church of Scotland's policy of charging for venereal disease treatment:

> It literally shocked me that a Christian Mission from my own country could profiteer on sin to the extent of charging 10/6d for an M and B injection. The combination of Calvin, Aberdeen, and if one believes Freud, subconscious guilt, so conditions my fellow countrymen that they believe that sin has to be paid for in this world as in the next.[60]

In the Colonial Office, meanwhile, the problem of the African 'epidemic' of venereal diseases was receiving attention from a special Sub-Committee of the Colonial Advisory Medical Committee set up to investigate it.[61] In 1943 the Secretary of State had sent a circular on the problem to all Colonial Governors. Their replies were discussed in this Committee, and evidence taken from experts, mostly doctors, with colonial experience. Many of the debates which we have seen to have been prominent in individual African territories were also discussed in this Committee. In particular, there were clear differences of opinion between those who regarded the ultimate solution to the problem as lying in a programme of social and moral

---

[59] Young papers, memo. to Chief Secretary, Tanganyika, n.d.
[60] MNA: M2/5/21: W. Watson to Director of Medical Services, Nyasaland, 25 October 1943.
[61] PRO, CO 994/5: Colonial Medical Advisory Committee: Venereal Diseases Sub-Committee, 1943–7.

reform, and those who held to the view that such intervention was inappropriate, and even counter-productive. Again this echoed the old debate between mission medics and their government counterparts, but it now took on a new secular form.

A variety of views was also evident in the replies from Colonial Governors and Directors of Medical Services. The Director of Medical Services for Kenya (A. R. Paterson) argued that what was required was not further legal powers in respect of notification, but 'further facilities for making treatment more readily and widely available'.[62] The Director of Medical Services in Uganda (de Boer) meanwhile placed more emphasis on the 'social' side of the problem, and echoed the earlier Ugandan debates by arguing that African sexuality was what needed to be reformed: 'It is not suggested that the local African is specially immoral or even that he is amoral but that his way of looking at sexual contact is different from that generally accepted to be that of the European Christian civilisation.' In an account very reminiscent of the earlier debates, he described how previous generations had enforced an indigenous morality, which had now broken down. The solution proposed to this problem was not, however, the same as that proposed at the beginning of the century by people like Lambkin. The sense conveyed by de Boer and others was that Africans were living in a kind of moral limbo, exaggerated by the war, and from which there was now only one possible exit, that was towards a 'new morality'. Giving evidence to the Committee in 1944, he explained that 'in many parts of the country the customary moral code had degenerated ... these areas being closely related to areas in which mission influence and the spread of Christianity was most marked'. The problem, as he saw it, was that there was necessarily 'a time-lag between the destruction of an indigenous moral code and the growth of a Christian code to replace it'.[63] Quite how to spread the new morality, however, was a problem in a largely illiterate country, and would take some time. Meanwhile, he argued, greater coercive powers were called for. There would have to be frequent examinations of women found soliciting, and there should be compulsory detention of those found to be infected. The official attitude so far taken in Uganda he considered to be entirely inappropriate as it

[62] PRO, CO 994/5: D. M. S. Kenya to Chief Secretary, Nairobi, 18 June 1943.
[63] PRO, CO 994/5: Minutes of the 5th Meeting of the Venereal Diseases Sub-Committee, 5 May 1944.

took no account of the fact that 'the African's outlook on sexual matters' was different.[64]

The Committee itself was divided on both the issue of legislation and that of 'moral education'. There was much discussion of the example of Nigeria, where far-reaching legislative powers had been taken by the government to control the spread of venereal diseases (in this case gonorrhoea was the major problem). Sir Wilson Jameson took the view that 'the only propaganda that was worthwhile was quick and free treatment', and that 'nothing could be done with the idea of chastity: it must be treated as a public health problem and when enough of the population had been treated, V.D. would disappear'. He added that there was 'some risk of killing people with treatment', but that this risk must be taken because it was 'a choice between that and letting venereal disease spread'.[65] This was not an unanimous view, however. Others on the Committee emphasised that this could never be a purely medical problem and argued that nothing should be done which would 'interfere with any growing realisation and acceptance of Christian standards of morality'.[66] Much reference was made to the social problems of the West Indies, where the 'breakdown of the family' was thought to be particularly evident, and which provided an example which was constantly held up before those with a concern for the African colonies.

One feature of the African response to the venereal disease epidemic was evident from all the replies to the Secretary of States's circular, and occasioned much discussion in the Committee. This was the alleged fact that there appeared to be very few African communities in which any sense of 'shame' attached to infection with syphilis or gonorrhoea. There were two views of this. Some regarded it as enormously advantageous – it meant that Africans came forward for treatment readily, and this made the job of the Medical Officer very much easier. Those who took this view also often argued that the African attitude to venereal diseases made legislation to control their spread unnecessary and inappropriate. To make treatment compulsory, argued the Director of Medical Services for the Gold

---

[64] PRO, CO 994/5: D. M. S. Uganda (H. S. de Boer) to Chief Secretary, Entebbe, 5 October 1943.

[65] PRO, CO 994/5: Minutes of the 6th Meeting of the Venereal Diseases Sub-Committee, 19 July 1944.

[66] PRO, CO 994/5: Dr Letitia Fairfield, Minutes of the 6th Meeting of the Venereal Diseases Sub-Committee, 19 July 1944.

Coast, when at the same time such treatment was not widely available, would be likely to create 'public discontent'. If effective means of treatment were available on a large scale, there would be no need of legislation to compel the public to make use of them.[67]

Others on the Committee or giving evidence to it, argued more along the lines of the missionary medics, that a sense of shame attached to venereal disease was a necessary step on the way towards the enforcement of a new moral code, and that this would ultimately be the only effective means of control. With a view to this discussion, an article by Morrison Rutherford, a Major of the Royal Army Medical Corps working in West Africa, was circulated to members of the Committee. In it he discussed the absence of stigma attached to infection with gonorrhoea, and cited a Sierra Leonian newspaper obituary for an African clergyman which read: 'In spite of being a martyr to gonorrhoea for many years, he continued his work as a missionary to the end.'[68]

The Committee appointed in Nyasaland to consider the venereal disease problem reported to the Colonial Office that in that territory there was a great deal of 'fear, shame and loss of face', alongside indifference. Whilst the increase in the incidence of these diseases was thought to have been brought about by social disintegration and the dissolution of African family life in a migrant economy, it was also argued that venereal diseases themselves contributed to this dissolution, a great number of marriages ending in divorce as a consequence of the sterility induced by the infection.[69] The Nyasaland Committee was also concerned to regulate the activities of local healers who professed to be able to cure these diseases, but whose treatments were said to be merely palliative, inducing a false sense of security in their patients, many of whom were still infective when they considered themselves cured. A rather imaginative experiment was set up in Zomba African Hospital, where a local healer was invited to demonstrate his curative powers on a controlled group of patients. The experiment had to be abandoned when no patients would come forward for such treatment. Clearly those who had

[67] PRO, CO 994/5: D. M. S. Gold Coast (J. Balfour Kirk), 4 September 1943.

[68] M. C. Rutherford, 'Some Observations on Gynaecology and Obstetrics in Nigeria', *Journal of the Royal Army Medical Corps*, 83 (1944), p. 60, enclosure in PRO, CO 994/5.

[69] PRO, CO 994/5: Report submitted by Committee appointed to consider and make recommendations on the problem of venereal diseases in Nyasaland (also in MNA: M2/5/56).

found their way to the hospital were already convinced of the superiority of modern medical treatments for these particular diseases.

A sense of frustration with the very rationality of African attitudes to venereal diseases is evident in this period. In the 1930s the South African Red Cross had produced a propaganda film on venereal disease for African audiences, entitled 'The Two Brothers' (later reissued as 'Mr Wise and Mr Foolish Go to Town'). This was a silent film, to which commentary had to be added at each showing, a feature which apparently led to considerable improvisation and the attachment of unintended meanings. The film took a rationalist medical position on the problem of venereal disease, and concentrated on demonstrating the superiority of western medical cures over local ones. Colonial authorities in Central Africa thought this might be an appropriate propaganda tool, but when shown before a select audience of soldiers, students, teachers and chiefs in Lusaka in 1945, it produced some unexpected reactions, not the least of which was a great deal of laughter. As W. V. Brelsford reported, the opening scenes of the film, set in 'an unfamiliar South African setting, with people of a strange tribe dressed in strange clothes caused much laughter and set the film off in the wrong atmosphere'. When shown again at the Jeanes School the film was 'half way through before the audience became serious'. Clearly some members of the audience regarded the film as an affront to their intelligence. Commenting on the character of Mr Foolish, one member of the audience expressed the view that 'he (Mr Foolish) would have to see "experimental films" for a year before he would understand about syphilis'.[70]

Apart from these efforts at propaganda, the wartime epidemic produced one or two 'great campaigns' against venereal diseases, along the lines of earlier campaigns against sleeping sickness and yaws. The most notable of these was the enormously ambitious and expensive 'Ila V.D. campaign' in Northern Rhodesia. Concern had been expressed for some time over the apparently low birth rate amongst the BaIla, a small group living on the Kafue river, amongst whom the incidence of syphilis was said to be very high. A campaign was organised through the chiefs, whose responsibility it was to bring all Africans under their authority for compulsory examination

---

[70] W. V. Brelsford, 'Analysis of African Reaction to a Propoganda Film', *Nada*, no. 24 (1947), p. 10.

and treatment. On the whole there was very little resistance to the campaign, the BaIla attitude to venereal disease being entirely straightforward, such as to occasion amused and derisory comment from one European observer:

> When a headman is told to bring the people for treatment, they all come along quite happily, and at first it was a constant source of amusement to see patients come out of the grass shelter after examination and announce that they were 'on treatment', each such announcement being greeted with cheers and laughter from their assembled friends awaiting their turn for examination.[71]

The BaIla sufferers from syphilis, it seemed, were happy to come forward for treatment, even when such treatment was made compulsory, provided that they did not have to travel too far to receive it. Impressed by the injection, they were less convinced by the exhortations to change their sexual customs. In the case of the BaIla, viewed as a 'primitive' group, it was their 'primitive' sexual customs which were held to be responsible for the spread of syphilis, not the degeneration of such customs under the impact of industrialisation. They were, remarked Evans, in exasperated tones, a 'painfully logical people' whose fears of venereal disease had been allayed by the knowledge that a certain cure existed.[72]

Similar campaigns were launched in the Namwala district of Northern Rhodesia, and later in the Eastern Province. These continued into the 1950s, falling under the Federal Ministry of Health after 1954. But in 1958 the Ministry announced a change of policy. There would be no more special campaigns against venereal diseases, and their treatment would now become a normal function of all medical units. The report went on to say that, whereas a few years previously the problem in Northern Rhodesia had been of such a magnitude as to require a specialist Medical Officer and a staff of field officers in mobile units, now no such measures were indicated for 'Even in the big cities, where venereal disease in Africans is still rife, the numbers treated have declined, although the population at risk has more than doubled.'[73]

Figures from Southern Rhodesia demonstrated this decline. As

[71] A. J. Evans, 'The Ila V.D. Campaign', *Rhodes-Livingstone Journal*, no. 9 (1944), p. 44.

[72] *Ibid.*

[73] Federation of the Rhodesias and Nyasaland, *Annual Report of the Public Health for 1958* (Salisbury, 1958), p. 13.

elsewhere in East and Central Africa, the incidence of gonorrhoea had greatly increased during the war years, overtaking that of syphilis. The more ready accessibility of penicillin in the 1950s, however, seemed to have effected a real decline in the incidence of both diseases. The figures for Salisbury, for example, showed a decline in reported new cases between the years 1948 and 1958. In 1948 there had been 1,693 new cases of syphilis reported, and 2,200 of gonorrhoea. By 1958 these numbers were down to 435 new cases of syphilis and 256 of gonorrhoea.[74] Elsewhere there was rather more caution in announcing the end of the post-war epidemic of venereal diseases. The incidence of syphilis and gonorrhoea declined more slowly in Uganda, for instance, despite widespread use of penicillin. Such an improvement, it was said in 1955, would only come about 'with an alteration of moral standards'. By 1957 a significant decline in the incidence of syphilis had been noted, but the number of gonorrhoea cases continued to rise. By 1958 there were 30,704 cases of gonorrhoea reported from government hospitals in Uganda, and 13,279 of syphilis, the black market in sulphanomides being held responsible for the emergence of resistant strains of gonorrhoea and its continued high incidence.[75]

By the late 1950s, then, the epidemic was over. Both syphilis and gonorrhoea were to remain serious medical problems in East and Central Africa, and ones for which a conclusive medical solution has still not been found. What was most remarkable about the epidemic of the Second World War, however, was its apparent universality. Apart from the discussion on the African's alleged absence of 'shame', there is very little in the material I have discussed which is very distinctly 'colonial'. The issues which emerge clearly from debates of this period in colonial medical departments are identical to those being discussed in Britain and North America. The targeting of the 'prostitute', the issue of compulsory examination, the 'public health' versus 'morality' issue, the discussions on the ethics of medical intervention, and the unease at the very effectiveness of penicillin: none of these were specific to the African epidemic. By the post-war period the increasing specialisation within the medical profession, and the increased confidence which came with the advent of improved chemical remedies, had their impact on Africa and on

[74] *Ibid.*
[75] Uganda Protectorate, *Annual Report of the Medical Department for 1958* (Entebbe, 1958), p. 27.

discussions of African health problems, which were now more likely to be viewed as technical problems, like any others. It would be a mistake, however, to see this period as representing the culmination of a long process by which a culturally neutral, scientific and universal medical analysis came to triumph over African disease problems. We only have to turn to the 1980s, and to representations of the African AIDS epidemic, to recognise that social constructions of disease remain (and will always remain) powerful, and that a century of colonial rule and of a medicalised discourse on the 'African' has had lasting effects.[76]

CONCLUSION

The notion of an epidemic of a sexually transmitted disease is in itself an interesting and curious one. Even if we take it that all epidemics are in some sense socially caused and socially constructed, epidemics of sexually transmitted diseases nevertheless stand out as being particularly unamenable to purely medical solutions and medical analyses. In this chapter I have tried to demonstrate the strong element of social construction inherent in the colonial concern with syphilis (and to a lesser extent, gonorrhoea) in Africa. The history of syphilis in Uganda, though still very sketchy, shows how colonial medics came to the 'virgin soil' of Uganda with their own preconceptions about the epidemiology of syphilis, with various moral positions and with often strong ideas about the nature of African societies. These views were not uniform, and they were not completely predictable. Although very strong continuities existed between the discussions in late nineteenth-century Britain on the problem of venereal diseases, and those in early colonial Uganda, the latter were clearly influenced by the particular circumstances of that territory, and especially the very powerful voice of the traditional political hierarchy. I am not suggesting that, in any sense, European medics invented the problem of syphilis in Uganda, rather that their construction of it as a particular sort of epidemic, and the shared discourse they developed with the male elite over female sexuality, were influential and seemed to sum up many of the tensions and dilemmas of colonial rule. This shared discourse was

[76] See Renee Sabatier, *Blaming Others. Prejudice, Race and Worldwide AIDS* (London, 1988); Richard Chirimuuta and Rosalind Chirimuuta, *Aids, Africa and Racism* (Burton-on-Trent, 1987).

evident later in other East and Central African territories where the issue of the spread of syphilis came to the fore in the 1920s and 1930s, when the effects of patterns of industrialisation and labour migration were being most strongly felt. Here also the scientific language of western medicine created a new way in which the very real problems of this period could be expressed. What interests me in this history is the way in which the sexuality of African peoples became so much a focus of European concern, and came to represent the problems of maintaining social order in a rapidly changing society. The development of this discourse on African sexuality took place in dialogue with African male elites in the practice of colonial rule. It was not simply 'produced' by the panic over sexually transmitted diseases, for there were many other strong influences (including colonial psychological studies and anthropology), but at times it found a ready focus in what appeared to be the indisputable facts of a medical problem.

How far this discourse on African sexuality was a peculiarly colonial one is a question which it is difficult to answer. Nineteenth-century British discussions of the sexuality of the 'under-classes' carried with them very similar notions of difference and distance, and the 'sanitation syndrome' was, of course, not peculiar to colonialism. In the twentieth century the influence of changing ideas about sexuality, and the rise of psychological explanation, can clearly be seen in colonial discussions of the African, though the nineteenth century lingered on with the intransigence of the concept of 'race' and its continuing influence. In mid-twentieth-century colonial Africa (and indeed in contemporary South Africa) it is possible to find very 'twentieth-century' psychoanalytical discourses alongside apparently unreformed Social Darwinian ones.

The question of how far medics in colonial Africa were responsible for the particular constructions placed on epidemics of sexually transmitted diseases is also a difficult question to answer straightforwardly. Throughout the period I have examined, Christian morality remained a strong influence on the approach to this medical problem. It is important always to remember that colonial African medical departments were chronically underfunded, and that throughout this period (at least until finances improved somewhat in the 1950s) colonial governments relied heavily on mission bodies to provide medical services to large sections of the populations under their control, especially those in rural areas. This meant that, although government medical officers might disagree with the missionary view on sexually transmitted disease, they were probably not often in a position to prevent this view from being promoted amongst Africans (although they could sometimes threaten to stop grants made to mission hospitals). By the 1920s and 1930s, whilst this basically Christian moralist view had been secularised and absorbed into welfarist policies in Britain, in colonial Africa the impoverished state was largely unable to respond to lobbies in the metropole on mother and child health, nutrition and the status of women, and thus the missions continued to lead the field in this regard. It was only in the post-war period, with the availability of Colonial Development and Welfare Fund grants that the welfarist ideology was promoted directly through state institutions.

The colonial state, then, was hardly in a position to intervene to reform African sexuality, no matter how much concern might be expressed over it. In any case, as we have seen, there was a great deal of squeamishness about such intervention, just as there was in Britain. As the century progressed, and as the medical profession became more specialised and professionalised, so its confidence in medical solutions to medical problems increased. As we have seen from the debates over control which took place throughout this period, but especially in and around the Second World War, the majority of medical officers in government departments were extremely reluctant to see the state intervening to control directly the sexual behaviour of African colonial peoples. Though many complained that the African patient was only interested in the injection, on balance most preferred this attitude to the development of a Christian sexual morality, which they saw as inevitably obstructing their work.

A more complete social history of venereal diseases in Africa is clearly necessary. This chapter has attempted to outline the history of colonial medical ideas on the epidemiology of these diseases in Africa, and has related those ideas to wider colonial concerns. Integral, though much less accessible, to such a history are the changing representations of and responses to these diseases in African communities, and in particular, the influence of Christianity on constructions of sexuality. It is possible, using documentary sources from both government and mission records, to identify an 'African voice' on these problems, but it is a very specific one in both cases. Work by scholars in Africa which examines the history of gender and sexuality, and which, in the process of so doing, deconstructs the African colonial subject will ultimately contribute a great deal to the social history of venereal disease there, and will complement this chapter's rather cursory examination of the 'official mind'.

12. The early years of AIDS in the United Kingdom 1981–6: historical perspectives

VIRGINIA BERRIDGE

INTRODUCTION

Anthony Sampson, author of that well-known cross between journalism and contemporary history, *Anatomy of Britain*, recently commented on the relationship between the two. His view was that historical perspectives and methodologies should be applied to very recent events. Otherwise, one could miss that 'real vibrant sense of history as happening just around the corner'.[1] This chapter, in that genre, focusses on the analysis of a very recent series of events – the advent of AIDS in the United Kingdom and the initial reactions in terms of policies and of conceptions of disease, between 1981 and 1986. It has two broad aims – first, to examine the ways in which the new disease was defined as an issue for health policy and as an issue for scientists and the public, and the ways in which expertise and experts also defined themselves in relation to AIDS. And secondly, it aims to draw from the particular instance of this analysis of AIDS policies, some more general reflections about history, in terms of content, methodologies and concepts, and the different forms of its relationship with public policy in the health area as illustrated through AIDS.

We have suggested the identification and categorisation of three distinct policy phases for AIDS in the UK.[2] The first (1981–6) saw

A version of this chapter was given at the conference on AIDS and Contemporary History at the London School of Hygiene and Tropical Medicine in April 1990. Thanks are due to the Nuffield Provincial Hospitals Trust for funding the research on which the chapter is based and to Ingrid James for secretarial assistance.

[1] A. Sampson, 'Journalism and Contemporary History' (paper given to the seminar on twentieth-century policy and administration, Institute of Historical Research, February 1990).

[2] V. Berridge and P. Strong, 'AIDS Policies in the UK: A Preliminary Analysis', in E. Fee and D. Fox (eds.), *AIDS: The Making of a Chronic Disease* (California, forthcoming).

the slow growth of AIDS into a national policy issue. Policy was essentially, and in particular at the beginning, formed in a bottom-up rather than top-down way. Policy was being formed at the local level both through gay groups and through the construction of clinical and scientific expertise. These coalesced to form an initial 'policy community' round public health interests in the Department of Health. The second, and briefer phase (1986–7) can be character-ised as the period of 'war-time emergency' when AIDS came to be viewed as a clear political priority rather than simply a departmental matter, and where sections of society were put on almost a war-time footing to meet what was seen at that stage as a national emergency. This has been followed (1987/8 to the present) by a phase of 'normalisation', where AIDS and the reaction to it are becoming part of normal policy and institutional processes. Thus, AIDS itself (or in a significant change of terminology, HIV disease) is in the process of becoming a chronic, rather than an acute, disease. The rate of growth of the epidemic has slowed and public interest and panic have markedly decreased. Official institutions have been established and formal procedures adopted; paid professionals have in many instances replaced the earlier volunteers.

Currently available interpretations of the development of AIDS policies in the UK and USA have advanced broadly two different forms of explanation. AIDS has been characterised as a heaven-sent opportunity for the populist New Right governments of the 1980s to roll back the moral frontier. Government reaction, underpinned by the gay plague reaction of the popular press, was slow because only gay men were initially affected; high level intervention came only when the threat to the heterosexual population became clear.[3] Another form of explanation comes in a cross-national comparison of AIDS policies in the UK, USA and Sweden. In this view, neither right-wing ideology nor public opinion had much effect. Policy, as in almost all health arenas, was dominated by the traditional liberal, bio-medical elite. AIDS was a classic example of top-down policy making; government sent signals about the preferred con-sensual reaction into the public domain.[4] The emphasis in both

[3] For example, see J. Weeks, 'AIDS: The Intellectual Agenda', in P. Aggleton, G. Hart and P. Davies (eds.), *AIDS: Social Representations, Social Practices* (New York and London, 1989), pp. 1–20.

[4] D. M. Fox, P. Day and R. Klein, 'The Power of Professionalism: AIDS in Britain, Sweden and the United States', *Daedalus*, 118 (1989), pp. 93–112; P. Day and R.

interpretations is on the period of high level government intervention – either in examining why it was delayed or in analysing why it came about.

This chapter, by contrast, focusses on the early period of AIDS policy making from 1981 to 1986, prior to the period of political emergency reaction. For both interpretations underestimate the openness and fluidity of policy making in its early stages. There were no established departmental, local or health authority mechanisms in which it could be encompassed. There were no established expert advisory mechanisms which could deal with it; in fact, there were initially no experts. AIDS did not have its pre-existing 'policy community'; this concept, developed by Richardson and Jordan to delineate the existence of sub-systems organised round particular issues at a departmental level, which develop close relationships and shared priorities with outside interests and pressure groups, provides a useful explanatory framework for this early period of policy development.[5] In 1981–6 a policy community developed around the disease. Gay activists, clinicians and scientists coalesced and consorted, sometimes uneasily, around the issue, and links were established with the Department of Health and in particular with the public health interests within that department. Policy was formed in a bottom up rather than a top-down way, with a volunteer rather than an official ethos. A clear policy line – of the danger of a heterosexual epidemic – united the departmental and external interests. The alliances formed in 1981–6 were in some senses only temporary. But they were important in establishing definitions of the issues around AIDS which were later adopted and expanded at a political level.

For the disease itself, too, this was an 'open' period. The nature of the disease was still to be established. The construction of the virus theory and the establishment of its hegemony provide a contemporary illustration of the processes around disease which are usually studied historically. The 'popular culture' of AIDS was also established at this time; the dynamics of its relationship with the emergent scientific discourse is worthy of study.

Klein, 'Interpreting the Unexpected: The Case of AIDS Policy Making in Britain', *Journal of Public Policy*, 9 (1990), pp. 337–53.
[5] J. J. Richardson and A. G. Jordan, *Governing under Pressure* (London, 1979) p. 44; see also C. Ham, *Health Policy in Britain* (London, 1985).

THE INITIAL GAY RESPONSE

Take, for example, the early gay response and how it developed. Some gay men travelled to the United States in the early 1980s and began to hear of people dying of strange cancers. A member of a student gay group in Cambridge recalled how their gay helpline began to get calls after a BBC *Horizon* programme, 'Killer in the Village', in the spring of 1983. They began to look around for information and to hold weekly meetings on AIDS and health issues. 'We were groping in the dark. There was no sense of there being anyone other than us to turn to.'[6] Some had seen the potential seriousness of the disease even earlier than this. 'My first encounter with AIDS was a tiny little one sentence in the *Guardian* in 1981 about two deaths in the States. A friend of mine pointed to it and said it was going to be the biggest issue in our lives.'[7] But this was far from being a general reaction. *Capital Gay*, the London-based free gay paper was publishing articles such as 'San Francisco – a safe route for visitors' and a regular 'cruising' section covering gay pubs and discos.[8] A man who was later among the first to be diagnosed sero-positive recalled: 'My reaction at that time insofar as I considered it a personal threat – my reaction was to distance myself from it – there were small numbers and so it was unlikely to affect one personally . . . I didn't take much notice, it seemed so remote . . . that was a general reaction.'[9] But in May 1983 that reaction began to change. The *Horizon* programme 'Killer in the Village' appears to have had a key impact on the gay response. Volunteers at the Gay and Lesbian Switchboard in London arranged to open up a special line after the programme and volunteers were specifically briefed. 'For a number of days after, a lot of very worried people were ringing . . . the "Killer in the Village" programme was absolutely crucial.'[10] The Gay and Lesbian Switchboard was of central import-ance in the initial response. In May 1983, more than 200 people attended the country's first public conference on AIDS organised by the Switchboard. Mel Rosen, director of the New York based Gay Men's Health Crisis, spoke. Some present at the conference

6   Interview, gay community worker, February 1989.
7   Interview, Lesbian and Gay Switchboard worker, January 1990.
8   See issues of *Capital Gay*, 1984–5.
9   Interview, Body Positive volunteer, March 1990.
10 Interview, gay community worker, March 1989.

remembered his words – 'There's a train coming down the track and it's heading at you.'[11] A member of the audience recalled: 'I was struck by the potential gravity of what was happening and the absolute silence on what was happening – there was very little in the mainstream press.'[12]

Organisations began to coalesce around the disease – AIDS helplines in Cardiff in 1984 and in Brighton in 1985, for example, and gay student meetings around AIDS in Cambridge at the same time. In the London context, the central organisation was the Terrence Higgins Trust, founded in 1982 and then refounded in the following year in the wake of the Switchboard public meeting. The Trust's early history highlighted some key features of gay organisation building. Originally founded by friends of Terrence Higgins (who had died of AIDS in 1982) as the Terry Higgins Trust, its initial image was working class ('They were East End wide boys really'), with an emphasis on Variety Club style fund-raising for research, and support from the Motor Sports Club, a gay leather and biking group.[13] After the 1983 meeting, however, it was refounded as an organisation focussed on health education, on AIDS care, and with the aim of securing influence on policy. It was organised by a group of primarily middle-class gay men with organisational experience at various levels of gay politics. One of the early leaders called them the 'alternative professionals', but voluntarism was also the keynote:

> There was only one office ... and then we got another to give us somewhere to sit ... there was one fairly naff photocopier, meetings in the corridors ... we were a small group of volunteers at that time ... people were doing their main job and then working thirty hours a week for the Trust ... There were the strains of having committee meetings until 12.00 or 1.00 a.m. and having to be at work and knowing that people were ill ... it gives astonishing highs.[14]

By the end of 1983, the Trust was producing its first leaflets on AIDS and early in 1984 it opened its own AIDS helpline. Articles in the gay press for example by Julian Meldrum in the 'Meldrum on AIDS' column in *Capital Gay* – opened up discussion of issues like

---

[11] Interview, gay activist, July 1989. See also the reports surrounding the organisation of this meeting in *Capital Gay*, 13 May 1983, 20 May 1983, 27 May 1983.
[12] Interview, gay activist, July 1989.
[13] *Capital Gay*, 26 November 1982, 18 February 1983, 4 March 1983.
[14] Interview, gay community worker, February 1990.

safe sex and the role of promiscuity among gay men.[15] There were different levels of volunteer expertise and organisation – as, for example, in the formation in 1984/5 of Body Positive, a group where, as a founder member pointed out, 'the first people were there because of the virus, not because of particular skills'. Yet this, too, developed as an effective organisational and public force, based on a network of locally autonomous organisations by contrast with the London-based central organisation of the Trust.[16]

AIDS organisations were new, but they also grew out of a decade of organisation building round gay health issues in the 1970s. AIDS has to be seen, in this as in other areas, against the 'larger agenda' of pre-existing policy objectives and debates. For the 'gay community' (a convenient short-hand term) AIDS intersected with two prevailing issues – the 1960s and 1970s agenda of gay liberation and the demedicalisation of gay sexuality; and the growing importance of health questions as a gay issue in the 1970s and 1980s. The defeat of the disease/medical model of homosexuality had, ironically, seen a rise of health as a matter of concern in gay organisations and as a specific focus of self-helping groups. Organisations like Switchboard and Friend had developed a clear health dimension to their advisory and counselling activities. Self-help groups, for example Group B for gay carriers of the hepatitis B virus, had been organised; and gay men were increasingly using the GUM clinics for non-judgemental primary health care. The response to AIDS thus fitted into pre-existing gay medical and health paradigms. The disease provided a gay organisational and political focus which was lacking after the disintegration of some of the gay political organisations (such as CHE, the Campaign for Homosexual Equality) by the early 1980s. For clear policy objectives were also developed. AIDS was seen as (in Jeffrey Weeks's words) an epidemic waiting to happen, a clear opportunity for the 'moral majority', resurgent in the 1980s, to attack the gay social and political agenda of the 1960s and 1970s. One objective was to defend that. A Switchboard organiser recalled: 'We held our first training session on AIDS in 1983 – but it broke up in a rout after about thirty minutes. People were saying AIDS was a

---

[15] For example, 'Meldrum on AIDS', in *Capital Gay*, 7 December 1984.
[16] Interview, Body Positive volunteer, March 1990; comments made by voluntary workers about relative organisational models at conference on 'HIV: The Local Authority Response', Kensington and Chelsea, June 1990.

weapon to re-medicalise gay male sexuality. People were denying that there was anything going on.'[17]

There was as a result a focus on the actual and potential heterosexual nature of the epidemic – a message publicly enunciated by, amongst others, members of the Gay Medical Association. In April 1983, members of the Association, in a letter to the *British Medical Journal* responding to an article which had advanced variants of the hot bed/gay promiscuity theory of the spread of AIDS, argued that this was a condition which potentially could affect the whole of society.[18] Around a quarter of cases to date had not been in homosexual males. The policy aims of AIDS organisations, but in particular the Trust, were threefold: to convey the message of the dangers of AIDS to gay men; to develop a public role (but without thereby sacrificing credibility among gays) by raising public and political awareness of the dangers of an AIDS epidemic; and to prevent the danger of an anti-gay backlash by stressing – as the Gay Medical Association had done – the idea of AIDS as, potentially and actually, a heterosexual disease.

This was not just pressure group politics. Because AIDS was such a 'new' policy area, there was a chance for effective policy input. Contact was early on established between Trust activists and doctors in the Communicable Disease Surveillance Centre at Colindale, who had begun to monitor AIDS on a national basis in August 1982.[19] There was also a congruence of objectives between gay organisations and public health interests in the Department of Health. A key figure in this process was Tony Whitehead, formerly a Switchboard volunteer (and at the centre of gay opposition to British Home Stores' employment policies in the 1970s) and later Chairman of the Trust Steering Committee. Contact was established via a gay activist who had stood in a by-election in the mid-1970s. Another participant recalled,

> I was involved in a meeting with the CMO (Chief Medical Officer), the Editor of *Capital Gay* and Tony Whitehead towards

[17] Interview, Lesbian and Gay Switchboard worker, January 1990. See also J. Weeks, 'AIDS: The Intellectual Agenda', in P. Aggleton, G. Hart and P. Davies (eds.), *AIDS: Social Representations, Social Practices* (Lewes, 1989).
[18] M. R. Farrell, J. A. Freston *et al.* (members of Gay Medical Association), 'Acquired Immune Deficiency Syndrome', *British Medical Journal*, 286 (1983), p. 1143.
[19] B. H. O'Connor, M. B. McEvoy and N. S. Galbraith, 'Kaposi's Sarcoma/AIDS Surveillance in the UK', *Lancet*, 16 April 1983.

the end of 1984 ... He'd heard about us from X, who'd been prominent as a gay activist in the early 70s. People from the Department of Health had been running around asking who to talk to.[20]

Gay men became part of the emergent policy lobby around AIDS. In 1985 that role was legitimated overtly through membership of the newly established Department of Health working group on AIDS and health education; and, indirectly, through gay medical membership of the main Expert Advisory Group on AIDS (EAGA). But much work also consisted of lobbying behind the scenes. Tony Whitehead recalled,

All my links were direct with Sir Donald Acheson. There was no AIDS Department at the DHSS at that time ... our funding [for the Trust] was negotiated through Sir Donald and John Patten ... A typical day would have been a morning with Sir Donald, an afternoon at a hospital, and an evening in a gay pub giving a talk on AIDS.[21]

This was a complex balancing act in terms of establishing public and departmental confidence while also retaining the confidence of the gay community. Both interests worked together – for example in 1985 to discredit the notion of AIDS as a notifiable disease. But the relationship later disintegrated. There was controversy in Whitehall about the Department's potential funding of explicit leaflets about gay sex. The establishment of a national AIDS Helpline in 1986/7 organised by Broadcasting Support Services rather than directly by the Trust emphasised its growing marginalisation. The failure of the UK AIDS Foundation, a proposed umbrella organisation bringing together eminent academics, politicians and medical men, as well as Trust activists ('a body to carry clout and respectability') and which would have given the Trust a share in national co-ordination, fell apart in recrimination over opposing policy objectives, in particular over the question of testing. But AIDS had initially opened an avenue for gay expertise which was professional, yet voluntaristic and self-helping, to help define the policy agenda and initially to become part of the policy community around AIDS. At the same time it provided a political issue with enormous cohesive power within the gay community. It united the gay health and gay radical

[20] Interview, Gay AIDS worker, January 1990.
[21] Interview, Tony Whitehead, July 1989.

agendas bringing professionals and activists into a broad alliance which the earlier gay liberation organisations had never achieved.[22]

CLINICAL AND SCIENTIFIC EXPERTISE

Another part of the policy lobby was also forming at around the same time. Clinical and scientific expertise on AIDS was in the process of being established. The AIDS experts came initially from a range of areas such as immunology and virology, and from cancer research, where work on retroviruses had been undertaken for the previous twenty years and where the change from studying chicken viruses to human retroviruses had already been made because of new direction in leukaemia research. Significantly, too, AIDS brought the area of sexually transmitted diseases and genito-urinary medicine in from the cold. One participant commented:

> It was a 'Cinderella speciality' with poor facilities and second rate people working in it ... You could go into genito-urinary medicine without a higher medical qualification ... It was a pretty poor service in terms of the quality of physicians and facilities, ... AIDS has helped – it's made genito-urinary medicine a primary career option.[23]

AIDS meant, too, that a speciality not normally close to the centre of policy formation in the health arena was drawn very directly into a policy advisory role. It also meant that 'new men', scientists and clinicians without much previous experience, or a track record in policy advice, found themselves in a position of direct influence. One commented, in relation to AIDS's role in the Medical Research Council: 'There may have been some jealousies on the Systems Board that AIDS was getting too much attention. It was not quite nice in scientific terms. People with no scientific track record were making public pronouncements about the MRC.'[24]

The early researchers in the AIDS area in Britain came from a mixed background. Jonathan Weber and Robin Weiss at the Institute of Cancer Research were virologists; Anthony Pinching at St

---

[22] Denis Altman has also made this point in relation to the impact of AIDS on gay communities in the United States: D. Altman, *AIDS and the New Puritanism* (London, 1986), pp. 98, 103; see also D. Altman, 'Legitimation through Disaster: AIDS and the Gay Movement', in E. Fee and D. Fox (eds.), *AIDS: The Burdens of History* (California, 1988), pp. 301–15.

[23] Interview, genito-urinary medicine consultant, February 1989.

[24] Interview, immunology consultant, February 1990.

Mary's and Richard Tedder at the Middlesex, immunologists, Michael Adler at the Middlesex and Charles Farthing at St Stephen's were specialists in genito-urinary medicine. The Social Services Committee report noted in 1987 what it called the 'haphazard pattern of recruitment of expertise' to AIDS.[25] There were undoubted tensions and differences as in any scientific community; but these new-fledged scientific and medical experts also developed a consistent policy line and means of airing it. Particularly noticeable was the high media profile they adopted in order to press the case for urgent action on the part of government. Certain of them adopted an overt public lobbying style which was initially characteristic of the AIDS area. In the absence of the type of established policy consultative machinery which would exist in a well-established area of health policy, the experts resorted to the press and to television. In doing this, they were consolidating existing patterns of health reporting, which rely heavily on the small circle of medical 'experts'. But they were also joined by gay AIDS activists. The Terrence Higgins Trust in particular was aware of the value of using the media – it became 'pretty clued up about news management' as one activist put it. They and the medical and scientific experts were prepared to be openly critical of lack of action on the part of government or the research councils. One commented 'we accepted a public profile to ensure the message was put across'. An often uneasy alliance was formed – 'we were united in front of the cameras – but outside the studios we'd be fighting for the same sources of funding'.[26]

THE PUBLIC HEALTH RESPONSE

The type of public reaction which would normally lead to exclusion from the 'corridors of power' in this case brought admission to them. For the external policy lobbies were complemented by the 'public health' reaction to AIDS within the Department of Health. Initially AIDS was dealt with via the low key: by classic public health routines of monitoring and surveillance and through the issue of advisory guidelines. AIDS cases were monitored on a voluntary basis by the Communicable Disease Surveillance Centre at

[25] Social Services Committee, *Third Report. Problems Associated with AIDS*, Session 1986–7 (London, 1987).
[26] Interview, gay activist, July 1989.

Colindale (part of the Public Health Laboratory Service, whose uncertain future was saved by its role in monitoring AIDS) from 1982 onward. Sir Donald Acheson, the Chief Medical Officer, as a public health epidemiologist himself, was also well aware of the disease's potential for spread. His annual reports made conscious references to the role of the great nineteenth-century public health pioneers, such as Sir John Simon, Medical Officer to the Privy Council Office. AIDS was, in his view, a disease which lay in this great tradition of the public health fight against disease. He commented,

> While the scourge of smallpox has gone and diphtheria and poliomyelitis are at present under control, other conditions such as legionellosis and AIDS have emerged. The control of the virus infection (HTLV III) which is the causative agent underlying AIDS is undoubtedly the greatest challenge in the field of communicable disease for many decades.[27]

It highlighted, in his view 'the need for the control of the spread of infection to be regarded as an issue of prime importance to the future of the nation'.

Acheson, universally hailed for his role in AIDS by members of the policy lobbies ('if any honours are deserved for AIDS, he deserves one'), had met with gay activists to register support for the nascent Terrence Higgins Trust and its activities in the gay community and remained in regular contact with Tony Whitehead. For the rest, his Department focussed its activities on issuing a number of warning and advisory circulars. The Advisory Committee on Dangerous Pathogens issued one to laboratory workers in 1984; there was the Health Education Council's leaflet, *Facts About AIDS*; and there was advice for doctors in 1985. Acheson notably opposed attempts to introduce a more stringent public reaction based on quarantine or notification. The death of Greg Richards, chaplain in Chelmsford prison, early in 1985, together with increasing public and political concern about the safety of the blood supply, brought overt demands for a harsher response. In that month MPs of all political parties joined in pressure for a change of stance.

The recently established Expert Advisory Group on AIDS was the justification for holding the liberal line. Kenneth Clarke, the Health Minister, in a Commons statement in February 1985, maintained that EAGA's view was that the present system of disease

[27] *Annual Report of the Chief Medical Officer of the DHSS for the Year 1984* (London, 1986), pp. 35–7.

surveillance was working well. Experience with other sexually trans-mitted diseases suggested that notification would not help. But in 1985 the Public Health (Infectious Disease) regulations made under the Public Health (Control of Diseases) Act of the previous year were extended to cover AIDS. Powers were reserved to detain patients when in a 'dangerously infectious condition'. There were also restrictions (including body-bags) on the removal of bodies from hospitals. Clarke stressed that powers of detention were not intended for the majority of AIDS cases – 'We need these reserve powers for the very rare case that might eventually arise somewhere some time.'[28] The regulation was used only once; and notification, perceived as the greater danger to civil liberties, was thereby deflected.

The Chief Medical Officer was chairing a committee on the Public Health Function in tandem with his close involvement with AIDS. The revival of infectious disease in Britain since the 1970s – with legionella, salmonella, and ultimately AIDS – appeared to offer an opportunity for a redefinition and revival of the much-reduced post-war role of public health.[29] The departmental public health response in its practical formulation epitomised many of the pre-existing themes in public health in the 1980s. In the 1900s public health had moved away from its broader environmental and social reforming focus towards an emphasis on individual responsibility for health, on prevention and health education. The 'new public health' of the 1970s and 1980s had much in common with these earlier social hygienist views of public health. These were expressed through AIDS in the focus on health education and prevention as a primary component of the public health response. In December 1985, Norman Fowler, as Social Services Secretary, in announcing a package of new measures costing £6.3 million to deal with AIDS, allocated £2.5 million for a national information campaign to begin the following spring and run throughout the rest of 1986. The campaign – in newspapers and leaflets only – was to be directed at the general public, with a series of targeted campaigns for those at

[28] *Hansard*, 20 February 1985, cols. 498–500.
[29] Department of Health and Social Security, *Public Health in England. The Report of the Committee of Inquiry into the Future Development of the Public Health Function* (London, 1988). For the redefinition of public health in the twentieth century and in particular post-war, see J. Lewis, *What Price Community Medicine? The Philosophy, Practice and Politics of Public Health Since 1919* (Brighton, 1986).

special risk.[30] Despite political pressure for an extension to television, that had to wait until the later period of emergency reaction
in late 1986–7. In its main features, then – advisory guidelines to
health professionals, a mass media health education campaign – the
initial departmental public health approach fitted neatly into the
pre-existing public health paradigm of the 1980s. It was similar in
many respects to the Department's anti-drugs activities at the same
time.

THE ISSUE OF HETEROSEXUAL SPREAD

Drug use was soon to come more centrally into AIDS as a policy
issue. For the question of potential and actual heterosexual spread
of the disease which united the AIDS policy community also began
to cause heightened political, public and departmental concern. A
number of issues brought it to the fore as a matter of more general
anxiety: the question of the safety of the blood supply, knowledge
of heterosexual transmission in Africa and the question of international travel; and the drugs issue.

Initial gay awareness of the disease was concentrated at a very
specific period in the spring of 1983. It was at this time, too, that
doubts about the blood supply began to surface publicly. Here
again, as with the gay response, the AIDS/blood issue fitted into pre-
existing agendas. There had previously been criticism of the government for its failure to develop self-sufficiency in Factor VIII and
other blood products after an outbreak of hepatitis B among
children at a special school in Hampshire in 1981. The development
of self-sufficiency, so critics argued, was being hindered by failure
adequately to invest in the expansion of the Blood Products Laboratory at Elstree with the extra blood it would need. Heat-treated
Factor VIII, introduced originally because of hepatitis, was available by 1984, but there were technical problems involved in getting it
into mass production. In the spring of 1983, reports of the possibility
of the transmission of the disease through blood first began to
appear in the medical press and thereafter in the press in general.

In May 1983, a report in the *Mail on Sunday* on hospitals which
were using 'killer blood' described how two men were in hospital in
London and Cardiff suspected to be suffering from AIDS after

---

[30] *Hansard*, 2 December 1985, cols. 1–2.

routine transfusions for haemophilia.[31] Exact knowledge of the virus and its transmissibility was limited at this stage and the priority was seen, both within the Department and the Haemophilia Society, the voluntary organisation concerned, as encouraging haemophiliacs to continue with treatment. A DHSS spokesman was quoted in May 1983 as saying that 'the advantage of using imported blood products far outweighs the "slight possibility" that AIDS could be transmitted to patients through Factor VIII'.[32] A consultant involved in treating large numbers of haemophiliacs at this period recalls the sense of uncertainty:

> The only investigative tool we had was their T-4 ratio – we did them on all the patients . . . A man I was following up with non A/ non B hepatitis . . . went on for months and months, feeling ill with glandular fever. I didn't know then, but I now know he was sero-converting to HIV. Over half had sero-converted by the time we were watching them.[33]

Information was spread at the clinical level by regular meetings organised by Adler and Pinching at the Middlesex or St Mary's; and that group was one of the clinical settings in which the idea of heterosexual spread was discussed.

But the blood question was also the issue which first brought AIDS to public and political attention. The first parliamentary question tabled on the subject – by Mrs Gwyneth Dunwoody, in July 1983 – asked Kenneth Clarke about the costs of ensuring British self-sufficiency in blood and blood products, and about numbers of haemophiliacs who had died of AIDS.[34] The response was two-fold: measures to protect the safety of the domestic blood supply through the National Blood Transfusion Service; and measures to establish the safety of blood products used in haemophilia treatment. The initial reaction in the former case was advisory only: a leaflet, in August 1983, asking high-risk donors not to give blood. For blood products, the situation was problematic. Heat-treated Factor VIII was not available from the United States until the end of 1984. Dr Charles Rizza, an Oxford haematologist, was reported as saying that, until it was available, 'I'm afraid our haemophiliacs are

[31] S. Douglas, 'Virus Imported from U.S. Hospitals Using Killer Blood', *Mail on Sunday*, 1 May 1983.

[32] Quoted in J. Hampshire, 'Probe on Imports of Killer Blood', *Daily Mail*, 2 May 1983.

[33] Interview, haematology consultant, January 1990.

[34] *Hansard*, 11 July 1983, col. 275.

in the lap of the gods.' Even the use of US heat-treated products was a matter of debate.

There was a terrible period from the end of 1984 until October 1985 ... Here we knew the epidemic was very small and we had a policy of education and turning people away ... The pool was thought to be safe ... Our problem was – did you give US stuff where the pool was terrible, or unheated British stuff from a safe donor pool? We gave at least two people untreated British stuff and they got infected. We didn't know that an unsafe pool was rendered safe by heating.[35]

NHS-treated products became available in March 1985. One early product, insufficiently heat-treated, was associated with a number of sero-conversions and had to be withdrawn from the market. By October 1985, a British HIV antibody test had been developed and all blood donations began to be screened. The issue opened up some divisions between different interests involved in the question of the blood supply. 'NBTS didn't start testing donors until October 1985 – and there was much criticism about this from the haemophilia world. They didn't want to use a test that might have false positives. They protect the donors and are not interested in the recipients – we do the opposite!'[36]

At the political level, the issue was of central concern: half the fifty-nine questions on AIDS in the 1984–5 parliamentary session dealt with this matter alone. Haemophiliacs themselves, by contrast with the gay reaction to AIDS, remained in the background. The essentially private haemophiliac culture (few sufferers would openly admit to their condition) was further isolated by AIDS.[37] Knowledge about the heterosexual spread of AIDS in Africa heightened anxiety. Despatches from the British ambassador in Kinshasa about the AIDS problem in Zaire 'demonstrated', as one senior civil servant put it, 'the real potential of the disease once loose in heterosexual society'.[38] Demands for immigration control and restrictions on travel to and from Africa were considered.

The advent of an AIDS dimension to the issue of illegal drugs in late 1985 and early 1986 added to the sense of urgency and to the focus on AIDS as a heterosexual disease. The discovery that drug

[35] Interview, haematology consultant, January 1990.
[36] Interview, haematology consultant, January 1990.
[37] Interview, Haemophilia Society worker, June 1989.
[38] Interview, senior civil servant, 1989.

users in Edinburgh were infected with the virus on a par with ghetto users in New York forced drug policy onto the AIDS agenda. A revisionist 'policy community' established round drugs in the 1980s had already been arguing for harm-minimisation approaches. AIDS eventually gave these pre-existing objectives some degree of political feasibility.[39] In the autumn of 1986, the McClelland Committee on HIV infection in Scotland declared the dangers of heterosexual spread of the disease to be a greater danger than the spread of drug use itself.[40] For Ron Brown, MP for Leith, the issue was a 'national emergency'. Sir Bernard Braine, chairman of the all party committee on the misuse of drugs drew attention to the 'appalling prospect' the AIDS/drugs question raised. But both he and the Scottish secretary, John MacKay, were unwilling initially to countenance a radical change of policy as a result. The establishment of a needle-exchange system would be, Braine argued, 'the equivalent of trying to control an epidemic of smallpox by issuing vats of smallpox to the population at large'.[41] In his view, there were no grounds for availability outside an authorised treatment programme.

The debates, ostensibly and immediately about AIDS, were also part of the 'larger agenda' of drug policy: they reflected the tensions between a medically dominated specialist treatment system, the advent of the voluntary sector as an important factor in drug policy and the revisionist desire to establish more liberal medical prescribing policies and even an alternative 'treatment system' outside the drug clinics. Research was the legitimating factor for a change of approach encompassing some of these objectives. It was only after research commissioned by the Department of Health had demonstrated that attenders at needle-exchanges did achieve behaviourchange (although a disappointingly small proportion of them stayed on to do so) that political support was reluctantly thrown behind a harm-minimisation rather than an eradication approach to illegal drug use.[42]

---

[39] For further discussion of the impact of AIDS on drug policy see V. Berridge, 'Aids and British Drug Policy: Continuity or Change', in V. Berridge and P. Strong (eds.), *AIDS and Contemporary History* (Cambridge, forthcoming).

[40] *HIV Infection in Scotland. Report of the Scottish Committee on HIV Infection and Intravenous Drug Misuse* (Edinburgh, Scottish Home and Health Department, 1986).

[41] *Hansard,* 6 March 1986, cols. 559–66.

[42] G. V. Stimson, L. Alldritt, K. Dolan, M. Donoghoe and R. A. Lart, *Injecting Equipment Exchange Schemes: Final Report* (London, Goldsmiths' College, 1988).

THE ECONOMICS OF AIDS

The question of heterosexual spread, which put the general population immediately at risk, also brought to the fore the question of cost. The potential future costs of AIDS in terms of treatment and the provision of services became a matter of parliamentary concern in the early years. Initially funding was left very much to local health authorities. Barney Hayhoe as Health Minister was of the opinion in December 1985 that it was too soon to make reliable estimates of levels of expenditure. Certainly no information was held centrally about the average cost of caring for AIDS sufferers, estimated in mid-1986 at between £10,000 and £20,000 per patient, depending on the infections involved. But health authorities were also asked to prepare plans for future AIDS services and their funding as part of short-term programmes to be submitted by the end of 1986.[43] AIDS initially was seen as a burden on existing resources.

As it assumed the dimensions of a major health issue by 1985–6, however, its status changed to a potential attractor of additional funding. The £680,000 for AIDS services which had gone to the North East, North West and South East Thames Regional Health Authorities in 1985–6 rose to £2.5 million in 1986–7. This funding was part of an additional package announced by Norman Fowler in December 1985: it included £2.5 million for the national information campaign; £270,000 for haemophiliac reference centres; £100,000 for counselling training; and £750,000 to the Public Health Laboratory Service for testing.[44] At the local level, where the development of AIDS services was concerned, this allocation led to determined battles to ring-fence funding and ensure it reached its intended AIDS destination.

> I came back from India and it was the very first time the Department of Health had given money to AIDS and everyone was up in arms – the Unit Manager was using it to offset the deficit. I rang all the people I knew on the Health Authority to say I'd go public. The money was clearly ring fenced for AIDS and I've not had problems since.[45]

[43] See parliamentary questions on this issue, *Hansard*, 16 December 1985, cols. 70–2, 20 December 1985, col. 427, 17 March 1986, col. 54, 17 July 1986, col. 616, 23 July, col. 308.

[44] *Hansard*, 2 December 1985, cols. 1–2.

[45] Interview, genito-urinary medicine consultant, March 1990.

Much of the political debate around the issue of costs was couched in a language of health and human capital which would not have been out of place in the nineteenth century. A particular proponent of this view was Michael Meacher, Labour party health spokesman. In the first Commons debate on AIDS in November 1986, he argued:

> Every £1 million spent on prevention will probably save £10 million which would otherwise have been spent in caring for AIDS victims . . . when faced with a death rate from AIDS which could – I hope to God that this does not happen – rise twofold in the next five years, and when the clinical care costs for nursing AIDS victims could rise to £300 million a year, any underprovision of prevention, counselling and research facilities could only constitute the grossest form of false economy.[46]

Health and economic efficiency were inextricably linked.

RESEARCH POLICY

Meacher had stressed the need for increased research funding as an economic measure, but the development of research around AIDS in Britain in the early years was uncertain. Within the Medical Research Council, the major funding body for science research, AIDS was initially seen – as in services – as potentially a drain on existing straitened resources. Sir James Gowans, secretary of the MRC, visited the United States in 1983. On his return, he met with Sir Henry Yellowlees, then CMO, and Dr Whitehead, then Director of the Public Health Laboratory Service. An AIDS Working Party was set up as a result in October 1983. Chaired by David Tyrrell, Director of the Common Cold Research Unit and a virologist, it was advisory only and its terms of reference were deliberately non-activist: it was to review knowledge and research; encourage research co-operation; and advise Council on knowledge and research.[47] As a result, AIDS research was 'very small fry'.[48] There was a feeling – publicly enunciated on occasion – that AIDS research was best left to the French and the Americans. This approach was criticised by researchers, by some members of the Working Party and through increased parliamentary questioning in 1984–5.

[46] Commons debate on AIDS, *Hansard*, 21 November 1986, cols. 799–864.
[47] Medical Research Council Working Party on AIDS, First Report, April 1984 (unpublished).
[48] Interview, immunology consultant, February 1989.

Researchers wanted to see more action. The virologist and early AIDS researcher Jonathan Weber criticised the MRC's role as 'leading from behind' and argued that research funding should not come through the 'stifling hands' of the MRC.[49]

The Working Party produced three reports between April 1984 and April 1986. The second, in February 1986, stressed the urgency of the issue. It recommended the maintenance of the peer-review system for research applications, but also a need for more direct guidance from the MRC. This produced no official response from the MRC Council.[50] The Council was proactive in one area, however. In October 1985, it set up an epidemiology committee as a sub-committee of the main AIDS Working Party, chaired by Sir Richard Doll, the eminent epidemiologist. This move arose from DHSS pressure; and the Department also provided the bulk of funding (£250,000) for the committee. But it ran into trouble over its proposal to establish a national co-ordinating centre for epidemiology: it was 'a terrible mistake . . . we underestimated the extent to which people working on AIDS were jealous of their positions'.[51] It was only at the end of the first stage of policy development that matters developed differently. Sustained parliamentary questioning on the research issue in late 1986, together with the formation of the Whitelaw Cabinet Committee that autumn and the Social Services investigation into AIDS in 1986–7, brought the possibility of increased AIDS funding. Sir James Gowans moved swiftly and adroitly to extract funding from the Cabinet committee and appeared before the Social Services committee as the advocate of AIDS research as a means to revitalise basic science.

The result was the MRC 'directed programme' on AIDS, a proactive and closely planned and managed departure from the usual reactive form of research funding. The economic possibilities inherent in AIDS's change of status as a policy issue brought a change of response, and, in the directed programme, a new organisational form of achieving it. The directed 'research initiative' model (based on the Rothschild 'customer-contractor' model of policy-relevant research) had been adopted as a model of social science

[49] Social Services Committee, *Third Report. Problems Associated with AIDS: Minutes of Evidence*, II, p. 53.
[50] Medical Research Council Working Party on AIDS, Second Report, February 1986 (unpublished).
[51] Interview, epidemiologist, March 1989.

research development in the late 1970s and 1980s, but had been resisted by the more politically powerful MRC. AIDS brought change in this sense, but a change which was used to further the MRC's long-established focus on basic science rather than public health or clinically focussed research.[52] As in policy making more generally, the heightened institutional response led to changes in key personnel. The area was no longer so open to the 'new men' of AIDS research. Research was now 'headed by the great and the good who'd never been previously involved . . . We had a sense that the whole leviathan of MRC research was bringing in the J.C.Ls [Johnny Come Latelys] – . . . All the people who'd been beavering away were ignored.'[53]

THE CONSTRUCTION OF SCIENTIFIC AND POPULAR CULTURES

The formalisation of research funding and research policy also called attention to the production and acceptance of scientific discourse around AIDS. Historians and others have drawn attention to the construction of ideas about illness and the negotiated relations between dominant and oppositional conceptions of disease and its treatment. With AIDS, it was possible to document these processes in play. The human immunodeficiency virus was first identified in 1983. The newness of the disease was initially marked by an absence of the type of scientific certainty which would be an expected concomitant of the fight against disease. Morality and science entwined, as in the 'hot bed theory': 'the traffic in human material in certain quarters by abnormal routes has reached such a level that, combined with the effects of drug abuse of various kinds, the sheer weight of chemical and microbial insult to the body in general, and to T-lymphocytes in particular, goes beyond the tolerable limit'.[54] The Chief Medical Officer's report for 1983 did not moralise, but was no less tentative: 'Expert opinion suggests that there is no risk of contracting AIDS as a result of casual or social contact with AIDS patients e.g. on public transport, in restaurants,

[52] For an historical introduction to these issues in MRC history, see J. Austoker and L. Bryder (eds.), *Historical Perspectives on the Role of the MRC* (Oxford, 1989).
[53] Interview, immunology consultant, February 1990.
[54] A. P. Waterson, 'Acquired Immune Deficiency Syndrome', *British Medical Journal*, 286 (1983), pp. 743–6.

or in private dwellings. The spread of AIDS appears to require intimate contact.'[55] A range of explanations was advanced in the scientific and medical press: possible links with African swine fever; the virus emerging from Africa, or Haiti. Nothing could be taken for granted. Science in many instances went back to earlier explanations of disease – in terms of morality, of alien influence, or external threat.

The construction of such scientific knowledge and its change over time had, as its oppositional counter-part, a developing belief in alternative and self-helping medical treatments akin in political context to the radical opposition embodied in medical botany and folk medicine in the nineteenth century.[56] But oppositional theories were not the whole picture; and the broader 'popular culture' of belief about AIDS should not be forgotten. This has been unfortunately entangled in the notion of 'moral panic', implying that public reactions were explicitly anti-gay and were stirred up by the 'gay plague' angle of the popular press. This ignores the heterogeneity of the press response: not all papers, even the popular ones, were uniformly anti-gay. It also implies a direct relationship between press content and audience reaction which was commonplace in older mass communication theory but which now stands discredited in favour of a more complex interrelationship.[57] Most importantly, it demonstrates the 'enormous condescension of posterity' to beliefs about illness and its transmission. Despite the discovery of the virus in 1983, there was still widespread belief in contagion in 1985–6. 'I'll keep my distance from anybody who has AIDS. I won't speak to the person. Fear will make everybody react this way. As long as I don't know how AIDS is transmitted, I won't take my chances.'[58]

Even MPs were not immune to a belief in contagion. After the

---

[55] *Annual Report of the Chief Medical Officer . . . for . . . 1983* (London, 1984), p. 45.
[56] For discussion of the relationship between orthodox and unorthodox medicine in historical context, see W. F. Bynum and R. Porter, *Medical Fringe and Medical Orthodoxy* (London, 1987); for an historian's perspective on self-help medicine in the context of AIDS, see J. Harvey-Young, 'AIDS and Deceptive Therapies' (paper presented to the conference on AIDS and the Historian, NIH, Bethesda, March 1989).
[57] For some discussion of these issues in relationship to media research, see V. Berridge, 'Content Analysis and Historical Research on Newspapers', in M. Harris and A. Lee (eds.), *The Press in English Society from the Seventeenth to the Nineteenth Centuries* (London and Toronto, 1986), pp. 201–18.
[58] Quoted in A. Vass, *AIDS: A Plague in US – A Social Perspective* (St Ives, Cambridge, 1986), p. 96.

death of Greg Richards, the Chelmsford prison chaplain, in 1985, Renée Short, MP, asked about the availability of screening facilities 'resulting from the investigations into the outbreak of acquired immune deficiency syndrome'.[59] Anxiety in church circles focussed on the possibility of transmission via the communion cup.[60] 'We'd have cleared the court if we had a sero-positive person in those days', recalled a London probation officer.[61] Such examples can be multiplied; and they continue to do so, despite market-research findings of a considerable increase in public knowledge about the nature of the virus following the major AIDS campaigns in the media.[62] Popular beliefs around AIDS have come under two forms of attack: from activists who have seen them simply as anti-gay prejudice; and from science and government whose perspective stressed the need to modify and educate public opinion. Historically, however, they have their own validity; and their existence in the 1980s rather than the 1800s should not lead to a Whiggish belief in the necessary superiority – or concreteness – of scientific formulations.

THE ESTABLISHMENT OF AIDS AS A POLICY ISSUE

Popular unease about the disease appears to have been common by 1985. The level of its impact on policy making remains to be assessed. But certainly AIDS was by then established as a more formal policy issue and this was marked by the organisation of policy advisory mechanisms. The Department of Health moved in late 1984 to set up administrative and policy advisory machinery focussed on the new disease. The Expert Advisory Group on AIDS (EAGA) first met in January 1985 to advise the Chief Medical Officer. Its members came from the clinical and scientific areas of expertise on AIDS. A 'social' group dealing with prevention and health education issues had a mixture of medical and gay activists. The Expert group met seven times in 1985 and set up a number of associated groups: on counselling, screening, resources, a group on

[59] *Hansard*, 5 March 1985 cols. 438–9. See also the question from Robert McCrindle, MP, implying contagion, on 7 February 1985, col. 657.
[60] Interview, senior civil servant, 1989. The Terrence Higgins Trust reacted to this with a leaflet on *AIDS and the Chalice*.
[61] Interview, London probation officer, 1988.
[62] Department of Health and Social Security, *AIDS: Monitoring Responses to the Public Education Campaign* (London, 1987).

AIDS and drug abuse; a surgeons', anaesthetists' and dentists' sub-group; groups on employment, renal units, artificial insemination; and on immunoglobulin. One early member recalled:

Acheson wanted advice – and pulled names out of a hat of those who'd written about it . . . it was more effective early on – so many big issues were dealt with on the run . . . EAGA was a force in developing policies very quickly – screening, blood transfusions, breastfeeding. Everything had to be developed over about two years.[63]

As well as external links, the Department also developed its own internal policy machinery on AIDS. In 1985, a direct phone line for professional inquiries was linked to a special AIDS Unit in the Department. Matters began to move outside the public health ambit in the Department and high-level generalist civil servants became involved. One recalled:

AIDS really hit us in 1985 . . . it didn't appear as a problem until it came up through the media more than anything else . . . It gradually bubbled up . . . and grew rapidly over a period of about eighteen months . . . it was an unfamiliar phenomenon, a disease which was unknown to medical science, which appeared fatal and growing.[64]

A ministerial steering group on AIDS, chaired by Barney Hayhoe, met in December. In January came the first meeting of an interdepartmental group on AIDS, with representatives ranging from the Department of Health through to the Foreign Office and the Treasury. Its purpose was to advise the ministerial steering group on the development of a co-ordinated strategy.[65] AIDS was beginning to move from a departmental to a high-profile political policy issue. As a departmental question, policy lines which most clearly united the community were a stress on the need for urgent action, and the need for public education to stress the heterosexual nature of the disease rather than the 'gay plague' angle of the popular press.

The way in which those objectives gained political feasibility in the period of 'war-time emergency' from 1986–7 has been discussed elsewhere.[66] But interpretations of the function of the initial 'policy

---

[63] Interview, genito-urinary medicine consultant, February 1989. For details of the membership of the expert group, see *Hansard*, 20 February 1985, cols. 498–500.
[64] Interview, senior civil servant, 1989.
[65] *Hansard*, 14 January 1986, cols. 556–7.
[66] In Berridge and Strong (eds.), 'Aids Policies in the UK'.

community' have varied. One senior civil servant's view was that 'the Advisory Group was hijacked by a homosexual group among the doctors ... the result was a publicity campaign which stressed the heterosexual spread of AIDS, all done to avoid creating a homosexual backlash'.[67] AIDS, in his view, was an example of 'the impact of a lobby on the conduct of policy'. From the gay perspective it was different: 'There is such a thing as realpolitik and we need to do business on that basis. We were a Broad Church drawn together. The gay community needed educating ... what the backbenchers were allowed to rant and rave about was not government policy.'[68]

Certainly these loose and often uneasy initial alliances were reconstructed in the latter stages of policy development. Some of the early experts moved out of key policy committees or were more marginal to policy development. The traditional bio-medical elite did come to predominate, 'the old boy network of British science': 'X tried to reorganise it in the MRC way ... Let's get an MRC person in who doesn't know anything about the subject, but at least he'll behave.'[69]

CONCLUSION: AIDS AND HISTORY

This chapter's secondary aim was to illustrate and analyse the role of history in relation to AIDS. Initially history was used in two ways: as a form of background knowledge, and also as 'historical partisanship', the use of historical example to advance particular policy positions. Both types of historical activity intermingled. Historians and, in the British context, key policy actors such as Acheson and Adler directly used the historical record to defend a liberal consensus response to AIDS. The political and public demand for compulsory notification was in part deflected by reference to the failure of past attempts at compulsion and the success of the voluntaristic and confidential tradition in the area of sexually transmitted disease. This 'lesson of history' approach was in turn refracted through different national political cultures. In the United States, the use of similar historical examples proved more open to debate; opponents of the voluntaristic approach likewise argued from historical

---

[67] Interview, senior civil servant, 1989.   [68] Interview, gay activist, July 1989.
[69] Interview, genito-urinary consultant, March 1990.

example.[70] The greater decentralisation of power in the United States mediated the nature of the historical response. The 'lesson of history' approach was not specific to AIDS, but has emerged in times of crisis, or of policy flux in other areas of health policy: as, for example, with the use of the history of British drug policy debates around American drug policy in the 1960s, or in the way in which the 'decarceration' debates in mental health were informed by critical historical work on the asylum.[71]

But history was also background to AIDS. Knowledge of reactions to past epidemics, the historical response to sexually transmitted diseases, conflicts between individual liberty and the public good in past public health debates, all fed indirectly into the discussion. There was an idea that the advent of AIDS itself, as a new infectious disease, marked a significant moment in history; historical consciousness was in general heightened. Thus the 'historical background' considered appropriate has itself changed with changes in the perception of the disease. Charles Rosenberg has recently discussed the stages of reaction to epidemic disease, encompassing AIDS within a model of chronic disease, not epidemic spread. Historical perspectives mirror the perceptions of the present.[72] This is not to argue for the abandonment of historical background, but rather for a richer and broader definition of what is of historical relevance to AIDS. Historical work on the way in which social and political relations are mediated by disease, on how disease comes in and out of focus because of particular political, social circumstances, and how national cultures and histories structure reactions to disease, is relevant and should form part of the historically informed discussion.[73] Historical parallels can still be instructive. Take, for example, the reproduction in the 1980s and 1990s of the social

---

[70] For examples of the 'lesson of history' approach, see R. Porter, 'History Says No to the Policeman's Response to AIDS', *British Medical Journal*, 293 (1986), pp. 1589–90; and A. Brandt, 'AIDS in Historical Perspective: Four Lessons from the History of Sexually Transmitted Diseases', *American Journal of Public Health*, 78 (1988), pp. 367–71.

[71] For the use of drug policy, see V. Berridge, 'AIDS, Drugs and History', *British Journal of Addiction* (AIDS Special Issue, forthcoming).

[72] C. Rosenberg, 'What is an Epidemic? AIDS in Historical Perspective', *Daedalus*, 118 no. 2 (1989), pp. 1–17.

[73] These comments arise from discussions of the role of history and anthropology in relation to AIDS at the conference on 'AIDS Research: Issues for Anthropological Theory, Method, and Practice', organised by the Wenner-Gren Foundation for Anthropological Research, June 1990. I am particularly grateful to Shirley Lindenbaum for her comments and to a paper by Sander Gilman.

hygienist concerns of the 1900s: an individualised public health focussed on prevention, the theme of national degeneration (or heterosexual spread), the particular focus on the role of women and children, and the way in which the interim phase of social research on AIDS, poised between activism and academics, mirrors the embryonic development of social research at the turn of the century.

This chapter has suggested two further roles for historians of the very recent past: the study of the 'larger agenda', the pre-history of AIDS policy issues, without which it is impossible to analyse the impact of the disease; and the study of AIDS itself. This is by no means a task unique to them. This chapter has aimed to show how the concepts of other disciplines such as sociology, anthropology or political science can be fruitfully incorporated. But there are particular historical strengths. History is, as Patrick Dunleavy has noted, generalist in its concerns, a unifying force in the fragmentation of social science research.[74] Peter Stearns comments: 'To the extent that policy issues typically involve change, a trained historical sense (beyond the factual historical background) is conceptually indispensable.'[75] There is also a different function for history: not through its direct contribution to policy, but through an analysis of the nature and determinants of the issues relevant to policy, sharpening their definition and specifying options. AIDS, which has highlighted the complexities of so many of the cultural, policy and social issues which surround health in British society in the late twentieth century, has also emphasised the unrealised potential in the relationship of history to policy.

[74] P. Dunleavy, 'The Study of Public Policy: Do Historians Have a Role?' (paper given to the seminar on twentieth-century policy and administration, Institute of Historical Research, May 1990).
[75] P. N. Stearns, 'History and Public Policy', in G. J. McCaw and G. H. Weber (eds.), *The Roles of Academic Disciplines in Policy Analysis* (Port Washington, NY, 1984), pp. 91–128.

Index

AIDS, 5, 9, 10, 14, 149; in Britain
1981–6, 303–28; development of
scientific knowledge and popular
beliefs, 239–40, 311–12, 322–4;
funding of research and treatments,
319–20; government policy (UK),
312–15, 324–6; issue of heterosexual
spread, 309, 315–8, 319; research
policy, 320–2; see also Africa; drugs
policy; haemophiliacs; homosexuals;
United States
Abbanus, St, 63
'Abd al-Razzâq, 97
abortion, 184, 185
Abû l-'Abbâs Muḥammad ibn Yazîd
al-Mubarrad, 79
Abû l-Ḥasan 'Alî ibn Muḥammad al-
Madâ'inî, 79
Abû Salama, 90
Abû 'Ubayd Allâh Muḥammad ibn
'Umrân al-Marzubânî, 79
Acheson, Sir Donald, 310, 313, 325, 326
Ackerknecht, E., 136
Adcock, F. E., 42
Adler, Michael, 312, 316, 326
Adomnan, Life of Columba, 64, 65
Advisory Committee on Dangerous
Pathogens, 313
Afghanistan, cholera in, 150, 161
Afra, conversion of, 59
Africa, 4, 7, 11, 16, 151; AIDS
epidemic, 299, 315, 317; colonial
discourse on African sexuality, 299–
302; influenza epidemic, 241, 245–6,
247; reponse of major religious
systems to human and animal
epidemics, 241–68; traditional

African religion and public health
ideologies, 75, 241–2, 246, 247–57
passim, 265–6; venereal disease, 269–
302; see also cattle; Central Africa;
East Africa; Islam; missionaries;
sexual mores; smallpox; southern
Africa; West Africa
Afrikaner response to influenza
pandemic, 264–5, 266
Ahmednagar, India, plague in, 235
Aix-en-Provence, cholera epidemic
(1835), 155
akhbâr literature, accounts of epidemic
disease in, 78–9, 90, 93, 96
Aladura prophetic healing churches,
Nigeria, 267
Alaska, Amerindians, 199
Albanian refugees, fifteenth-century,
113
Albergo dei Poveri, Genoa, 122
Alcibiades, 32, 41, 43
alcoholism in Hawaii, 184
Alexandrian anatomy, 31
Alison, Dr W. P., 133, 142, 143 n. 31,
144, 145
Amand, St, 60
Amerindians: impact of imported
diseases on, 175–6, 179–80, 193, 196–
7; relationship between sexual mores
and population decline, 198–201
'Amr ibn al-'Âṣ, 87
Anand detention camp, Gujarat, 233,
235
Anas ibn Mâlik, 95
Anatolia, cholera in, 151
anatomy, morbid, 141, 143–4, 165
Anaxagoras, 42

329

Andrew the Apostle, 60
Angers, plague avoidance, 108
Anglican missions in southern Africa, 264, 267
Ankleshwar, India, plague in, 235
anomie, as factor in population decline, 183–4, 188
anti-contagionism, 13, 136, 145, 146, 168
anti-medicine movements, in Africa, 267, 268
Anuak territory, Nuer invasion of, 253
'Aphrodisian' cultures, 194, 199, 201
Apollo, cult of, 42, 43
Apostolic church in South Africa, 265
Apt, Provence, plague avoidance, 108
Arab traders, 277, 285
Archidamos, king of the Lacedaimonians, 22
Argentine, slaughter of Amerindians, 180
Aristophanes, 21, 28
Armstrong, Dr John, 140, 142, 143, 144
Arnold, D., 10, 14, 223, 224, 225
Arnott, Dr Neil, 136
Arthur Road Hospital, Bombay, riots at (1896), 218
Asclepius, cult of, 41
'Âṣim ibn Sulaymân al-Aḥwal, 95
Athens, plague of, 4, 7, 9; account of, 21–36; impact on Athenian society, 37–44
Attica, 21, 22, 27
Austria, 158, 161, 163, 166
Austro-Prussian War, 158
Aztecs, 149

Babukusi, 250–1
Bacchanalianism, 37
bacteriology, 14, 172
Baden, imposition of *cordons sanitaires*, 166, 169
Bagamoyo, prophetic movements in, 260
Bagandan society, 269–75 *passim*, 278–83 *passim*
Baker, Surgeon Major, of Indian Medical Service, 230
Bancroft, Edward, 146
Bandra, India, plague in, 224
Bantu, 243, 261, 280
Banyaruanda, 279

Barcelona, plague in, 105
barefoot theory of plague, 215, 216
Barry, Surgeon Major, of Indian Medical Service, 230
Baṣra, plague in, 90, 94, 95
Bassano, Italy, 115, 117
Bassein, India, evacuation of, 219
Bastiano (pedlar at Volterra), 113
Bateman, Dr Thomas, 142–3
Beddoes, Thomas, 139, 140
bedouin attitudes to contagious diseases, 84, 87, 89
beggars, segregation of, 101–4 *passim*, 120, 121
Beinart, William, 243
Bembo, Agostino, 116
Benaglio, Dr Marc'Antonio, 114, 118, 122
Bendis, cult of, 37
Bentham, Jeremy, 143, 146
Bergamo, Italy, 114, 118, 119, 122
Berlin, 162 n. 35, 168, 169, 172
Bermondsey, cholera mortality rates, 156
Bertrand, Dr J. B., 106, 108, 118
Bingley, A. H., 224
bird malaria, 191–2
Bishop, Reverend Artemas, 182
bishop-saints, Frankish, 73–5
Black Death (1348–50), 4, 15, 16, 37–8, 158, 170, 210; in Middle East, 78, 86, 98
Blackman, William F., 198
Blainey, Dr Thomas, 227
blood-letting, 131, 138, 139, 140, 142, 143
Blood Products Laboratory, Elstree, 315
Boa, Uganda, 277
boards of health, 15, 18, 121
Boccaccio, Giovanni, 16
Body Positive (AIDS organization), 308
Boers, 264
Bombay, 6, 9, 12, 203 n. 3; Contagious Diseases Hospital, 229; plague in, 204, 206–7, 210–24 *passim*, 227–39 *passim*; riots, 218, 220, 222 n. 89, 223–4
Bonitus, bishop of Clermont, 74
Borromeo, St Carlo, 102
Bowman, J., 199
Bragadin, Antonio, 106

Braine, Sir Bernard, 318
Brandt, Johanna, 265
bread supplies, 107–8, 116
Brelsford, W. V., 296
Brenta river detention camp, Italy, 121
Brescia, Italy, plague in, 116
Briggs, Asa, 1, 152
Brighton, AIDS helpline, 307
Bristol medical school, 139
Britain, 14, 19; AIDS 1981–6, 303–28;
    cholera epidemics, 152, 158, 161–2,
    165, 168, 169, 170, 171; public health
    1750–1850, 125–48; *see also*
    colonialism
British Home Stores, employment
    policy, 309
British Medical Journal, 269, 271, 309
Brittany, monster myths, 65–6
Broach, India, plague in, 235
Broadcasting Support Services AIDS
    helpline, 310
Broicsech (Irish badger monster), 67
Broussais, François J. V., 144, 147
Brown, John, 147
Brown, Ron, MP for Leith, 318
Brunswick, cholera mortality rates, 156
bubonic plague, *see* plague
Budansab, Fakrudin, 236
Buer, M. C., 131
Buffon, Comte de, 201
Buganda, syphilis epidemic, 269–70,
    274, 275, 276, 278, 280, 282–3
al-Bukhârî, Muhammad ibn Ismail, 97
Bunyoro, 274–5
Buom (Nuer prophet), 254
burial customs, 40, 164, 170, 244, 254
Burke, William, 165, 169
Burke's Peerage, and AIDS, 240

Cadorino, Giacomo and Lucia, 112
Calcutta, 207, 222 n. 89
California, epidemics, 90
Caluppa, St, 59–60
Calvi, G., 9–10, 109
Cambridge, gay student group, 306,
    307
camel mange, cited as example of
    contagious disease, 83, 89, 92, 93
Campaign for Homosexual Equality
    (CHE), 308
Canada, Amerindians, 193
Canning, George, 189

Canton, 181, 189 n. 34
Cape Colony, 241, 245, 246, 263
Capello, Vincenzo, 111
Capital Gay, 306, 307, 309
Cardiff, AIDS in, 307, 315–16
Carib Indians, 199
Carmichael, A., 17, 18
Carthaginians, epidemic among
    (397 BC), 27, 28–30
Cartigliano, Italy, 115
Catherine the Great, 19
cattle: cattle-killing, Xhosa, 252, 255–7;
    diseases, *see* lungsickness; rinderpest
Caucasus, cholera in, 151
Celtic dragon myths, 63–7
Central Africa, venereal disease, 284,
    285, 286, 288–9, 290, 296–7, 298, 300
Central America, cholera epidemics,
    151
Chadwick, Edwin/Chadwickian ideas,
    13, 126–8, 133–7 *passim*, 142, 144,
    145 n. 35, 147
Chalcideans, Athenian expedition
    against, 26
Chambars, plague among, 235
Chapin, Dr Alonzo, 192, 193
charitable response to epidemics, 106,
    107, 119–20
Charles Mallory (ship), 190
Cheever, Henry T., 184
Chester Infirmary, fever wards, 131
Chevalier, Louis, 1, 69, 158
Chibi district, Southern Rhodesia, 265
China, 151, 181, 189 n. 34, 197, 199
Chinook Indians, 199–200
Chisholm, Dr Colin, 142
cholera, 1, 10, 149–73; differential
    impact on rich and poor, 154–7;
    government policies, 166–70, 171–3;
    mortality rates, 6, 170, 203–4;
    occupational analysis of victims,
    155–6; physical symptoms 8, 153–4;
    relationship between social unrest
    and, 149–50, 157–66, 170–1
Christianity: Christian prophetic
    churches in Africa, 266–7; rejection
    of, during epidemics, 37–8; response
    to epidemic disease, 5, 17, 242, 263–
    4, 273–4; syphilis epidemic in
    Uganda attributed to introduction
    of, 269, 270, 271–2, 277, 293; *see also*
    missionaries

Church Missionary Society (CMS), 270, 271, 273
Cicogna, Pasquale, 111
Cipolla, C. M. 121
Cividale, Friuli, 111, 115, 118, 121
Clark, William, 199
Clarke, Kenneth, 313–14, 316
class conflict, 116–17, 163–4, 165
Clement, St, 74
Cleopompus (leader of Athenian forces besieging Potidaea), 26
clerical culture, medieval, dragon lore in, 53, 55–6
Clovis, Merovingian king, 71
Clutterbuck, Henry, 140, 144
Coady, Inspector, of Bombay, 220
Cobb, Richard, *Paris and its Provinces*, 69–70
Cochrane, C. N., 30, 31
Coemgen, St, 64
Colindale, Communicable Disease Surveillance Centre at, 309, 312–13
Colman Ela, St, 63–4, 66
Colonial Medical Advisory Committee, sub-committee on venereal diseases, 292–5
colonialism, 11, 13, 150, 244; African prophetic response to, 242–3, 249–50, 251–57 *passim*; and British reactions to epidemics in India and Africa, 205–40 *passim*, 264–5, 269–302 *passim*; and impact of exotic diseases on native populations, 149, 175–6, 241
Columba, St, 64
Columbus, Christopher, 175, 198
commerce: bans and controls on, 15, 115–16, 210–11; as channel for spread of disease, 18, 112, 122, 150–1, 159, 160–1, 269, 277; relaxation of plague measures in interests of, 12, 167–8, 172
Communicable Disease Surveillance Centre, Colindale, 309, 312–13
concealment of plague victims, 219, 235, 236
conspiracy theories, 4, 113, 164, 165
Constantin, F., 260
Constantine, Donation of, 57
Constantinople, plague in, 27
contagion theory, 3, 13, 138, 142, 216; and AIDS, 323–24; Arab, 83–5, 86,

88–91, 98; classical Greek, 33–6; in early modern Europe, 105, 112–13; *see also* anti-contagionism
Contagious Diseases Act, 283
Cook, Albert, 271–2, 273, 277, 280, 281–2, 284
Cook, J. H., 273–4
Cook, Captain James, 176–9 *passim*, 182, 193–6 *passim*, 199
Cooper, F., 258–9, 260
Cooter, R., 136
cordons sanitaires, 12, 17, 115, 163, 164, 166, 167, 208
Cortés, Hernán, 149, 179
countryside, flight to, 108, 115
crime, increase in, during epidemics, 232–3
Crimean War, 157, 161
Cripps, Arthur, 267
Criscentia, St, 70
Crom Conaill (Celtic monster), 67
Cullen, William/Cullenian view of fever, 130, 133, 138–45 *passim*, 148
Cuneo, Michele de, 198–9
Cybele, cult of, 37

dancing mania, 37
Darwin, Charles, 188
Darwinism, Social, 175
Davies, J. N. P., 281
Dawson, M., 244–5
de Boer, H. S., 293–4
dead, disposal of, 117, 118; *see also* burial customs
dearth, as cause of illness, 126–8, 133, 134, 245; *see also* malnutrition
death, attitudes to, 16, 39–40, 244
debility theory of fever, 130–1, 144; *see also* dearth
Defoe, D., *A Journal of the Plague Year*, 9, 104, 109, 117
Delian Games, 43
Delos, purification of (426 BC), 42–3
Delumeau, J., 158
demons, as cause of epidemics, 82–3, 86–7
Deng Laka (Nuer prophet), 254
Department of Health (UK), response to AIDS, 305, 309–10, 312–15, 316, 318–22 *passim*, 324–6
Desiderius of Cahors, Bishop, 73
detention camps, 208, 222, 234

Devil, 59, 60, 61, 123
Dharwar, India, 219
Dickens, Charles, *Bleak House*, 112
diet, 107–8, 116; *see also* malnutrition
Digo people, Kenya, 261
Dinka religion, 253
Diocletian, Emperor, Edict against the
   Manichaeans, 61
Diodorus Siculus, account of Syracusan
   epidemic, 27, 28–30, 42, 43
Diopeithes, 42
diphtheria, 217, 313
disinfection: during cholera epidemics,
   163, 169–70, 172; measures in India,
   207–8, 216, 217, 222
dispensaries, 131, 133
dissection, 141, 143–4
Dobson, M. J., 7
doctors, *see* physicians
Dok Nuer people, 254
Doll, Sir Richard, 321
Dols, M., 17
Donatus, bishop of Epirus, 58
Donzellini (Venetian physician), 107–8
dragons and dragon-slayers, Dark Age
   myths, 45–76 *passim*
drainage schemes, 73, 74, 75
drugs policy and AIDS, 315, 317–18;
   needle-exchange system, 318
Dunleavy, P., 328
Dunwoody, Gwyneth, 316
Durey, M., 152, 161–2, 167, 168, 170
Duvalier, 'Baby Doc' Jean-Claude, 149
dysentery, 192, 193

EAGA, *see* Expert Advisory Group on
   AIDS
East Africa, 151; epidemics and
   religious systems, 241–61 *passim*, 266;
   venereal disease, 269–300 *passim*
ecological equilibrium, notion of, 75
Edinburgh: drug users and AIDS, 318;
   Medical School, 128, 130, 133, 136,
   139, 140 n. 25, 165; New Town
   Dispensary, 133; Royal Infirmary,
   133; typhus epidemics, 132
El Tor cholera bacillus, 151
Elbourne, E., 261–2
Eleanora (ship), 180
Eleusinian Mysteries, 41
Elliott, Robert, 270
Ellis, Reverend William, 184

Elphick, R., 243
employment, impact of plague on, 115–
   16, 117
endemic infections, distinction between
   'new' epidemics and, 5, 7–8, 281–2,
   284
Epidemics (Hippocratic Corpus), 35
Eritrea, rinderpest in, 247
Ethiopia, alleged origin of Athenian
   plague, 22, 27
evacuation of at-risk populations, 12,
   120–1, 219, 233, 234
Evans, A. J., 297
Exeter riots (1832), 158
exhalations, pestiferous, theories of, 46,
   59, 61, 65, 67, 130, 134, 144
Expert Advisory Group on AIDS
   (EAGA), 310, 313, 324–5, 326

Factor VIII (blood product), 315, 316
famine, *see* dearth
Farcinatore, Matteo, 112
Farr, Dr William, 127
Farthing, Charles, 312
fear, as cause of illness, 114
Feierman, Steven, 247–8, 249–50
Felix, bishop of Nantes, 73
feudal regimes, 163
fever theories and British public health
   1780–1850, 125–48; fever hospitals,
   131–5, 138, 148
Filate (Ethiopian villager), 45, 46
flagellant movement, 37
flight from plague, 4, 94, 108, 115, 219,
   232
Florence, 106; plague (1630s), 9–10,
   109, 110, 112, 115, 117–20 *passim*;
   public health measures, 15, 18–19
Fortunatus, *see* Venantius Fortunatus
Foucault, Michel, 104
Fowler, Norman, 314, 319
Fracastoro, Girolamo, 108, 110
France: cholera in, 158, 161, 162, 165,
   166; hospital medicine, 139, 143;
   plague in (*see also* Marseilles), 9, 106,
   108, 118
Franco-Prussian War, 159–60
Franks, 55, 56, 59, 62; *see also*
   Merovingian period
French Revolution, 163
Friend (AIDS organization), 308
Friuli, 106, 111, 122

fumigation, 117, 118, 163, 208

GUM clinics, 308
galley slaves, as providers of essential
    services during plague, 117, 118
Gallipoli, 161
Gallus I, bishop of Clermont, 74
Gallus II, bishop of Clermont, 73
Gay and Lesbian Switchboard, 306,
    308, 309
Gay Medical Association, 309
Gazaland, control of tsetse in, 75
genito-urinary medicine, impact of
    AIDS on, 311, 312
Genoa: pesthouse, 122; plague in, 109,
    111, 112, 116, 117
Genovefa, St, 71
George, St, 50, 59
George IV, king of England, 189
Gerbaldo, Giovanni G., 122
Germanus, bishop of Paris, 50
Germany, 19; cholera epidemics, 157–8,
    159, 166, 171; colonialism, 249
Ghanchis, plague among, 235
Ghori, India, attack on plague search
    party, 235, 236
Gildas, legend of Maelgwn, 66
Gilks, J. L., 280
Glasgow: epidemics, 128, 132, 158;
    Medical School, 140
Glass, D. V., 127
Gold Coast, 294–5
Gomme, A. W., 42
gonorrhoea, 283, 284, 290, 294, 295,
    298
Gonzaga princely house, rulers of
    Mantua, 19
government responses to epidemics, *see*
    public health
Gowans, Sir James, 320, 321
grain trade, 107–8, 116
Granger, R. O., 144
grave-robbing, 165
'great internment', 104, 120
Gregory I (the Great), St, 57, 58
Gregory of Tours, St, 57–8, 59–60,
    61–2, 69, 70
Grenada, fever in, 142
Grey, Sir George, 256
Group B (hepatitis self-help group),
    308
Guardian, early AIDS report, 306

Guest, Lady Charlotte, translation of
    Mabinogion, 66
Gulu, Uganda, yaws in, 279
Guy de Chauliac, 38

HIV (human immune deficiency virus),
    239, 240, 304, 316, 317, 322; *see also*
    AIDS
Habsburg empire, 158, 167
ḥadîth literature, references to
    epidemics in, 78, 81, 84–5, 90, 92, 93,
    94, 95–6
Haemophilia Society, 316
haemophiliacs and AIDS, 315–17,
    319
Haffkine, W. M., 228
Hagnon (leader of Athenian forces), 26,
    27, 34
Haiti, AIDS in, 149
Hamburg, 14; cholera epidemics, 156,
    157, 159, 160, 167–8, 169, 171, 172
Hampshire, outbreak of hepatitis B,
    315
Hankin, Ernest Hanbury, 208, 215, 224
Hansen's Disease, *see* leprosy
Hare, William, 165, 169
Harford, Charles, 270, 271
Harvey, Surgeon-General (Director of
    Indian Medical Department), 209
Hashim Dada of Nagpada, 218
Hastings, marquess of (formerly earl of
    Moira), 160
Hawaii, factors contributing to
    population decline, 4, 7, 176–201;
    see also missionaries; venereal
    disease
Haygarth, John, 131, 139
Hayhoe, Barney, 319, 325
Health Education Council, *Facts About
    Aids*, 313
Heckewelder, John, 201
Henderson, J., 19
Henry VIII, king of England, 19
hepatitis B, 308, 315
Heraclitus of Ephesus, 39, 40
Hermae, mutilation of the, 41
Herodotus, 32
Hesiod, 41–2
Higgins, Terrence, 307; *see also*
    Terrence Higgins Trust
Hijâz, 93
Hilary, St, 58

Hillebrand, William, 195
Hippocratic medicine, 30, 31, 34, 35, 36
Hirst, L. F., 217
Holladay, A. J., 33–4, 35, 36
Holmes, G., 20
homosexuals and AIDS, 304–13 *passim*, 315, 323, 324, 326; in United States, 239, 240
Hong Kong plague epidemic, 215
Honolulu, 186, 189, 196
Hopkins, D., 243
Hopkins, Sarah Winnemucca, 184–5, 199
Horizon programme (BBC TV), 'Killer in the Village', 306
hospital medicine, development of, 138–9
hospitalisation of plague victims, fear of in India, 226, 229–30, 233
'Hottentots', *see* Khoikhoi
housing conditions, 120, 121, 157; *see also* overcrowding; sanitarians
Howard, John, 108, 121
Howard, R. B., 134
Hubli, India, 210, 235
Hudson, E. H., 281
Hume, David, 76
Hungary, cholera in, 163
Huron Indians, 176
Husack, Dr, of Boston, 142

Ibn Abî Shayba, 97
Ibn Ishâq, Abû 'Abd Allâh Muhammad, 84
Ibn al-Nadîm, 79
Ila V. D. campaign, Northern Rhodesia, 296–7
immunity, acquired, 34; *see also* survivors
Inca empire, 149
India, 4; cholera epidemics, 150, 151, 203–4; epidemics of plague 1896–1914, 203 40; government measures to combat plague, 207–18; popular reaction to government plague measures, 218–38
Indian National Congress, 205, 239
Indian Plague Commission, 216
Indians, American, *see* Amerindians
industrialisation, 150, 152, 283, 286, 289

infanticide, in Hawaii, 182, 184, 185–8, 198
influenza, 7, 190, 193, 241; pandemic 1918–19, 203, 245–6, 247, 260, 264–7
International Sanitary Convention (1897), 210
Iraq, 90, 93
Ireland: monster myths, 63–4, 67; public health, 128, 132
Irish saints, *Lives* of, 63–4
Iroquois Indians, 176
Isidore of Seville, 58
Islam, 5, 11, 17; charismatic brotherhoods in Africa, 260–1, 268; discussion of epidemic disease in early Islamic society, 77–99; East African Muslims' responses to plague, 242, 245, 257–61, 268; Indian Muslims' hostility to plague measures, 219, 235–6
isolation of the sick, 163, 164, 169–70, 172, 207; isolation hospitals, 15, 135, 216; *see also* segregation
Israelites, 91, 92
Italy, 4, 15–16, 17–19, 20, 161; influence of epidemics on perceptions of the poor, 101–23

Jalgaon, India, 236
Jameson, Sir Wilson, 294
Japan, 8, 18, 151, 197
Jarves, James J., 196
Jeanes School, 296
Jeeva, Govind, 228
Jefferson, Thomas, 201
Jews, 160; suspected of spreading disease, 4, 37, 113–14, 162, 163 n. 40
Jewson, N., 129–30, 138
jinn (spirits), as cause of epidemics, 83, 85, 86–7
Johnson, D., 252–54 *passim*, 268
Johnston, Sir Harry, 270
Jones, E. L., 19
Jordan, A. G., 305
Journal d'un Bourgeois de Paris, 69
Judd, Dr Gerrit P., 193

Kagwa, Sir Apolo, 272
Kaira district, Gujarat, 233, 235
Kamakau, Samuel M., 191
Kamamalu, Hawaiian queen, 189
Kamba, smallpox among, 245

Kamehameha I, Hawaiian king, 180, 184, 190
Karad, India, plague in, 232, 236
Kauai, Hawaii, 190
Kavirondo, Kenya, syphilis in, 280, 286
Kay (-Shuttleworth), James Phillips, 136–7
Keane, Major G. J., 274, 275, 276, 277, 279
Kensington, cholera mortality rates, 156
Kenya, 261; prophets, 250–1; rinderpest outbreak, 247; smallpox in, 244–5; venereal diseases, 280, 286, 290, 293
Kenyatta, Jomo, 250
Khoikhoi ('Hottentots'), 241, 243, 261–3, 264
Kikuyu prophets, 245, 250
Kimbangu, Simon, 267
Kiponda b. Selemani, *shaikh*, 260
Kitâb al-anbiyâ' ('Book of the Ancient Prophets'), 81
Kitâb al-quadar ('Book of Divine Will'), 81
Kitâb al-ṭibb ('Book of Medicine'), 81
Kitasato, S., 214
Koch, Robert, 172
Königsberg, cholera riots (1831), 158, 164, 166
Kotzebue, Otto von, 183, 184
Krusenstern, Adam Ivan, 179
Kulkarni, Shripat Gopal, 221

La Pérouse, Jean François, Comte de, 179, 194, 196
Lambkin, Colonel, 269, 270, 271, 272–3, 281, 293
Lamont, Dr, 276
Lamu, slavery in, 259
Lancet, The, 269, 270, 271
Langogne, Lozère, wolf of, 72
Laws, Dr Robert, 285
lazzaretti, 12, 15, 19
Lazzaretto di San Gottardo, Friuli, 122
Le Goff, J., 53–4, 55, 62, 63, 71–2
legionella, 313, 314
Lemnos, plague in, 22, 27
leprosy, 18, 19; in Hawaii, 191, 194–5, 196; Islamic attitudes, 85, 88
Levi, Carlo, 46
Lewis, Meriwether, 199, 200
Liholiho, Hawaiian king, 189

Limoges, 74
Lisiansky, Captain Urey, 194
Liverpool: cholera riots (1832), 158; Fever Hospital, 131
London, 158, 315–16; cholera mortality rates, 156–7; Fever Hospital, 131, 132, 140, 142–4; medical schools, 139–40, 141
Lorenzo Giustinian, St, 102
Lovato, Pietro Antonio, 112
Lübeck, cholera in, 168
Luckin, W., 166
Lucretius, account of Athenian plague, 9, 27
Lukiko (Bagandan chiefly council), 274
lungsickness, 241, 246, 247, 251, 254, 255
Lusaka, showing of propaganda film on venereal disease, 296

Mabinogion, 66
Mac Reiche, St, 67, 71
McGrew, R., 152–3
MacKay, John, 318
Maclean, Charles, 136, 145
McClelland Committee on HIV infection in Scotland, 318
McNeill, W. H., 149
Madagascar, cholera epidemic, 151
Maelgwn, king of Gwnedd, 66
magistrates, public health, 15, 102, 131
Mahars, plague among, 235
Mail on Sunday, report on infected blood products (May 1983), 315–16
Makila, F. E., 250–1
malaria, 8, 48, 70–1, 73, 75, 191–2, 200, 203
Mâlik ibn Anas, 96–7
Malindi, prophetic movements, 260
malnutrition, 122, 134, 158–9; *see also* dearth
Malo, David, 195
Malthusianism, 109, 121, 127
Manchester, 134, 136, 140 n. 25, 158; Fever Hospital, 131
Manchester and Salford Sanitary Association, 148
Manchuria, bubonic plague in, 75
Mantua, 15, 19
Maranke, Johana, 266–7
Marathas, campaign against (1817), 160
Marcellus, St, 49–59 *passim*, 62, 67–73 *passim*, 75

Marduk (Babylonian deity), 50
Maria Francesca, Sister (nun of
  Genoa), 109, 111, 112, 117–18
markets and fairs, role in spread of
  disease, 159, 161
Marranos, expulsion of, 113–14
Marseilles, 161, 207; plague (1720), 9,
  106, 108, 118
martyrdom, Muslim view of plague as,
  4, 17, 95–6, 97, 98
Masaniello, revolt of (1647), 116, 117
Masowe, Johana, 266–7
maternal welfare programmes in
  Africa, 284–5
Mdalidephu (African deity), 254
Meacher, Michael, 320
measles, 8, 189, 190, 192
'medical police', 13, 19, 129, 132 n. 11
medical profession, *see* physicians
Medical Research Council (UK), 311,
  322, 326; Working Party on AIDS,
  320, 321
medical science, 13–14, 129–33 *passim*,
  138–46 *passim*, 204; African attitudes
  to western, 286, 296, 297; Indian
  attitudes to western, 226–7, 230–2;
  Islamic, 96–7
'medicalisation' of society, 14, 138–9,
  172
Medicean regime in Florence, public
  health projects, 19
Medina, 97
Meldrum, Julian, 307–8
Melisandros, 28
Memel, cholera riots (1831), 158, 164
meningitis, 291
Mercy and Truth, 273–4
Merovingian period, 4, 11, 50, 55, 56,
  75; hagiography, 60, 63; Parisian
  environment in, 67–9, 71
Messina, Black Death in, 37
Metcalfe, Captain Simon, 180
Methodist missionaries in Africa, 263,
  264–5
Mexico, 197
miasmatic theory of disease, 3, 13, 36,
  71, 214; in early modern period, 112,
  113, 122; in nineteenth-century
  Europe, 134, 143, 144, 168
middle-class view of cholera, 154–5, 166
Middlesex Hospital, London, AIDS
  research, 312, 316

migration, and spread of disease, 159,
  160, 245
Mijikenda people, Kenya, 261
Mikalson, J. D., 28
Milan, 102; plague epidemics, 112, 118,
  121; public health measures, 15, 18
military cordons, see *cordons sanitaires*
'military model' of public health, 14, 15
millenarianism, of African prophetic
  movements, 252, 254, 255, 256, 262,
  263, 265, 267
missionaries, Christian, 5; in Africa,
  245, 261–7 *passim*, 269–302 *passim*;
  in Hawaii, 179, 181–2, 184, 186, 189,
  190, 193; medical, 190, 264, 266,
  273–5 *passim*, 277, 284, 292, 295,
  300–1; response to epidemics of
  venereal disease in Africa, 270–4
Mlanjeni (Xhosa prophet), 255, 263
Mlozi war, 285
Mocenigo, Giovanni, 122
Mokapu, Hawaii, excavation of
  prehistoric skeletons, 178
Molua, St, 63
Moore, R. I., 19
moral issues, 104–5, 122–3, 293–4, 300–
  1; in discourse over AIDS, 322, 323;
  see also sexual mores; sin
Morris, R. J., 152, 170, 171
mortality rates, 6, 170, 203–4
Moscow, expulsion of Jews (1891), 160
Motor Sports Club, 307
Mu'âdh ibn Jabal, 87
Mu'âwiya ibn Abî Sufyân, 93
Muhammad, the Prophet, 78, 79–80;
  pronouncements on epidemic disease,
  84–5, 87, 88, 89, 91
Mulago hospital, Uganda, 275, 278–9
mumps, 36
Musisi, Nakanyike, 283
Muslims, *see* Islam
Mutonyi wa Nabukelembe, 250–1
Mwali (African deity), 266
Mwapodzo, Kivoyero (Mijikenda
  elder), 261

Nâfi' ibn Jubayr, 94
Namwala district, Northern Rhodesia,
  campaign against venereal diesease,
  297
Naples, plague in, 116, 117
Narcissus, Bishop, 59

Nasik district, India, plague in, 235
National Blood Transfusion Service,
    measures to protect safety of blood
    supply, 316, 317
Ndava, Zvidzai, 265–6
Ndebele, 244
New England, 7, 179
New Zealand, *rewa-rewa* epidemic, 190
Ngundeng Bong (Nuer prophet), 253,
    268
Nicetius, bishop of Trier, 73, 74
Nicias, Peace of (420 BC), 41
Nigeria, 267, 294
Nijhni-Novgorod, autumn fair, 161
njovera (non-venereally transmitted
    syphilis), 282 n. 36, 286
nobility, feudal, peasant attacks on,
    163–4
Noble, Dr Daniel, 134
Nongqawuse (Xhosa prophet), 255,
    256, 263
North-Western Provinces, India, 238, 239
Northern Rhodesia, 288, 290, 296–7
nosology, 141, 143
Novarsenobillon (arsenical treatment
    for syphilis), 286
Nuer prophets, 251, 252–3, 257, 268
Nxele (Xhosa prophet), 254–5
Nyabuor Yoal (Nuer prophet), 254
Nyasaland, 288; venereal disease in,
    282 n. 36, 285, 290, 295

Oahu, Hawaii, 178, 186, 190
oku'u epidemic, Hawaii, 190, 192
'Orange County Connection', 240
Ottoman Empire, 17
outsiders, as bearers of plague, *see*
    strangers
overcrowding, as factor in spread of
    disease, 21, 24, 29, 108, 112, 137,
    156–7, 166

Padua, plague epidemics, 110–11,
    119–20
Page, D. L., 30
Paiute Indians, 184, 196
'panic' reaction to plague, 114; in
    India, 12, 204–40 *passim*
Panzac, D., 17
Paris, 167; Faubourg Saint-Michel, 68–
    70, 71; in Merovingian period, 67–71;
    riots (1832), 164; sanitary reform, 171

Parry, A., 30
Paterson, A. R., 293
Patten, John, 310
Paul Aurelian, St, 65
Paula Marin, Francisco da, 192
Pausanias, 43
Peires, J. B., 243–4, 246, 252, 254, 255,
    256, 263
Pelagius, 58
Pele (Hawaiian deity), 184
Pelling, M., 134, 153
Peloponnesian War, 21, 22, 32, 33
Peloponnesians, 21, 22, 26, 27, 32
penicillin, 290, 298
Pentecostal church, 265, 267
Pericles, 26, 28, 32, 42, 43
personification/embodiment of disease,
    8–9, 48–9, 67, 71, 248, 258
pesthouses, 121–2
Petit Mills, Bombay, 230
Philadelphia, fever in, 142
Philip II, king of Spain, 19
Philip the Fair, 69
Philippines, 197
Phillips, H., 264, 265
Phormio, 28
physicians; conduct during epidemics,
    38; popular attitudes to, during
    epidemics, 164–6, 169; and public
    health, 18
Pinching, Anthony, 311–12, 316
Piraeus, plague in, 22, 27
Pizarro, Francisco, 149
plague, bubonic, 1, 6, 8, 9, 73, 74;
    association between poverty and, 17,
    101–23; epidemics in India, 203–40;
    Islamic response to, 5, 17, 81, 85–6,
    87, 93–4; rat-flea hypothesis, 14, 216,
    217; *see also* Athens; Black Death
Plato, reference to Athenian plague, 28
Plummer, C., *Lives* of the Irish saints,
    64, 65, 66, 67
Plutarch, 28, 42
poisoning, rumours of, 9, 22, 27, 37,
    163, 165, 224
Poland, cholera epidemic, 158, 161
Polynesians, 176, 178, 184, 191
Poole, J. C. F., 33–4, 35, 36
Poona, India, plague in, 207–8, 209,
    214, 230–1, 232, 235, 239; popular
    resistance to plague measures, 219,
    221–2, 224, 238

poor, the, 17, 145, 158–9, 235; belief that epidemics were conspiracy against, 4, 163, 164, 165; as beneficiaries of the plague, 107, 116, 117–19; as incubators and spreaders of disease, 106–14, 118, 129, 209, 238; poor relief, 119–20, 121, 133; as victims of disease, 114–16, 133, 134, 154–7; *see also* dearth; Italy

Poor Law, 135, 137, 146, 148

popular culture, distinction between clerical culture and, 53, 55–6

population: control, 184–8; decline in Hawaii, 176–201; venereal disease and low birth rates, 195–6, 284–5, 289; *see also* Amerindians

Porto, Luigi da, 114

Portugal, 108, 161, 197

Potidaea, siege of, 26, 27, 34

Pouwels, R. L., 258

poverty, *see* poor

Powhaten, Chief, 200

'pox', 10

Prato, Italy, 110

Prichard, James Cowles, 139

Priestley, Joseph, 147

Prins, G., 256–7

prisoner-of-war camps, Franco-Prussian war, 160

prisoners, used to provide essential services during epidemics, 117

Procopius, description of Constantinople plague, 27

prophetic movements in Africa, 242–3, 245, 247–57, 260, 261–2, 266–8

prostitution, 113, 120, 121, 235, 288, 290, 298

Prussia, cholera epidemics, 163, 164, 165, 167, 168–9, 171

public health, 12–13, 14–16, 18–19; government reaction to fever epidemics in Britain, 125–48; response to AIDS in Britain, 312–15, 324–6; response to cholera epidemics in nineteenth-century Europe, 163–73 *passim*; state intervention to control spread of plague in India, 204–40 *passim*; traditional African systems, 75, 247–8

Public Health (Control of Diseases) Act, 314

Public Health Laboratory Service (UK), 313, 320

Punjab, plague epidemics, 204, 238, 239

quacks, 118, 233–4

Qu-Appelle reservation, Canada, 193

quarantine, 12, 17; during cholera epidemics, 163, 164, 166–7, 168, 169–70, 172; in early modern Italy, 15, 115, 120

Queensberry House barracks, Edinburgh, as emergency fever hospital, 132

Qur'ân, 86, 92, 259

Quraysh attitudes to smallpox, 84

racial segregation, 211, 212, 287–8

Ragnimodus, bishop of Paris, 70

Ragusa, 15, 18

Rajapur, Ahmednagar district, 235

Ramiya, *shaikh*, 260

Rand, W. C., 207, 214, 219, 221

rats, 62, 120; rat-flea theory of plague, 14, 216, 217

Read, James, 262

Reade, W. L., 214

Reform Bill (1832), 157, 158, 161–2

refugees, as bearers of disease, 113, 160, 161

religion: impact of epidemics on, 4, 11–12, 16, 37–41 *passim*, 44; view of disease as divine punishment, 4, 17, 30, 42, 91, 95, 104, 122; *see also* Africa; Christianity; Islam

revolution, conjuncture of epidemics and, 149–50, 153, 157–8, 162, 170–3; *see also* riots

Revolution of 1848, 157, 158, 162

rewa-rewa epidemics, New Zealand, 190

Richards, Reverend Greg, 313, 324

Richardson, J. J., 305

Righi, Alessandro, 110

Riley, J. C., 128–9

rinderpest (cattle plague), 13, 241, 245, 246–7, 251, 253, 263–4

riots, 9, 12, 116–17; during cholera epidemics, 158, 162–7 *passim*, 169–70; in response to plague regulations in India, 204, 208, 209, 218–20, 223–4, 226, 236; *see also* revolution

ritual practices, 4, 12, 37, 39, 41, 62, 105–6

Rizza, Dr Charles, 316–17
Rollins, Mr (surgeon-major on La Pérouse's ship), 196
Rome, flooding and plague (AD 589), 57–8
Roscoe, Reverend, of Church Missionary Society, 271
Rosen, Mel, 306–7
Rosenberg, C. E., 8, 153, 327
Rotherhithe, cholera mortality rates, 156
rumours about epidemics, 223–6, 239–40
Rush, Benjamin, 142, 147
Russia, 19, 163; cholera epidemics, 150, 153, 158, 160, 164, 165, 167, 169–70, 172
Rutherford, M. C., 295

Sabazius, cult of, 37
Sahlins, M., 194, 199
St Mary's Hospital, London, 311–12, 316
St Vitus's Dance, 37
saints, as dragon-tamers and restorers of health, 49–76
Saleh, Sharif, 259–60
Salisbury, Rhodesia, 298
'Salvarsan' treatment, 275, 285
Sampson, Anthony, 303
Samson, St, 65–6
Samthanne, St, 63
San Bonaventura, Father Antero Maria di, 109
San Diego, 239–40
San Francisco, gay community, 306
San Lazzaro dei Mendicanti, Venice, 104
San Martino a Gangalandi, 113
sandalwood trade, Hawaiian, 181
sanitarians/sanitary reform, 13, 126–8, 133–8 *passim*, 142, 146–8, 156–7, 173; in Germany, 166, 171–2; in India, 211–12
'sanitation syndrome', 288, 300
Sant'Erasmo island, detention camp on, 121
Santo Stefano, Italy, 115
Sarhili (Xhosa chief), 256
Savoy–Piedmont, accusations of plague-spreading, 118
Schadewaldt (butcher in Memel), 164

Scotland: fever epidemics, 128, 132, 146; *see also* Edinburgh; Glasgow
scrofula, 193
search parties, as feature of plague operations, 221–2, 233, 235, 236
Second World War, African venereal disease epidemics, 290–9
segregation of plague victims, 211, 212, 216, 287–8; camps, 208, 222, 234; *see also* isolation; quarantine
Seine-et-Oise department, cholera epidemic (1832), 155–6
self-help medicine, and AIDS, 323
Sepúlveda, Spain, plague epidemic, 110
serpent legends, 58–61 *passim*, 65–6, 71, 72, 88
sexual mores: of Amerindians, 198–201; connection between Hawaiian depopulation and, 193–6; impact of western 'civilisation' on African, 269–72 *passim*, 277–8, 283, 289, 293–4, 300, 301
shaikhs, East African, 260–1
Shambaa people, Tanzania, 247–8, 249–50
Shepherd, W. D., 230–1
Shilts, R., 240
Short, Renée, MP, 324
Shoshangane (Gaza chief), 75
Sidonius, bishop of Mainz, 73
Siegfried, A., 162
Sierra Leone, 295
Silene, Libya, 59
Silvester, Pope, 57
Simon, Sir John, 135, 313
Simond, P. L., 14, 215–16
sin, perceived connection between disease and, 17, 273–4
Singleton, M., 248
Sirur, India, 235
skin infections, 193
Slav refugees in Venice, 113
slaves, East African, 258–60; *see also* galley slaves
sleeping sickness, 269, 271
smallpox, 5, 8, 15, 176, 313; African epidemics, 241, 243–5, 247, 247–54 *passim*, 258, 261; Arab attitudes, 83–4; impact on Hawaiians, 189 n. 34, 190–1, 192; Indian epidemics, 203–4, 217; 'personalisation' of, 248, 258; transmission of, 130, 138, 159–60;

vaccination, 11, 173, 190
smells, foul, dangers of, 3, 59–60, 112, 114; *see also* exhalations; miasmatic theory
Smith, Captain John, 200
Smith, Thomas Southwood, *see* Southwood Smith
snake-venom, rumours of poisoning by, 224, 225; *see also* serpent legends
Snow, John, 155
Snow, P. C., Municipal Commissioner for Bombay, 224
social disorder, epidemics and, 12, 39–40, 116–17, 118–19, 152–3, 232–3, 243–4; *see also* class conflict; revolution; riots
Social Services Committee (UK), report on AIDS, 312, 321
Society for Bettering the Conditions of the Poor, 132
soldiers: as carriers of disease, 112, 122, 159–60, 161, 290–1; fever among, 141–2; used to enforce plague regulations (see also *cordons sanitaires*), 208, 216, 221, 225
Sophocles, 40, 41
South Africa, 296, 300; epidemics, 243, 245, 247, 282 n. 36; missionaries, 262–5 *passim*
South America, 149, 151, 198–9
southern Africa: epidemics and ideological systems, 241–57 *passim*, 261–7 *passim*; venereal disease, 284, 286, 288, 296
Southern Rhodesia: influenza epidemic, 245, 265–7; venereal disease, 282 n. 36, 286–7, 288, 290, 297–8
Southwood Smith, Thomas, 136–7, 138, 143–6
Spain, 19, 108, 110; conquest of South America, 149, 198–9
Spalato, 121
Sperber, Dan, 45, 50
Sperling, D. C., 261
state and epidemics, *see* public health
Stearns, P. N., 328
Stettin, cholera riots (1831), 158, 164–5
Stevenson, Robert Louis, 194
Stevenson, William, 184
strangers/outsiders, tendency to blame epidemics on, 4, 112, 113, 234–5, 243
Strazzolini, Canon Jacopo, 111, 115, 121

Strzelecki, Sir Paul Edmund, 195–6, 198
Sudan, prophets in, 251
sulphonamide drugs, 298
Surat, India, plague in, 219, 231
survivors of plague, as privileged body, 118–19
Sweden, AIDS policy, 304
Sydney, confirmation of plague theory, 216
symptoms of disease: description of, 30, 31, 143; social effects of, 8, 153–4
syphilis, 2, 5, 8, 194, 200; 'epidemic' in East and Central Africa, 10, 269–302; impact of Christianity and 'civilisation' as cause of, 269–73, 277, 278, 283; issue of compulsory examination, 276, 291, 296–7, 298; missionary medical services and attitudes, 273–5, 278–9, 292, 300–1; non-venereally transmitted form, 281–2, 284, 286; treatments, 275, 279, 285–6, 292
Syracuse, siege of, 27, 28–9
Syria, plague in, 85–6, 87

Taliesin, 66
Tanzania/Tanganyika, 247–8, 258, 290, 291
Tedder, Richard, 312
Terrence Higgins Trust, 307–10 *passim*, 312, 313, 324 n. 60
Thasos, epidemic on, 35–6
Thrace, plague in, 26, 27
Thucydides, account of Athenian plague, 9, 22–44 *passim*
Tilak, Bal Gangadhar, 238–9
Times of India, 208–9
Tnugdal, *Vision* of, 65
tobacco addiction, Hawaii, 183
Tolonyane (Tswana prophet), 249, 252
trade, *see* commerce
Transvaal, 264
Trento, Italy, 112
Treviso, Italy, 105, 115
Trier, 73, 74
tropical medicine, 204
trypanosomiasis, 75
tsetse fly, 75, 253
Tswana tribe, 249, 252
tuberculosis, 2, 153, 173, 193, 203
Tucker, Albert, bishop of Uganda, 270

Tuscany, 110, 113
typhoid, 173
typhus, 130–1, 132, 137, 138, 140, 141, 142
Tyrrell, David, 320

UK AIDS Foundation, 310
Udine, Friuli, 122
Uganda, 14; venereal disease in, 10, 269–83, 284, 289, 290, 298, 299
ulama, East African, 258
'Umar ibn al-Khaṭṭâb, 85, 86
Umayyad, 84, 92, 93, 95
undertakers, 117, 118
Undhera, India, inoculation of villagers, 228
Unitarianism, 143, 146, 147
United Kingdom, *see* Britain
United States, 151, 160; AIDS epidemic, 239–40, 304, 306, 316–17, 320, 326–7
untouchables, 4, 235
urbanisation, 151, 171, 283, 286, 289
utilitarianism, 143, 145

vagabonds/vagrants, 112, 113, 117–18, 120
Van Rensburg, Niklaas, 265
Vancouver, Captain George, 179, 180, 195
Vanderkemp, J. T., 262, 263
Vapostori movements, 266–7
Varna, 161
Venantius Fortunatus, 50, 52, 54–9 *passim*, 65, 68, 70, 73
venereal disease: attitudes to, 11, 273, 274–7, 279, 283, 294–6, 297; in Hawaii, 182, 187, 193–6, 198–200; *see also* gonorrhoea; syphilis
Venice, 18, 116, 118; board of health, 15, 121; Great Council, 111; International Sanitary Convention (1897), 210; plague epidemics, 101–5, 106, 111, 112, 113–14
Verona, 116
Viegas, Dr A. C., 206, 207, 209, 227
Virgil, portrayal of cattle plague, 27
Virginia, Indian tribes, 200–1
Visconti family, rulers of Milan, 18
Volterra, Italy, 113

voluntary subscription societies, 131, 132, 148
votive churches, 105
votive offerings, 62

Wales, monster legends, 66
warfare, 32, 141; and spread of epidemics, 159, 161; *see also* soldiers
Watchtower Movement, 265
water supplies: polluted, 112, 155, 166; suspected poisoning of, 22, 27, 165, 224; *see also* wells/springs
Watson, W. H., 292
Weber, Jonathan, 311, 321
Weidauer, K., 30
Weindling, P., 14
Weir, T. S., 213, 229
Weiss, Robert, 311
wells/springs: infested by dragons, 59, 61, 62, 63; rumours of poisoned, 9, 37, 163
West Africa, 294, 295
West Indies, 294
Westminster, cholera mortality rates, 156
Whig medicine, 10–11, 139, 146, 324
Whitehead, Dr, Director of Public Health Laboratory Service, 320
Whitehead, Tony, 309–10, 313
Whitelaw Cabinet Committee, 321
whooping cough epidemic, Hawaii, 190, 192
witches: accused of spreading plague, 118, 123, 162; persecuted in Africa, 255, 256, 266, 267
wolf of Langogne (*Bête de Gévaudan*), 72
Wolsey, Thomas, Cardinal, 19
workhouse fever wards, 135
Wrmonoc, *Life* of St Paul Aurelian, 65
Wyandot Indians, 176

Xenophanes of Colophon, 39
Xhosa: epidemics, 243–4, 246; prophets and cattle-killing movement, 251, 252, 254–7, 262–3

yaws, 7–8, 179, 279–81, 282, 286, 292
yellow fever, 142, 145
Yellowlees, Sir Henry, 320
Yersin, Alexandre Emile, 214

Young, Dr W. A., 291–2

Zaire, 267, 317
el Zein, Abdul Hamid, 259

Ziyâd ibn Abî Sufyân, Umayyad
viceroy of the East, 93
Zomba African Hospital, 295–6
Zulu spirit churches, 267

Past and Present Publications

General Editor: PAUL SLACK. *Exeter College, Oxford*

Family and Inheritance: Rural Society in Western Europe 1200–1800, edited by Jack Goody, Joan Thirsk and E. P. Thompson*
French Society and the Revolution, edited by Douglas Johnson
Peasants, Knights and Heretics: Studies in Medieval English Social History, edited by R. H. Hilton*
Towns in Societies: Essays in Economic History and Historical Sociology, edited by Philip Abrams and E. A. Wrigley*
Desolation of a City: Coventry and the Urban Crisis of the Late Middle Ages, Charles Phythian-Adams
Puritanism and Theatre: Thomas Middleton and Opposition Drama under the Early Stuarts, Margot Heinemann*
Lords and Peasants in a Changing Society: The Estates of the Bishopric of Worcester 680–1540, Christopher Dyer
Life, Marriage and Death in a Medieval Parish: Economy, Society and Demography in Halesowen 1270–1400, Zvi Razi
Biology, Medicine and Society 1840–1940, edited by Charles Webster
The Invention of Tradition, edited by Eric Hobsbawm and Terence Ranger*
Industrialization before Industrialization: Rural Industry and the Genesis of Capitalism, Peter Kriedte, Hans Medick and Jürgen Schlumbohm*
The Republic in the Village: The People of the Var from the French Revolution to the Second Republic, Maurice Agulhon †
Social Relations and Ideas: Essays in Honour of R. H. Hilton, edited by T. H. Aston, P. R. Coss, Christopher Dyer and Joan Thirsk
A Medieval Society: The West Midlands at the End of the Thirteenth Century, R. H. Hilton
Winstanley: 'The Law of Freedom' and Other Writings, edited by Christopher Hill
Crime in Seventeenth-Century England: A County Study, J. A. Sharpe†
The Crisis of Feudalism: Economy and Society in Eastern Normandy c. 1300–1500, Guy Bois†
The Development of the Family and Marriage in Europe, Jack Goody*
Disputes and Settlements: Law and Human Relations in the West, edited by John Bossy
Rebellion, Popular Protest and the Social Order in Early Modern England, edited by Paul Slack
Studies on Byzantine Literature of the Eleventh and Twelfth Centuries, Alexander Kazhdan in collaboration with Simon Franklin†
The English Rising of 1381, edited by R. H. Hilton and T. H. Aston*
Praise and Paradox: Merchants and Craftsmen in Elizabethan Popular Literature, Laura Caroline Stevenson

The Brenner Debate: Agrarian Class Structure and Economic Development in Pre-Industrial Europe, edited by T. H. Aston and C. H. E. Philpin*

Eternal Victory: Triumphal Rulership in Late Antiquity, Byzantium, and the Early Medieval West, Michael McCormick†*

East-Central Europe in Transition: From the Fourteenth to the Seventeenth Century, edited by Antoni Mączak, Henryk Samsonowicz and Peter Burke†

Small Books and Pleasant Histories: Popular Fiction and its Readership in Seventeenth-Century England, Margaret Spufford*

Society, Politics and Culture: Studies in Early Modern England, Mervyn James*

Horses, Oxen and Technological Innovation: The Use of Draught Animals in English Farming 1066–1500, John Langdon

Nationalism and Popular Protest in Ireland, edited by C. H. E. Philpin

Rituals of Royalty: Power and Ceremonial in Traditional Societies, edited by David Cannadine and Simon Price*

The Margins of Society in Late Medieval Paris, Bronisław Geremek†

Landlords, Peasants and Politics in Medieval England, edited by T. H. Aston

Geography, Technology, and War: Studies in the Maritime History of the Mediterranean, 649–1571, John H. Pryor*

Church Courts, Sex and Marriage in England, 1570–1640, Martin Ingram*

Searches for an Imaginary Kingdom: The Legend of the Kingdom of Prester John, L. N. Gumilev

Crowds and History: Mass Phenomena in English Towns, 1780–1835, Mark Harrison

Concepts of Cleanliness: Changing Attitudes in France since the Middle Ages, Georges Vigarello†

The First Modern Society: Essays in English History in Honour of Lawrence Stone, edited by A. L. Beier, David Cannadine and James M. Rosenheim

The Europe of the Devout: The Catholic Reformation and the Formation of a New Society, Louis Châtellier†

English Rural Society, 1500–1800: Essays in Honour of Joan Thirsk, edited by John Chartres and David Hey

From Slavery to Feudalism in South-Western Europe, Pierre Bonnassie†

Lordship, Knighthood and Locality: A Study in English Society c.1180–c.1280, P. R. Coss

English and French Towns in Feudal Society: A Comparative Study, R. H. Hilton

An Island for Iself: Economic Development and Social Change in Late Medieval Sicily, Stephan R. Epstein

Epidemics and Ideas: Essays on the Historical Perception of Pestilence, edited by Terence Ranger and Paul Slack

* Published also as a paperback
† Co-published with the Maison des Sciences de L'Homme, Paris